THE CAMPHOR FLAME

THE CAMPHOR FLAME

POPULAR HINDUISM AND
SOCIETY IN INDIA

Revised and Expanded Edition

C. J. FULLER

PRINCETON UNIVERSITY PRESS

PRINCETON AND OXFORD

Copyright © 1992, 2004 by Princeton University Press
Published by Princeton University Press, 41 William Street,
Princeton, New Jersey 08540
In the United Kingdom: Princeton University Press,
3 Market Place, Woodstock, Oxfordshire OX20 1SY
All Rights Reserved

First published 1992

Revised and Expanded Edition, 2004

Library of Congress Cataloging-in-Publication Data

Fuller, C. J. (Christopher John), 1949–
The camphor flame : popular Hinduism and society
in India / C. J. Fuller.—Rev. and expanded ed.
p.   cm.
Previous ed.: Princeton, N.J. : Princeton University Press, c1992.
Includes bibliographical references and index.
ISBN 0-691-12048-X (pbk. : alk. paper)
1. Hinduism—India. 2. India—Religious life and customs.
3. India—Social life and customs. 4. Religion and sociology—
India.   I. Title.
BL1150.F85   2004
294.5′0954—dc22   2004044776

British Library Cataloging-in-Publication Data is available

This book has been composed in Linotron Sabon

Printed on acid-free paper. ∞

pup.princeton.edu

Printed in the United States of America

10 9 8 7 6 5 4 3 2

ISBN-13: 978-0-691-12048-5

ISBN-10: 0-691-12048-X

25.00

For Penny and Alexis

CONTENTS

MAPS AND TABLES

PREFACE TO THE REVISED AND EXPANDED EDITION

S INCE THIS BOOK was first published in early 1992, Hindu nationalism has become an increasingly powerful force in India. For this second edition, I have therefore written a new Afterword that discusses the arguably most important development of the last decade by examining the relationship between Hindu nationalism and popular Hinduism. Two new sections have been added to update the Bibliographical Guide, the Bibliography has been reset to include the additional works cited, and the Index has been revised to incorporate new material from the Afterword. Otherwise, the original text is unaltered, for in the book's overall argument and presentation of material, I would not want to make significant changes, even though there certainly are errors of fact and judgment that I would ideally like to correct. In particular, in the light of recent events, I would now give much more attention to the mixture of Hindu and non-Hindu beliefs and practices that did and still does form part of popular religion, despite attempts by Hindu nationalists (and their Muslim and Christian counterparts) to insist otherwise.

I thank Véronique Bénéï for her critical comments on an earlier version of the Afterword and Mary Murrell for her editorial support.

PREFACE

THE MODERN social and cultural anthropology of India, based
on intensive fieldwork, began in the late 1940s, but during the
next twenty-five years, most anthropologists paid relatively little
attention to popular Hinduism, the living religion of the vast majority of
the population. Since the mid-1970s, however, anthropological research
on popular religion has developed significantly, in both quantity and
quality, and there has also been a marked improvement in scholarly cooperation between anthropologists and Indologists working on the textual
traditions of Hinduism.

By 1985, when I began to plan this study, I had become convinced that
the rapidly growing literature could be synthezised into an up-to-date
account of popular religion, which would also counterbalance the philosophical bias apparent in other general books about Hinduism. I wanted
to respond as well to the reasonable complaint, repeatedly heard from my
colleagues and students, that the anthropology of Hinduism has become
so abstruse that only experts can be expected to make sense of it. A principal objective of this book is to place the more important specialist literature in a broader anthropological framework, which is also intelligible to
a wider readership interested in Hinduism and India. My text is unlikely
to delude anyone into thinking that popular Hinduism is a simple matter,
but I hope that I can show that it is not incomprehensible.

My own experience of popular Hinduism has mostly been gained in
the south Indian city of Madurai, especially in the Shri Minakshi-Sundareshwara temple, and it is right that I should start my acknowledg-
ments by thanking the priests and other officiants who work there, because they taught me so much of what I know about their religion. Given
the nature of this book, the second debt to be acknowledged is a general
one to the community of scholars whose work forms the indispensable
basis for my own. I also thank the many friends, colleagues, and students
who have discussed the book with me, commented on sections of it delivered as seminar and conference papers, provided useful information from
their own research, and encouraged me to keep writing.

I owe particularly deep debts to Johnny Parry, for giving me sound
advice and detailed comments on numerous draft chapters; to Nick Dirks
(who also read the penultimate version), Tony Good, David Shulman,
and Sylvia Vatuk, for closely scrutinizing an earlier, unsatisfactory version of the manuscript and then persuading me to continue; and to Alf
Hiltebeitel, for carefully reading the penultimate version of the manuscript. I also thank Penny Logan, Adrian Mayer, Gloria Raheja, and Jon-

athan Spencer for commenting on individual chapters. At various critical points, the encouragement of André Béteille, Maurice Bloch, David Brent, Margaret Case, Jean and John Comaroff, Wendy Doniger, Jock Stirrat, and Peter van der Veer was invaluable, and I owe special thanks to the late Sir Edmund Leach, whose loyal support was vital at an early stage.

Much of this book was written during my tenure of a Social Science Research Fellowship from the Nuffield Foundation; I thank the foundation's trustees and its deputy director, Patricia Thomas, as well as the London School of Economics and my colleagues in the Department of Anthropology for allowing me leave to take up the fellowship. The research in Madurai on which parts of the book are based was supported by grants from the Social Science Research Council (now Economic and Social Research Council), the British Academy, and the London School of Economics.

The verses from *Love Song of the Dark Lord: Jayadeva's* Gītagovinda, edited and translated by Barbara Stoler Miller, copyright 1977 by Columbia University Press, are reproduced by permission of Columbia University Press. Parts of chapter 4 have appeared, in different form, in articles in *Man*, and they are reprinted by permission of the Royal Anthropological Institute of Great Britain and Ireland.

Last but not least, I owe an immense debt of gratitude to my wife, Penny Logan, and my son, Alexis, which cannot be repaid.

NOTE ON TRANSLITERATION

IN ACCORDANCE with conventional practice among writers on Hinduism, names and terms are transliterated from Sanskrit forms, unless the form in a modern, vernacular language is plainly required. Diacritical marks are omitted, and the normal adjustments to the transliteration system are therefore employed: *ri* for *r̥*, *ch* for *c*, *v* or *w* for *v*, and *sh* for *ś* and *ṣ*. In transliterating Tamil terms, more extensive adjustments are employed to compensate for the peculiarities of the Tamil alphabet: in particular, the consonantal sounds *g*, *j*, *d*, *b*, *sh*, and *s* are all indicated. When correct orthography is unclear, the spelling of some local words reproduces the cited sources. Proper names of people, places, and castes appear in their usual English forms.

Since this is a book about popular religion, I must stress that my use of Sanskrit rather than vernacular forms is designed only to enhance intelligibility. It does not imply any acceptance of the religious literati's assumption that Sanskrit—the "perfected" speech of the deities themselves—is the only proper language for Hinduism.

NOTE ON DOCUMENTATION

THROUGHOUT this book, when specific facts or arguments are quoted from a particular author's work, it is cited in the text. When presenting information or analysis that is either well known to scholars in the field or derives its support from a range of works, however, I omit references so that the text is not cluttered by long lists of names, dates, and numbers. A principal purpose of the Bibliographical Guide is to supply missing sources. Anthropological and other literature on Indian society—and its distinctive features, such as the caste system—is only cited when directly pertinent.

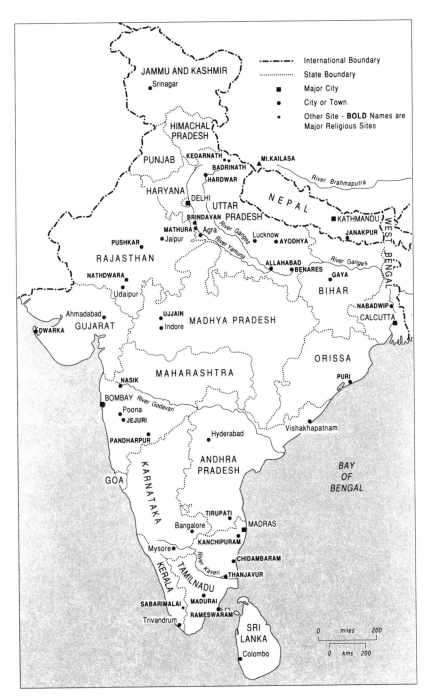

JAMMU AND KASHMIR
Srinagar

HIMACHAL
PRADESH

PUNJAB **KEDARNATH**
BADRINATH Mt. KAILASA
HARDWAR

HARYANA
DELHI
UTTAR
BRINDAVAN PRADESH
MATHURA Agra River Ganges Lucknow
PUSHKAR Jaipur River Yamuna **AYODHYA**

River Brahmaputra

N E P A L

■ KATHMANDU
JANAKPUR

WEST BENGAL

RAJASTHAN
NATHDWARA
Udaipur
ALLAHABAD
BENARES River Ganges
GAYA
BIHAR

Ahmadabad
UJJAIN
MADHYA PRADESH
Indore
NABADWIP
■ CALCUTTA

DWARKA GUJARAT

ORISSA

MAHARASHTRA
NASIK River Godavari
BOMBAY
Poona
JEJURI

PURI

PANDHARPUR

Hyderabad
Vishakhapatnam

GOA
KARNATAKA
ANDHRA
PRADESH

BAY
OF
BENGAL

TIRUPATI
Bangalore ■ MADRAS
KANCHIPURAM
Mysore
CHIDAMBARAM
River Kaveri
KERALA **THANJAVUR**
TAMILNADU

SABARIMALAI **MADURAI**
RAMESWARAM
Trivandrum

SRI
LANKA

Colombo

0 miles 200

0 kms 200

Major Hindu Religious Sites in India and Nepal

THE CAMPHOR FLAME

Chapter 1

POPULAR HINDUISM AND INDIAN SOCIETY

HINDUS GREET and show respect to their many deities, both gods and goddesses, by a simple and perfectly graceful gesture: they raise their hands, with the palms pressed together and fingers pointing upward, and slightly bow the head. Often, while walking past a temple on a city street or a little shrine on a country path, this gesture is made quickly, but it can be much more measured and elaborate. People may bow down before a deity's image, kneel with the head lowered to the ground, or even prostrate themselves completely with the arms stretched out in front.

It is not only human beings who graciously show respect, greet, and bid farewell to gods and goddesses with this gesture, for the deities do so to each other. The goddesses Lakshmi and Parvati perform the gesture to their husbands, the great gods Vishnu and Shiva, respectively, but sometimes Vishnu shows his respect to Shiva or Shiva does the same to Vishnu. Indeed, as their sculptured images and pictorial representations show, any deity may sometimes salute any other by the same gesture of raised hands and bowed head.

In exactly the same way, Hindus welcome and part from each other. If two people of similar status meet formally, each raises the hands and slightly bows the head to the other, while simultaneously saying the Sanskrit word *namaskara*—which also denotes the gesture itself—or, more usually, a vernacular synonym like Hindi *namaste*. If the two people are of markedly different status, then only the inferior is likely to perform the gesture, and may even fall down in prostration at the superior's feet. On the other hand, at the informal meetings that occur throughout an ordinary day as people run into their relatives or friends, colleagues or workmates, the formal gesture is typically simplified to no more than a rapid lifting of the right hand and a nod of the head.

As a symbolic act, this gesture—with its variants from full prostration to informal flicking of the head and hand—expresses two of the most critical features of Hindu religion and society. First, as we have seen, exactly the same gesture is made by people to deities, and by both deities and people to each other. This reflects a supremely important fact about Hinduism: unlike Judaism, Christianity, and Islam, it postulates no absolute distinction between divine and human beings. In many contexts, human beings are seen as actually divine in one way or another. The Hindu who told Lawrence A. Babb that the gesture is made to salute "that bit of god which is in every person" (1975: 52) caught in a simple phrase one of Hinduism's axiomatic truths.

Second, the Hindu gesture of respect—unlike, say, the handshake—expresses an inherent asymmetry in rank, because it is made by an inferior to a superior. In other words, the gesture symbolizes in a condensed form the principle of hierarchical inequality that is so fundamental in Hindu religion and society. Thus a human worshiper, like a lower deity, gestures in respect to a superior deity, but the same pattern may be discerned in an entire range of interactions between people: a wife makes the gesture to her husband, children to their parents, a low-caste person to a high-caste person, an employee to an employer, a student to a teacher, and so on and so forth. In all these cases, the superior typically makes no reciprocating gesture or does so only cursorily. Therefore, when two people do raise their hands and bow to each other in greeting—as does in fact commonly occur—they mutually represent themselves as equals, but only because one person's expression of respect is exactly balanced by the other's.

If the inequality in a relationship is very marked, the inferior normally prostrates instead of performing the standard gesture, as a subject does to a king or a disciple to a spiritual guru. "All this part above the neck belongs to God," one Hindu told G. Morris Carstairs (1957: 77); in prostration, therefore, the expression of asymmetry is reinforced by lowering the head, the highest and most godlike part of the body, to the level of the superior's feet, the lowest part.

Of course, in all circumstances, people may make a gesture of respect (or fail to do so) with ironical, insulting, or groveling intent, but the sense of their action still derives from the fact that the gesture should express respect toward a superior being. Moreover, I must make it clear in introducing a study of religion that the gesture of respect or prostration, especially when made before a deity, often primarily signals devotion or adoration—a vital aspect of much Hindu worship—rather than mere inferiority. But even when this is so, the gesture extends, rather than displaces, the symbolization of inequality that is so fundamental, because the object of devotion is almost invariably superior as well.

Thus the principle of hierarchical inequality, as well as the partial continuity between divinity and humanity, is always symbolically present in the gesture of greeting and respect, and although these are not the only important themes to be explored in this study of popular Hinduism and Indian society, they are certainly central. To begin with the *namaskara* is therefore to begin in the right place.

Popular Hinduism and Its Anthropological Analysis

By "popular Hinduism," I conventionally refer to the beliefs and practices that constitute the living, "practical" religion of ordinary Hindus. In 1981, Hindus formed approximately 83 percent of India's population (*Census of India* 1981, Series-1 India, Paper-4 of 1984, Table HH-15). By 1991, when the Census recorded the country's population at 844 million, they would have numbered around 700 million. Except for some references to Nepal, this book is confined to Hinduism within India and does not discuss overseas Hindus.

My subject matter, to be a little more precise, is principally popular theistic Hinduism, because I shall be mainly concerned with beliefs and practices focused on the multiplicity of deities with whom Hindus interact and communicate in ritual. Ethnographic evidence shows that ordinary people see relationships with the deities as fundamental in their lives. In this respect, the people of Rampura village in Karnataka represent most, if not all, Hindus. According to M. N. Srinivas, they "lived in a theistic universe in the sense that everyone in the village believed that god did exist, or more precisely, deities, male and female, and spirits, did exist" (1976: 323). And because they existed, deities could be prayed to for help and were "the source of hope for undertaking the multifarious activities essential for day-to-day living," although deities were also demanding, for they "had to be worshipped, offered sacrifices, and made much of," and were liable to punish people if neglected or transgressed (ibid.: 329). It is Rampura's religious world, writ large on a diverse pan-Indian frame, that is described in the following chapters.

Let me quickly say, without belaboring the point, that this book does not pretend to be a comprehensive study of popular Hinduism. A lot of material is included, but a lot is also left out, and on many topics we still have very little sound evidence. My own experience of Hinduism comes mainly from my research in the great temple of the goddess Minakshi and her husband Sundareshwara (Shiva) in the south Indian city of Madurai, and I have tried hard to overcome the south Indian, urban, Brahmanical, temple-centered bias that this may have induced in me. I have also carried out earlier fieldwork in rural Kerala among non-Brahmans, although I did not do much research on religion then, and the principal antidote to any Madurai-centric myopia has been the published work of other scholars.

Popular Hinduism can be distinguished from "textual Hinduism," the "philosophical" religion set out and elaborated in the sacred texts that are the principal subject matter for Indologists, Sanskritists, historians of religion, and other textual scholars. The sacred texts of Hinduism—and the concepts, ideas, and speculations contained in them—are often vitally important to popular religion, and the latter cannot be studied successfully unless textual scholarship is taken into account. In many places in this book, therefore, textual material will be discussed or even used to open an analysis of ethnography. Nevertheless, themes central in the scriptures are not always central in ordinary people's beliefs and practices, and textual scholars' conclusions do not necessarily provide good guides to the workings of popular religion. For the anthropologist of popular Hinduism, ethnography—not scripture—is both the major source of evidence and the touchstone of interpretation.

Obviously, I take it for granted that popular Hinduism is an authentic religion, equal in standing to any other, and that it would be sheer prejudice to dismiss it as superstition. In particular, the view that popular Hinduism is degenerate textual Hinduism—as some scholars have supposed until remarkably recently—is completely indefensible in the light of ethnographic evidence about the subtle complexities of demotic belief and practice.

I now need to explain my approach to the analysis of popular Hinduism. Except for chapter 5 on rituals of kingship, where I take my main case studies from the past because monarchs no longer rule in India, most of my discussion is based on ethnographic data collected in the field by modern anthropologists since the end of the Second World War and Indian independence in 1947. Hence this is a book about contemporary religion, and on the whole, despite many references to historical change, I pursue a synchronic, structural method of analysis. Hinduism, like India itself, has always been changing, especially during the modern era, but it has not altered so much that we must describe it as "transformed," as is Buddhism in modern Sri Lanka (Gombrich and Obeyesekere 1988).

No serious student, of course, continues to credit the myth of timeless India; moreover, despite the clear tendency in much Hindu religious discourse to devalue temporal change, I do not subscribe to the more sophisticated claim that the Indian worldview is definitively unhistorical. I also fully accept that the religion and society of today are a product of history and can be fruitfully studied as such. But none of these points undermines the insights to be gained from a mainly synchronic, ethnographically based analysis. The ethnographic record clearly shows that there are enduring structures within Hindu religion and Indian society, at both the institutional and ideological or symbolic levels, and the objective of this book is to reveal and analyze some of the most important of them. Unapologetically, I mostly write in the "ethnographic present" to refer to the period since, approximately, the 1940s.

As an anthropologist (who would probably be classified as a sociologist in India itself), I see popular Hinduism, like every religion, as a social and cultural construction. By this I mean that popular Hinduism is created and recreated in and by a collective ordering of experience. All Hindu members of Indian society—and sometimes non-Hindus as well—participate in constructing or constituting Hinduism, and in so doing they make for themselves a meaningful world. Moreover, insofar as Hinduism then provides one significant framework for meaningful social action, it only does so because its structure is adequately—although not totally—consistent with the structure of society as a whole. Consequently, in order to understand popular Hinduism as a social and cultural construction, it is necessary to grasp its interdependent relationship with the society of which, at a more inclusive level, it is itself a part.

Before expanding on these admittedly abstract statements, I need to say that although this book is about Hinduism and mainly concentrates on Hindu institutions, I am not suggesting that Indian society is the same thing as Hindu society. It is not and I deliberately refer to popular Hinduism and *Indian* society, because a large proportion of Hindus—even though most of their religious activity involves them alone—do have significant social relationships with Muslims, Christians, Sikhs, and other minority groups. Hindus, whatever the chauvinists among them like to believe, belong to a religiously plural society.

I now turn to the social and cultural construction of religion itself. In the last hundred years, a vast literature on the anthropology and sociology of religion has grown up, and many different styles of analysis and interpretation have been developed. This is not the place to review them, but I can illustrate some salient points by reconsidering the symbolic act that is the Hindu gesture of greeting and respect.

As we have seen, the gesture expresses inequality between the two individuals involved. We could also say, however, that the gesture's function is to sustain institutional inequalities and that it publicly legitimates unequal relationships. Moreover, because the gesture is made to deities as well as people, it represents the inequality between people as homologous with that between them and deities, so that human superiority is justified by godlike attributes. Or instead of justified, it is mystified, so that the gesture tends to disguise behind a religious veil the objective bases of social inequality that lie, for instance, in unequal control over politico-economic resources.

In contrast with the "analytical" approach, which emphasizes social function and the legitimation or mystification of underlying social inequalities, there is an alternative "interpretative" approach, which insists that the gesture of respect puts into play a set of symbols that are meaningful for the actors, Hindus themselves, so that our principal aim is to interpret those symbolic meanings in their own terms. The gesture, as I explained above, also symbolically expresses the absence of any absolute distinction in Hinduism between deities and people, and we must therefore see human society itself, as well as religion, as products of a wider cultural system that represents both deities and humans as "actors." To make the gesture of respect, therefore, is to participate in a hierarchical world populated by both deities and human beings, and in a small way to reiterate, through symbolic action, the meaningfulness of that world.

A sharp distinction is often drawn between the "analytical" approach more prevalent in British social anthropology and its "interpretative" counterpart, which has been most fully developed in American cultural anthropology. Social, analytical approaches—which tend to define religion and society as analytically separable domains—are defended as rational analyses uncontaminated by religious mysticism and exaggerated cultural relativism, whereas cultural, interpretative approaches—which tend to portray religion and society as mutually constitutive of each other—are extolled as sensitive readings of "the native's point of view" free from distortion by imposed western categories. In reality, however, both perspectives are indispensable. Thus, for example, the Hindu gesture of respect—depending on the context in which it is made—certainly can be an act that legitimates social inequality between two people, such as husband and wife. Simultaneously, however, it can also be an act that equally plainly represents two people's relationship as part of a distinctively Hindu cultural system of hierarchical relationships linking both divine and human persons: a wife is the devotee of her husband as a god and she acts in the image of Lakshmi, the perfect wife who bows down at the feet of her husband Vishnu. More generally, no social analysis can be undertaken successfully unless we grasp adequately the people's own culturally constituted understandings of their action. Conversely, we cannot accomplish the latter task unless we interpret social action in relation to the ideologies and institutions of society, which are apprehended as an external reality by people of flesh and blood living in a material world.

To sum up and refocus the discussion: all symbolic interaction with the gods and goddesses of popular theistic Hinduism is about relationships among members of Indian society, as well as between them and their deities. Let me close this section with a final illustrative example. When a male priest belonging to the high-ranking Brahman caste worships a deity in a temple, he does so in accordance with the deity's presumed wishes. By analyzing the ritual we can learn a lot about how deities, and their connections with human worshipers, are indigenously conceptualized. At the same time, however, the priest expresses, legitimates, or reconstructs his own position within society. His action says something about him in relation to other members of society—his wife (who cannot deputize for him), other priests (who serve in different temples), other Brahmans (who look down on him because he is a priest), or non-Brahmans (who cannot do his work). In the anthropological investigation of worship and popular Hinduism in general, we can focus on the deities, as much of this book will do, but we cannot understand them properly unless we also look at their priests and other members of society.

INDIGENOUS CATEGORIES AND ORIENTALIST MISCONSTRUCTIONS

My theoretical approach to the social and cultural construction of popular Hinduism, as outlined above, would probably still attract severe criticism from some scholars committed to the cultural, interpretative perspective. They would insist that any argument postulating an analytical separation between religion and society is dependent upon the categories of western thought, because no such separation is made by Hindus themselves. By the same token, they might argue that the structures revealed by comparative analysis of ethnographic data on popular Hinduism, as pursued in the body of this book, are an artifact of western epistemological assumptions embedded within either the ethnography itself or my treatment of it. In other words, my subject matter is no more than a western, "orientalist" misconstruction of indigenous Hindu culture. Although no one writer has written in exactly these terms, they do sum up a currently influential intellectual stance particularly associated with American "ethnosociology" and the critique of "orientalist discourse." Thus an article by McKim Marriott, the leading advocate of an "Indian ethnosociology," begins as follows: "It is an anomalous fact that the social sciences used in India today have developed from thought about Western rather than Indian cultural realities." He continues: "Attending to what is perceived by Indians in Indian categories should at least promote a more perceptive Indian ethnography" (1989: 1).

The contribution made to the study of religion and society in India by ethnosociological anthropologists has been valuable, and I shall draw on some of it later. Yet in the light of the influence—mainly within the United States—which ethnosociological ideas now enjoy, partly because of their convergence with critiques of orientalism (Inden 1986), I do need to register my disagreement with Marriott and those who think like him. The social science of India has not in fact developed from thought about western as opposed to Indian "cultural realities," but from thought about their interaction, and such interactive reflection is precisely the mechanism by which all comparative anthropology and sociology develops.

Therefore, when we look closely at "Indian categories"—as we must—we have to do so through a comparative, cross-cultural lens.

Consider the very terms "Hindu" and "Hinduism." The Persian word *hindu* derives from Sindhu, the Sanskrit name of the river Indus (in modern Pakistan). It originally meant a native of India, the land around and beyond the Indus. When "Hindu" (or "Hindoo") entered the English language in the seventeenth century, it was similarly used to denote any native of Hindustan (India), but it gradually came to mean someone who retained the indigenous religion and had not converted to Islam. "Hinduism," as a term for that indigenous religion, became current in English in the early nineteenth century and was coined to label an "ism" that was itself partly a product of western orientalist thought, which (mis)constructed Hinduism on the model of occidental religions, particularly Christianity. Hinduism, in other words, came to be seen as a system of doctrines, beliefs, and practices properly equivalent to those that make up Christianity, and "Hindu" now clearly specified an Indian's religious affiliation.

Nowadays, of course, the term "Hinduism" belongs to contemporary Indian discourse alongside the term *dharma*, stripped of its more complex connotations of socioreligious moral order, law, and duty to mean much the same thing, especially in the neologism *sanatana dharma*, "eternal religion." That linguistic development significantly reflects the impact of modern Hindu reformist thought and the Hindus' own search for an identifiable, unitary system of religious belief and practice. Nonetheless, "Hinduism" does not translate any premodern Indian word without serious semantic distortion, and it still does not correspond to any concept or category that belongs to the thinking of a large proportion of the ordinary people whose popular Hinduism I shall discuss.

Yet that is not a decisive objection against employment of the term. Anthropological or sociological analysis abstracts from empirical data and also attempts to make them intelligible by using concepts and deploying generalizations that are formulated comparatively and rarely correspond precisely to indigenous categories in any particular society. That "Hinduism" is not a traditional, indigenous category, concept, or "cultural reality"—albeit an important negative fact—in no way nullifies an analysis that demonstrates that Hinduism is a relatively coherent and distinctive religious system founded on common structures of relationships.

The point can be brought home by considering a converse case. "Islam," meaning submission to God, is the term given to that religion by Muhammed himself, and in the eyes of most Muslims a Muslim is quite simply someone who accepts the "five pillars": the profession of faith that "there is no God but Allah and Muhammed is his prophet"; the observance of the Ramadan fast; the giving of alms; the observance of the five daily prayers; and the ideal obligation to make a pilgrimage to Mecca. "Islam" and "Muslim," in other words, are indisputably Muslim categories, and that they are is an important positive fact about the religion. Nevertheless, that fact in itself is no more decisive than the absence of such categories. In reality, there is a lot of dispute about the meaning of the categories among Muslims themselves and much variation in forms of Islam even within the Arab world, let alone outside it. A comparative anthropologist of Islam, Michael Gilsenan, therefore rightly sees it as his task to "dissolve" conceptions that suggest, for instance, that the religion is "a single, unitary, and all-determining object," and to explain "what the term *Islam* comes to mean in quite different economic, political, and social structures and relations" (1982: 19). In other words, a major objective for anthropologists of Islam is to qualify the unity postulated in the indigenous category (without neglecting its significance), whereas an anthropologist of Hinduism (although also concerned with variation) must reveal the relative unity that exists despite the absence of an equivalent category. In both projects, however, the method is comparative analysis using concepts and generalizations produced by reflection on the interaction between alternative "cultural realities."

One other important point deserves to be mentioned here. Even without an indigenous category "Hinduism," Hindus (like other people) are able to take a partly distanced view of their own religion. As David F. Pocock observes (1973: 65–66), ordinary Hindus commonly display a "kind of sociological awareness" that enables them to look at rituals by considering not only the deities' wishes, but also the socially structured customs of different groups of worshipers. Every ethnographer has benefited immeasurably from such an awareness, and every sound account of popular Hinduism—including those written by Indian scholars—is the product of an enriching interaction between indigenous and foreign ways of thinking. The comparative analysis presented in this book continues along the same path; to try to construct a picture of popular Hinduism through indigenous categories alone would not do justice to the Hindus' own capacity for self-reflection.

THE STRUCTURE OF INDIAN SOCIETY

Modern research on Indian society by anthropologists and other scholars shows that, beneath the myriad disparity of social and cultural forms to be found in a vast and ancient land that is now home to one-sixth of the world's population, there are common principles, institutions, and structures. As I have already said, one of the most fundamental principles in Indian society is hierarchical inequality. This is revealed not only by ethnographic research, but also by textual scholarship; the discussion below will draw on both fields of knowledge.

The Varna and Caste Hierarchies

Because the principle of hierarchical inequality is most distinctively expressed in Indian society by the concepts of *varna* and caste, I shall start with them and it is appropriate to do so by referring to an ancient scriptural text.

To begin at the beginning: the gods created the world and everything in it by sacrificing the primeval Man, Purusha.

> When they divided the Man, into how many parts did they apportion him?
> What do they call his mouth, his two arms and thighs and feet?
> His mouth became the Brahmin; his arms were made into the Warrior, his thighs the People, and from his feet the Servants were born.

These two verses come from a famous hymn describing Purusha's sacrifice, the *Purusha sukta*, which is found in the *Rig Veda* (10.90, vv. 11, 12; O'Flaherty 1981: 29–32). The *Rig Veda*, the first and most important of the four Vedas that are the earliest Hindu scriptures, is thought to have attained its extant form around 1500–1000 B.C. (although the dates have always been subject to dispute). The Vedas are collections of Sanskrit hymns that reveal a ritualistic religion of sacrifice, very different in many respects from the Hinduism of medieval and modern times, although sacrifice does remain a core ritual and the Vedas are still regarded by the majority of Hindu teachers as authoritative texts.

The *Purusha sukta* contains the first mention of the four "classes" or *varna*s of Hindu society: the Brahmans (Brahmins), the Kshatriyas or Warriors, the Vaishyas or People, and the Shudras or Servants. In their origin from the parts of Purusha's body, the hierarchy of four classes is directly represented by passing from the head to the feet. The Vedic verses' image of the *varna*s has remained current to this day, although the duties of the four classes have been elaborated over the centuries in the corpus of religiolegal texts—mostly written by Brahmans—known as the *dharmashastra*. In brief, these duties are normally held to be religious scholarship, especially learning and teaching the Vedas, as well as priestcraft, for the Brahmans; protecting society as kings and soldiers, and sponsoring rituals, for the Kshatriyas; agriculture, cattle herding, and trade for the Vaishyas; and service of the other three classes for the Shudras.

The fourfold *varna* system, emergent at the origin of the world, represents a scripturally authoritative, ideal religious model of Hindu society as a complementary hierarchy: a unity constituted by ranked classes, each with the different functions necessary to sustain the whole. There is no sound historical evidence that the castes of medieval and modern India actually emerged from subdivision of the four classes. Rather, the *varna* system is important because it is an ideal model for the caste system, despite the latter's more complex structure.

No Indian village is exactly like any other, but across the agricultural plains where the vast majority of the country's population lives, there are about half a million villages, most of them containing people belonging to several Hindu castes, often as many as twenty or thirty. Many predominantly Hindu settlements also have small Muslim or other non-Hindu populations as well. The term "caste" translates *jati* that, in all the main Indian languages, literally means "kind" or "species," so that the social unit that we describe as a "caste" is but one of these kinds. Any unit conventionally labeled as a *jati* or caste within a particular local community is commonly divided into subcastes, sub-subcastes, and so on, which may be seen as the most significant units by their own members, even if the larger caste is perceived as a single unit by outsiders. Conversely, across a wider region, castes differentiated at the local level may coalesce into supercastes or caste blocs. Castes, therefore, normally lack hard and fast boundaries, and they stand in relation to each other within a relatively fluid segmentary system. This system explains why people, if asked for the name of their *jati*, may answer in various ways. Depending on context, they may, for example, say that they are Brahmans, or they may give the name of their Brahman subcaste or even a division of the subcaste.

Within multicaste villages, the distinctions among castes and subcastes are manifested in many different ways. The houses of people belonging to different castes often form clusters that are separated, more or less sharply, from each other. The spaces in which people gather to talk are often also identified as belonging to different castes or sets of castes. The use of village wells, as well as access to public eating places, is typically restricted by caste; the lowest castes tend to be debarred from facilities used by the higher castes. When people of different castes do eat together—for example, at a wedding feast—they may sit in separate caste lines and be served in order of rank. How people dress, how they talk, and even how they walk typically reveal their caste membership, and in any one place everybody knows the caste of everybody else. If for some reason a stranger comes, it will not be long before that person's caste is known as well. Caste, in other words, is not an abstract, hidden principle of social organization; it is a visible dimension of everyday life in rural India, which is part of everyone's social and personal identity in a very real sense. Even now, when caste distinctions carry less weight than they used to, they show no sign of fading away completely. This is true in towns and cities as well, in spite of the fact that so much urban social activity involves anonymous strangers.

Although non-Hindus in India do have castes, the caste system is fundamentally a Hindu institution, and I shall restrict my discussion of its most important features to Hindu castes. Every Hindu is born into one and only one caste, and remains a member of that caste until death. In other words, castes are ascriptive social groups; there is no individual social mobility among them. Castes are normally endogamous, so that husband and wife belong to the same caste, which is also their children's caste. If marriage does take place across caste boundaries, then it is almost invariably hypergamous, so that a woman marries into a higher caste. Even today, very few Hindus outside the liberally minded urban elite freely make "love marriages"; the vast majority of unions are arranged by a couple's parents according to endogamous (or hypergamous) rules. The pattern of arranged marriage is probably the firmest foundation for the continuing survival of the caste system.

In theory, the caste system defines a division of labor, which reproduces in a more complicated pattern the division of functions in the *varna* system. In practice many occupations are caste-specific, especially in the service and artisan sectors. Thus, for example, throughout India there are castes of washermen and carpenters who have a virtual monopoly on their work, so that almost all laundry or carpentry is actually done by members of the appropriate caste. It is fairly rare for members of one caste to take up the traditional occupation of another, but it has always been common for people of every caste not to pursue their own caste occupation. In particular, most agricultural work—the occupation of vast numbers of people—is not specifically assigned to particular castes, even though many landholding castes are classified as "farmers" or "cultivators." Further, almost all occupations in modern sectors of the economy are caste-free in the sense that members of any caste can take them up, although in practice many such occupations do recruit disproportionately from particular castes. Hence the extent to which castes actually are closed occupational groups, in the past or present, should not be exaggerated. The division of labor has never been fully determined by caste, despite the force of the ideological principle of complementary hierarchy set out in the *varna* model.

The caste system is pan-Indian because everywhere in the land, despite local variations, it has the same basic structure. It is a hierarchical system and in principle all castes within a locality can be ranked vis-à-vis each other in a single hierarchy. At the top of the hierarchy are the Brahmans and at the bottom are the various castes of untouchable Harijans or Dalits, as their own protest movements have begun to call them. The Brahman castes, of course, correspond to the Brahman *varna*; the Harijans are classically defined as *avarna*, outside the fourfold system and below the Shudras. In between the Brahmans and Harijans are a large variety of other castes, which putatively belong to the Kshatriya, Vaishya, or Shudra classes, although in south India it is traditionally said that all castes that are neither Brahman nor Harijan are Shudra. In reality, the consistency with which different castes are ascribed to particular *varnas*—by their own members or outsiders—varies greatly and often causes argument. Moreover, the mutual ranking of all castes, particularly those in the middle, is frequently disputed, and quarrels about *varna* affiliation are but one expression of such disagreement. Nonetheless, it is generally accepted that in principle a clear rank order of castes within a locality ought to obtain, so that the ideal model of a complementary hierarchy is not erased by existing disputes over relative status among caste members.

One important principle underlying the caste hierarchy derives from the opposition between ritual purity and pollution. The Brahmans are the purest caste and the Harijans the most polluted; those in between are partially ranked according to their relative purity. Ritual pollution derives from many sources. For example, virtually all bodily emissions and waste matter are sources of pollution (saliva, semen, menstrual blood, feces, urine, hair, and nail clippings in particular). Organic life, in other words, is the most immediate source of pollution, which is mainly controlled by a daily bath and other ablutions as required. But pollution is also controlled by allocating to specific, low-ranking castes duties like barbering, laundering, and removing nightsoil, so that the purity of Brahmans and high-caste people is preserved by others who perform polluting tasks for them. Hence the complementary division of labor among castes has a ritual dimension and is not simply "economic." A caste's purity, and thus its contingent status in the caste hierarchy, are also protected in many other ways—notably by the rules of endogamy and hypergamy, and the complex restrictions governing the consumption of food and water cooked or supplied by members of lower castes. By these means, caste members ensure that their own purity, which is sometimes thought of as a quality of their blood and "bodily substance," is not sullied by either marital and sexual relations with lower-status outsiders—which could also lead to the birth of impure children—or by consuming food and drink polluted by other hands.

As well as the bodily pollution to which everyone is liable on a daily basis, there is also a more severe form occasioned by birth, death, and menstruation. These events pollute respectively the mother and her baby (and sometimes her husband and close kin as well), a range of the deceased's kin, and the menstruating woman herself. Menstrual pollution, traditionally observed for four days each month, is frequently cited as the reason why mature women are always more polluted than men and therefore inferior to them; conversely, the prepubertal girl, but rarely the post-menopausal woman, is sometimes glorified because of her purity. Thus the purity-pollution opposition can underpin the inequality between men and women (and indeed other categories of people, such as wife-taking and wife-giving affines) as well as that among castes.

Those suffering serious bodily pollution are subject to a variety of restrictions designed to ensure that they do not transmit their pollution to others. For instance, menstruating women should not eat with unpolluted family members and should not cook for them. Additionally, no polluted person should approach the gods and goddesses to worship them in their temples or shrines, because to do so could pollute those sites and the divine images within. The environment of the deities must always be kept as pure as possible. If it is not, they become angry and punish people who insult them by approaching in a contaminated condition. For this reason, untouchable Harijans were permanently excluded from most public temples until they were admitted by "temple-entry" legislation from the 1930s, fully consolidated after Indian independence in 1947. But even today, especially in rural areas, Harijans are still kept out of many temples. Moreover, no Hindu in a severe state of pollution, such as that caused by birth, death, or menstruation, would contemplate entering a temple or shrine.

In Louis Dumont's highly influential and theoretically sophisticated treatise on the caste system, *Homo Hierarchicus*, the opposition between the pure and impure is presented as the fundamental ideological principle of the hierarchical caste system (1970a: chap. 2). Ritual purity and pollution certainly are important for Hindus, and the caste system certainly is a central institution, but Dumont's work—like much of the anthropological literature—accords them exaggerated prominence, for other principles and institutions of Indian society matter a great deal too.

Brahmans, Renouncers, and Kings

The Brahman, the renouncer, and the king: each of these three key figures can, depending on context, claim superiority over all others. Hence there are, as Richard Burghart shows (1978a), at least three "hierarchical models" of Hindu society, which alternatively afford supreme rank to the Brahman, renouncer, or king.

Brahmans, as we have seen, are ritually purer than non-Brahmans, but their superiority within the caste hierarchy also depends on other factors, notably their traditional command of religious learning as given by their monopolistic right to teach, study, and recite the authoritative Vedas. In the Hindu world, Brahmans ideally constitute a class of religious literati, who alone have the power of sacred knowledge. Moreover, the Brahmans' status is also a function of their relationship with renouncers, whose role and importance must now be outlined.

The ascetic renouncer, the *sannyasin*, is a crucial figure in Hinduism and he (for female renouncers are rare) enjoys a very special place in the social and religious imagination. The renouncer typically makes his appearance as a calm, tonsured monk clad in ochre robes or, perhaps more charismatically, as a gaunt, half-naked figure, crowned by ropes of uncut, matted hair, who subsists only on what he can beg and dedicates himself to lonely meditation and awesome austerities. Although only a small minority of Hindus become renouncers, they are sufficiently numerous to be prominently visible in every major religious center, and they enjoy a significance out of all proportion to their actual numbers.

To explain this significance, I must briefly consider the rationale for world renunciation, drawing on the work of textual scholars. Post-Vedic texts, especially from the Upanishads onward (after 500 B.C.), reveal a turning away from the ritualistic religion of the Vedas, despite the dogma that the Vedas remain truly authoritative. This development is generally interpreted as a sign of the growing prominence of the ideal of world renunciation, seen as the path to the ultimate religious goal now identified as liberation (*moksha*) from the eternal cycle of rebirth (*samsara*). All action in the world, meritorious or unmeritorious according to its consistency with the moral code (*dharma*) appropriate to the actor, has its inevitable "fruit" or consequence, so that—according to the famous doctrine of *karma*—a person's condition is determined by past deeds in this or previous lives. Because the aim is to escape rebirth and redeath, however, mundane action—even if it is meritorious ritual—is devalued in comparison with transcendental knowledge and is ideally avoided through renunciation, the surest route to that knowledge. From the sixth century B.C. onward, Buddhism and Jainism were also influential in extolling the renouncer; when Hinduism established itself as predominant in India during the early centuries of the Christian era, the ideal of ascetic world renunciation became firmly entrenched within the religion and remains so to this day.

Renouncers quit the world and mundane society by performing their own funeral rites. Yet, if they are understood to have left this world, they are still visibly present to those remaining within it. Assuming that they believe a man's renunciation to be genuine (which is not always the case), ordinary householders accord a renouncer great respect as the exemplar of a supreme religious ideal. They typically treat him as spiritually preeminent and may seek his assistance in their own religious life or even in other, more worldly matters. Hence renouncers can be drawn back into the world's affairs, and many of them actually command considerable power and wealth. This is particularly true of renouncers belonging to influential monastic and devotionalist orders, who often live comfortably in settled communities owning vast estates donated to them by pious kings and laymen. And, as one might expect, well-regarded and powerful renouncers are treated as men of very high status, entitled to all the privileges of rank enjoyed by eminent Brahmans and majestic kings. Indeed, in the presence of a great ascetic renouncer—at his temporary camp or in a monastery—even Brahmans and kings will bow down to acknowledge his superiority.

A vital aspect of the relationship between Brahmans and renouncers is that the former, although they are mostly householders living in the world, have come to be partially assimilated with the latter, so that the "ideal Brahman" is or is like an ascetic renouncer. The concept of the ideal Brahman has been pertinently questioned, but the ideological significance of the Brahman-renouncer assimilation is indisputable. In particular, it means that the social and religious supremacy of Brahmans partly depends on their likeness to renouncers. Hence Brahmans can represent themselves as independent of inferiors, just like renouncers who ideally avoid all entangling ties with members of the society they have left, even though the Brahmans' purity is still partly preserved by the lower castes who carry out polluting tasks for them. Paradoxically, therefore, Brahman supremacy is a function of both their asymmetrical, complementary relationships with inferior castes, and their ideal detachment from such relationships.

One important corollary of the Brahman-renouncer assimilation is that the Brahman priest is portrayed as unlike a renouncer; he has to carry out rituals to preserve a devalued world that others can renounce, and he has to maintain social ties with worshipers from whom he receives gifts or payment, a main source of his livelihood. The Brahman priest is therefore inferior to the Brahman who is not a priest, at least in the eyes of the latter. The classical duties of the Brahman are divided. Religious scholarship and mastery of the Vedas are seen as consistent with the renouncer's transcendental objective, but priestcraft is not. Priestcraft is delegated to an inferior class of supposedly unlearned Brahmans, often belonging to subcastes that cannot intermarry with nonpriestly Brahmans. In explaining the Brahman priest's relative inferiority, other factors are involved as well, but it is important in a study of Hinduism to emphasize that, in general, no priest is a respected personage enjoying very high status.

Let me now turn to the king, who is in many ways the converse of the renouncer as the paramount protector of the world. In the modern republic of India, no *raja* or *maharaja*, "great king," now rules, but (as we shall see in chap. 5 in particular) kingship is still an important concept and institution. The Hindu king is almost invariably male and is paradigmatically a Kshatriya, so that many kings were historically proclaimed as Kshatriyas irrespective of their birth. In the *varna* hierarchy (as the *Purusha sukta* makes plain) and in Brahmanical ideology (as set out in *dharmashastra* texts), Kshatriya kings are inferior to Brahmans. The king's power and authority cannot alter his lower status, which partly depends on the necessary involvement of kings and warriors in polluting violence and bloodshed. Hence, as Dumont shows (1970a: chap. 3), politico-economic power cannot be transmuted into superior religious status within the *varna* and caste hierarchies, whose common structure is itself sustained by the complementary relationship between Kshatriya kings and Brahmans who legitimate their authority.

On the other hand, Dumont exaggerates the extent to which the Hindu king is a "secular" figure who universally assumes a rank inferior to Brahmans. The king plays a central role in Hinduism by guaranteeing the overarching moral order of society and the cosmos—the *dharma* in a holistic sense. Without a king, there is anarchy and the "law of the fishes" (when the big just swallow the small) prevails. The king is the earthly regent of the deities and sponsors their worship, like the lordly patron (*yajamana*) of the Vedic sacrifice. At temples under his protection and of course in his court, the king is (or was) supreme. In these arenas his supremacy has to be recognized by all his subjects, including the Brahmans who are granted privileges by him. In the hierarchical ordering of Indian society, therefore, the relationship between an authoritative king and his subjects is one fundamental dimension.

In the countryside, locally dominant castes enjoying preponderant control over the land—the primary means of production—frequently identify themselves as Kshatriyas; the most celebrated case is the Rajputs, dominant across much of northern and western India. But there are many other landholding castes that also claim Kshatriya status or, even if they do not, represent themselves as kinglike, as petty rulers of their local settlements. The members of non-Brahman dominant castes tend to be ambivalent about Brahman claims to preeminence; usually they are not denied openly, but nor is too much made of them. A royal, military model of status ranking is instead given prominence, and landholders demand and commonly receive due deference from their subordinates, often clients bound by political and economic ties. None of this is a mere matter of naked force, for political power and landed wealth are themselves positively valued and constitute a recognized basis for claiming a widely acknowledged lordly superiority. Kingly hierarchy—albeit less splendidly than in the courts themselves—is therefore reproduced at the local level within a network of patron-client relations anchored in the landholding pattern.

In a fuller study of Indian society, we would now have to look at the agrarian class system, trading networks, industrialization and urbanization, and many other factors. For a work on Hinduism, however, *varna* and caste, and Brahmanhood, renunciation, and kingship, are the most crucial ideological and institutional components in the hierarchical structure of Indian society, although one other form of inequality—that between men and women—cannot be overlooked.

The Position of Women

> Yes, a husband is a god. Even as we believe in God . . . so we must consider our husband equal to God. . . . [Whatever he may be], he's fine for me. Even if he beats me, then beat away, Brother. He's my husband. (Jacobson 1978: 118)

These words are Bhuribai's, an elderly, poor, and illiterate high-caste woman living in a Madhya Pradesh village, who told her life-story to Doranne Jacobson in the early 1970s. The quotation starkly reveals the position of Hindu women as seen by one of them, whose views are not exceptional. As a description of female subordination, Bhuribai's words are no less graphic than the following famous verse from the *Laws of Manu* (*Manusmriti* 5.148; Basham 1971: 182), the most influential *dharmashastra* text, which attained its extant form nearly two thousand years ago.

> In childhood subject to her father,
> in youth to her husband,
> and when her husband is dead to her sons,
> she should never enjoy independence.

According to virtually all traditional Hindu authorities, a woman is a minor at law, who has rights of maintenance and residence, but normally no rights in her patrilineal family's immovable property. (In matrilineal communities such as the Nayars of Kerala, a woman generally enjoys greater rights, but matriliny is the custom of only a small minority of Hindus.) In general terms, Hindu women, in the past and the present, are plainly inferior in status to men and subordinate to their power and authority. Scripturally, women are assimilated with Shudras. Whereas men of the first three *varnas* undergo an initiation rite in early adulthood, so that they are "twice-born," women do not and, like all Shudras, remain disprivileged in religious and legal terms.

The position of women is most clearly set out in relation to wifehood; according to P. V. Kane (1968–77, 2:561–62), all *dharmashastra* texts "are agreed that the foremost duty of a wife is to obey her husband and to honour him as her god," just as Bhuribai said. The virtuous wife is a *pativrata*, "devoted to her husband," who remains ever faithful. Sexual fidelity is consistently stressed and many well-known stories tell of the dreadful misfortune visited on the husbands and families of adulterous women. The status of her family and caste also depend heavily on a woman's sexual conduct. An unmarried girl who is unchaste and a wife who is unfaithful bring dishonor; but if they have sexual relations with men of a lower caste, they are also polluted and hence endanger the purity of their group. Outcasting was the traditional punishment for such transgressions. The preoccupation with purity is a major reason for the insistence on female sexual probity. Among Brahmans and many high castes, girls used to be married before puberty. This practice was partly intended to prevent any sexual liaisons compromising to family and caste status that might result in the birth of illegitimate, mixed-blood offspring. Partly because men do not bear children and do not absorb women's polluting sexual fluids during intercourse as fully as women absorb men's semen, the sanctions on illicit male sexual behavior are far less strict. Obviously, these physiological considerations neatly rationalize greater sexual liberty for men, but they are nonetheless consistent with basic assumptions about bodily purity and its connection with the purity of the group. Moreover, as Bhuribai's words—and indeed her whole story—show, the ideal of the virtuous wife is not just a dogma propounded by men, for it is often fully internalized by women themselves. Wifely devotion and faithfulness are vital to a woman's self-esteem.

Yet women are not uniformly inferior and subordinate. Many women, especially later in life, have considerable power and influence, not only in the home itself, but also in the arrangement of their children's marriages, the organization of work on the family farm, the buying and selling of property, and many other matters. Publicly, such women may consistently defer to their menfolk, but in reality many weighty decisions are made by them. Furthermore, the ideal of the virtuous wife, although pervasive throughout Indian society, is more explicitly stressed among higher castes and the well-to-do, whose female members are therefore more likely to present a passive and deferential appearance. The custom of prepubertal marriage, for example, has rarely been practiced by the lower castes, whose obsession with group purity—and hence male control over women—is generally less consuming.

The status of women, moreover, is interdependent with other indices of status. Take as an illustration the case of work. A family's status, in the eyes of its own members and outsiders, is significantly affected by the kind of work done by its womenfolk. Likewise, a caste's status is also partly a function of the work its female members typically do. Women belonging to high-status, wealthy families are often confined to the home and may be fully veiled if they must go out; in general, they do no work at all beyond supervision of their servants, unless—as is now common in India—they have "respectable" clerical or professional employment (which can often place them in senior positions). In lower-status, poorer families, women do domestic tasks and may, in a farming family, work when required on their own family land. In the lowest-status, poorest families (typically landless and low-caste), women go out to work for others as servants, agricultural laborers, or manual workers in factories and on building sites. There are notable exceptions; for example, in fishing communities, women often control marketing and have a major economic role outside the household. Among most of the population, however, the extent of female participation in work inside or outside the home is an inverse index of family and group status. Because this is understood by everybody, women are fully aware that wage-work for others outside the home is degrading, and so are likely to aspire to a life of domestic idleness. What applies to women applies to men as well, if less forcefully. A high-caste, wealthy landlord commonly delegates all responsibility for his estate to an employed supervisor, so that he can devote himself to lordly patronage, religious study, or some other dignified pursuit.

Idle women secluded at home may bemoan their fate and envy the apparent freedom of lower-status, poorer women who work together in fields or factories, earning wages that reduce their economic dependence on their husbands. But most such work is hard, badly paid, and demeaning. Furthermore, the institutionalized inequalities of Indian society ensure that, in most social settings, women at the top perceive few common interests with women at the bottom, or vice versa. The very logic of the status system also means that the women who are most inferior and subordinate relative to their own husbands are, in broad terms, the ones who belong to the highest social strata. They are therefore unlikely to want to change places with women from the lower strata. That this is so emerges clearly in Bhuribai's story, for through her seemingly self-abased faithfulness she "has also helped to uphold the high status of her caste, a status from which she has derived much benefit" (Jacobson 1978: 134), not least for her own self-esteem.

Everywhere in India, however, despite the inferiority and subordination that attach in varying degrees to wifehood, marriage makes a Hindu woman "auspicious" (*shubha, mangala*). She epitomizes goodness, prosperity, well-being, health, happiness, and creativity, which will be confirmed—she and her family hope—when she becomes a mother, a status idealized in both popular culture and scripture. But the wife is an auspicious, perfect Hindu woman only while her husband is alive. The widow is inauspiciousness personified and epitomizes every negative quality. Especially among Brahmans and other high castes, for whom the idea of auspicious wifehood is most fully elaborated, widows cannot attend auspicious rituals, such as weddings. Unlike wives, widows should not wear jewelry or colored saris, and they cannot put an auspicious red mark (*tilaka*) on their foreheads or a vermilion streak (*sindura*) in the parting of their hair; indeed, widows should keep their hair short or shaved off, whereas other adult women do not cut their hair. Such quasi-ascetic restrictions have always been harshest among the high castes, who traditionally prohibited widow remarriage as well. Today they tend to be rigorously observed only by a minority of rather old-fashioned widows. Nevertheless, the widow remains the living symbol of inauspiciousness in contrast to the auspicious wife. It is still widely believed that she has suffered a great misfortune in surviving her spouse. She may even be blamed for his death, because a good wife predeceases her husband.

Bhuribai, then, expresses a characteristic wish when she prays: "Please take me first. Let him [my husband] live, but take me" (ibid.: 129). If the husband does die first, a woman can escape widowhood to remain an auspicious wife by immolating herself on his funeral pyre as a *sati*—also a "faithful wife"—since she does not strictly become a widow until her husband's funeral rites are complete. The self-immolation of widows, often known by the anglicism "suttee," was almost entirely confined to high-caste communities in particular regions of India. Even where it did occur quite often (such as nineteenth-century Bengal), only a small minority of women died in this way. Suttee was first prohibited by law by the British government of India in 1829. Since then it has been very rare, although it is not extinct even today, as the highly publicized case of Roop Kanwar, an eighteen-year-old Rajput girl who burnt herself in Rajasthan in 1987, made clear to the world. Ghastly as the ritual of self-immolation seems to most Indians, a widow who chooses to follow her husband on to the fire is still widely seen as an acme of wifely perfection. When poor Bhuribai did eventually lose her husband, she too wanted to die with him, although she was not allowed to do so (ibid.: 133).

It is, of course, true that widowhood can and often does enhance a woman's power, precisely because she is no longer subject to her husband's authority. Throughout India, many widows are virtual matriarchs over their households and younger family members, including adult sons, and they display the kind of steely authority wielded by the most powerful of all modern Indian widows, Indira Gandhi, who ruled as prime minister for most of the period between 1966 and her assassination in 1984.

Nevertheless, widowhood consistently carries a powerfully negative symbolic load among Hindus, and it is crucial that the inauspiciousness of widows reverses the auspiciousness personified by women with living husbands. Complete wifely auspiciousness, moreover, is dependent upon sexual maturity, the precondition for natural creativity through childbirth. Yet the mature woman is subject to birth and menstrual pollution, whereas the immature girl is not. Hence in simple terms, a pure girl normally grows up to become an impure wife, who is nonetheless auspicious until she becomes an inauspicious widow. A wife is less pure than her husband and, partly for that reason, she is his inferior, but she is simultaneously the personification of goodness in life, notably because she can bear the sons who will succeed her husband and continue his family line.

A mature woman's sexual fertility, heralded by her polluting menstruation, is also conceptualized as a manifestation of the feminine power (*shakti*) that she shares with Hindu goddesses. Later I shall explore the goddesses' significance for the position of Hindu women; here I only want to make one crucial point. In many respects, the relationship between men and women, especially husbands and wives, patently reflects hierarchical ideology and epitomizes institutionalized inequality in Indian society. Yet women are not just the second sex; quite apart from any real power and influence that they may in fact have, women do, as wives, personify auspiciousness and, like goddesses, they possess a ritual power upon which men (and gods) partly but significantly depend. The position of women in Hinduism and Indian society is much more complex than Bhuribai's assertion and *Manu*'s edict initially suggest.

SANSKRITIC HINDUISM AND THE GREAT AND LITTLE TRADITIONS

Because the principle of hierarchical inequality is so fundamental in Hinduism and Indian society, anthropological analysis of the popular religion has often been preoccupied by the problem of religious stratification. Put simply, the problem is this: is Hinduism divided into higher and lower strata, forms or levels, so that the beliefs and practices of higher-status social groups are distinct from and superior to those of lower-status groups? Answering this apparently easy empirical question has turned out to be very difficult, but I need to look at it now because debate about the problem of religious stratification has been central to analysis of the relationship between popular Hinduism and Indian society.

In modern anthropology, the debate was opened by Srinivas in 1952 in his pioneering monograph, *Religion and Society among the Coorgs of South India*. In that book, Srinivas introduced the concept of "Sanskritic" Hinduism, defined as "Hinduism which transcends provincial barriers and is common to the whole of India" (1965: 75). In contrast to "All-India Hinduism," there are "Peninsular," "Regional," and "Local Hinduisms" (ibid.: 214), but most striking throughout Srinivas's study is the dichotomy between Sanskritic Hinduism and local, village-based, non-Sanskritic Hinduism.

The phrase "Sanskritic Hinduism" clearly implies a definitive connection with Sanskrit scriptural texts. In fact, Srinivas does not define "Sanskritic" in such terms, but he does list a series of features characteristic of Sanskritic Hinduism, such as worship of great deities like Vishnu and Shiva, the pan-Hindu sacredness of rivers, the importance of major pilgrimage centers, the currency of the two classical epics (the *Ramayana* and the *Mahabharata*), the sanctity of the cow, belief in the concepts of *karma* and *dharma*, and the preeminent role of Brahmans (ibid.: chap. 7).

In Srinivas's analysis, Sanskritic Hinduism is coupled to another concept, "Sanskritization"—the historical process by which the beliefs and practices of lower castes tend to converge toward those of higher castes, especially Brahmans, as the former try to raise their status by emulating the latter. Sanskritic Hinduism is thereby given a sociological foundation as, in principle, the religion of the high castes, whose pan-Indian universality derives from its roots in the Sanskrit scriptural tradition mainly perpetuated throughout the country by the Brahman literati. In other words, the division of Hinduism into higher Sanskritic and lower non-Sanskritic strata is explained sociologically as the functional correlate of a caste-based, hierarchical social structure.

Also in the early 1950s, in connection with his wide-ranging examination of the contrast between "folk society and civilization," Robert Redfield introduced into anthropology the concept of the "great" and "little traditions." In 1954, Redfield and Milton Singer published an influential article on the cultural role of cities, in which they discussed India in a wider comparative perspective. They argued that in all major civilizations "primary urbanization"—the early, internally generated growth of cities—has been instrumental in transforming the mainly rural, eclectic, "folk" little traditions into a coherent great tradition. This transformation is accomplished by the urban literati, who create the great tradition by intellectual, aesthetic, and ritual systematization, so that it becomes the "core culture of an indigenous civilization" and "a vehicle and standard for those who share it to identify with one another as members of a common civilization" (1954: 63).

Although Redfield's and Srinivas's concepts are far from identical, they have generally been merged in Indian anthropology. Thus Singer easily refers (despite some minor qualifications) to the "Great Tradition of Sanskritic Hinduism" (1972: xiii, 384, 386) and by implication contrasts it with the little tradition of non-Sanskritic Hinduism. Like Singer, most anthropologists of Hinduism, irrespective of their preferred terminology, have implicitly accepted this fusion of alternative ways to describe Hinduism's higher and lower strata, and nothing would be gained by trying to separate them anew. The fundamental question is not in fact terminological, but substantive: what are these higher and lower strata first identified by Srinivas, Redfield, and Singer?

Clearly, Srinivas's list of Sanskritic Hinduism's characteristic features (as summarized above) is very miscellaneous. Moreover, as J. F. Staal

(1963) shows, many of them are only tenuously Sanskritic, if that term is taken to signify a real connection with Sanskrit language, literature, and culture. To give one brief example: although the standard recensions of the *Ramayana* and *Mahabharata* are in Sanskrit, their stories are told among ordinary people in vernacular languages, and some versions of the epics—such as the *Ramayana* in Hindi and Tamil—themselves enjoy the status of popular religious classics. Further, many epic stories reappear, more or less transformed, in other vernacular mythologies (and associated ritual celebrations) that eulogize local deities and sacred centers, rather than great deities and all-India centers. Difficulties of a similar sort can be raised about every feature in Srinivas's list, so that the dividing line between Hinduism's two strata dissolves. In the end, we seem to be left with a concept of Sanskritic Hinduism that has no definable empirical content at all.

Recognizing this problem, Srinivas and other writers have tried to be more precise, but their efforts have only produced a range of variant definitions, more or less apposite for the particular contexts in which they have been deployed. Significantly, too, the anthropologist who probably searched for Sanskritic Hinduism most assiduously in the field frankly admits his failure. "The structure of Sanskritic Hinduism was not so simple as I had thought," writes Singer, because there are actually "several variant versions"; "I stopped looking for *the* Great Tradition and gave up the effort to select *the* orthodox version of Sanskritic Hinduism" (1972: 82).

All competent anthropological studies of Hinduism over the last thirty years or so have reached similar conclusions. It is now generally accepted that the religion is not split into two (or more) separate strata, each with its own body of distinctive beliefs and practices. In fairness to Srinivas, Redfield, and Singer, it must be said that they always insisted that the higher and lower strata are interconnected. Yet their work does tend to represent the whole as if it were a combination of two strata, so that it mistakenly implies that Sanskritic and non-Sanskritic Hinduism, or the great and little traditions, are separate—or at least separable—components of the religion.

Partly reacting to criticism of Srinivas, the Sanskritist J. A. B. van Buitenen observes that the term "Sanskritic," although a misnomer, "has reference to a rather complex notion of normative self-culture, of which it is more or less consciously felt that the Sanskrit language was its original vehicle. . . . 'Sanskritic' is that which is the most ancient, therefore the most pure, and therefore hierarchically the most elevated" (1968: 34). Thus the sense of the term is undeniably Hindu, "if not in fact Brahmanistic," and it draws attention to one vitally important indigenous criterion of evaluation: is a belief or practice authorized by Sanskrit scripture, whose interpretation preeminently belongs to learned Brahmans? Seen in this light, the category of Sanskritic Hinduism primarily connotes a Brahmanical standard for evaluation, a paradigm of the normatively most distinguished or prestigious. As my quotation from their article showed, Redfield and Singer had said something very similar, but Srinivas himself did reify his concept by postulating a real separation between Sanskritic and non-Sanskritic Hinduism. In other words, Srinivas made a stock anthropological error; he converted an indigenous, ideological distinction into an analytical concept, and then applied it to the empirical evidence to try to divide what is actually united by common underlying themes and principles.

At the level of ideological discourse rather than empirical fact, however, Srinivas's concept of Sanskritic Hinduism appositely captures an indigenous frame of reference. It is true, as we shall see in later chapters, that the Brahmanical standard of Sanskritic Hinduism is neither monolithic nor unchallenged by alternatives. Nonetheless, it represents the single most important evaluative norm within Hinduism. By reference to it, higher-status groups tend to regard their own beliefs and practices as superior to those assumed to belong to lower-status groups.

Let me illustrate this point by a brief reference to Jonathan Parry's ethnographic report on evaluation among Brahmans in the sacred city of Benares (Varanasi). Benares Brahmans make "a sharp distinction . . . between the *shastrik* (or scriptural) and the *laukik* (or popular)." If a belief or practice can be established as *shastrik*, it is "eternally valid and binding on all Hindus, and in [its] interpretation the Brahman is preeminent"; if *shastrik*, it is "unquestionably authoritative," but if *laukik* it is not. The *shastrik* is "that which is sanctioned—or held to be sanctioned—by the ancient Sanskrit texts," by which is meant the entire corpus of scripture, although there is "no general consensus on what belongs to which category." Hence, and crucially, the *shastrik-laukik* opposition is an evaluation made with reference to the supposed contents of the *dharmashastra* and other Sanskrit texts, not on the basis of any scrutiny of their actual subject matter (Parry 1985a: 204–5).

Parry's account clearly shows that Benares Brahmans (and others in the city as well) consistently evaluate religious belief and practice by reference to the *shastrik-laukik* distinction. They also assume that the scriptural and popular are two more or less stable and separate religious strata, whereas in reality they are not, owing to the lack of any general consensus about their constituent elements. As Parry (ibid.: 203) also observes, however, the very distinction between scriptural and popular is predicated on putative heterogeneity between the higher and lower strata, which are imagined as truly disconnected as if the scriptural and popular—Sanskritic and non-Sanskritic, great and little—originated in two totally different domains. Hence among Hindus themselves, especially Brahmans and others keen to assert their own superiority, there is a marked disposition to reify the putatively separate strata. This indigenous tendency to reification has itself contributed to anthropological misconstruction of empirical separation within the one religion.

Yet it is equally mistaken to overstate the unity of Hinduism. Impatient dismissal of the concepts of Sanskritic Hinduism and the great and little traditions as uselessly distortive, as well as their uncritical adoption, have both contributed to misunderstanding popular Hinduism and its relationship with Indian society. It is crucial to that relationship that social inequality is frequently reflected, expressed, and constructed in the religious domain by asserting that my beliefs and practices, and my group's, are superior to yours. Hence there are significant social factors that generate and sustain a measure of institutional separation between different bodies of religious belief and practice. The temples of great deities like Vishnu and Shiva, for example, tend to attract more high-caste worshipers, and they are mainly served by Brahman priests, who make only vegetarian offerings and use Sanskrit as the ritual language. By contrast, the temples of many other deities tend to be patronized by the low castes, and they generally have non-Brahman priests, who make both vegetarian and nonvegetarian offerings and use vernacular languages in ritual. Clearly, there are complex historical reasons for such institutional separation, but the relevant sociological point is that the separation is reinforced by the higher-status groups' need to differentiate themselves from their inferiors by patronizing institutions, like the great deities' Brahmanical temples, which are evaluated as superior religious arenas. Moreover, by the circular logic typifying ideologies of social inequality, the existence of institutional separation is often taken as proof of the very validity of an evaluative distinction between Sanskritic and non-Sanskritic Hinduism.

Institutional separation, however, is always incomplete, precisely because the beliefs and practices of popular Hinduism are always interconnected and rest on common structures of relationships. Hence the measure of separation that does exist cannot sustain the claim that the religion comprises two (or more) separate strata. Nowhere is this clearer than among the deities themselves, the gods and goddesses with whom a study of popular Hinduism must begin.

Chapter 2

GODS AND GODDESSES

> Lord Vishnu spoke:
> Long ago, when everything animate and inanimate was lost in that one awful ocean, Shiva himself appeared in order to awaken Brahma and myself. There was only this dreadful undifferentiated ocean made up of darkness in the midst of which I myself, with one thousand heads, one thousand eyes, one thousand feet and one thousand arms, lay sleeping, self-controlled, bearing conch, discus and mace. Meanwhile I saw at a distance a god of boundless light, shining like ten million suns, circled by luster, the four-faced god whose Yoga [ascetic power] is great, the person of golden color, wearing a black antelope skin, the god who is hymned with Rig, Yajur and Sama Vedas.
> (*Kurma Purana* 1.25; Dimmitt and van Buitenen 1978: 205 [diacritics omitted])

A S THE SUN sinks quickly in a blaze of redness below the Indian horizon, women light oil lamps symbolizing the goddess Lakshmi's presence in their homes and temple priests prepare for evening worship. At most temples, the crowd of worshipers is thickest after dark, and at Shiva's temples in Gujarat it is said that the greatest spiritual merit can be gained then, because all the deities are in attendance. To gaze on the phallic emblem of Shiva standing in his temple is as beneficial as a vision of every god and goddess separately, all 330 million of them (Stevenson 1920: 394–95). The ancient sage who first advanced this figure no doubt thought of it as almost unimaginably large. And even if India's human population, now more than twice as numerous, has rather reduced its impact, the proverbial total of 330 million still conveys to us popular theistic Hinduism's superabundance of divine beings.

Giant numbers are invoked too to describe the indescribable dimensions of the gods, of Shiva shining 10 million times as brightly as the radiant sun in the Indian sky. Above all else, it is the vast and variously imagined power of the deities that Vishnu's speech intends to convey, and it is that power over the world and its inhabitants that is taken for granted by the overwhelming majority of Hindus. They therefore see ritual communication with the gods and goddesses as imperative.

HINDU POLYTHEISM

Before we can explore the rituals of popular Hinduism, we have to understand the distinctive nature of its polytheism. The dictionary defines polytheism as "belief in or worship of many gods." Although this definition broadly applies to Hinduism, all Hindus sometimes and some Hindus always insist that there is in reality only one God, of whom all the distinct gods and goddesses are but forms. To ask if Hindus do or do not believe in more than one god is therefore too simple, for they may say that there is one god and many in almost the same breath. For example, Hindus often talk about different deities whom they worship, identify the god or goddess considered to be most powerful or sympathetic, and simultaneously insist that all deities are ultimately one. This manner of speaking is not self-contradictory. Conventionally and simply, we can say that the polytheistic Hindu pantheon comprises a large number of deities, the term I use throughout to refer collectively to both gods and goddesses. Most deities have numerous forms or manifestations and most have a multitude of names. Chanting standard lists of their names is itself a common way to praise deities. There is, however, no sharp opposition between distinct deities or forms of them, on the one hand, and variant names for the same deity or form, on the other. Thus a single deity with different names may be seen, in another context or from another perspective, as a set of distinct deities. This fluidity—which means that one deity can become many and many deities can become one—is a supremely important characteristic of Hindu polytheism.

Also crucial in Hindu polytheism is the relationship between the deities and humanity. Unlike Jewish, Christian, and Islamic monotheism, predicated on the otherness of God and either his total separation from man or his singular incarnation in Christ, Hinduism postulates no absolute distinction between deities and human beings. The idea that all deities are truly one is, moreover, easily extended to proclaim that all human beings are in reality also forms of one supreme deity—Brahman, the Absolute of philosophical Hinduism. In practice, this abstract monist doctrine rarely belongs to an ordinary Hindu's stated religious beliefs. Yet, examples of permeability between the divine and human can easily be found in popular Hinduism in many unremarkable contexts.

As we have seen, a wife ideally venerates her husband as a god, but a more forceful and reciprocal expression of a like idea is that the bride and groom are divine on their wedding day. They are usually identified as particular deities—the groom as, say, Shiva or Rama, an incarnation of the great god Vishnu, and his bride as their respective consorts, Parvati or Sita. During the wedding ritual, the couple are worshiped in much the same way as deities are worshiped before their images in temples, so that at least once in their lives, almost all Hindus assume a divine form before their family and friends.

There are many other comparable examples. For instance, a priest, particularly in temples dedicated to Vishnu or Shiva, should carry out a ritual to make himself a form of the god during worship. More generally identification with the deity, so that the human worshiper becomes divine, is a fundamental objective in Hindu worship (*puja*). Again, a man or woman, or even a child, who becomes possessed by a deity is, while in this state, regarded as a bodily manifestation of the deity within. A more particular instance is the pure virgin girl adored as a goddess in *kumari puja*, "virgin worship," a cult most prevalent in northern and eastern India and Nepal.

The most dramatic cases, however, are certainly the Hindu "holy men" and "god-men" (gurus, sadhus, swamis, and so on) who have sometimes found fame and fortune beyond India as well as within it. All these holy men are in principle ascetic world-renouncers. Ordinary Hindus are rarely credulous about their holy men (or occasionally women), many of whom are treated with healthy skepticism because their complete renunciation is doubted. But those who do command conviction are often revered and worshiped as divine, even though no one would normally deny that they are also human beings. Men of this kind include leading monks, such as the Shankaracharyas who head the monasteries founded by the great philosopher Shankara around A.D. 700–800, as well as the founders of new religious movements, such as the god-man Sathya Sai Baba, who claims to be a form of Shiva. In contemporary India, millions of Hindus worship the Shankaracharyas, Sai Baba, and other similar personages as deities.

None of this means that Hindus cannot or do not differentiate between deities and people. For most people most of the time, the difference between divinity and humanity is patent and never dissolves one ineradicable distinction: in the current age anyway, gods and goddesses are immortal, but human beings must die. Because the religion is premised on the lack of any absolute divide between them, however, human beings can be divine forms under many and various conditions, and the claim to divinity is unsensational, even banal, in a way that it could never be in a monotheistic religion lacking 330 million deities. By a western reader in particular, this fundamental point must be understood. A Hindu claiming to be divine is rarely saying anything extraordinary, let alone heretical, and human divine forms are no more and no less than a logical corollary of Hinduism's fluid polytheism.

Most of the principal deities worshiped by Hindus are, however, fully divine and not, at one and the same time, partly human. The multiplicity of their names does not make it easy for readers unfamiliar with them. But I shall try to simplify by using single names for each deity consistently, overlooking other epithets and regional variants whenever possible. Moreover, the impression of inchoate abundance given by so many names will be mitigated once the main dimensions of the polytheistic pantheon have been grasped.

VISHNU AND SHIVA AS GREAT GODS

Vishnu and Shiva are preeminent as the two great gods (*deva*) of Hinduism. They are worshiped by Hindus everywhere and there are thousands upon thousands of temples and shrines dedicated to them. They are also the leading characters in Hindu mythology and other scriptures, and most accounts of theistic Hinduism, since they are based on textual scholarship, focus on this pair. Because the place of Vishnu and Shiva in popular Hinduism significantly reflects the textual design, my account partly derives from that scholarship. A third great god, Brahma, has a prominent place in classical mythology and is sometimes important in popular religion as well, although he is not widely worshiped and normally assumes a subsidiary role in relation to Vishnu, Shiva, and other deities.

Vishnu's name means "the pervader" and Shiva's "the auspicious," usually interpreted as a propitiatory epithet to avert his ferocity. Like all deities, each god has many names—classically 1,000 (or 1,008)—and in fact many Hindus rarely use the names "Vishnu" and "Shiva." In much of north India, for example, Shiva is usually known as Mahadeva (or a vernacular synonym), "great god," and both gods (in common with others) are ordinarily addressed by terms such as *bhagavan* or *swami*, translated as "god" or "lord."

Vishnu and Shiva are sometimes described as celestial, not simply because they inhabit a heavenly world, but also because they primarily oversee the universe as a whole. Their vast powers are very general and their stage transcends the world inhabited by human beings. The perennial theme of their dramas is the tension between order and chaos, creation and destruction, on a cosmic scale. Typically, this tension is expressed through the eternal opposition between Vishnu and Shiva (allied with other deities) and the "demons" (*asura*), who strive to usurp the gods' place and thereby destroy the proper order (*dharma*) of the cosmos. The greatest and most powerful of the demons, however, are normally devotees of Vishnu and Shiva, who originally gave them their powers as a boon. Their hostility spent after defeat in battle, demons are often saved by their divine conquerors. Hence deities and demons are symbiotically linked to each other, and personify respectively the order and chaos that are, in the Hindu worldview, ultimately inseparable. The narrower moral connotations of good and evil implied by the English terms are less in evidence.

Let me now look at the two preeminent gods in a little more detail. Vishnu's consort is the auspicious goddess of fortune, Lakshmi, although in his temples he often has a second, lower-status wife as well, frequently identified as Bhudevi, goddess of the earth. Although Vishnu is a celestial god, he has ten distinct incarnations or avatars (*avatara*). Nine have successively "descended" into this world already and the tenth will appear to herald the dissolution of the world at the end of the degenerate era in which we now live, the *kaliyuga*. Each incarnation is always contemporaneously present as well, however, and by far the most important in popular Hinduism are the seventh, Rama, and the eighth, Krishna. Vishnu himself, in one form or another, is widely worshiped, but he is probably more frequently adored in his incarnations as Rama or Krishna. There are sizable devotionalist movements whose members worship Rama or Krishna, and many temples are dedicated to them throughout India. In all their temples, Vishnu or his incarnations are normally represented by anthropomorphic images. Vishnu in particular is often shown wearing a high crown. On his forehead, the god wears one of the distinctive "sectmarks" of the Vaishnavas (Vishnu's devotees)—typically a vertical red line within a white V-shape.

Rama, the hero of the *Ramayana*, was the king of Ayodhya, in north India. Among other feats he vanquished Ravana, the demon king of (Sri) Lanka, who was a devotee of the gods (Brahma, Shiva). For most Hindus, Rama is the very model of a just and righteous king and husband to his wife Sita.

Krishna's story is recounted in various mythological sources and he also appears prominently in the *Mahabharata*, particularly in the section known as the *Bhagavad Gita*—nowadays the most celebrated of all Hindu scriptures—which is believed to have been spoken by Krishna. Krishna, like Rama, was a king and conqueror of demons, but his cult frequently turns on his exploits as a child and youth, especially his love affair with the beautiful cowherdess, Radha.

Shiva's wife is Parvati in classical mythology, but in his temples he has many different consorts. Unlike Vishnu, Shiva has not descended to earth in a series of incarnations, although he does have a huge range of contemporaneously existent forms or manifestations (*murti*) that include, for example, Bhairava (the terrible), Bhikshatana (the beggar), Dakshinamurti (the guru), and Nataraja (lord of the dance).

The principal cultic symbol of Shiva is the aniconic *linga*, a round-topped pillar that represents his phallus and stands on a base representing the female sexual organ (*yoni*). In virtually all his temples, the main shrine houses a *linga*, which is the object of worship in almost exactly the same way as anthropomorphic images of other deities. But Shiva can be represented anthropomorphically as well. He is commonly shown with a head of matted locks and other distinctive marks of the world-renouncer, who generates fiery heat (*tapas*) and hence creative power within himself by practicing asceticism. On his forehead (or the *linga*) he wears the mark of the Shaivas (Shiva's devotees)—three horizontal stripes of white ash (*vibhuti*), sometimes surmounting a dot of red powder (*kunkuma*) or red lead (*sindura*) above the bridge of the nose. The ash, which comes from the funeral pyre, is associated with Shiva himself, but the red mark is a symbol of his female consort.

Unlike Vishnu, Shiva has children, normally two sons, Ganesha and Skanda, who figure prominently in their father's cosmic dramas. In general, Ganesha and Skanda are subject to Shiva's superior authority and derive their power from him. Ganesha, the elder son, is the celebrated elephant-headed god and as Vighneshwara, "Lord of the obstacles," he is ubiquitously worshiped before starting any ritual or enterprise. Ganesha is often, but not always, represented as unmarried, whereas the younger son Skanda has two wives. Ganesha and Skanda are worshiped in association with Shiva, but there are also many temples independently dedicated to each of them. Ganesha's cult is especially popular in Maharashtra and Skanda's in Tamilnadu, where he is usually called by his Tamil name, Murugan.

The relationship between Vishnu and Shiva is fundamental in Hinduism, as is shown by much of their mythology, both classical and vernacular, and by the rituals performed for the two gods. In the Tamil country, the gods' relationship is conspicuously expressed by portraying Vishnu and Shiva as brothers-in-law, with Vishnu's sister, the goddess, being Shiva's wife. In other areas of India, however, the two gods' relationship is seldom given such an elemental form, and everywhere it can be partly obscured by the tendency to ascribe every godly quality to both of them. For several centuries, Vaishnavas have been more inclined to assert the absolute supremacy of Vishnu at the expense of Shiva, than Shaivas have been to do the same for Shiva in relation to Vishnu. Both sets of devotees, however, are consistently inclined to claim that each god fully possesses the other's powers as well. Similarly, in exact conformity with the premise that many can be one, it is not hard to find Hindus praising Vishnu as Shiva, Shiva as Vishnu, and Vishnu-Shiva as the supreme God. Nonetheless, there is an underlying structural relationship between the two gods defined by their distinctive divine personalities.

To oppose Vishnu "the preserver" to Shiva "the destroyer" (with Brahma as "the creator"), which used to be common in the literature, is certainly simplistic. Yet in broad terms, Vishnu is principally associated with the preservation of the cosmos and its proper order, over which he is sovereign. Through his incarnations, it says in one myth, Vishnu "was born among men for the maintenance of Dharma" (Dimmitt and van Buitenen 1978: 67). Hence, Vishnu is also linked to kingship, for the Hindu king must guarantee order in the world. As we have seen, Vishnu is iconographically distinguished as a monarch wearing a crown. Shiva, by contrast, is preeminently a lone ascetic—the greatest of them all—who has renounced the world so that he is outside and beyond its institutional constraints. Shiva's place is the cremation ground, whence comes the ash he smears on himself, as well as the forests and mountains, at the margins of the settled realm over which the king reigns. Describing himself to Parvati, Shiva says: "He is not a normal man. His hair is unkempt. He is always alone by himself. Above all, he is indifferent to the world" (ibid.: 162). The summit of Mount Kailasa in the Himalayas is Shiva's favorite place of meditative repose, so that he is linked with the exterior and the beyond, whereas Vishnu is sovereign over the civilized center. Vishnu upholds the morality of the Hindu social system and its elaborate hierarchical institutions, because the order of society is intrinsic to and continuous with the order of the cosmos. Shiva, by contrast, rejects and transcends that order.

Of the two great gods, Vishnu seems more easily comprehensible, at least to the western mind. As preserver of the sociocosmic order, he is generally perceived as benevolent, as well as a god of orthodox righteousness. In his various incarnations, he has come into the world to save it, and Rama in particular is the quintessentially ethical king and husband. Shiva, however, is immediately discerned as complicated and even paradoxical. A renouncer performing austerities in his mountain fastness, he is often immoral, violent, or ferociously destructive as well (for example, in his terrible form as Bhairava). The supreme ascetic is also distinguished by his wanton adultery and unmatched erotic powers, symbolized by his phallic *linga*. His myths and rituals celebrate his repetitive transgression of conventional social and moral codes, so that those who worship Shiva ostensibly adore an antisocial god indifferently opposed to the order upheld by Vishnu the king.

It is not surprising that foreign observers of Hinduism have often been simultaneously repelled and fascinated by Shiva and his cult. Certainly Wendy Doniger O'Flaherty's claim that Shiva "is in many ways the most uniquely Indian god of them all" (1973: 1) is just. At the same time, in both myth and ritual, the preservation of the cosmos is shown to depend on Shiva's involvement with it, as he partly comes out of his ascetic state, so that the god is not depicted as a willful destroyer of the world. Conversely, the complex character of Vishnu, who is neither an unambivalent figure of righteousness nor always a preserver, must not be oversimplified. Thus Krishna for instance—the delightful child and beautiful lover who plays the trickster's role—crushes his enemies during the *Mahabharata* war and proclaims himself the final destroyer of the universe. Moreover and more subtly, in Hindu cyclical cosmology the powers to preserve and destroy, which in the end are both fully possessed by Vishnu and Shiva, are but two sides of the same coin; the world is created out of sacrificial destruction (as the hymn of Purusha's sacrifice explains), preserved by destroying the demonic enemies of order, and finally destroyed so that it can be created and preserved anew.

Lastly, many apparent paradoxes in Shiva's divine character are, to the Hindu way of thinking, hardly paradoxes at all. For example, the ascetic austerities practiced by a renouncer generate great power, not least erotic power. Logically and not paradoxically, therefore, the renouncer possesses far more sexual potency than ordinary men in the world. Hence Shiva the great ascetic is also the great lover, able to keep his phallus erect indefinitely without spilling his semen. Many other ostensible contradictions in the god's attributes are equally explicable in the light of Hindu ideas about world renunciation.

Vishnu and Shiva, as great gods with general powers over the cosmos, are normally thought to distance themselves from mundane problems affecting ordinary people. For this reason, Hindus rarely ask them for help either with collective afflictions, such as epidemics or drought, or with personal troubles, such as illness or childlessness. Requests of this sort, as we shall see, are usually addressed to other deities who are more likely to respond, although it is certainly not uncommon for people to pray to Rama and Krishna, or to some of Shiva's forms and his sons Ganesha and Skanda, for divine aid in this world. Moreover, although celestial Vishnu and Shiva command the universe, they are also represented here on earth in their temples.

VISHNU AND SHIVA IN THEIR TEMPLES

Every Hindu temple—from the vast edifices of the great gods to the crude shrines of little deities—is dedicated to a presiding deity. The temple contains that deity's image (or *linga* in Shiva's case) and normally bears its name. In a large temple, the image is housed in the main central shrine, which is surrounded by other shrines containing images of subsidiary deities; in a very small temple or simple shrine standing by itself, there may be only the one image. Sometimes, a temple has more than one presiding deity, but this does not materially affect the following discussion.

In principle, each temple (unless designed to be a duplicate of another) is unique, because it is dedicated to the particular form of the deity whose image is housed within it. In their major temples, Vishnu and Shiva always bear distinctive names. Vishnu, for instance, is Venkateshwara at Tirupati in Andhra Pradesh, today the richest temple in India, and Krishna is Jagannatha at Puri, his celebrated temple in Orissa; Shiva is Vishwanatha in the temple at Benares, which is widely accepted as his holiest site, and Sundareshwara in his great temple at Madurai in Tamilnadu, which is popularly known by his consort's name as the Minakshi temple. In their smaller temples, Vishnu and Shiva are commonly distinguished only by a suffix indicating the name of the locality. Nonetheless, all their temples are in principle dedicated to specific named forms of Vishnu or Shiva, which are distinct from their counterparts in other Vishnu or Shiva temples, so that the two gods' temples effectively define a set of their localized forms.

These localized forms are governed by the same polytheistic logic as other forms of Vishnu and Shiva appearing in mythology without affiliation to any specific locality. Thus, for instance, Dakshinamurti and Nataraja are normally identified in myths as two different forms of the universal Shiva, but in some contexts they may be seen as variant names for the one god Shiva. Moreover, there is no insuperable barrier to treating them as two fully distinct gods, although in practice this is rarely done by Shaivas. In the same way, two localized temple forms of Shiva, such as Vishwanatha and Sundareshwara, are normally said to be different forms of Shiva: Shiva as the "Lord of all" (Vishwanatha), who reigns over the city of Kashi (Benares), which is preeminently his own, and Shiva as the "Beautiful lord" (Sundareshwara), who is also the king of Madurai. But because both gods—like all Shiva's temple forms—are credited with all his powers, both Vishwanatha and Sundareshwara may also be regarded as only alternative eponyms for the one, universal Shiva. The same logic, of course, applies at successive levels not only to forms of Shiva himself but also, for instance, to distinguishable forms of Nataraja or Sundareshwara.

Since Vishnu and Shiva are celestial great gods with general powers over the cosmos, the existence of localized temple forms raises the problem of their actual affiliation to sites fixed in space. In fact, the problem arises for other deities too, but it is sharpest for Vishnu and Shiva precisely because they, more than others, most fully exercise general, cosmic powers. Every temple, or at least every large one, has its own legend that, in addition to extolling the benefits of worshiping the deities enshrined there, purports to solve the problem of "the tension between the limitation implicit in the localization of the deity and the universalism proclaimed by the god's devotees" (Shulman 1980: 40). Venkateshwara at Tirupati, for instance, is Vishnu on Venkata hill. The hill was brought to its site at the command of Vishnu, who decided to rest there after he—in his third incarnation as the boar—had rescued the earth from the waters covering the universe after its dissolution. Sundareshwara at Madurai is husband to Minakshi. She was queen of the Pandyan kingdom and her campaign to conquer the world ended in the Himalayas, when Shiva came down from Mount Kailasa to the battlefield. Afterwards, Shiva came to Madurai to marry Minakshi and remained there as Sundareshwara, the joint sovereign of the Pandyan kingdom.

Every temple's legend is different, but each draws on common mythical themes, and each provides an explanation of why Vishnu or Shiva, in a particular form, has chosen to situate himself at that temple site. David D. Shulman (1980) has analyzed the Tamil temple myths of Shiva and shows that they consistently explain the localization of the god's forms by linking him to a local goddess, as in the myth of Minakshi and Sundareshwara. Similar analyses of other sets of temple legends would reveal comparable patterns underlying alternative solutions to the problem posed by the great gods' localized temple forms.

VISHNU AND SHIVA AS KINGS AND VILLAGE DEITIES

The king, as we know, plays a central role in Hinduism, and Vishnu and Shiva in their localized temple forms are widely represented as reigning monarchs. Frequently, these forms of Vishnu and Shiva rule over lands that are undefined; Marie-Louise Reiniche (1979: 83–111), for instance, describes the rituals at Shiva's temple in a south Indian village where there is considerable emphasis on the god's sovereignty, but not in relation to any specific realm. In many cases, though, the temple form is identified as the monarch of a specific kingdom. Then Vishnu and Shiva are "state deities," taking on forms that portray them as eternal, true kings, for whom human rulers act as regents in this world; "That the palace and the temple are two faces of the same center reminds us that the [human] king by himself would be nothing" (Biardeau 1981: 20). In spite of Vishnu's primary identification in classical texts as the king as opposed to Shiva the ascetic renouncer, both gods do in practice assume the royal function. Out of many examples, four well-known ones may be cited: Eklinga (Shiva) at Eklingji, for centuries god of the powerful Rajasthani kingdom of Mewar; Jagannatha at Puri, god of the kingdoms of Orissa from medieval to modern times; Padmanabha (Vishnu) at Trivandrum, to whom the king of Travancore (southern Kerala) dedicated his new state in the eighteenth century; and Sundareshwara at Madurai, the ruler with Minakshi of the ancient Pandyan kingdom and its successor regimes. Puri, Trivandrum, and Madurai are the capital cities of their respective kingdoms, but the village of Eklingji is some distance from Udaipur, the Mewar capital since the seventeenth century.

As kings, Vishnu and Shiva's principal responsibility is protection of the royal house and the kingdom, its people and territory. Thus in their royal forms, the gods' general powers over the universe become more specifically deployed within the boundaries of a kingdom situated on earth, whether or not such a kingdom actually corresponds to an extant polity. However, the Hindu kingdom—the largest and most perfect ordered system that can exist in the world—is also conceptualized as a microcosm of the universe, and ideally it is coextensive with India (classically Bharatavarsha) and the whole world. The boundaries of all these spaces should coincide and every Hindu king should strive to expand his realm until it reaches the outermost limits of the world. Thus the descent of Vishnu and Shiva to earth as monarchs only partially implies territorial circumscription of their universal powers.

Yet the great gods' powers are made more limited and specific when they become linked to smaller localities and social units. Thus, for instance, in many regions of India, the countryside is dotted with small temples to Shiva, as in central Gujarat, where every village contains one or more, each in principle distinguished by a particular name and legend (Pocock 1973: 82–84, 89–90). In some cases, as with the Tamil Pramalai Kallar caste, Shiva is the principal god of the lineage temples, so that he is the protector of the Kallars' local kin units (Dumont 1986: 393–401). It is difficult to say how commonly Shiva, as such, is the presiding deity in rural shrines and temples, but we do know that in many regions a particular form of Shiva, the terrible Bhairava, is the focus of ritual attention. Bhairava (Bhairon, Bheru, etc.) is then a "village deity" (*gramadevata*), who may be worshiped as the tutelary deity of a village or another local settlement unit, such as an urban quarter (despite the term "village deity"). Sometimes, while still classified as a *gramadevata*, Bhairava's protective functions are less clearly identified, although he can also be the protective deity of a kin group, that is, a "clan (or family) deity" (*kuladeva*; *kuladevata*). Two villages in which Bhairava takes such roles are described later in this chapter. In one region in particular, Maharashtra, another form of Shiva known as Khandoba frequently replaces Bhairava. The two gods are commonly seen as forms of each other, although Khandoba is also a regional god of the Maratha people as a whole.

It is significant that Bhairava is also present in many Shiva temples as the fierce watchman, standing near the gateway to guard the temple against evil spirits and human thieves. He plays a similar and important role in Benares, Shiva's city, where he is popularly known as its "police chief," a protector who punishes transgressors. Almost always, a guardian deity of this kind is inferior and subordinate to the greater deity, the source of its power, whose temple or domain he watches over. These are the characteristics of Bhairava generally; he is a form of Shiva, but a subordinate one, who has been given his specific power to protect a re-

stricted domain or group by the universal Shiva or a higher form of the
god, such as a king. Hence Shiva the great god, particularly as Bhairava,
can take his place in the pantheon alongside other little, village deities,
but he then assumes a lower, localized form with narrower and more
particularistic powers. Much the same applies to Vishnu when he takes
the form of his fourth incarnation, the "man-lion" Narasimha (Nar-
asingh), whose role closely resembles Bhairava's in some regions, especially Andhra Pradesh and Orissa. Overall, though, Narasimha's cult is
less extensive than Bhairava's, and Vishnu—as Narasimha or alternative
forms—is less closely associated with other little deities than Shiva/
Bhairava. Why this is so will be considered shortly.

I end this section with some brief remarks about Shiva's sons Ganesha
and Skanda, and about Hanuman. Throughout India, Ganesha is widely
worshiped in both towns and villages (for instance, as a guardian of water
sources). He is sometimes a clan deity. But there are few large temples
dedicated to Ganesha, even in Maharashtra, where he is an especially
popular deity for the entire region, so that his cult rather lacks the splendor of his father's or of Vishnu's. In most of India, Skanda is fairly unimportant, but in Tamilnadu, as Murugan, he is the presiding deity of large
and wealthy temples in which he is commonly represented as a king.
Murugan is almost certainly the most popular deity among Tamils, and
he is firmly identified as their regional deity. Murugan is not a tutelary
deity of villages, but sometimes he is a clan deity. The most prominent
Vaishnava deity to take a comparable role is probably Hanuman, the
"monkey god," who is in mythology Rama's most fervent devotee. Hanuman is popularly said to possess gigantic physical strength. Across
much of central India (where he is sometimes seen as a form of Shiva),
Hanuman is an important village deity, but he is widely worshiped everywhere, especially by people who believe that his sheer strength can crush
the malevolent agencies afflicting them.

THE GODDESS AND HER FORMS

O Goddess who removes the suffering of your supplicants,
    have mercy!
O mother of the whole world, be gracious!
O mistress of the universe, protect the world!
    Have mercy!
You are the mistress of all that moves and moves not!

You alone are the foundation of the world,
    residing in the form of earth.
O you whose prowess is unsurpassed,
    you nourish the world in the form of the waters.

In these two verses from an invocation (*Markandeya Purana* 88.2–3; Dimmitt and van Buitenen 1978: 219), both the awesome majesty and the enfolding protectiveness of the Hindu goddess are tellingly conveyed.

Devi (feminine form of *deva*) means "goddess," but in the vernacular goddesses are more frequently called *mata* or *amman* (or cognate terms) in north and south India, respectively. The connotation of the vernacular terms is "mother"—"mother of the whole world" and all who live in it—but it should be stressed that the goddesses themselves often have no children.

In their temples and shrines, sculptured images of goddesses are invariably anthropomorphic. Almost all goddesses wear a red mark on the forehead and the red-white contrast symbolizes the opposition between female and male deities. Goddesses linked to Shiva commonly wear three stripes of white ash above the red mark as well.

All goddesses may be regarded as forms of (Maha)devi, *the* (Great) Goddess, who is praised in the verses above. The logic of polytheism applies to them, so that different goddesses, whether they appear in mythological or ritual contexts, can be seen as either distinct deities or diverse forms of the one goddess who bears a multiplicity of names.

The great gods' consorts are Lakshmi, Parvati, and Saraswati, the goddess of learning and music, who is Brahma's consort and much more widely worshiped than her husband. These three goddesses are generally conceptualized as distinct beings, but they are also forms of the one goddess. In both myth and ritual, however, Devi—*the* Goddess—appears in her own right as well, as "mistress of the universe" and a celestial deity on a par with Vishnu and Shiva. Like the two great gods, Devi fights demons across the cosmos, notably in her form as Durga, who slays the gigantically powerful buffalo-demon Mahishasura in a war celebrated annually in the autumn at Navaratri ("Nine nights"), one of India's most popular festivals. But perhaps the most dramatic form of the single goddess is ferocious Kali, who reveals her supremacy over the gods when she is iconographically portrayed as trampling on the corpse of Shiva. In her single form, the goddess is also known as Shakti, "power," and her devotees are described as "Shaktas." As a first approximation, we can therefore say that there is an unmarried, independent, or autonomous goddess, Devi/Shakti, who can also take distinct wifely forms as Lakshmi, Parvati, and Saraswati. Further, when single the goddess's powers—whether represented as completely independent of the gods' or derivative from theirs—are deployed free of male constraint, whereas a wifely goddess is a subordinate partner lacking powers separate from her husband's.

Yet there are significant differences in how Lakshmi, Parvati, and Saraswati manifest themselves. Normally, partly because of Brahma's subsidiary role in popular Hinduism, Saraswati is represented in iconography and worshiped by herself (for example, by students who supplicate her before examinations). Lakshmi too is popularly represented and worshiped alone, often as Mahalakshmi, the goddess of good fortune and wealth; businessmen, for instance, commonly worship her at the start of the financial year. Lakshmi also appears prominently as Vishnu's loyal and subordinate wife, his constant consort in his temples. Parvati, by contrast, is really Shiva's wife only in classical mythology. She is not worshiped as a single goddess and in Shiva's temples, although his different consorts can be regarded as forms of her, each consort has her own distinct name, and the equation with Parvati is rarely stressed. Far more often, Shiva's consorts are simply said to be forms of Devi or Shakti, and everywhere the pairing Shiva-Shakti is a prominent one. In other words, Shiva's consorts—to a far greater extent than Vishnu's—are systematically treated as distinctive married forms of Devi/Shakti, the goddess who otherwise has no active male partner. This in turn is consistent with the widespread belief that Shiva's wives were originally single, local goddesses. Thus in popular Hinduism the relationship between the autonomous goddess and Shiva is far more striking than that between her and Vishnu, for his wife Lakshmi's identification with Devi/Shakti is played down.

Like Vishnu and Shiva, the goddess can also assume localized temple forms identified as monarchs, so that her powers are more specifically directed to the protection of a kingdom. Minakshi, who shares the Pandyan throne with Sundareshwara, is one example, but she is exceptional. More commonly, a form of autonomous Devi is the state deity. Unmarried Chamundeshwari (a form of Durga) is, for example, the state deity of the Mysore kingdom; Taleju played a similar role in the old Malla kingdom of Nepal. In this context, it is notable that the state deity of modern India is a goddess, Bharat Mata, "Mother India." The worship of goddesses, particularly Durga and Kali, is especially popular in Bengal, and it was a prominent Bengali nationalist and novelist, Bankim Chandra Chatterjee (1838–94), who virtually created Bharat Mata as the protector of the people and land of an embryonic nation. In effect, he brought into being the first Indian national deity. Bharat Mata now has a modern temple in Benares where, instead of an image, there is a large map of India. Bharat Mata is not in fact a widely worshiped goddess, but she was the first Hindu state deity to become sovereign over a secular republic with boundaries fixed on a map.

The most important category of localized forms, however, comprises the "village goddesses," female *gramadevata*, many of whom also serve as clan deities. The vast majority of these goddesses (*mata, amman,* and so on in ordinary parlance) stand alone in their temples and shrines, and are represented without any male consort, although they are not necessarily said to be unmarried. The Tamil village goddess Angalamman, for example, is normally represented as an auspicious married woman with sons, but she is also a virgin without a husband (Meyer 1986: 50–51, 54–58). Angalamman's ambiguous status is quite typical and the critical feature is not so much that the goddess is unmarried, but that any male consort is absent.

A significant proportion of village goddesses, although by no means all, are the tutelary deities of specific social units—villages or other local settlements—whose boundaries define the spatial extent of their powers. Throughout the southern peninsula of India, but not so uniformly in the rest of the country, virtually every local settlement has its own tutelary goddess(es). Or rather every tutelary goddess has her own settlement: "The village topocosm is her domain, its destiny is in her hands, and its inhabitants are her people" (Brubaker 1979: 129). However, in any one region the same goddess—in the sense that she has the same name and characteristics—commonly serves as the tutelary goddess of many different villages; in much of Tamilnadu, for instance, this goddess is usually Mariyamman. At another level, though, Mariyamman is normally regarded as a different goddess in each village: Mariyamman of this place as opposed to Mariyamman of that place or another. Such differentiation does not prevent people identifying all village Mariyammans as localized forms of the one goddess. Moreover, a village goddess sometimes transcends her own boundaries and comes to be worshiped by people from farther afield. Nonetheless, tutelary village goddesses are preeminently represented in both ritual and mythical contexts as distinct deities who belong to different places and are jealous of their power in relation to neighboring settlements' goddesses.

This material brings us back to one aspect of the relationship between gods and goddesses. Throughout India, lone village goddesses are more commonly seen as actual or potential consorts of Shiva rather than Vishnu. As we have seen, the consorts of Shiva's temple forms are often believed to have once been local, unmarried goddesses. Even for goddesses who are represented without any husband, however, a marriage ritual may be held and at it the spouse is typically identified, implicitly or explicitly, as a form of Shiva. Alternatively, such a goddess may be the sister of a great god's consort, and again that god is usually Shiva. It is true that in Tamilnadu, for instance, people say that Shiva's wife is also Vishnu's sister and that Bhudevi, Vishnu's second wife in his temples, was once a local village goddess. Furthermore, in areas where Vaishnava cults are strong, such as Orissa within the sphere of Jagannatha's influence, village goddesses are linked to Vishnu instead of or in addition to Shiva. All the same, in most of India, Shiva—very often in his form as Bhairava—is more closely connected to the band of single village goddesses than Vishnu. Shiva's linkage with them is itself another expression of the archetypal Shiva-Shakti pairing, and it is in turn correlated with the fact that Shiva, more often than Vishnu, assumes the form of a localized village deity with specific powers.

THE QUALITIES OF THE GODDESS

One striking aspect of the relationship between male and female deities is the overarching structural opposition between the great gods' link to the universe as a celestial space and the goddess's link to this world and the earth as both soil and territory. Thus, for example, Bhudevi is the earth (*bhu*) divinized, and in the mainly Bengali concept of *shakti-pitha*, "seat, bench of Shakti," goddesses are affiliated with specific geographical sites. According to myth, Parvati as Sati, the "virtuous wife," killed herself when her father insulted Shiva. Her corpse, borne on his shoulders, was cut up by Vishnu to end Shiva's dangerously violent grief. The parts of Parvati's body then fell to earth at the *shakti-pitha* sites. Bhudevi and the "seats of Shakti" both exemplify the way in which the goddess is linked with the earth and this world, in complementary opposition to transcendent Vishnu and Shiva. Thus the goddess, when contrasted with the great gods, always retains an earthly aspect; in a significant sense, Devi ascends from and unites in herself her multiple earthbound forms, particularly the village goddesses, whereas Vishnu and more especially Shiva descend from celestial unity partially to dissolve into localized forms.

But the goddess also has a more distinctive and vital set of characteristics, signaled by the very name "Shakti," which is critical to her relationship with the gods. To describe the power of gods and goddesses, Sanskrit and vernacular languages have numerous and often polysemous terms, such as *tejas*, "fiery splendor, glory, energy, luster," which is characteristic of all deities, or *tapas*, "heat of asceticism," which is particularly but not exclusively associated with Shiva. *Shakti*, too, denotes divine power and is probably the most commonly used term among ordinary Hindus to refer to the power of any deity. However, *shakti* also specifically labels the power, potency, or activating energy—not political power of domination—that is incarnated in goddesses and, according to one classical idea of divinity, goddesses personify the dynamic female principle (*prakriti*) as opposed to gods who personify the passive male principle (*purusha*). *Shakti*, therefore, is the energizing power of deities that is marked as female and, reflecting the classical idea, in popular Hinduism the gods commonly require female consorts—their *shaktis*—in order to act. That is why temple images of Vishnu and Shiva, for example, frequently show them accompanied by consorts, whereas images of goddesses stand alone.

Goddesses can stand alone because they actually embody power as *shakti* and can therefore act by themselves. But when they do they are dangerous. Unmarried goddesses in particular, unlike wifely goddesses, are ferocious and quickly angered. Durga and Kali, who are especially popular in Bengal, are the most famous goddesses of this kind. Durga is, above all, the fearsome killer of the buffalo-demon; she rides into battle on a lion wielding a score of weapons. Kali likes to dwell in the cremation ground, and her horrific appearance as a murderous hag garlanded in skulls is devastatingly portrayed in her iconography. The vast multitude of single village goddesses have similar characteristics and many of them, such as Shitala Mata and Mariyamman, are the goddesses of smallpox, as well as cholera and other epidemic diseases. These diseases are thought to be inflicted by village goddesses, either to announce their presence or because they have been angered by disrespectful communities under their protection, although the individual victims are not normally held to be particularly blameworthy. Moreover the victims, especially of smallpox (until the 1970s the most feared and dreadful epidemic disease), must be revered as forms of the goddess who possesses them, lest her rage grow to lethal proportions. Consistent with their ferocity, which is sometimes thought to turn them bloodthirsty, most single goddesses demand animal sacrifices. Epidemic diseases, for example, are often countered by sacrificing animals to appease the goddesses, but at a few major temples like Kali's famous Kalighat temple in Calcutta, animals are slaughtered daily to please her.

Why are single goddesses, especially those who are actually unmarried, more violent and testy than wifely goddesses? To start to answer this crucial question, we can look at the concept of ritual "temperature," whose most salient aspect in everyday Hindu life is related to food and drink classified as more or less "hot" or "cold," "heating" or "cooling." Thus among the Tamils described by Brenda E. F. Beck (1969), a long list of foodstuffs can be classified as heating or cooling, some more extremely than others. For instance, among fruits, mango is heating and papaya strongly so, whereas coconut is cooling and lime very cooling. In detail, such classifications vary from place to place, but in general Hindus believe that good health is preserved by maintaining a balance between the heating and cooling foods consumed, so that illness may be diagnosed as imbalance in the body, which has grown too hot or too cold. But the body's thermal state also varies "naturally"; for example, a pregnant woman is hot and must therefore avoid excessively heating foods, whereas after parturition she is cold and must ensure that she does not get even colder.

Deities, like human beings, are subject to the regime of hot and cold. Most germane to our present discussion is the conviction that single goddesses are normally very hot. Their power is symbolically equated with both heightened sexual energy and a capacity for angry violence. Sexual maturation augments the bodily heat of females, and so too does unsated sexual desire. Although sexual intercourse is itself a heating activity, release brings about a subsequent cooling. Single goddesses—except for the minority portrayed as young girls—are represented as sexually mature adults, but because they lack a partner, they are consistently hotter than wifely goddesses. Rage also typifies the abnormally hot and in turn raises the heat still farther. Unreleased sexual energy and violence are therefore closely linked, and both are characteristic qualities of single goddesses.

Consistent with this thermal pattern, the goddesses who control epidemic diseases stand alone, often being portrayed as unmarried. Their hot anger is manifested in the feverish diseases of people whom they possess. Smallpox—especially associated with Shitala Mata and Mariyamman—also usually struck during the hottest months (approximately April to June). Cooling rituals are a key part of the worship of a smallpox victim possessed by the goddess, and propitiatory animal sacrifice—although it heats those who carry it out—cools the goddess by placating her. Conversely, it is sometimes desirable to heat a hot goddess still further. Durga, for instance, before she sets out to wage war against the buffalo-demon during the Navaratri festival, is offered hot foods and sacrificial animals to stimulate her vengeful violence.

If single goddesses are very hot, all goddesses—because they personify an energetic power symbolically equated with female sexuality—are collectively represented as relatively hot compared with gods, although it must be noted that Shiva's ascetic power (*tapas*) is also equated with fiery heat. The contrast between hot goddesses and cool gods is pervasively and economically symbolized by the red forehead marks prominent on goddesses, because one connotation of the red-white contrast is heat as opposed to cold. Unsurprisingly, the power of goddesses, especially single goddesses, is represented ambivalently in Hindu myth and ritual because it can be terribly destructive but also, especially as sexual power, supremely creative. Let me now look more closely at this ambivalence.

The goddesses' sexual fertility is not a simple matter. Many popular Hindu rituals directly connect women's fertility with the goddesses' power, from which it is shown to derive; indeed, such rituals identify women as forms of the goddess and rest on the premise that all mature women share her power, *shakti*. Hindu goddesses are "mothers" to their human flock, whom they protect and also punish, but many of them are themselves childless. Unmarried goddesses, who are sometimes explicitly said to be barren, never have offspring and therefore display the destructive jealousy imputed to all childless women, who cannot fulfill the supremely valued role of motherhood. Much of the unmarried goddesses' anger is driven precisely by their childlessness. Yet many married goddesses also lack children. Lakshmi has none for Vishnu has no offspring, and although Shiva does have sons (Ganesha and Skanda) the myths say that Parvati (and other forms of his consort) never give birth to them after a "natural" pregnancy. Children imply replacement of their parents, particularly the father, and a Hindu son's principal religious duty is to light his father's funeral pyre. Were deities to have children born like humans, it would therefore suggest lost immortality, especially for the gods. It would also raise the spectre of overpopulation in the divine world, because in Hindu mythology, "death arises only when sexual increase appears" (O'Flaherty 1976: 28). For the deities, therefore, sexuality is often divorced from procreation and hence from death; despite their sexual fertility, the goddesses' divinity tends to preclude them from motherhood, the status so deeply desired by most Hindu women, who frequently seek assistance from their divine childless "mothers" in attaining it.

Connected with their link to the earth, the goddess's fertility is also identified with the soil's, which in turn combines with the notion that rivers are forms of the goddess, "nourishing the world in the form of the waters." Thus agricultural production, as well as human reproduction, are predicated upon the power of the goddess, whose sexual fertility is ritually celebrated to ensure that both processes are guaranteed. Plainly, if the world and its people are to survive and prosper, the goddess must exercise her power. But because that power is so potentially dangerous, a basic dilemma ensues: how can the goddess's power be active without becoming uncontrollably destructive?

The passive gods, as we have seen, need the energy of the goddesses. But union between a goddess and a god also checks the threat of her power. When united with a god, a goddess inevitably becomes an inferior wife and relinquishes control of her power to her husband, who acts for both of them as a married pair. The goddess becomes pacific, sexually restrained, and cool, and largely ceases to be a potential source of danger. But then she can no longer fully deploy the power that is hers alone and is still needed in the world. The general resolution to this dilemma—insofar as it can be resolved—is to let the goddess potentially transform herself from hot independence (her dark form) into cool wifehood (her light form), and vice versa. Hence the goddess exists in a kind of dynamic state—sometimes unmarried and able to wield her power with all its attendant hazards, sometimes united with a god and restrained by the bond of marriage, and sometimes in an intermediate position in which she is married but apart from her husband. Actually, many goddesses largely remain in one particular state; nonetheless, in both myth and ritual, the same transformative solution to the ambivalence of the goddess's power perennially emerges, so that dark and light forms of the goddess are never truly parted from each other. Black Kali, dancing on Shiva's corpse, repeatedly transforms into golden Gauri (an epithet of Parvati), Shiva's constant consort, and back again. And that in turn is yet another reason why even unmarried, autonomously powerful goddesses can never be entirely separated from the gods who could be their consorts.

Finally, we can complete the earlier discussion of Shiva's special association with village goddesses. Shiva oscillates continually between eroticism and asceticism, between his duties as a husband and householder and his unconcern as a renouncer and adulterous wanderer on the cremation grounds, so that his character is partly homologous with the goddess's. When displaying his immorality, violence, and destructiveness, Shiva resembles the dark, unmarried goddesses, and particularly as Bhairava, he is the village goddesses' counterpart and is often worshiped with them. Shiva/Bhairava, even if less consistently than the goddess, also has dark and light forms, and although he does not cause epidemics, his dark form is vengeful and violent. Dangerous Shiva therefore has a closer affinity with the goddess, especially in her single, village goddess forms, than the generally more equable Vishnu.

VILLAGE GODS AND OTHER LITTLE DEITIES

Of many little, village gods like Thakur Dev in Chhattisgarh (eastern Madhya Pradesh), it can only be said that "His formal attributes are few, and . . . he is associated with no iconographic tradition" (Babb 1975: 192). But if these gods, and many other little deities, are rather shadowy figures in the sense that their distinctive characteristics are ill defined, they are still vitally important, powerful presences for millions of ordinary Hindus. People worship these deities at their shrines and petty temples, where they are often represented only by uncarved stones or other simple emblems.

The little village gods commonly lack consorts. The classical idea that a lone god is passive is not systematically extended to them, so that all little gods tend to share the qualities of fierce Bhairava, as well as the village goddesses. However, little village gods hardly ever control human epidemic diseases, the goddesses' most devastating demonstration of their power.

Many little deities, male and female, are believed to have a nondivine origin. The great deities—Vishnu, Shiva, and Devi—are and always have been immortal and fully divine. On the other hand, many localized forms of the goddess are said to have once been women. I shall now look at a sample of instances of nondivine ancestry among the very large and diverse category of little deities.

Throughout India, many little deities are said to be former malevolent ghostly spirits, a miscellaneous category often referred to as *bhuta-preta* and distinguished from *asuras*, the great demons of classical mythology, such as Durga's foe Mahishasura, the buffalo-demon. Malevolent ghostly spirits, a major source of misfortune in popular Hinduism, will be discussed in detail in chapter 10, but some of their features need to be briefly outlined here. The spirit of anyone who meets a "bad" death is likely to linger on earth to harm the living, instead of passing over to the world of the dead. The causes of bad deaths are numerous—murder, suicide, accident, epidemic diseases, infant and maternal mortality, and so on—but the principal defining feature is that the death is premature, so that the victim dies unfulfilled.

As we shall see later, one of the commonest means of dealing with afflictions caused by malevolent ghostly spirits is deification. In other words, the ghost is enshrined and worshiped as a deity, so that its malevolent power can be controlled and even turned to the benefit of the living. Many deified ghosts are worshiped only by members of their former families, but in principle and sometimes in practice they can acquire a wider circle of worshipers. Conversely, many a little deity is said to be a deified ghost, even though no one claims to know its original human identity. Thus, for example, in Tamilnadu the gods Karuppan and Madan, who are both prominent village gods, are believed to have originally been *pey*, the ubiquitous and anonymous evil spirits or malevolent ghosts of the region. Karuppan and Madan exemplify the general principle involved here; in Louis Dumont's words (1986: 449): "Often a spirit is malevolent only as long as it lacks a cult; once the cult is provided, it becomes tutelary." Although such a deity is likely to retain much of its ancestral cussedness and continue to be capricious and demanding, the danger posed by the presence of a dead person's harmful spirit can be averted by transforming it into a god or goddess.

Deification of the dead is not restricted to the victims of bad deaths. Two of the most prominent kinds of little deity are *vira*s, heroes who died gloriously in battle, and *sati mata*s, heroines who chose to die on their husbands' funeral pyres. Everywhere in India, deified heroes and heroines are widely worshiped as powerful beings, often at stones erected as monuments and treated as their shrines. All heroes and heroines are particularly favored as clan deities by their descendants, but many of them also serve as tutelary village deities and some attract a much wider circle of devotees because they gain a reputation as extraordinarily powerful. In Rajasthan, for instance, countless *sati mata*s are enshrined in elaborate temples visited by huge numbers of people coming from far afield.

One heroic deity with a well-developed mythology and an extensive cult across Punjab, Haryana, western Uttar Pradesh, and Rajasthan is Guga. Guga, whose chief shrine is in Rajasthan, was a Rajput prince and many north Indian villagers revere him as a powerful protector. But Guga also illustrates the spectacular eclecticism of popular Hinduism. Some people claim that Guga *bir* (*vira* colloquially), "Guga the hero," converted to Islam before his death, so that he is really Guga *pir*, a *pir* being a Muslim saint. Although Guga *pir* naturally attracts Muslim devotees, he still attracts Hindus too (Lapoint 1978: 283–86; Lewis 1958: 210–13). And although most *pir*s are not confused with *bir*s, throughout India Muslim saints are widely worshiped at their tombs by Hindus who typically present offerings to them as if they were deities' images. Numerous cases of deified Europeans, often but not always soldiers, are also recorded (O'Malley 1935: 173–79); more than forty years after the British left India, some of them linger on as little deities.

The catalogue of little deities who have a human origin could be expanded almost indefinitely, but in closing it, there are several important points to make. First, the existence of these deities is itself an illustration of the absence of any absolute distinction between divine and human beings. Second, an ex-human deity is often thought to be particularly understanding about the needs of ordinary people, especially members of its former family and neighborhood. For that reason among others, such a deity may be favored when personal misfortune strikes. Third, the power wielded by little deities is usually limited and specific. Although some, like Guga, do have wider powers, the majority deal only with particular problems in particular places for the particular people who choose to worship them. Fourth, the narrowness of their power is correlated with their human origins, so that they are often identified as the inferior subordinates of greater, fully divine gods and goddesses, a pattern most explicitly displayed when they act as guardian deities protecting their superiors' temples. On the other hand, all little deities, irrespective of origin, can be associated or merged with other deities to become forms of them. Thus a deified hero might be identified as a form of Bhairava or a deified heroine as a form of a village goddess. To this kind of development there is no real limit and a little deity's cult may flourish until, like that of the "Old Gentleman"—the deified combined spirit of two Muslims in an Uttar Pradesh village—it is "but a short distance" from that of an "authenticated" great deity (Marriott 1969: 213).

RELATIONSHIPS AMONG VILLAGE DEITIES: TWO ETHNOGRAPHIC CASES

To complement the synoptic discussion in this chapter, I now present some ethnographic material to illustrate the relationships among village deities as they actually exist in particular rural settlements. Popular Hinduism in the countryside, as in the towns, is a complex phenomenon. One village of average size commonly contains thirty or more different temples and shrines, and villagers as a whole often recognize and worship up to a hundred identifiable deities of all kinds. In some, but by no means all villages, there are a few permanent large temples. Everywhere, however, the majority of shrines are either crude shelters or amount to no more than a roughly hewn image or painted stone standing in the open air.

In many villages, especially those with sizable Brahman populations, there are temples dedicated to Vishnu and Shiva, distinguished as great gods apart from the rest of the village's deities. In general, though, Vishnu and Shiva, as great gods protecting the universe, are thought to be less involved than village deities with the affairs of ordinary people and places, and by some villagers—especially of lower castes—they are practically ignored.

As no truly typical villages could be selected, I shall choose as case studies one principal example from north-central India, to be supplemented by a comparative sketch from the south. Ramkheri village lies in Malwa, western Madhya Pradesh. It is in the Hindi-speaking region and its religious style is, in broad terms, characteristically north Indian. Adrian C. Mayer lists forty-four shrines in Ramkheri, most of which are just red-painted stones (1960: 17, 101–2). They can be classified as follows: two Vishnu temples; one Shiva temple; eight Mata shrines; three Sati Mata shrines; six Village Lord shrines; thirteen Bheru (Bhairava) shrines; eight other little deity shrines; and three sites of special significance.

Although Ramkheri's largest temple, located in the village center, is a Vishnu temple, the most important shrines for the majority of villagers are those of the Matas, Village Lords, and Bherus. As always in northern India, the term *mata* is used for the goddesses; they comprise *the* village goddess, Shakti Mata, who protects Ramkheri; Shitala Mata, the smallpox goddess; two other minor goddesses of smallpox and cholera; four others lacking specific functions; and the three Sati Matas. Shakti Mata has a permanent shrine in Ramkheri's main square, near the Vishnu temple, and people say that she—with Hanuman Kherapati, Lord of the village, whose shrine is at the southern edge of the settlement, as well as Bheru—must be installed in a shrine before any house is built in a newly founded village (ibid.: 17). Shakti Mata is specially worshiped at the major annual festivals of Navaratri (in autumn) and Holi (in spring). If there is drought the village headman should call on Indra, god of the rains, at a ritual held at her shrine (ibid.: 101, 107, 112). Shitala Mata is not regularly worshiped, but approximately every twenty years all women with children who have survived smallpox hold a special ritual for her (ibid.: 111, 249). As well as the goddesses with shrines in the village, the people of Ramkheri do pay some attention to their clan goddesses (*kul mata*), who ought to be periodically worshiped by all members of a clan, although in practice this is rarely done (ibid.: 184–87). The Sati Mata shrines are memorials to deified local women who died on their husbands' funeral pyres. Sati Matas are mainly worshiped by members of their deceased husbands' clans, but they do attract other worshipers, especially women asking them to cure barrenness (ibid.: 193).

Hanuman Kherapati is the principal Lord of the village. The other five are three Lords or Maharajs ("great kings") of the village gates and two of the village boundary. Hanuman Kherapati also receives ritual attention at Navaratri and he may be worshiped in times of danger, such as when village fields are threatened by locusts (ibid.: 72, 101). Similarly, a sacrifice can be offered to one of the Lords of the village gates when there is an epidemic among village cattle (ibid.: 111–12). Hanuman is an important protective village deity across much of central India, while Kherapati, "Lord of the village," is clearly a form of Kshetrapala (Khetrapal, Ketrappa, etc.) who is, in many areas, the principal protector of the village fields and the site itself. In Ramkheri, the god, standing at the edge of the village, takes this role, complemented by the Lords who guard the gates and boundary, although Ganesha is also said to protect fields and is invoked before sowing begins.

Bheru is Bhairava and also a protector of the village. Villagers claim that he is a son of Shiva—another expression of his subordinate position—and they distinguish (as is common in this part of India) between "light" and "dark" Bherus (ibid.: 188–89). Unlike Shakti Mata and Hanuman Kherapati, however, all Bheru's shrines belong to particular lineages (clan-segments) of particular castes. Nonetheless, at Navaratri the headman visits all Ramkheri's forty-four shrines, which shows how "*all* sacred places are treated as the concern of the entire village, and their propitiation made a prerequisite for its welfare during the coming year" (ibid.: 101). The "most important function" of a Bheru "is to protect and make prosper those who acknowledge his power." He also particularly guards wells (ibid.: 189). A lineage's Bheru image in Ramkheri is said to be a copy of the main Bheru image in the ancestral village, so that although Bheru is a lineage deity, he is always linked with a particular place (ibid.: 190).

It is clear that the majority of the major village gods and goddesses in Ramkheri are primarily conceptualized as localized deities, with specific powers to protect the village and its people, or the kin groups to which they belong. It is because of these deities that Ramkheri possesses "divine sanctions for its foundation, and divine protection for its continuance" (ibid.: 17). However, Mayer's evidence also reveals a division of divine functions, which is a common feature among village deities. Shakti Mata (with Shitala Mata) primarily protects the people of the village against disease, Hanuman Kherapati (and the other Lords) protect its territory, while the Bherus protect the members of different lineages and the wells. In addition, the clan goddesses (and Sati Matas) protect those who belong to different clans. Note that Vishnu, even though he stands in the village's central temple, takes no real role in these matters. Although not rigidly drawn, the contrast between Shakti Mata at the center and the Lords at the periphery is striking. Whereas the goddess has an earthly, localized aspect in opposition to the great gods' celestial universality, among the tutelary village deities themselves, the goddess's role as motherly protector of her people is prominent and the gods—who also stand guard around the goddess—are complementarily responsible for the territory.

Popular religion in Mel Ceval village in southern Tamilnadu, studied by Reiniche, is distinctively south Indian in style. Mel Ceval has a sizable population of Brahman landholders and contains a fairly large temple dedicated to Shiva, who reigns over the village. In a sense, this temple is the fixed point around which the settlement is organized. Partly owing to Shiva's prominence, the network of relationships among deities appears more complicated in Mel Ceval than Ramkheri, and I can only sketch some of its basic features. In all, there are about thirty-five temples and shrines in Mel Ceval, mostly dedicated to little village deities (1979: 19–35).

One important temple is dedicated to Shasta, who is locally classified as a *deva*, a great god. In mythology, Shasta is the son of Shiva by Vishnu in his female form as Mohini. Shasta's principal function is to protect the territory of Mel Ceval and he particularly guards its boundary, for his temple is actually outside the village. Shasta is also a clan deity and thus protects the kin groups settled in the village, although any particular person's clan deity is always the Shasta enshrined in the ancestral village (ibid.: 30–31, 35–36, chap. 4). Owing to his close links with other little deities, Shasta—despite being a great god—is often viewed as a prototypical village deity like Aiyanar, his near equivalent farther north in Tamilnadu. At Shasta's temple in Mel Ceval, there is an image of the little deity Madan who guards the site, as Karuppan does at Aiyanar temples. Superior Shasta and Aiyanar are said to rule over the subordinate guardian deities and the relationship between these two categories of deities is an important one in Tamil popular Hinduism.

A little temple at the northern boundary of Mel Ceval, just beyond the area of habitation, is dedicated to the single goddess Chelliyamman. Linked to the foundation of the village itself, she is also its main tutelary goddess, protecting all the villagers living in the locality and the social order that embraces them. She is also said to be the elder sister of other local goddesses. Particularly important is her relationship with two goddesses within the settlement area. The first is Saundari, Shiva's consort in his temple, and the second is Muppidariyamman, a single goddess whose little temple lies south of Shiva's. Chelliyamman is frequently present in southern Tamil villages and towns, guarding them (and their Shiva temples) on the northern boundary. She is then a subordinate guardian of Shiva and his wife, represented as the latter's sister or as an inferior consort of Shiva himself. Chelliyamman in Mel Ceval is explicitly described as celibate; she is also superior to her partner or double Muppidariyamman who, unlike Chelliyamman, is offered animal sacrifices. We may note too that Bhairava is present near Chelliyamman as her devotee and also, further protecting the village, as a subordinate guardian form of Shiva himself. Like various other goddesses and little deities worshiped there, Mariyamman, the smallpox goddess, does have shrines in Mel Ceval, but she is particularly linked to one caste rather than the village population as a whole, so that collective protection against disease, like other dangers, is mainly assumed by Chelliyamman and Muppidariyamman (ibid.: 26–28, chap. 5).

Comparing Mel Ceval with Ramkheri, several points of similarity and contrast can be seen. Although both gods have temples at the heart of their settlements, Shiva in Mel Ceval plays a more prominent role than Vishnu in Ramkheri. Shasta in Mel Ceval, rather like Hanuman Kherapati and the Village Lords in Ramkheri, stands outside the village and protects its territory, although as a clan deity Shasta plays a role that mainly belongs in Ramkheri to Bheru and the clan goddesses. In Mel Ceval, Bhairava is not a clan deity. As protectors of the people of the village, Chelliyamman and Muppidariyamman resemble Shakti Mata, but the former appear to have a more general responsibility for the order of local society than the latter does. Furthermore, whereas Shakti Mata is at the center of Ramkheri, Chelliyamman stands outside the inhabited area, although she is linked to Shiva's consort and Muppidariyamman within it. In both places, however, if we leave aside Shiva's sovereign role in Mel Ceval, comparable protective functions are exercised by a set of localized village deities. Their connections with each other are particularly defined by the relationships between gods and goddesses, and superior deities and subordinate guardians, as well as by the contrast between people and territory, village and clan, and center and periphery.

CONCLUSION: CONTINUITY AND DIFFERENCE AMONG THE DEITIES

As I have said, neither Ramkheri nor Mel Ceval is a truly typical village. How protection is provided by village deities, how they are linked to different social units, and how they are related to each other (as well as to fellow deities without precise tutelary functions), vary in shape, content, and significance, especially between regions. On the other hand, ethnography shows that localized little deities who protect their particular villages and kin groups are very widespread in popular Hinduism, and they do have many comparable characteristics throughout most of India. Looking at the array of deities as a whole, one critical dimension is the overarching opposition between the great deities—principally Vishnu, Shiva, and Devi, the goddess—who have general powers to command and protect the universe, and the localized little village deities with narrower tutelary powers. Moreover, this opposition partly underpins a hierarchical structure (further discussed in chap. 4 and elsewhere), wherein the little deities are inferior to the great deities, often as subordinate guardians deriving some or all of their power from the great deities who ultimately control them.

That connection between great and little deities within a hierarchical structure exemplifies the importance of relationships among them, and it is one reason why I have not been using the terms "Sanskritic" and "non-Sanskritic" (or "great" and "little tradition") to classify the deities. As I explained in chapter 1, these terms—as often used—can imply that the two categories of deities really are separate or separable from each other. At one place in his study of the Coorgs, M. N. Srinivas, referring to a folksong about village deities, observes that "The important point . . . is that every intelligent and educated Coorg interprets [the song] as meaning that the various village-deities are forms of Shiva or his wife Parvati" (1965: 209). But this affiliative "rule" is not, as he implies, an objective one; the rule is not applied by everyone and it is actually, as the quotation shows, the product of a discourse in which educated Coorgs redefine their local deities as all-Indian and Sanskritic, and thereby represent themselves as superior worshipers of superior deities. The religion's higher and lower strata, and the allocation of deities to them, are constituted by an ideological discourse of evaluation, which we must not reify as if there actually were two separate strata with two separate categories of deities.

In this chapter, I therefore have emphasized relationships and continuities, because they—not misconstructed separation—are where a study of popular Hinduism's deities should begin. There is no clear-cut separation between great and little deities. Shiva, for example, is the superior of his own form as Bhairava, as Vishnu is of Narasimha, and Devi, *the* goddess, is of her village goddess forms. Vishnu and Shiva as such are relatively little worshiped by very large numbers of Hindus, especially in rural areas, but without taking proper account of the two great gods, it is impossible to make sense of Bhairava, Shitala Mata, or any other little deity, and impossible to comprehend the relationships among different deities and their forms. These relationships, which define the structure of the whole—the pantheon of deities in the widest sense—are built on difference, but difference emergent from a polytheistic logic of fluid continuity. In this logic, one deity can always become many and many become one, like Shiva at a Gujarati temple who is also the 330 million forms of himself and every other god and goddess.

Chapter 3

WORSHIP

PUJA, "worship," is the core ritual of popular theistic Hinduism. Every day, in temples and homes throughout India, *puja* is being performed before the deities' images by both priests and laypeople. *Puja* in a large temple, especially in the blackness enveloping the innermost shrines, has a powerful sensual impact, often amplified by the press of a large crowd of devotees in a hot, confined space. Frequently, there is a deafening and even discordant sound as the music of pipes and drums combines with ringing bells and the chanting of sacred texts. Scented smoke pours from the burning incense and camphor, and the heavy perfume of sandalwood, jasmine, and roses hangs in the air. The bright silks and gold, silver and jewels covering the images scintillate as priests wave oil lamps through the darkness. And when the ritual reaches a climax, devotees lift their hands in the *namaskara* gesture to show their respect to the deities whose names they loudly praise.

In a small temple or house, where *puja* is performed with fewer people present, the ritual is usually more restrained, so that its personal and almost homely aspect is more apparent than in a large temple. In *puja*, the deity in its form as an image is typically welcomed with a drink of water; it is undressed and bathed, and then clothed again, decked in jewelry and garlanded with flowers. A mirror may be provided so that the deity can gaze upon its own beauty. The deity is offered a meal, ideally of sumptuous splendor, and entertained by music, singing, and dancing; incense is wafted over it and decorated lamps are waved before it. At the end, the deity is bade farewell with the standard gesture of respect. In a temple in the early morning, a deity may be gently woken and at night put to bed, perhaps alone with a lullaby, perhaps with its consort to the accompaniment of erotic hymns. *Puja*, at its heart, is the worshipers' reception and entertainment of a distinguished and adored guest. It is a ritual to honor powerful gods and goddesses, and often to express personal affection for them as well; it can also create a unity between deity and worshiper that dissolves the difference between them.

THE NATURE OF DIVINE IMAGES

Like other rituals addressed to the deities of popular Hinduism, *puja* is normally conducted with images (*murti*; *vigraha*), and I must begin with them. All larger temples, as well as many domestic shrines and other places of worship, contain sculptured images. Most readers, even if they have never visited a Hindu temple, will have seen images in museums or photographs of them in books. Sculptured images are anthropomorphic (or sometimes theriomorphic) representations of deities, carved in stone, cast in bronze, or made out of wood, terra-cotta, or other materials. Sometimes images are made out of painted clay, so that they disintegrate when thrown into the river or sea at the end of a festival. In almost all large temples, the majority of images are stone or bronze, and they are often exquisitely beautiful. In a temple, the immovable image (*mula murti*, "root image") of the presiding deity, generally made of stone, is housed in the main shrine; around it stand images of subsidiary deities, sometimes placed inside shrines and sometimes not. Movable images (*utsava murti*, "festival image") of the presiding (and subsidiary) deities, which are usually cast in bronze, are used in festival processions and other rituals performed away from the immovable images. Although most sculptured images are anthropomorphic or theriomorphic, the aniconic *linga* of Shiva (as mentioned in chap. 2) is an important exception.

Plainly, since many images represent gods and goddesses with several heads, eyes, or arms and a host of other fantastic features, they are not designed to be exact likenesses of ordinary people or animals. The deities have powers and attributes transcending those of earthly beings, which their images are intended to display. However, the design of sculptured images (including *linga*s) is strictly governed by traditional iconographic rules, which in principle define precisely their proportion and shape, as well as the features particular to the deity whose image it is. Thus the number of arms, or the weapons and animals held in their hands, are specified uniquely for each deity or form of a deity, who can easily be identified once the rules of Hindu iconography are known.

Images are normally man-made artifacts. They are not usually considered to be sacred objects until they have been consecrated by installing divine power within them. However, some aniconic images are actually uncarved rocks. The *linga*s in many of Shiva's grandest temples are believed to have emerged naturally from the ground, "self-existent" and already full of divine power. A comparable example is the special type of fossil known as *shalagrama*, considered sacred to Vishnu. As it is imbued with Vishnu's powers, it can be revered just like any other image of the god. The same applies to the dried berry of a shrub (*Elaeocarpus ganitrus*), known as *rudraksha*, which is sacred to Shiva. Various other "naturally" sacred mineral and vegetable objects are treated similarly.

In the category of aniconic images, we can also place the unhewn or perhaps roughly etched stones, sometimes painted red, that serve as little village deities' images throughout India; they are either housed in crude shrines or left standing under a tree or in the open air. These stones serve exactly the same function as the sculptured images and *linga*s found in larger temples, even though they do not fit the classical iconographic rules. The same applies to other representations, such as the metal tridents or pots that stand at small shrines in some areas of India. Pots in particular, when filled with water in which a deity's power has been installed, are often used as the functional equivalents of sculptured mobile images at little deities' temples.

Frequently, a picture of a deity substitutes for an image. Pictures have probably always been used, but the advent of cheap color printing has made an enormous selection available in contemporary India. Carved images are relatively expensive and in millions of poorer homes, the household shrine contains only pictures of the family's favorite deities, which are consecrated and worshiped just like images.

Completeness requires us to stretch the category of images still further to embrace, for instance, natural phenomena such as rivers, as well as animate beings. For example, although any deity may be installed in a water-pot, the consecration ritual is generally said to turn the water into the water of the river Ganges (Ganga), the phenomenal form of the goddess Ganga. The Ganges (and indeed all rivers) are both "images" of Ganga and Ganga herself. In some contexts, much the same holds true for the soil in relation to the goddess of the earth, Bhudevi. A comparable but distinct example is the burning oil lamp, commonly identified with the goddess Lakshmi. Among living beings, various animals can be understood in a similar way. The cow is probably the best known example; it is frequently, although not invariably or exclusively, identified as an "image" of Lakshmi and Lakshmi herself. And most important, in the last analysis the same can apply to a human being. For example, when a priest becomes a form of Vishnu or Shiva during temple worship, his body is really an animate image, a literally anthropomorphic form of the god and, as such, the priest worships himself just as he worships the deity in its image. The case of the human "image" is important for understanding the relationship between a deity and its image, but let us first go back to ordinary sculptured images.

THE RELATIONSHIP BETWEEN DEITY AND IMAGE

When Hindus visit a temple, just gazing on the images for a "sight" or "vision" (*darshana*) of the deities is one of the most important things that they do. *Darshana* brings good fortune, well-being, grace, and spiritual merit to the seeing devotees, especially if they go to the temple early in the morning just after the deities have woken up. But *darshana* is not merely a passive sight of the deity in its image form; the deity is also gazing on the devotee with eyes that never blink, unlike those of human beings. Hence in *darshana* there is the "exchange of vision" (Eck 1981a: 6) that is so central to Hindu worship before images. In Hindu iconography, the eyes have a special place, and painting on or "opening" an image's eyes is frequently said to vivify it in an essential preliminary to consecration and worship. Shiva in particular is often represented with a third eye in the center of his forehead, from which his fiery power flows out, but on all divine images (as well as on men and women) the mark above the bridge of the nose symbolizes the third eye, the point from which power emanates. Thus when devotees look at images, they are also standing in the field of the deities' power and absorbing it like light through their own eyes.

So in the act of *darshana*, what exactly is a Hindu looking at? Is it the deity, its iconic representation in an image, or something in between? The answer is not easy, but it is crucial for understanding popular Hinduism.

We can begin by saying that a deity is *in* an image. It may be there because it has been installed by a consecration ritual, as with a manufactured image, or it may be "naturally" there, as with a self-existent image or *linga*. The deity may be permanently present in the image, as is generally said to be true in temples, or it may be there only temporarily, as with images made for a festival and discarded afterwards. A distinction between a deity and its image is plainly presupposed in many contexts. For example, the consecration ritual itself is premised on the notion that the image is "empty" before the deity is installed. By some more theologically sophisticated Hindus, such as the priests of the Minakshi temple in Madurai with whom I worked, the relationship between a deity and its image is commonly explained in terms of the power, *shakti*, possessed by all deities, even though *shakti* itself is personified as feminine. According to this explanation, the image actually contains some or all of the deity's power, so that the purpose of consecration is to install that power in a particular location, the image. There is no limit to the number of separate images within which the deity's power can be installed and the deity is never shackled by locating its power in images. Hence an image itself cannot be equated with its corresponding deity; the object of worship is not the image, but the deity whose power is inside it. Devotees who gaze upon an image do not directly see the deity, although they are touched by the power flowing out of the image. Certainly, much Hindu ritual is most consistently and economically explained by treating the image as a repository of divine power and, therefore, by distinguishing clearly between the image and its corresponding deity.

Yet this distinction between container and contained must not be overplayed. It is true that the identification of an image can be disputed, so that different people disagree about which deity's powers are in an image;

sometimes, too, the accepted identification of an image changes over time. Nonetheless, if an object—sculptured or otherwise—is a divine image, it must in principle be the image of a particular deity (or occasionally deities). Hence an image, unlike an ordinary container, is defined precisely by what it contains—the power of a particular deity—so that in the final analysis there can be no absolute distinction between an image and its corresponding deity. Thus people commonly point to an image and observe that it is, say, Vishnu or Shiva, of whom they have had *darshana*; this is not a metaphorical but a matter-of-fact statement that identifies the image as a specific, named deity. Similarly, the term *murti* is widely employed to denote a deity's form (especially Shiva as Dakshinamurti, Nataraja, etc.) as well as a deity's image. Consequently, we must understand the relationship between a deity and its image in a double sense, for the deity can either be distinguished from the image or identified with it, so that the image itself is then a "bodily" form of the deity, made concrete and visible in mundane time and space. Thus worship is addressed to a deity whose power is *in* an image and also to a deity *as* an image.

The double relationship between deity and image is particularly striking in the case of the human "image." Take for example the priest who, in south Indian Shiva temples, should install Shiva's powers in himself before he worships the god; according to the Shaiva ritual texts known as the Agamas, "only Shiva can worship Shiva." Plainly, the formula implies that the only perfect worship is the one performed by the god for himself, but here on earth it is commonly taken to mean that the priest must become, at one level, Shiva himself. As a form of the god, the priest then worships himself as part of Shiva's worship in the temple. At another level, though, the priest is a man who can be distinguished from the god Shiva, like a container from the contained. Hence in these temple rituals, Shiva assumes a form as the priest, but he is also the god whose power is in the priest, his animate image. In general terms, the same applies to anyone identified as divine, whether it is someone possessed by a village goddess, or a bride and groom treated as deities on their wedding day, or a holy man widely revered as a living god. In all these cases, to identify a person as a form of a deity also implies that that person is an "image" of the deity, for every image is also a divine form.

Finally, let me note that because no deity is constrained by its embodiment in images, a deity can be—and sometimes is—adored in imageless form; specifically, the divine "without qualities" (*nirguna*) is worshiped instead of the divine "with qualities" (*saguna*) made visible iconically. Some religious virtuosi, as well as Hindus opposed to so-called idolatry, have persistently argued that material images are needed only by the simple-minded and spiritually immature, who cannot turn their minds to the godhead without visible representations on which to focus. Muslims in India have long decried the Hindus' reverence for images, but in the last two hundred years or so, partly in reaction to Christian censure during the colonial period, image worship has been increasingly criticized by reformist Hindu intellectuals as a superstitious deviation from the true, original religion of the Vedas, which only marginally refer to the ritual use of images. But apart from some adherents of movements like the Arya Samaj in northern India, which has vigorously opposed image worship since its foundation in 1875, the vast majority of ordinary Hindus have been untroubled by criticism of their "idolatry." They know, as any sympathetic observer must also recognize, that in popular Hinduism devotion and respect for the deities are not diminished, but most completely expressed, through the use of images in worship.

THE CONTEXTS OF *PUJA*

Hindus perform *puja* in a wide range of settings. In temples, where priests are usually responsible for performing it before the deities' images, *puja* should be carried out regularly. Typically, in the great deities' major temples, it is done at least once a day, but in very grand and well-endowed ones, the daily cycle of worship includes a number of separate acts of worship, held at different times of day. In small and poorly funded temples, by contrast, worship may be done no more than once a week or even less often, and at the simple shrines of little deities, it tends to be sporadic. Worship at public temples is classically said to be "for the benefit of the world," because it is addressed on behalf of all to the deities who protect the whole population and preserve the entire sociocosmic order. At private temples belonging to particular families, kin groups, castes, or other social units, worship is mainly intended to benefit those who own the temple. When worship is performed by priests, especially in public temples, ordinary devotees have no active role and the value of the ritual is unaffected by the presence or absence of an audience. In all public temples, however, worship can also be performed for the deities either by individual devotees themselves or by priests acting on their behalf, although most ordinary people are usually content simply to salute the deities with the gesture of respect and to have *darshana* of them.

In addition to the worship conducted regularly, a temple's ritual cycle normally includes a range of periodic festivals (*utsava*) as well. (Confusingly, the term *puja* can also refer to such festivals, such as the annual Bengali goddesses' festivals of Durga Puja and Kali Puja. In this chapter, however, only *puja* as a single act of worship is under discussion.) In very large temples, many different festivals occur weekly, fortnightly, monthly, and annually, whereas in smaller temples there may be at most only one annual festival. During festivals, various kinds of rituals take place, such as processions, dramatic performances, dancing by the divinely possessed, and, at some temples, animal sacrifice. Festivals always incorporate acts of *puja* as well, and in its basic structure worship during festivals does not differ from worship performed on other occasions. At public temple festivals, the rituals—including the *puja*—are again for the benefit of all, whereas the beneficiaries of private temple festivals are particular groups.

Besides temples, *puja* is performed in many other institutions, such as monasteries, as well as in Hindu homes, normally at the household shrine where images or pictures of the deities are kept. Ideally, worship at home is done regularly, daily or perhaps weekly; although men do participate, especially during the more important festivals, domestic worship is often mainly the responsibility of women. Interestingly—and probably typically—a Marathi Brahman woman saw this as crucial in succinctly explaining why ritual power primarily belongs to females: "Everyone has some *shakti*, but women have more of it because they do more rituals and fasts" (Slocum 1988: 208). Some richer, high-caste households employ Brahman domestic priests to conduct their *puja*s, at least at major festivals, but the vast majority of domestic worship is done by ordinary householders. The principal purpose of domestic *puja*, of course, is to protect the household, but in addition many people perform personal worship at home, often addressing it to their own favorite deity (*ishtadeva*; *ishtadevata*).

In each and every context, *puja* is often one component of a longer sequence, so that it is performed in conjunction with hymn singing, offering oblations into a fire, festival processions, animal sacrifice, or a host of other rituals. Naturally, *puja* can also vary enormously in its elaborateness and correspondingly in the quantities of time and money spent on it. Between the spectacular worship conducted during a major festival at a great temple and the minimal rite held in a simple shrine or a poor home, there is a wide and obvious divergence. But despite this, and despite significant variations in the style of worship among different groups of Hindus in different regions of India, all rituals of *puja* have the same fundamental structure, which I shall now begin to investigate.

WORSHIP IN THE MINAKSHI TEMPLE

Let us begin with one particular example of *puja*, which comes from the Minakshi temple in Madurai. Rituals of worship in the Minakshi temple vary considerably. The one to be described is neither as elaborate as some, nor as simple and almost perfunctory as many others. I should make it clear that I shall not describe one specific event. Instead, I shall present a composite account of a ritual that occurs repeatedly in almost exactly the same way on similar occasions, mainly during major festivals for Minakshi and Sundareshwara (Shiva), the presiding deities of the temple.

At such a ritual, movable, festival images are the objects of worship. Minakshi's movable image, which is about two feet high, represents her standing alone, like her larger immovable image. Sundareshwara's movable image, of similar size, is not a *linga*, but an anthropomorphic image of Somaskanda, which represents the god sitting beside a female consort (Uma), with a small figure of their son Skanda between them.

Before a festival procession, the two images are normally placed side-by-side in a hall inside the temple complex. They are clothed—Minakshi in a sari and Somaskanda in a white cloth—but these garments are rarely neat, and the few garlands draped on the images have obviously been there for some hours. Priests and other temple officiants, including musicians, wait near the images and a small crowd of devotees sits or stands in front of the hall. At the start of the *puja*, a curtain is drawn in front of the images to shield them from the gaze of onlookers, but it is usually easy to see round the curtain and no one really objects.

Parenthetically, I should note that a *puja* of the kind to be described is rarely preceded by a preparatory ritual of purification. The latter is generally omitted in the Minakshi temple, although it is recognized that it always ought to be performed, as it is before certain very important rituals. The preparatory ritual is made up of a sequence of several separate rites. The priest states his earnest intention (*sankalpa*) to perform the main ritual that will follow and he worships Ganesha, lord of beginnings and obstacles, to ensure success. In the course of the rites that complete the sequence, the priest, the site, and the instruments of worship (the lamps, vessels, and so on, in addition to any special object to be used in the main ritual) are successively more highly purified. Charged with the power of the deities that has been installed in them, the priest and the instruments of worship are then worshiped as well.

Puja begins when the musicians start to play and a chanter, a Brahman officiant who is not a priest, starts to recite *mantras* (ritual formulas) in Sanskrit. The *mantras* derive from the Agamas and almost all rituals performed in the Minakshi temple include their recitation. The priest presiding over the ritual, assisted by others, first removes the clothes and garlands from the images of Minakshi and Somaskanda in preparation for the bathing ritual, known as *abhisheka*. He pours or rubs over the images a series of mostly liquid substances, such as (in this order) sesame-seed oil, milk, curds, a sweet confection known as *panchamrita*, green-coconut water, and finally consecrated water into which divine power has been invoked beforehand by the chanting of *mantras*. When this water is poured, the musical accompaniment reaches a climax, signaled by loud and rapid drumming.

The next stage is the decoration ritual, *alankara*, when the images are dressed in new clothes, given new sacred threads, sprinkled with perfume, and adorned with jewelry and fresh garlands of flowers. (Although Minakshi is a goddess, she—like her husband—wears over her shoulder the sacred thread that is the prerogative of adult male Brahmans.) A dot of red powder (*kunkuma*), symbolizing the goddess, is placed above the bridge of the nose on the images, and three stripes of white ash (*vibhuti*) are drawn horizontally on their foreheads, so that the images themselves bear the Shaivas' distinctive mark. The decoration during a major festival is often highly elaborate: an expensive, colored silk sari for Minakshi and a white silk cloth for Somaskanda, immensely valuable ornaments of gold and precious stones for both images, and several heavy garlands of flowers.

After decoration comes the food-offering ritual, *naivedya*. A covered plate of food, normally plain boiled rice (although there are alternatives), is held before each image in turn by a Brahman assistant to the priests. The presiding priest continuously rings a bell while sprinkling water around the plate, whose lid is slightly raised by the assistant. In this way, the priest offers the food to the god and goddess. The food (to be consumed later by priests or other temple officiants) is then taken away, and the curtain that has screened the whole of the worship thus far is drawn back. Its purpose is partly to protect the deities, especially Minakshi, from prying eyes while they are bathed and dressed, and partly to hide them from evil spirits, who are particularly jealous of the deities' splendid fare and always try to snatch it during the food offering.

Removing the screen lets all the devotees see the final stage, the display of lamps, *diparadhana*. In this ritual, the priest waves a series of oil lamps, and finally a candelabra burning camphor, in front of the images. On various occasions, different lamps are used, but a typical series comprises five oil lamps, each with its own design and number of wicks. The closing candelabra has seven camphor flames (one on each of its six branches and one in the center); although not strictly part of the *diparadhana*, we can include the candelabra here. Although there are variations in style among priests, it is generally agreed in the temple that the lamps should be waved separately before the head, body, and feet of an image, each time describing in the air the almost circular shape (as written in Tamil) of the ancient mystic syllable *om*, which represents the totality of the universe. The priest, facing the images, waves the oil lamps with his right hand and continuously rings a bell with his left; he does lay down the bell to take the camphor candelabra in both hands. Usually, the candelabra is waved with special care, high in the air, so that everyone can see it; at the same time, the musicians drum very loudly and rapidly to signal the culminating climax of the worship. At this point, many watching devotees raise their hands to gesture in salutation and call out the praises of the god and goddess. Many of them crowd round the priest, who will bring them the still burning candelabra, so that they can cup their hands over the flames before touching their eyes with the fingertips. From the priest devotees also accept red powder or, more usually, white ash to put on their own foreheads. They then start to walk away, and the priests and their assistants begin to move the images in readiness for the next event in the festival.

Ideally, just as every *puja* should be preceded by a preparatory ritual of purification, so it should also be completed with a sacrificial fire ritual. Briefly, this involves kindling a fire, invoking the deity—in this case Shiva—in the fire, and worshiping him there, pouring oblations of clarified butter and other foodstuffs into the flames (the rite known as *homa*), and then making offerings to the temple's guardian deities around the fire, including an extra offering to the guardian deity of the northeast quadrant, who is himself a form of Shiva. Like the preparatory ritual, the fire sacrifice is carried out in conjunction with acts of worship during certain very important rituals, but otherwise it is omitted. In a *puja* of the kind described, the distribution of powder and ash to devotees normally completes the ritual.

THE STRUCTURE AND MEANING OF *PUJA*

In theory, we might uncover the general structure of *puja* and elucidate its meaning by comparing a series of ethnographic accounts, for which my description of the Minakshi temple *puja* would be one starting point. However, there is a better and simpler approach. The Agamas, which in principle govern the ritual in Shiva's south Indian temples, belong to a body of Sanskrit texts that are treated as authoritative because they contain the deities' own directions for their proper worship. But these texts, since they are the products of an indigenous intellectual desire to abstract and systematize, also provide us with paradigmatic descriptions of *puja*. Only for the worship of the great deities—notably Vishnu, Shiva, and Devi in major temples served by Brahman priests—are texts like the Agamas taken as authoritative. Elsewhere, especially for little village deities worshiped by non-Brahman priests, even putative reference to ritual texts is rare. Nevertheless, the evidence shows that all *puja* rituals share the same fundamental structure and that structure is most clearly laid out in the paradigmatic descriptions contained in the Sanskrit texts.

According to the texts, *puja* consists of an ordered sequence of offerings and services, each of which is known as an *upachara*. Different texts contain variant lists of offerings and services, but their overall sequence is always much the same and the most common total number is sixteen. Jan Gonda (1970: 186, n. 196) provides a typical list of the sixteen *upachara*s in order, which I reproduce with some added clarifications in table 1.

The sixteen items in this sequence can be grouped into partly distinct phases. First, the deity is invoked (or invited to enter the image) and then installed there (nos. 1–2). Second, water for washing is offered (nos. 3–5). Third—the heart of the ritual—the image is bathed, dressed, adorned, shown incense and a lamp, and offered food (nos. 6–13). Fourth, after a series of gestures of respect, the deity is bidden farewell (nos. 14–16).

The Minakshi temple *puja* described above comprises four rituals that are separately identified: bathing, decoration, food offering, and waving of lamps. These four rituals are normally considered to constitute the full *puja* for Minakshi and Sundareshwara both during festivals and in daily worship, when *puja* is performed before their immovable images. Each ritual is classified as an *upachara* and they correspond—comparing them with the list in table 1—to bathing (no. 6); dressing, putting on the sacred thread, sprinkling with perfume, and adorning with flowers (nos. 7–10); offering food (no. 13); and waving an oil lamp (no. 12). Quite often the lamp service is immediately preceded by waving a censer of incense as well (no. 11). In the Minakshi temple, the rest of the offerings and services (nos. 1–5, 14–16) are usually omitted, to leave only the central, third phase (nos. 6–13).

TABLE 1
The Sixteen Offerings and Services of *Puja*

1. Invocation of the deity
2. Offering a seat to or installation of the deity
3. Offering water for washing the feet
4. Offering water for washing the head and body
5. Offering water for rinsing the mouth
6. Bathing
7. Dressing or offering a garment
8. Putting on the sacred thread
9. Sprinkling with perfume
10. Adorning with flowers
11. Burning incense
12. Waving an oil lamp
13. Offering food
14. Paying homage by prostration, etc.
15. Circumambulation
16. Dismissal or taking leave of the deity

Does this mean that the Minakshi temple *puja* is incomplete and therefore imperfect? The answer is certainly not. In Hinduism, ritual abbreviation and simplification are ubiquitous procedures that are allowed by the texts themselves, and the practice in the Minakshi temple is entirely conventional. Admittedly, temple officiants—if directly questioned—sometimes concede that the missing offerings and services should be included, although they often plead as well that because the images are permanently installed in the temple, they always contain the power of the deities, whose invocation and dismissal are therefore redundant. Arguments of this sort, though, are largely beside the point. A full series of sixteen offerings and services is best, but a shorter sequence, albeit less good, still constitutes a properly performed ritual of worship. Moreover, although the "full" worship in the Minakshi temple comprises only four rituals, which leaves out at least eight of the sixteen textual *upacharas*, it is common practice merely to offer food and wave the lamps. This is done for Minakshi and Sundareshwara on many occasions and for the subsidiary deities almost always. None of this is peculiar to the Minakshi temple and in most temples, which the former dwarfs in size and resources, a *puja* as full as its four rituals is fairly unusual. Frequently, in the Minakshi temple and elsewhere, *puja* is further reduced to no more than the showing of a one-flame camphor lamp with a plantain on the side as a food offering. Hindus commonly refer to the lamp service—and especially the camphor flame display—as *arati*, a term widely used throughout India as a synonym for *puja*. In the final analysis, the camphor flame, as the culmination of worship, stands synecdochically for the entire ritual. Synecdoche, indeed, is a basic principle of all Hindu ritual, including *puja*. As ordered parts of the whole, short and simple rituals, even if they are described as less good, still reproduce the structure and meaning of their fuller homologues.

It should now be clear that *puja* is, in the first place, an act of respectful honoring and that this meaning is inherent in its structure as an ordered series of offerings and services, most fully displayed in the paradigmatic textual model, but no less present in the Minakshi temple worship that I have described, as well as in more attenuated versions of the ritual. Honor is shown to the deities by presenting offerings and services to their image forms that are (or should be) as luxurious, sumptuous, and delightful as possible, and they should also fit the preferences that each deity is believed to have (for example, elaborate bathing rituals for Shiva and beautiful decorations for Vishnu). That worship is an act of homage to powerful, superior deities is explicitly understood by priests in the Minakshi temple and by many, if not most, Hindus throughout India.

It is common to liken the honor shown to deities with that due to kings, and Gonda's interpretation is echoed by other writers: *puja* "originally and essentially is an invocation, reception and entertainment of God as a royal guest" (1970: 77). Certainly, the idea that the deities are royal guests is important, especially in major temples where they are actually proclaimed as sovereign rulers. On the other hand, it would be wrong to conclude that *puja* always represents deities as supereminent kings. As I remarked earlier, Hindu worship has a personal and homely aspect too, and Diana L. Eck rightly observes that it can reveal "not only an attitude of honor but also an attitude of affection" (1981a: 36). Gods and goddesses are often the honored guests of humble worshipers, and the offerings and services of *puja* closely resemble the acts that ordinary people perform for each other or their guests at home. Respectful honoring is the first meaning and purpose of worship, but it elaborates the hospitality of the home as much as the grandeur of the palace, even if the latter is more striking in great temples.

THE DEITIES' NEEDS AND THEIR RESPONSE TO WORSHIP

Plainly, it is men and women who worship; they have to honor the deities. But do the deities need to be honored, and do they need the offerings and services rendered to them? Eck points out that worship is shaped by human ideas about honoring guests, rather than being a response to "God's necessity" (ibid.: 37). She is right and it is crucial that *puja* compromises neither the deities' power nor their other attributes. Nonetheless, the question of divine needs is not simple and there are divergent answers to it, which also suggest that worship, despite its fundamentally uniform structure, can have varying significance for different groups of Hindus.

In the Minakshi temple ritual, as in the vast majority of *puja*s, the images have a key role because the various offerings and services are actually made to them. The images of Minakshi and Somaskanda are physically bathed and decorated, real food is placed before them, and lamps illuminate them. Inasmuch as the images are forms of Minakshi and Sundareshwara, the divine couple themselves accept the offerings and services, or at least they are presumed to do so.

Yet it does not follow that the deities really require these ministrations. In the Minakshi temple, I was repeatedly told that *puja*, like other rituals, is designed "to please the gods." If worship, especially in public temples, is performed properly and does please the deities, they can be expected to respond by protecting the whole community so that it flourishes; if worship is not performed properly so that the deities are displeased, they are likely to withdraw protection, causing distress and misery. Many Minakshi temple priests blame contemporary India's problems on what they see as persistently poor performance of temple ritual. That in turn is put down to excessive interference in temple affairs by the Tamilnadu government, whose control over the temple they fiercely resent. However, even when temple worship is performed properly, divine protection cannot be guaranteed because the deities cannot be directly induced to act beneficently by honoring them in worship. Ultimately, the action of deities is determined by their own will, not that of mortals on earth.

But for my informants in Madurai, the impossibility of compelling divine action also depends on the premise that the deities' pleasure does not derive from the offerings and services in themselves. Gods and goddesses do not actually need offerings and services, because they never are dirty, ugly, hungry, or unable to see in the dark. Hence the purpose of worship is not to satisfy nonexistent divine needs, but to honor the deities and show devotion by serving them *as if* they had such needs. By this method alone can human beings adopt a truly respectful attitude toward the deities. Such an explanation of how *puja* pleases deities is logically consistent with a relatively emphatic distinction between a deity and its image, the container of divine power, because then the deity itself is not directly touched by the offerings and services made to its image. The outlook of Minakshi temple officiants is intellectually consistent and echoes the Agamic ritual texts, which make it clear that Shiva never requires anything from human beings. Many Hindus share a perspective close to the temple officiants' on the purpose of *puja*, the deities' needs, and the role of images, even if they articulate it less systematically.

Yet there is an alternative view, which is more consistent with the tendency to play down the distinction between container and contained, so as to equate an image with the deity of which it is a form. This view is more prevalent among Vaishnavas, notably devotees of Krishna, who tend to insist more forcefully than many Shaivas that the image is fully a form of the deity. Correspondingly, in the Vaishnava tradition, the god himself is often thought to need the offerings and services provided for him in worship. Devotees typically portray Krishna—especially in his form as a child—as willingly dependent upon them, so that the god, and the image that is his physical manifestation, actually suffer if they are not worshiped. In other words, Krishna has bodily needs that must be met by the offerings and services of *puja* and he is—in the form of the image receiving them—pleased because his worshipers meet those needs.

Even in this case, though, Krishna's needs are satisfied by human beings because he permits it, thereby expressing a mutual dependence between god and devotee that is more prominent in Vaishnava than Shaiva cults. It is all part of Krishna's "play" (*lila*) in this world; he has chosen to make himself dependent on his worshipers, most patently as a child, but his choice implies no qualification of his divine power. As John S. Hawley says, Krishna "allows us the game of feeding him for our benefit; it is symbolic action and would have no value but for the belief, the mood with which it is infused. God dines on our love, not our food" (1981: 18). Consequently, whether worship is addressed to Vishnu, Shiva, or any other deity, its fundamental purpose is human ministration to *putative* divine needs, in which the action of offering and serving, rather than the offerings and services themselves, is critical. Furthermore, Vaishnavas are equally insistent that worship does not constrain the deities. Therefore, irrespective of whether a deity actually has needs, or an image actually receives the offerings and services, *puja* is still an act of respectful honoring whose objective is to please a deity in the hope or expectation—but not the certainty—that it will protect and favor human beings.

Not all Hindu worship, however, is so high-minded and it frequently is motivated by a conscious intention to persuade or induce a deity to bestow reciprocal favors on the worshiper. Many Hindus, like the priests in the Minakshi temple, insist that it is always wrong to worship in such a spirit, as well as counter-productive, because the deities will be displeased by worship done with blatant ulterior motives. In some regions, especially western India where Vaishnava devotionalism is influential, a linguistic distinction is made between *puja* and *seva*. *Puja* is an exchange, a transaction "made in connection with benefits for the worshiper," whereas "worship through *seva* . . . represents the 'loving care' of those devoted to the deity without thought of benefit or return by the latter" (Mayer 1981b: 167). Elsewhere, the term *puja* rarely carries this negative connotation, but the distinction identified by Adrian C. Mayer is a more general one, and *puja* (to revert to the one term) often is performed by or on behalf of individuals or groups, who want to win boons from the deities. For instance, ordinary Hindus in Madurai have often told me that they regularly worship deities in connection with specific requests. Some deny that they bargain and say that they ask a priest to do the worship while simultaneously praying to the deity, but other people frankly admit that they try to make a deal. Some people even ask first and only offer worship afterwards if their request is met, arguing that it is senseless to spend time and money worshiping deities who will not demonstrate that they can help.

There is no doubt that the great deities, especially Vishnu and Shiva, are generally held to be unresponsive and even angered by futile efforts to persuade them to act in specific ways. Many little deities, by contrast, notably deified malevolent spirits, are thought to voice particular demands, and to be open to more or less direct bargaining about what they will do if such and such an offering is made during worship. In such cases, respectful homage is almost completely overshadowed by the real and assumed motives of worshiper and deity, respectively. Yet other deities—for example, many forms of the goddess—are not thought to take the lofty attitude of Vishnu and Shiva, but are still impervious to blatant cajolery. All these assumptions about the deities are themselves significant elements in the ideological discourse of evaluation, for superior deities are partly distinguished from inferior ones precisely by their ostensible refusal to enter into demeaning bargains with men and women about possible favors. Similarly, as part of the same discourse, educated, high-caste Hindus are generally more inclined to dismiss and condemn attempts to bargain with deities than uneducated, low-caste people, although the latter certainly do worship deities without ulterior motives as well; we must be careful not to endorse wholesale elitist disparagement of the faith of the lower strata. It is, however, clear that there is considerable variation among Hindus about the feasibility and morality of seeking personal benefits from worship. *Puja* is first of all an act of respectful honoring, and this is plainly inscribed in its structure. Yet how and why it is such an act, and whether honoring the deities excludes treating with them, are issues on which real differences of opinion exist among Hindus themselves.

THE ACHIEVEMENT OF IDENTITY BETWEEN DEITY AND WORSHIPER

Let us now turn to one of the most important and distinctively Hindu aspects of *puja*. This is the movement toward identity between deity and worshiper, which is partly revealed by the sequential logic of the ritual as it unfolds.

In the words of Penelope Logan, whose analysis of domestic worship in Madurai I draw on here, a fundamental process in *puja* is "embodying the deity and disembodying man" (1980: 123). In this process, the image plays a crucial role. Worship, whether in the home or elsewhere, is normally performed before an image precisely because the deity is then represented "with qualities" discernible by people and it takes on a tangible, fixed, and embodied form, proximate to the human being's condition. In its form as an image, the deity, so to speak, has come "down" toward the human level; through the performance of worship, the worshiper goes "up" toward the divine level to achieve, finally, identity with the deity.

In the course of most of the offerings and services that constitute worship, the deity is treated like a human guest embodied in its image, and the ritual reinforces the deity's embodiment in a physical form resembling the worshiper's own. Moreover, since the offerings and services are enjoyed by the deity alone, the separation between deity and worshiper has not yet disappeared. The partial exception to this is the display of lamps, an intangible service seen by both deity and worshiper. In many acts of worship, the lamp service precedes the food offering (as in table 1); in many others, as in the Minakshi temple and most south Indian cases, it follows it. Very frequently, however, in the ritual as performed by Hindus today, *puja* is closed by waving a camphor flame either by itself or in conjunction with other lights.

Showing the camphor flame is the climax of worship and, as mentioned above, it synecdochically represents the entire ritual. Quite commonly, an *arati*, a service of lights that includes a camphor flame, is performed by itself as a standard temple ritual. It is true that a camphor flame is not always shown and the lamp service may include only lamps, or sometimes long wicks, burning oil or ghee. Nonetheless, as Logan argues (ibid.: 124), camphor has particularly powerful symbolic properties because it burns with a very strong light and fragrance. The flame symbolizes both the deity's embodiment during *puja*, by appealing directly to the physical senses, as well as the deity's transcendence of its embodied form, for the burning camphor, which leaves no sooty residue, provides an intangible display of incandescent light and fragrance. As the all-consuming flame acts upon the senses of the worshiper, as well as of the deity, it simultaneously symbolizes the total disembodiment of the human worshiper. And although the deity was and remains in an embodied form, to be treated like a human guest, this state is now partly dissolved, so that both deity and worshiper together can transcend their embodied forms. When a camphor flame is shown at the climax of *puja*, therefore, the divine and human participants are most fully identified in their common vision of the flame and hence in their mutual vision of each other—the perfect *darshana*. God has become man and a person, transformed, has become god; they have been merged and their identity is then reinforced when the worshiper cups the hands over the camphor flame, before touching the fingertips to the eyes. By this means, the deity's power and benevolent, protective grace, now in the flame, are transmitted to the worshiper and absorbed through the eyes, again the crucial organs. In principle, moreover, all who see and touch the flame participate in the identification, for they also benefit from the transformation undergone by the worshiper who is often, as in a temple, a priest whose place cannot be taken by ordinary devotees.

Light, most especially the camphor flame, is thus an extraordinarily potent condensed symbol of the quintessentially Hindu idea, implied by its polytheism, that divinity and humanity can mutually become one another, despite the relative separation between them that normally prevails in this world where men and women live and must die. So it is fitting, too, that the camphor flame, through which the identity of deity and worshiper is achieved, should also stand for the whole ritual of *puja*.

The *Prasada*

At the end of the Minakshi temple worship, the priest brings the camphor flame to the waiting devotees and also gives them white ash or red powder, which they normally put on the forehead, although a little ash may be swallowed. The priest usually keeps a stock of ash and powder in a little bag, but ideally he has taken them from the images' feet. The ash and powder are kinds of *prasada*, literally meaning "grace," and the distribution of *prasada* is the indispensable sequel to all acts of worship in popular Hinduism.

There are several different types of *prasada*. Ash and powder are normally handed out in south Indian temples of Shiva and his consort, but in Vishnu's temples the principal item is a little consecrated water, some to be sprinkled over the head and some to be swallowed. Water and other liquids used in bathing rituals are similarly taken by devotees to be sprinkled or sipped, and flowers that have been placed on the images during worship may be presented to devotees at the end. Other examples could be added, but in many contexts—in temples, houses, or elsewhere—the main type of *prasada* is food that has been offered to the deity during worship and is subsequently eaten by priests, attending devotees, lay worshipers, or indeed anyone else, such as absent friends or relatives to whom it has been sent. In the literature on popular Hinduism, *prasada* is often defined as sanctified food, but this is an error; *prasada*, despite the undoubted importance of food, comprises a wide range of sanctified substances.

Prasada is the material symbol of the deities' power and grace. During *puja*, different substances—ash, water, flowers, food, or other items—have been transferred to the deity, so that they have been in contact with the images or, as with food, have been symbolically consumed by the deity in its image form. As a result, these substances have been ritually transmuted to become *prasada* imbued with divine power and grace, which are absorbed or internalized when the *prasada* is placed on the devotee's body or swallowed. Whenever *puja* is concluded by waving a camphor flame, taking in the *prasada* is a process that replicates and consolidates the transfer of divine power and grace through the immaterial medium of the flame. Hence the flame and *prasada* together divinize the human actor to achieve the identity between deity and worshiper (including nonparticipatory devotees), which completes the transformation initiated by the offerings and services made during *puja*.

Because food *prasada* is actually eaten, it most strikingly symbolizes human internalization of divine qualities and the "physiological engagement" between deity and devotee, to borrow from a slightly different setting a phrase of Lawrence A. Babb (1987: 69). No doubt, the powerful and patent symbolism of eating explains the prominence of food as *prasada*. In some Vaishnava cults in particular, the offering of food and its consumption as *prasada* are highly elaborated. But other items can be swallowed as well, and all *prasada* is absorbed by the body, literally or figuratively, so that food *prasada* has no unique efficacy. Moreover, the ritual in its entirety—the *puja* plus the taking of *prasada*—is required to effect the ideal merging of deity and worshiper.

The structure of Hindu worship also suggests that the identification of deity and human is sustainable for only a short period, despite the mutual vision through the camphor flame and the divine power and grace absorbed from the *prasada*. The normal temporariness of the state of identity is aptly marked by the impermanence of almost all the main materials used. Liquids used in bathing rituals drain away; flowers on the decorated images quickly fade and lose their scent; incense, oil, and camphor all disappear in smoke; foodstuffs are consumed; and the ash, powder, or water smeared or sprinkled on the person at the end rapidly rub off or evaporate. Taking *prasada* does not prolong the identity of the divine and human for very long. The whole ritual then has to be repeated and, in a sense, there is so much repetitive worship in Hinduism precisely because it has so much obsolescence built into it. Hence, although *puja* ideally brings about identification between deity and worshiper, the very need for the ritual and its repeated performance are themselves testimony to the relative differentiation of the divine and human that is an ever-present reality for most people most of the time. In the divine world, we are told, flower garlands do not fade, but in this world where men and women blink and die, they do (Blackburn 1985: 256).

Worship and Social Hierarchy

All Hindu rituals, as I stressed in chapter 1, are about relationships among members of Indian society, as well as between them and their deities. *Puja* is obviously no exception, and how different sets of social relationships among priests, lay worshipers, and devotees are reflected, expressed, and constructed through worship could be discussed from many angles. However, I shall focus on two particular problems that have stimulated anthropological discussion: the connection between *puja* and social hierarchy, and the relationship of *puja* with precedence and kingship.

The terms of the first problem are initially given by the importance of purity and pollution in Hindu society. With more or less analytical sophistication, some writers have argued that the relationship between deities and worshipers in *puja* is homologous with that between the higher castes, particularly Brahmans, and the lower castes: in short, that deities are to people as pure high castes are to impure low castes. In this vein, Edward B. Harper, relying on fieldwork data from Karnataka, argues that the great gods (*devaru*), who are served by Brahman priests employing a Sanskrit liturgy, "must be fed, their temples must be swept, and their bodies and feet must be bathed. By performing these services, the Brahmin absorbs the god's impurity" (1964: 195). The Brahman priest can remove pollution from the god only if he is in the highest possible state of purity, which in turn requires the lower castes to remove his pollution: washermen clean his dirty clothes, barbers shave him and cut his hair, untouchables clean his latrine, and so on. Hence, according to Harper, Hindu society "is organized around the task of caring for its gods, and a division of labor among the castes is necessary to attain this end" (ibid.: 196).

Although initially attractive in its cogency, Harper's argument fails to withstand close scrutiny for a number of reasons. The most crucial is that he misconstructs *puja* as primarily a ritual to remove impurity from the deities, particularly by bathing them. Although a state of purity in both temple and worshipers is a precondition for worship, the basic aim of the ritual, as we know, is to honor powerful deities, not to purify them. Whether deities themselves are actually susceptible to pollution is an issue on which Hindu opinion varies; some people insist that they are not, and others say that they are, pointing to myths and rituals that are concerned with polluted deities. It is, however, clear that worshipers must purify themselves before beginning *puja* in order to make themselves fit to honor the deities and benefit from the ritual, and not simply to avoid polluting the deities. If people do pollute temples and the images within by entering when suffering, for instance, from birth, death, or menstrual pollution, the deities are normally said to be angered, whether or not they are also polluted, so that the offenders suffer their wrath and gain no benefit from any ritual that they perform. Above all else, therefore, infringing the rules of purity offends deities much like any misperformance of worship, but it does not necessarily mean that deities themselves are seriously affected by pollution, whereas all human beings are, irrespective of their status.

Moreover, although some deities are said by some Hindus to suffer from death or menstrual pollution, no deity is subject to the day-to-day pollution caused by ordinary bodily functions. The Brahmans' purity partly depends on lower castes removing such pollution from them, but the deities' does not depend on Brahman priests acting in like fashion. Thus the relationship between deity and worshiper is not homologous with that between pure and polluted persons—specifically Brahmans and the lower castes—and *puja* does not express any such homology.

A more fruitful line of enquiry looks to the significance of the food *prasada*. In the course of his analysis of *puja*, Babb argues that "An asymmetrical transaction in foods . . . lies at the heart of *puja*, a transaction both expressive of and supportive of hierarchical distance between the divine and the human" (1975: 57). This argument rests on the proposition that *prasada* is food that has been partly consumed by the deity before being "returned" to the worshiper. A transfer of this kind expresses hierarchical ranking—specifically the worshiper's inferiority before the deity—because people who eat food that has been partly consumed by someone else openly acknowledge their inferiority by accepting "leftovers" or "remains," known in Hindi as *jutha*.

Jutha (or its synonym in other Indian languages) primarily refers to food that has been half-eaten and could therefore pollute anyone else who finishes it, because it may have been touched by the first person's hand and polluting saliva. Under most circumstances, Hindus never eat such food. There are, though, some well recognized exceptions. The most important is when a wife eats food left on her husband's plate, which is a common custom throughout India and, among many Hindus, is done for the first time during their wedding.

But can *prasada* be identified with *jutha*, as the polluted leftover food of the deities? Many Hindus, presumably including those studied by Babb in Chhattisgarh, do call *prasada* the deities' *jutha*, and this is quite widely reported, especially from north India. Other Hindus, such as my informants in the Minakshi temple, flatly deny that *prasada* is a species of polluted leftovers and stress the semantic opposition between the two categories; their view may be commoner in south India, although it is also prevalent among devotees of Krishna in western India, who insist on the "exceptional mystical powers" of *prasada* (P. J. Bennett 1990: 199). But despite differences in the classification of *prasada*, the ritual logic is essentially the same everywhere. Since purity and impurity are invariably relative qualities, leftovers that are polluted from the point of view of the superior party may still appear pure to the inferior. Hence, whether food *prasada* is actually described as the deities' *jutha* or not, it is not polluted, but pure, for the consumer, the worshiper. Nonetheless, to eat food that has first been tasted by another is always a demonstration of relative inferiority, as it is when a wife eats from her husband's plate. In that sense, all consumption of *prasada* does express the deities' hierarchical superiority over their worshipers.

Yet the deities' superiority over human worshipers is not the real issue, which is rather the extent to which *puja* also expresses the principles of hierarchical inequality within human society. Babb himself, although his argument has several twists and turns, claims that it does, particularly because he emphasizes the parallel between the "transaction in foods" during worship and the exchange of food between castes of different rank: "in its expression of hierarchy the asymmetrical exchange of foods that takes place in *puja* is in consonance with more general principles that order Hindu life" (ibid.: 56).

Although Babb's conclusion is not wholly wrong, as we shall see, the line of argument is flawed. Some anthropologists have placed even more stress than Babb on food transactions and exchanges in *puja*, but in fact there is no real "transaction in foods" during *puja* at all. The deity is not given food, which it has to reciprocate with a "counterprestation" (ibid.: 57) of *prasada*. Instead, the deity is served a meal, which the worshiper later consumes. The food *prasada* is not a return gift, but the same food transmuted—like all other substances that become *prasada*—by its contact with the deity in its image form. There are no food transactions and prestations in *puja*, because they are not what the food offering together with the receipt of *prasada* amount to.

Furthermore, food exchanges between castes do not mirror any salient dimension of *puja*. The rules that traditionally govern intercaste food exchanges—now greatly weakened in much of contemporary India—are complicated. They vary according to the kind of food involved and they are not the same for all groups everywhere in the country. In general, however, ordinary boiled foods such as rice and vegetable dishes—which typically constitute the core of a meal offered to the deities—are subject to the tightest restrictions, because these foods are thought to transmit pollution to the eater most easily. Consequently, to protect their own purity, nobody will traditionally accept such food if it is cooked and served by someone of a lower caste. The very refusal to accept is itself an assertion of higher-caste status. Deities, however, self-evidently accept food cooked by human beings, who are nevertheless their inferiors. Thus deities do not act in relation to people as the members of high castes act in relation to those of low castes, and *puja*—inasmuch as it is about the offering of food to deities—does not obey the rules governing food exchanges within the caste system. Once more, we see that the relationship between deity and worshiper is not homologous with that between high and low castes.

Far more pertinent is the relationship between husband and wife. In most households, the wife cooks and serves food to her husband, so that he takes it from his inferior partner; in the same way, the deity takes food from the inferior priest or lay worshiper. In temples, food is often prepared by someone other than the priest, but obviously the cook is also the deity's inferior. When we recall that the closest analogue to eating the deity's left-over food is a wife's consumption of her husband's, it makes good sense to say that a worshiper stands in relation to a deity as a wife to her husband. Such a comparison is indeed drawn in many contexts, so that priests and devotees are commonly described as wifely servants of the gods and goddesses. That in turn is consistent with the fact that *puja* is really about honoring a respected guest, for the quality of hospitality in a Hindu home always depends on a wife's work in her kitchen. Thus in a real sense, it is the institutionalized hierarchical inequality between husbands and wives, not between castes, that is most patently reflected in the ritual of *puja*.

WORSHIP, PRECEDENCE, AND KINGSHIP

Let me now take up the second problem, the relationship among *puja*, precedence, and kingship, which has attracted considerable attention in recent scholarship. Especially in temples, worship frequently provides the context for displaying and establishing distinctions of rank, and this occurs in two main ways, the first being the order of *prasada* distribution. At a temple, the priest normally gives *prasada* to the person of highest rank first. He (or occasionally she) may be the temple's patron or manager, who has overall supervisory responsibility for its affairs and must ensure, among other things, that its rituals are properly conducted. In the past, particularly at an important temple, the patron was often a king, and even today there are many temples at which an ex-king or his descendant retains the supervisory role. In most smaller temples, the patron was and is a local magnate, often a village or dominant-caste headman, acting in his role as a petty ruler. Especially in south India, most large and many small temples are now controlled by the state, so that the government official in charge assumes the patron's role. Although much temple ritual is paid for by funds controlled by patrons, particular events are often sponsored by outside bodies, such as families or caste associations, and then the leading party who receives *prasada* first is the senior representative of the sponsoring body. Sometimes, too, the sponsor is a wealthy individual. From time to time, the highest-ranking person in attendance at worship is a dignitary visiting a temple, such as a government minister, an influential holy man, or even a famous film-star. Often, of course, nobody important is present at ordinary temple worship, so that the priest just goes to the nearest person first. But if there are several people of high rank, the priest distributes *prasada* in their order of precedence before turning to anybody else. In India today, distinctions are rarely made among ordinary members of the public in temples, but in the past, at some major temples, *prasada* was carefully given to Brahman devotees first and then casually handed out to the lower castes or even, as in Suchindram (southern Tamilnadu), just thrown on a platform for them (Appadurai 1981b: 212–13; Pillay 1953: 265).

The second way to signal rank, particularly in south Indian temples, is by the receipt of "honors" (*mariyadai* in Tamil). Honors come in various forms, but one of the most common is a silk cloth, which is draped across the image's shoulders during worship and then tied by the priest, like a turban, round the recipient's head at the end of the ritual. This cloth is usually the principal honor given to a ritual's sponsor; if several representatives of the sponsoring body are entitled to cloths, they are tied in order of seniority. Normally, the recipient of the first (or only) cloth was also, immediately beforehand, the first recipient of *prasada* as well, so that his primacy is doubly marked. *Prasada* and honors have some similarities, but there are also crucial differences; in particular, honors are restricted in number and always single out dignitaries, whereas *prasada*—although distributed in rank order—can be offered to everyone.

To many Hindus, again especially in south India, the order of precedence at temple worship is of paramount importance, because it publicly confirms the rank of individuals, the offices they hold, or the groups they represent. For this reason, powerful men—on behalf of themselves, their offices, or their groups—have long competed vigorously and even bitterly for precedence in temple worship. Frequently, in temples great and small, disputes over precedence have actually ended in absurd stalemate. For example, two groups of Kallars, the dominant landholding caste in Pudukkottai in Tamilnadu, have joint control of one temple. For years and years, they have argued about which group has precedence in the receipt of *prasada* and other honors. Today, the priest has to give to the two groups' headmen simultaneously, "with his hands crossed to blur any possible precedence accruing to the receipt of honors from the right hand as opposed to the left." But that will not do either, so that recently, "the dispute over precedence took the form of quarreling about which hand would be crossed over or under." No strategy could ever settle this ancient quarrel once and for all; as Nicholas B. Dirks comments, "Equality in a situation involving honor is a virtual impossibility" (1987: 254–55).

But why do people go to such lengths over precedence at temples? Although the distribution of *prasada* allows everyone to receive a deity's power and grace, someone given *prasada* first, and an honor as well, is openly singled out as the deity's first worshiper. That in itself is constitutive of superior status and authoritative rights within the temple, principally because the first worshiper can claim to be the highest-ranking subject of the deity in its capacity as a sovereign ruler. In other words, precedence as emergent from worship depends upon the idea that the deity is quintessentially honored as a king, whose worshipers form a court arranged in order of rank according to their proximity to him.

As we have seen, this idea is an important one, especially in temples where deities are proclaimed as sovereign rulers, and it is the basis for

Dirks's contention that *puja* "operates as a root metaphor for political relations" centered on kingship (ibid.: 134). Arjun Appadurai and Carol A. Breckenridge (1976), who initially developed the thesis about temple honors, as well as other writers like Dirks who have extended it, have greatly contributed to our understanding of the temple as a political arena. But as analysis of *puja* itself, their approach is less convincing. These scholars overlook the fact that the distribution of *prasada* and presentation of honors are the sequel to *puja*, not its core, and they do so because they rely on a transactionalist, exchange model of worship. Thus Dirks, for instance, argues that "The highlight of puja is feeding the god and then returning some portion of the offerings used in worship as *pracatam* [*prasada*]" (1987: 38). As I have already shown, the food exchange model is defective. Dirks's argument fails to explain how the ritual of *puja* itself represents the worshipers' relationship with the deity. More generally, by placing so much emphasis on honors and kingship, this school of writers comes perilously close to reducing *puja* to its political component, as if it were a ritual whose primary function is to constitute rank and authority among powerful men. Clearly in some contexts, that function is very important, but *puja* as a whole is never about "politics" alone, however culturally sensitive is the definition of that term.

Conclusion

Puja, to conclude, is an act of respectful honoring for powerful deities, which comprises a series of offerings and services. The ritual owes as much to notions of domestic hospitality as it does to obeisance in the king's court. In general the worshiper is as much a deity's wifely servant as its royal subject. Correspondingly, an attitude of devotion, as well as deference to a powerful superior, is commonly central in worship, although there are also contexts in which respectful honoring largely gives way to interested bargaining for favors from the deity. A ritual that always has the same fundamental structure can therefore be variously interpreted and modified by Hindus, so that its emphasis tends toward homage, devotion, or negotiation.

Participation in *puja* plainly expresses and constructs relationships between powerful deities and their worshipers, and also among worshipers themselves. Such people are often unequal, as we have just seen. Sometimes inequality is most dramatically displayed by complete exclusion from the assembly of worshipers, as in the case of Harijans who were formerly kept out of public temples. Moreover, the constitution of social groups as communities with shared qualities and interests is itself significantly shaped by their common participation in worship, notably worship offered to deities who protect a particular group, such as a family or village. Various examples of worshiping communities will be further discussed in later chapters.

Finally, let me stress again that fundamental to *puja* is the ideal achievement of identity between deity and worshiper; it is inherent in the ritual's internal sequential logic and it is consolidated by the taking of *prasada* afterwards. Ethnography shows that this identity is not explicitly sought by all ordinary Hindus whenever they perform *puja*, and I do not mean to imply that every act of worship is motivated by this lofty objective; more pragmatic ends, such as seeking divine aid in times of trouble, are often far more in evidence. Yet this movement toward identity is worship's most distinctively Hindu aspect and it must be given due significance in understanding the ritual. Through worship, an inferior, less powerful mortal here on earth potentially transcends the human condition to become one with a deity present in its image form. Like *namaskara*, the gesture of respect made to the deities, but more elaborately, *puja* expresses the principle of hierarchical inequality between deity and worshiper. But the ritual simultaneously—even if only temporarily—can also overcome the relative separation between divinity and humanity.

Chapter 4

SACRIFICE

IN 1972, AT A temple in Cuttack in Orissa, the presiding goddess Chandi, a form of Durga, was decorated as Kali on one night during the great annual festival of Durga Puja (Navaratri), which celebrates her victory over the buffalo-demon. Around midnight, a goat was led to a site near the temple gateway, some distance from Chandi's shrine but within the image's line of sight. The goat was purified and promised to the goddess by sprinkling it with consecrated water. It was then worshiped by the temple's Brahman priests, who offered it flowers, incense, food, and water. A prayer was whispered into the goat's ear to cut it free from its life and to promise liberation for its soul. A sword, infused with divine power, was also worshiped. Another man, a non-Brahman, then raised the sword and severed the goat's head with a single stroke. The head was taken to an altar near Chandi's shrine, and the Brahman priest went inside, closed the shrine doors and completed the act of offering the goat to her. The carcass was returned to the person who gave the animal, so that he could take it home to cook the meat, which would be shared with his family and friends. By dawn, over five hundred goats and some thirty fowls had been immolated for Chandi as Kali. Later in the day, the goddess's image was given a purificatory bath and a meal of cooked goat-meat was served to her, although normally she is given only vegetarian dishes. Some devotees said that the meat actually went to the Chamundis, Chandi's subordinate guardian goddesses (Preston 1980: 63–67).

ANIMAL SACRIFICE IN POPULAR HINDUISM

Animal sacrifice on the scale seen in Chandi's temple on that Durga Puja night occurs only on special festival occasions, and even then it is rare outside eastern India (Bengal, Orissa, and Assam) and Nepal. Moreover, everywhere in the subcontinent, Hindus kill animals in lesser numbers and less frequently than they used to. Nevertheless, animal sacrifice is still practiced widely and is an important ritual in popular Hinduism. It contrasts strikingly with nonviolent *puja* at which the food offered to the deities is normally vegetarian; the relationship between sacrifice and worship is thus a vital one.

The word "sacrifice" conventionally translates several Sanskrit and vernacular terms, which name a variety of different rituals. However, our concern is with latter-day animal sacrifice, for which *bali* is probably the most common single term, although a descriptive vernacular phrase, such as "cutting the animal," is often used.

Everywhere, the animals most frequently immolated are male goats, pigs, and fowls, although the greatest of all sacrificial victims is a male buffalo. The smaller animals are offered to both male and female deities, but the buffalo is reserved for goddesses. It is the ideal animal for Durga/Kali during Navaratri, when its slaughter reenacts her conquest of the buffalo-demon, but it is also killed for a variety of fierce goddesses on other occasions. In contemporary India, however, buffalo sacrifices are now rare. The usual method of killing all animals is decapitation with a sword or knife, ideally in a single stroke, but other means, such as suffocation or impalement, are sometimes used. Vegetables (including fruits) are commonly sacrificed as substitutes. Pumpkins and melons, for instance, are regularly proffered; they are sliced in two as if they were animals and sometimes red powder is rubbed into the pulp to simulate blood. Such surrogate sacrifices, also widely described as *bali*, must be placed within the same category as true animal sacrifices. A vegetable is offered if an animal is unavailable, either because nobody will agree to supply it—doubting the real need for such a costly victim—or because it has been decided to replace blood sacrifice with a bloodless equivalent. The grandeur and complexity of sacrifices do, of course, vary greatly, but only for goddesses in eastern India (as discussed below) are animals regularly killed at major temples served by Brahman priests. Elsewhere, animal sacrifice is today mainly confined to the smaller temples and shrines of little deities, where non-Brahmans officiate.

As the description of Chandi's sacrifice illustrates, the animal has to be purified, promised, and worshiped before the sword, which has also been worshiped, descends on its neck. It is a common adage that an animal should tremble when water is sprinkled over it to show that it is accepted as an offering, but the full preparatory ritual makes it plain that the deity only takes a victim that already participates in its divinity. Thus the ritual of sacrifice merges the victim with the deity, a process completed by the immolation. However, in Hindu sacrifice—as is true of sacrifice in many religions—the victim is both an intermediary between the deity and the human sacrificer (the donor), and a substitute for the latter. The perfect sacrificial victim, as many myths demonstrate, is always the human sacrificer himself. Animal sacrifice approximates that ideal by merging the sacrificer with the deity—as *puja* does in a different way—but sacrifice also cuts the two parties apart when the victim dies, so that only the animal's life passes to the deity. The human sacrificer remains alive, able to reap the benefits of pleasing the deity by making a sacrifice.

It is, then, an animal's life that is taken by a deity in place of the sacrificer's. The primary material symbols of the animal's life are its blood, its head, or both. Sometimes the blood is directly offered to the deity, but even when it is not, it is normally regarded as a principal symbol of the life tendered during the sacrifice. The animal's head is often specifically presented to the deity, either in a special ritual (as for Chandi in Cuttack) or by simply turning it toward the shrine. Afterwards, the head may be taken by the priests (as in Cuttack, where it is cooked for offering later to Chandi) or by the person who gave the animal; sometimes, the head is buried instead. The carcass of a slaughtered animal is occasionally buried, but it is usually cooked and some of the meat is offered to the deity. In this sense, deities who are offered animal sacrifice are "meat-eating," whereas those who are not are "vegetarian," but such a dietary contrast oversimplifies the picture.

The deities offered animal sacrifice are fierce, violent, and "hot." Particularly prominent among them are single, dark forms of the goddess—Durga, Kali, and many village goddesses, such as Shitala Mata and Mariyamman, the goddesses of smallpox. Gods such as Bhairava and Narasimha—fierce, lower forms of Shiva and Vishnu—are also offered animal sacrifices, as are a host of other little deities, especially those deemed to be former malevolent ghostly spirits. The great gods, notably Vishnu and Shiva in most of their forms, as well as Ganesha and Skanda, are hardly ever offered blood sacrifices. Nor are benign light forms of the goddess, who are prototypically identified as wives.

Although the act of sacrifice is "heating," it is often done to propitiate angry deities. Goddesses of disease, for example, are offered blood sacrifices to assuage their rage, to cool and placate them. Fierce deities are sometimes said to want animal sacrifice precisely because they crave blood, the only offering that can really satisfy them. "The Devi likes blood," say some people in Chhattisgarh (Madhya Pradesh) with reference to the dark goddess (Babb 1975: 225). With many troublesome little deities and malevolent spirits, propitiation is frequently the sole motivation; the people give deities and spirits blood so that they go away. But at many sacrifices, even to allegedly bloodthirsty goddesses, it is rarely so straightforward. The goddesses' protection, not their departure, is normally being sought and, as we have just seen, sacrifice (like *puja*) does symbolically identify the sacrificer with the deity. Moreover, sacrifice can express honor and devotion toward the deity whose wishes have been met. And when the sacrificer and others eat the cooked meat after offering it to the deity, or (sometimes) drink the animal's blood, they consume a kind of *prasada* containing divine power and grace, just as they do after *puja*.

TANTRISM AND THE GODDESS

Worship of ferocious goddesses is most fully developed within the stream of Hinduism known as Tantrism, named from its texts, the Tantras. As we saw in chapter 2, because the goddess incarnates power, *shakti*, she can be worshiped by herself. In the most extreme version of this idea, the gods become inferior and redundant, as spectacularly portrayed by Kali dancing on Shiva's corpse. Kali, garlanded in skulls and drinking blood in the cremation ground, is the quintessential goddess of Tantrism, adored by her devotees as the supreme deity. Her cult enjoys its greatest popularity among Bengalis. In West Bengal the annual festival of Kali Puja is widely celebrated; in Calcutta, one such celebration, which attracts big crowds, is held at a large cremation ground. In Calcutta, too, at Kalighat, is Kali's most famous temple, where several black goats are sacrificed to her daily, although many more are killed at major rituals (Kinsley 1975: 124). In Bengal, Durga is widely worshiped too, especially at her annual Durga Puja, and although Durga's character is less extreme than Kali's, the two goddesses share a lot. Durga is also portrayed as a ferocious murderess, slayer of the buffalo-demon, and is offered animal sacrifices; indeed, Kali is often considered to be a specially violent form of Durga. A similar equation applies to Chandi in Cuttack, for she, as Kali, is offered the sacrifices during Durga Puja. Chandi's cult in Orissa has been heavily influenced by Bengali Tantrism, which—at least since the eighteenth century—has had a pervasive impact on popular Hinduism throughout eastern India.

As we saw, at Chandi's temple, Brahman priests preside over the sacrifices and complete the offering of animals to her, but a non-Brahman actually beheads the goats, and for most of the year the goddess is offered only vegetarian food. In a Tantric temple, there are no such compromises. For example, at Tarapith temple in West Bengal, which is dedicated to Tara (who closely resembles Kali), several goat sacrifices occur almost every day. In this temple, where ritual is ideally governed by the Tantras, Brahman priests decapitate the animals and afterwards offer some of the blood to the goddess in a short *puja*. Devotees also dip their fingers in the blood, which they touch to the forehead or lips, so that the blood is absorbed like *prasada* (Morinis 1984: 184–85).

Tantrism's fundamental premise is reversal of conventional religious values, so that what is normally proscribed as impure, inauspicious, and abominable is instead eulogized as pure, auspicious, and desirable, the most perfect expression of devotion and the only true path to spiritual enlightenment. Hence the notorious formula for Tantric rituals, which require the offering and consumption of meat, fish, alcohol, and parched grain, and involve worshiping the goddess in the form of a naked woman with whom devotees have sexual intercourse. These rituals, described in the texts of the extreme "left-hand" Tantrics, plainly demonstrate the central significance of reversal in Tantric ritual. Kali's worship exemplifies the same thing. She is a murderous goddess who has left the gods powerless and dead. Brahmans, who rarely participate in ritual violence in any other setting, actually kill animals for her and offer blood, instead of vegetarian food, in *puja*. None of this puts Tantrism outside Hinduism, because it is demonstrably a logical, albeit extreme, development of many of the religion's central concepts. It has also had a profound impact on more conventional and ostensibly antithetical streams such as devotionalist Vaishnavism, as exemplified by the Tantric-influenced Sahajiyas in Bengal (Dimock 1989). After all, Kali is only the most absolute and uncompromising form of the dark goddess, whose characteristics cannot be defined apart from those of the light goddess. Yet Tantrism is the most fully developed antithesis to the values of "orthodox" Brahmanical Hinduism, to which we must now turn because their significance for grasping the place of sacrifice in popular Hinduism is crucial.

THE RELATIONSHIP BETWEEN WORSHIP AND SACRIFICE

Some of Chandi's devotees in Cuttack said that her subordinate Chamundis, not the goddess herself, take the meat offerings after the sacrifice. The assertion is typical and often pressed more forcefully. The true recipient of sacrifice is not the deity ostensibly offered it, but that deity's inferior, subordinate guardian, or even any evil spirits who happen to be in the vicinity. Many of Chandi's devotees, even those attending the sacrifice, also voiced their dislike of and opposition to the slaughter, although others said that it pleases the goddess and must be done (Preston 1980: 68). These opinions reflect some of the antipathy to Tantrism's reversals that has long existed, even in Bengal itself. However, hostility toward animal sacrifice is found among contemporary Hindus everywhere, although often, even for the same people, it sits alongside a belief that because some deities want it, it must go on.

Some of the opposition to animal sacrifice is relatively recent, as I explain below, but it rests on a much older foundation. Let us look first at the conventional picture presented by scholars of the classical texts, ignoring the qualifications that some of them have raised. The Vedas, the earliest Hindu scriptures, are collections of hymns that particularly describe a ritualistic religion centered on sacrifice (*yajna*), the horse being the greatest of animal victims. In post-Vedic texts, as I explained when discussing renunciation in chapter 1, there is a movement away from the animal sacrifice prescribed by the Vedas. Sacrifice, like all ritual action to sustain the world, becomes devalued in comparison with transcendental knowledge gained through ascetic world renunciation. Furthermore, the connected impact of Buddhism and Jainism contributed much to the accrescent belief that nonviolence is supremely valued, which stimulated growing hostility to the sacrificial slaughter of live animals. From the early centuries of the Christian era, ascetic renunciation and nonviolence became indissolubly linked as normative values in the "orthodox" Brahmanical synthesis, which emerged in conjunction with the decline of Buddhism and Jainism in India. That synthesis continues to shape Hinduism in a number of decisive ways, despite the existence of non- or anti-Brahmanical currents as well.

One component in the Brahmanical synthesis is the ideological assimilation between Brahman and ascetic renouncer, and one of its important corollaries is the notion that the Brahman should completely separate himself from violence. Violence compromises the Brahman's attachment to the renouncer's values, as well as his ritual purity, since killing pollutes the perpetrator. Brahmans involved in violence are therefore degraded and Brahmans, including priests, never normally participate in animal sacrifice. Even those who do, like Chandi's temple priests, delegate the work of killing to a non-Brahman, so that only priests in Tantric temples like Kali's normally engage fully in blood sacrifice. For the same reasons, Brahmanhood tends to be normatively identified with vegetarianism; a high proportion of Brahmans eat no meat or fish, although there are significant exceptions, especially in Bengal, Kashmir, and some other parts of north India. To a considerable but incomplete extent, therefore, vegetarianism is established as the dietary rule of the highest caste, and nonviolence and vegetarianism are taken as indices of purity and superior status. Conversely, violence (including participation in sacrifice) and meat eating tend to be associated with impurity and low status.

A second important component in the Brahmanical synthesis is the dogmatic belief that animal sacrifice—despite copious instructions for its proper performance in the Vedas and some later texts (Kane 1968–77, 2: chap. 32)—is an inferior ritual that does not belong to Brahmanical Hinduism. Compared with *puja* in which the food offering must, consistently with this belief, be vegetarian, animal sacrifice is an improper way to worship the deities, for it inevitably produces pollution and is therefore appropriate only for inferior deities worshiped by inferior people. Animal sacrifice, in short, is ideologically devalued in relation to vegetarian worship.

At the same time it is clear that *puja* can be interpreted as a transforma-tional variant of sacrifice, specifically Vedic sacrifice. This could be shown in many ways, but one simple illustration is given by the food offering (*naivedya*) in *puja*, which closely resembles a sacrificial oblation, because it is transferred to the deity by sprinkling water around the plate in an act almost identical to the victim's aspersion before immolation. Afterwards the food, like the blood or meat of a dead animal, is taken as *prasada* (or its equivalent) by worshipers who consume it to absorb the deities' power and grace. Thus we can argue, as Madeleine Biardeau most forcefully does (1976: 139–54 and *passim*), that *puja* is a distinctively Hindu spe-cies of nonviolent sacrifice. Biardeau further argues, convincingly, that *puja* as nonviolent sacrifice has to be understood as a ritual that stands in a complementary relationship with animal sacrifice; taken together, the pair of rituals testifies to the perennial centrality of sacrifice as Hindu-ism's primary ritual. Yet, as she says (ibid.: 140), the ritual of worship prescribed by the texts governing ritual in the temples of Vishnu and Shiva is never described by Hindus as "sacrifice," for linguistically and conceptually *puja* is sharply demarcated from blood sacrifice (*bali*) for inferior deities. Thus the complementary, structural relationship between the two rituals is hierarchical; as Biardeau pithily puts it elsewhere, "The mere mention of blood implies hierarchy" (1989b: 136). Moreover, com-plementarity is obscured by the stress on difference, because in the Brah-manical synthesis, *puja* must be completely distinguished from animal sacrifice.

Sacrifice and Relational Divinity in South India

My task in this and the next section is to show how the Brahmanical synthesis—despite its textual roots and the existence of alternative val-ues—is relevant to animal sacrifice in popular Hinduism and specifically to the ranking of deities in relation to sacrifice. I shall do so by looking at ethnographic data from south India, because it is there, particularly in Tamilnadu and adjacent regions, that the pantheon of deities is most plainly shaped by their connection with sacrifice. Elements of the south Indian picture exist elsewhere as well, but the argument in these two sec-tions is basically confined to the south.

Let us begin with a particular case. In the Madurai region, among the Pramalai Kallars, temples dedicated to the Tamil village god Aiyanar gen-erally include a shrine to the little deity Karuppan as well, just as Shasta temples include Madan farther south. Aiyanar is the master of his servant Karuppan, who is a subordinate guardian god watching over the temple from his place at the edge of the site. A favored gift for Aiyanar is a terra-cotta horse; the horse is associated with kings in India and the gift reflects Aiyanar's royal characteristics. But when Aiyanar is given a horse, another must be given to Karuppan, even though it does not befit him, because the two gods together preside over the temple. Partly because he is a former evil spirit (*pey*), Karuppan is also thought to desire animal sacrifices. When they are offered, the shrine of Aiyanar, who receives only vegetarian offerings, is screened so that he cannot see the killing. Some people say that in fact the sacrifice, like the horses, is offered to both deities, but the ritual suggests that it is not (Dumont 1970b: 27–31).

Louis Dumont's much-quoted analysis of Aiyanar's relationship with Karuppan has several complex strands, not all of which I find convincing. His basic proposition, though, is that Aiyanar is a pure, vegetarian god and Karuppan is an impure, meat-eating god. In part, this is directly symbolized by their spatial configuration, because Aiyanar stands at the temple's center, the pure interior, whereas Karuppan is at the impure exterior, where sacrifice must be carried out so that it cannot pollute the center. Aiyanar and Karuppan exemplify the two fundamental categories of deity—pure vegetarian versus impure meat-eater—and the relationship between them is homologous with that between high-ranking vegetarian castes and low-ranking nonvegetarian castes. Aiyanar is to Karuppan as the high castes are to the low castes. Moreover, Dumont's most crucial, general thesis is that Hindu divinity is *relational*; it must be comprehended as a relationship between superior and inferior parts structured by the same principle that governs the caste hierarchy, namely, a complementary opposition between purity and impurity, expressed here by a dietary contrast. For Dumont, therefore, the connection between the pantheon of deities and the caste structure of society is a function of the common principle upon which they rest.

In this argument, one specific problem requires notice. Although Dumont describes Aiyanar as vegetarian and Karuppan as meat-eating, this is inexact. Karuppan is fundamentally distinguished from Aiyanar by his desire for animal sacrifice. Both deities, like *all* deities, are the objects of *puja* at which vegetarian food offerings are made, but Karuppan is additionally offered animal sacrifices and it is those that Aiyanar must not see. No deity is offered only animal sacrifice, for if it were it would not be a deity at all, but a demonic spirit craving blood alone. Deities are therefore not differentiated according to whether they are offered *puja*, whose food offering is normally vegetarian, but according to whether or not they are offered sacrifice. We must therefore focus first on the relationship between *puja* and animal sacrifice, rather than the dietary distinction. Furthermore, as my discussion of the Brahmanical synthesis showed, vegetarianism is itself only one aspect of the principle of nonviolence belonging to the values of the ascetic renouncer. Aiyanar's purity relative to Karuppan's therefore depends not only on his vegetarianism as such, but also on his firm rejection of animal sacrifice.

I should also note that in some of his writings, including parts of his analysis of Aiyanar, Dumont practically claims that popular, theistic Hinduism is an epiphenomenon of hierarchical caste ideology. Most forcefully, in an article jointly signed by David F. Pocock, he writes that "belief in gods" is "subject to an overriding belief in the necessary co-existence of opposites, in the complementary relationship of pure and impure. The religion of gods is secondary; the religion of caste is fundamental" (1959: 34). This kind of sociological reductionism, which implies that worship of the deities is but sublimated worship of hierarchical society, is surprising in a writer as subtle as Dumont and must surely be rejected.

On the other hand, Dumont's thesis about relational divinity contains a penetrating insight, which we can extend to Tamil village goddesses, such as Mariyamman, who are also offered animal sacrifices and are often designated as "meat-eating." At the edge of a goddess's temple, there is commonly a shrine to Karuppan (or a similar little deity), and he is also a subordinate guardian to whom sacrifices are made. However, especially at her annual festival, sacrifices are generally offered to the goddess herself, but significantly not before her immovable stone image inside the central shrine of her temple. Instead, the sacrifice is carried out before another form of the goddess, such as a pot of water into which her powers have been invoked at a site away from the temple. Preparing and carrying the pot are often the responsibilities of men who have been possessed by the goddess—or "seized" in the local idiom—so that they too embody her. In many cases, the actual sacrifice is conducted by possessed people, and it is always done some distance away from the central shrine, often right outside the temple buildings. The sacrifice is hardly ever carried out by the priest who performs worship at the central shrine, and he sometimes leaves the temple entirely for the duration of the sacrifice. The priest, whether or not he is a Brahman, usually belongs to a caste higher than that of the possessed men, so that the sacrificer is inferior to the priest responsible for worship inside the temple. This division of labor is itself an expression of the hierarchical relationship between *puja* and animal sacrifice.

The climax of a Tamil festival for a goddess like Mariyamman is the sacrifice, but it requires her to be split into high and low forms. The high form, manifested in the immovable image at the pure center of the temple and served by a higher-ranking priest, is offered vegetarian food in the context of *puja*, whereas the low form, manifested in, say, a pot of water and possessed men of lower rank, receives the sacrificial offering at an exterior site. Sometimes, there is also a distinct intermediate form that is given meat offerings after the sacrifice, but often the meat is presented to the form receiving the sacrifice. In either case, the polar opposition between high and low forms remains the critical feature. Moreover, this opposition is structurally isomorphic with the one between a single high deity like Aiyanar and another low deity like Karuppan, who is the former's subordinate guardian, or indeed between a goddess like Mariyamman at the village center and her inferior partner Ellaiyamman ("goddess of the boundary") at the edge. Hence Dumont's paradigm of relational divinity has to be extended to cover not only paired distinct deities, but also differentiated, ranked forms of the one deity.

Empirically, the situation can be more complicated, as three brief examples will suggest. In a Tamil temple of Angalamman, Shiva and Vishnu have been cursed to become her inferior guardians, Shiva being Karuppan, so that the usual hierarchical pattern is inverted (Reiniche 1988: 372–73). In Draupadi's temples in northern Tamilnadu, there are two guardian deities, Pottu Raja and Muttal Ravuttan, a converted Muslim; the first is normally superior to the second, although not invariably, but in any case the relationship between the pair is itself a developed and significant feature (Hiltebeitel 1989: 340–48). There can, too, be further differentiation within the category of sacrificial deities and in an Andhra Pradesh village, goddesses are divided into two kinds according to the types of animals offered and the manner of their immolation (Herrenschmidt 1989: 93–98).

Yet in spite of these added layers of complexity, they all rise upon a basic binary opposition and Dumont's insight remains invaluable; it comes from his stress on the complementary *relationship* between high and low deities (or deities' forms), which are pure or impure relative to each other, as shown in ritual by their respective rejection or acceptance of animal sacrifice. Dumont's structuralist argument does not imply that the relationship between deities is substantively identical to that between castes; an "impure" deity, for instance, is enshrined in a temple whose purity must be preserved and such a deity is rarely, if ever, said to pollute a "pure" deity like a low-caste person can pollute someone of higher caste. Rather, the argument is that the structural opposition between pure and impure defines a principle of hierarchical ranking that is central to caste and also to the pantheon of Tamil village deities. Thus the complementary, hierarchical relationship between deities—so often given by the link between a higher, more powerful deity and its subordinate guardian—is also expressed in terms of relative purity.

CASTE AND HIERARCHY AMONG THE DEITIES

A key part of Dumont's general theory of caste is that the system rests on complementary relationships between the pure, high castes and the impure, low castes—paradigmatically between Brahmans and untouchable Harijans. This claim, like the rest of Dumont's theory, has been subjected to exhaustive critical evaluation since the late 1950s, and I shall not review the discussion here. What is, I believe, clear is that hierarchical complementarity, based on the pure-impure opposition, is one crucial structuring principle of the caste system, notwithstanding the existence of others, and that this is very plain in south India, especially Tamilnadu.

There is considerable regional variation in the caste system across India, and in Tamilnadu the division between Brahmans and others— middle-ranking non-Brahmans together with Harijans—is exceptionally sharp. André Béteille (1965a: 52–53) admits that it may be "an exaggeration to say that Brahmins, on the one hand, and Non-Brahmins and Adi-Dravidas [Harijans], on the other, represent two cultures," but the differences in their styles of life are prominent everywhere in Tamilnadu, if not always so extremely as in Thanjavur District, where Béteille carried out research. In Thanjavur, along the banks of the Kaveri, Brahmans are unusually numerous and powerful. In addition, modern political rivalry between Brahmans and non-Brahmans has tended to deepen differences between them all over the state. Nonetheless, one vital marker of Brahman culture in south India is and long has been strict vegetarianism. Some higher-ranking non-Brahman castes, or sections of them, are also vegetarian, such as many subcastes of Vellalars, one of the largest landholding castes in Tamilnadu. All the same—and despite being described as a Shaiva tradition as well—vegetarianism is persistently identified as a Brahmanical caste custom, and non-Brahmans who are vegetarian claim higher status partly because they are following the Brahmans' superior dietary code. Thus the pronounced opposition between the two great categories—Brahmans versus non-Brahmans and Harijans—also tends to be assimilated to that between vegetarians and nonvegetarians.

As we move away from Tamilnadu and the adjacent regions of southern and coastal Andhra Pradesh and southern Karnataka, the caste system changes its shape. For example, far to the north in the Hindi-speaking area, most Brahmans are also vegetarians and vegetarianism is generally evaluated highly. Yet in quite a lot of northern Brahman groups—for example, many subcastes of the large Kanya-Kubja community—some kinds of meat or fish are widely eaten, and individual Brahmans are more likely to "lapse" into meat eating, so that strict vegetarianism is less an index of Brahmanhood than it is in the south. Also, many populous, dominant landholding castes in the north, notably the Rajputs, claim to be Kshatriyas, members of the royal, warrior *varna* ranking second to the Brahmans. Kshatriyas traditionally eat meat, which is thought to build up their martial strength, and meat eating is esteemed by them, even though they may also recognize that vegetarianism has higher prestige. In south India, all non-Brahmans, including landholding castes like the Vellalars, are generally assigned to the fourth and lowest *varna*, the Shudras, so that meat eating is not held up as a sign of high-ranking Kshatriya status. In north India, too, there are large and powerful merchant castes classified as Vaishyas, members of the third *varna*, and they are traditionally vegetarian, often more strictly so than many Brahmans. Vegetarianism is hence associated not only with Brahmans, but also with Vaishyas, who rank below Kshatriya castes like the Rajputs. But in the south, predominantly vegetarian merchant castes like the Chettiyars in Tamilnadu tend to be seen as Shudras, whose dietary code is Brahmanical in style, rather than Vaishya in contrast to Kshatriya. Overall, therefore, the sharp dichotomous distinction found in Tamilnadu between vegetarian Brahmans and other meat-eating Shudras (and Harijans) is considerably weaker in north India.

In the Hindi-speaking north, the ethnography also shows that, among the little village deities, the distinction between "pure" deities who are not offered animal sacrifice and "impure" ones who are is less systematically elaborated. Lawrence A. Babb's evidence from Chhattisgarh is illustrative. There, as everywhere, a distinction is drawn between light, wifely goddesses who are not offered animal sacrifice, and dark, single goddesses who demand it; a parallel distinction is also made between Shiva and his lower form as Bhairava, to whom sacrifices are offered. In the region, the main tutelary village god is Thakur Dev, who is also the subordinate guardian deity of the tutelary village goddess; he is represented by stones in front of her shrine. The unmarried village goddess, who goes by a variety of names but is invariably identified in part with Shitala, goddess of smallpox, is believed to demand bloody sacrifice, as is Thakur Dev (1975: 223–30, 241–43).

Babb's evidence, however, like other data from north India, does not reveal a pattern of the Tamilnadu kind. In northern ethnography, with the partial exception of the Himalayan foothills (cf. Galey 1986), temples presided over by clearly defined, ranked pairs of deities like "pure" Aiyanar and "impure" Karuppan are not reported. Thakur Dev, for example, is not systematically paired with a local equivalent of Aiyanar. Moreover, although Babb (ibid.: 241) refers to the insistence at some temples that animals offered to a goddess must be killed outside by low-caste menials, she does not appear to divide into higher and lower forms, or to have an inferior partner who actually accepts blood sacrifices. Elements of the southern pattern, especially the general notion that sacrifice is polluting and demanded by lower deities, are of course present, but they do not coalesce into a clear-cut, structural opposition between higher and lower deities or forms.

One reason why relationships between little village deities vary regionally lies in the shape of the caste system. In Tamilnadu, the systematic distinction between two categories of deities or deities' forms, according to whether or not they are offered animal sacrifice, reflects the sharp divide between superior, vegetarian Brahmans and inferior, nonvegetarian non-Brahmans. In short, relational divinity founded upon the complementary link between higher and lower deities is a symbol of Tamil caste society. In the north, on the other hand, the lack of systematic distinctions between deities is correlated with the weak contrast between less strictly vegetarian Brahmans and other, lower castes. Everywhere, except in the Tantric context, deities given blood sacrifice are normally seen as inferior to those offered solely vegetarian food in *puja*, but only in the south, apparently, does this distinction generate a clear hierarchical dichotomy in the pantheon, homologous with that between vegetarian and nonvegetarian castes.

To leave the matter there, though, is to imply that south Indian deities hypostatize Tamil caste society in a crudely reflective manner. Let me reiterate that relationships among different categories of deities, some of which I explored in chapter 2, are highly complex. Throughout India, however, one crucial relationship is that between a superior deity and an inferior subordinate, who typically protects the former's temple at its periphery. In Tamilnadu, though, that relationship is also expressed—more systematically than elsewhere—in terms of relative purity as defined by rejection or acceptance of animal sacrifice, a ritual consistently devalued in comparison with purely vegetarian worship by Brahmanical, renunciatory values. Starting from Dumont's analysis of Aiyanar, I have argued that the castelike relationships between deities and their forms in Tamilnadu is consistent with the structure of the Tamil caste system. To that extent, when Tamils sacrifice animals to Karuppan after drawing a screen before Aiyanar, they engage in symbolic action that reflects one central, structuring principle of their caste society.

In the Pramalai Kallars' Aiyanar temples only Kallars are normally present. The reader may therefore object that any such symbolic action would be meaningless for people who all belong to the same meat-eating low caste. So let me present a more patent illustrative case. A few miles north of Madurai, at Alagarkoil, there is a major temple dedicated to a form of Vishnu called Kallalagar, "Beautiful Lord of the Kallar." As his name indicates, Kallalagar is specially linked to the Kallars, who take a key role at one of his main festivals, although the Pramalai subcaste is actually not much involved. In the outer gateway of Alagarkoil temple there is a massive door, which is rarely opened. Behind that door Karuppan is believed to be present, although there is no image of him. Karuppan is Kallalagar's subordinate guardian deity and the temple's divine watchman. Kallalagar's priests are Vaishnava Brahmans. Every night, after the final act of daily worship, the officiating priest brings a food offering to Karuppan, which he shows to the door. Just before, this food has been offered to Kallalagar, so that Karuppan is given his superior's left-over meal—a patent sign of his inferiority. Otherwise, except very occasionally, the Brahman priests never serve Karuppan, whose own priests are non-Brahmans, carrying out his worship in front of the door outside the temple. But these priests make only vegetarian offerings to Karuppan and although animals for sacrifice are led to the door, where they are sprinkled with water to offer them to the god, the killing is done some distance away by other people, often Kallar devotees themselves.

Events in Alagarkoil plainly represent Karuppan, the recipient of sacrificial offerings, as inferior to Kallalagar, a form of strictly vegetarian Vishnu. But equally important is that everything also represents the Brahman priests—and by extension all Brahmans—as superior to the non-Brahmans who act as Karuppan's priests and a fortiori to the Kallars and other low-caste people, who eat the meat from animals they sacrifice. Actually, despite Vishnu's vegetarianism, many low-caste devotees say that they sacrifice animals to Kallalagar himself, rather than to Karuppan, and nothing happening at Alagarkoil means that Kallars and those like them go home convinced that Brahmans are superior; in present-day Tamilnadu that is inconceivable. Nonetheless, although Kallalagar is the Kallars' Vishnu, the organization of the work of worshiping him and Karuppan in the door plainly symbolizes the vegetarian Brahmans' socioreligious superiority over the meat-eating Kallars and other non-Brahmans. The ritual at Alagarkoil temple exemplifies precisely how the hierarchical social relationships of caste, in their Tamil guise, can be reconstructed through the rituals of worship and sacrifice.

Substantial Divinity among the Great Deities

Karuppan's prominence as a guardian deity at Alagarkoil is, however, rather unusual and at other major Vishnu temples in the region, the god's left-over food is offered at the end of the day to another Vaishnava deity inside the temple, who is said to be its principal guardian. In Shiva's temples, it is offered to Bhairava the watchman (and another Shaiva deity called Chandeshwara), who also stand inside. This is the practice at the Minakshi temple in Madurai, which I shall now discuss.

Just outside the Minakshi temple, there is a shrine for Karuppan; alongside several other little deities enshrined nearby, Karuppan is regarded by some people as a guardian deity of the great temple. But only very occasionally and hastily are any of these putative, exterior guardians worshiped by the Brahman priests who serve Minakshi and Sundareshwara.

The one major exception is the single village goddess Chellattamman, whose temple lies a few streets north of the Minakshi temple. Throughout southern Tamilnadu, Chellattamman (or Chelliyamman) is typically located on the northern edge of a settlement, and in Madurai she guards the northerly approaches to the Minakshi temple and the city as a whole. Chellattamman has a special link with Sundareshwara, because on one evening during her annual festival, her movable image is brought before the god's central shrine for a ritual conducted by the Minakshi temple priests. At this ritual, which is formally described as her "coronation," Sundareshwara is said to give the goddess the power she needs to guard his temple and the city during the year to come—a clear example of the delegation of power from superior to inferior deity. After the ritual, Chellattamman is taken back to her temple by her own non-Brahman priests. Later that night, the climax of the festival, the priests sacrifice pigs to the goddess.

In the Minakshi temple's ritual cycle, Chellattamman's visit is a minor event within the elaborate round of festivals that succeed each other throughout the year. In all Minakshi temple rituals, the food offered to the deities is vegetarian and animal sacrifice is never performed, although from time to time there are vegetable sacrifices, which are understood as surrogate blood sacrifices. The details are complicated, but the key points are that real animal sacrifice never occurs in the Minakshi temple and, furthermore, that its ritual cycle represents Minakshi, Sundareshwara, and other deities in the temple as only marginally connected to those who are offered animal sacrifice. Hence any complementary relationship between "pure" Minakshi-Sundareshwara and "impure" guardian deities, such as Karuppan or even Chellattamman, is weakened to the limit.

As a result, we find substantial divinity, not relational divinity, in the Minakshi temple. By the term "substantial," Dumont refers to the condition in which the reality imputed to a construct, such as a deity, is primarily given by its own inherent qualities, its "substance," rather than by its complementary relationship with another equivalent construct. Thus the divinity of Minakshi and Sundareshwara is not ritually represented as contingent upon their relationship with inferior deities who receive blood sacrifice, as is so for Aiyanar in relation to Karuppan. Instead, their divinity is independently given, so that their godhead has an absolute quality wherein highness appears divorced from lowness.

It is consistent with this ritual representation that the Brahman priests of the Minakshi temple are dismissive about the link between Sundareshwara and Chellattamman. This may be partly because the link does tend to compromise the god's substantial divinity, but anyway the priests treat the goddess's visit to the temple as a trivial episode, necessary only because she must have her powers renewed. They scornfully dismiss the notion of a wedding, popular among Chellattamman's own devotees. The latter say that her visit to the Minakshi temple is the high point of Chellattamman's year because she marries Sundareshwara, although she then returns to her own temple in a rage, probably because the god will not allow a meat-eating deity to stay with him. Back home, Chellattamman has to be propitiated by a nocturnal animal sacrifice, a ritual surrounded by terrible danger that ordinary people see at their peril because the goddess is so angry. One and the same ritual in the Minakshi temple therefore has a different significance for the two deities and their attendants. For Sundareshwara the great god, his meeting with Chellattamman is a minor episode in a vast annual cycle of ritual, which barely compromises his substantial divinity and separation from inferior deities; his priests correspondingly treat the occasion as trivial too. For Chellattamman the village goddess, whose divinity is relational and quintessentially defined by her link with Sundareshwara, their meeting—even though its aftermath enrages her—is her greatest moment, and many of her devotees claim that it is her wedding.

Among south Indian deities, there is therefore an important distinction to be drawn. Unlike little village deities, great deities such as Minakshi and Sundareshwara, who are worshiped in major temples by Brahman priests in charge of a completely vegetarian cult, do not symbolize the complementary hierarchical relationships of caste. Instead, their substantial divinity is a mirror of an imaginary world in which superiors can remain aloof and apart from inferiors. But that is exactly how, according to the Brahmanical synthesis, a Brahman should ideally be: an ascetic renouncer who is dependent on nobody. The great deities symbolically negate complementarity, and instead stand for the absolutely independent superiority that is also assumed by the perfect renunciatory Brahman.

The ritual representation of the great deities' substantial divinity also finds its parallel in the discourse of Brahman priests, who indirectly emphasize their own socioreligious superiority by insisting that the deities whom they serve are only barely connected with the village deities served by non-Brahmans. This is another striking example of ideological evaluation, whereby the great deities—Srinivas's Sanskritic deities—are portrayed as truly separate from their non-Sanskritic, village counterparts. The great deities' independence is, of course, partly institutionalized in the ritual domain because the two categories of deities have, in particular, separate priesthoods and different modes of worship. Among the village gods and goddesses themselves, however, there are castelike relationships between superior and inferior deities or their forms, and the non-Brahmans who mainly worship them emphasize their relationship with the great deities, in spite of partial institutional separation between the two categories.

These apparently paradoxical findings need to be stressed. We have here a religious image of the world that gives rise to an extraordinarily powerful double process of symbolic construction and legitimation. The great deities display an autonomous superiority that does not depend on the existence or meaningfulness of inferiors, and they mimetically command an imaginary society in which Brahmans in particular claim superiority for the deities they worship—and by extension for themselves—by asserting their absolute, substantial reality. The little village deities, who are mainly served by non-Brahman priests, are linked to each other—and, it is claimed, to the great deities as well—by complementary hierarchical relationships like those on which the caste system is founded. Thus worship of the village deities, not the great deities, predominantly legitimates in religious terms the caste hierarchy whose summit is occupied by Brahmans. In the end, the ritual representations of both categories of deity converge to legitimate Brahman superiority within caste society, in a profoundly revealing illustration of how deeply rooted hierarchical values are in popular Hinduism.

REFORMIST OPPOSITION TO SACRIFICE

Although the contrast between relational and substantial divinity in its Tamil form is less evident elsewhere in India, it also matters in the context of modern Hindu reformism, where substantial divinity tends to displace relational divinity. Let me begin to explore this topic by returning to sacrifice itself.

Nowadays, throughout India, blood sacrifice attracts criticism and condemnation. Animals are certainly killed on a lesser scale than they used to be and the greatest victim, the buffalo, is rarely offered now. Thus for instance, by the 1940s, M. N. Srinivas was finding growing opposition to animal sacrifice in Coorg, now in Karnataka. Some Coorgs opposed buffalo sacrifice on the grounds that buffaloes were akin to cows, which should never be slaughtered, and "the local leaders of the Indian National Congress have been everywhere more or less successfully opposing the propitiation of village-deities with blood-offerings" (1965: 182). And at the festival of a village goddess observed by Srinivas, the number of animals offered in 1941 was many fewer than in the remembered past (ibid.: 194).

Contemporary opposition to animal sacrifice derives, in large measure, from modern Hindu reformism. Reformism has never been a unitary phenomenon, but it was and is a powerful current within Hinduism, and its roots mainly lie in India's encounter with the west during the colonial era. The crucial features of modern religious reformism, which distinguish it from its precursors, are its patent adoption of ideas originating in the west and its fusion with social reform movements and political nationalism.

Modern reformism began in Bengal around 1800 and its first great figure was Ram Mohun Roy (1772–1833), sometimes called the "Father of modern India." Ram Mohun, deeply influenced by Christianity and other western currents of thought, attacked what he saw as idolatry and superstition. He formulated a new vision of "rational," monotheistic Hinduism, which he claimed to have rediscovered in the Vedas and Upanishads. In finding the "true" religion in Hinduism's most ancient and authoritative scriptures, Ram Mohun followed the path of almost all Hindu reformers, before and since, but his systematic criticism of superstition was unusually vigorous and set a definitive precedent for modern reformism. Also new was Ram Mohun's intensive involvement in social reform, especially the campaign against suttee. Against the opposition of conservative Hindus, he denounced widow burning as a horrific, superstitious custom with no legitimation in authentic scripture. The campaign was one powerful factor behind the government's decision to prohibit suttee in Bengal in 1829; the law was extended to the rest of British India in the following year.

There were many other strands in Ram Mohun Roy's thought and action, and in subsequent decades, both in Bengal and later in other regions of India, numerous disparate elements also became part of the reformist movement. The main preoccupations of different reformist groups, and the forces driving them, varied considerably and changed over time. The Arya Samaj, for instance, gained a huge following across northern India after 1875 and was far more populist than Ram Mohun's Brahmo Samaj, even when the latter expanded its influence in the second half of the nineteenth century. The Arya Samaj, like other powerful movements of the period, was also more revivalist and less radical than the "progressives" descending from Ram Mohun Roy, and it was instrumental (with other groups) in the growth of "conservative" Hindu neotraditionalism, often strongly colored by ethnic communalism.

By the end of the nineteenth century, however, religious and social reformism—in both its progressive and conservative guises—was increasingly tied to Indian nationalism. The Indian National Congress, which led the campaign for independence and afterwards became the ruling Congress party, was founded in 1885. The Congress leadership tried to avoid open involvement in religious controversies, especially because they tended to divide Hindus and Muslims, but the steady growth of nationalism both inside and outside Congress went hand in hand with the "rediscovery" of Hindu (and Muslim) cultural and religious values, acclaimed as at least equal to those coming from the west.

For the more progressive Hindu reformists, rediscovery also meant regeneration of their civilization, corroded from within by a host of indefensible, barbaric medieval customs such as untouchability, suttee, child marriage, and the ban on widow remarriage (which prevented child brides from marrying again after the death of older husbands). For more conservative neotraditionalists, at least some of these customs—like child marriage and the ban on widow remarriage—were part and parcel of authentic Hindu culture and they resisted reformist attacks on them. But in one crucial respect, both camps shared a common stance—hostility to a large part of the popular Hinduism of the masses. For all the nationalists rediscovering Hinduism, many "superstitious" beliefs and practices were objectionable because they did not belong to the authentic religion. Blood sacrifice was a clear case in point; to both progressives and conservatives (who were active in campaigns to ban cow slaughter), sacrifice was a barbarity inconsistent with Hinduism's central tenet of nonviolence. In other words, as many writers have observed, the modern reformist vision of Hinduism—even in its putatively antireformist, neotraditionalist form—has a strongly elitist, Brahmanical dimension. Given all this, it is not so surprising that Congress members in Coorg in the 1940s were taking time and trouble to campaign against animal sacrifice, at first glance a rather odd preoccupation for political nationalists.

In many key respects, modern reformism plainly reasserts the values of the Brahmanical synthesis discussed above. That is why I said earlier that contemporary opposition to animal sacrifice rests on an old foundation, although it also stems from the very widespread influence of reformism, whose antipathy to ritual killing has spread well beyond the self-consciously nationalist political classes. Moreover, if reformism is traditionally Brahmanical in tone, it also introduces something both radical and new. Popular "superstitious" practices, like animal sacrifice, are no longer just devalued as inferior; they are now condemned as wrong and not even part of authentic Hinduism. Hence the complementary relationship between high and low gives way to a bifurcation into true and false. This is a very significant alteration and I shall start to discuss it with an example.

Consider an apparent paradox. Except for those participating in Tantric rituals, Brahmans generally avoid any involvement in animal sacrifice. But suppose that a Brahman is ill with a disease that he, like others, believes has been sent by an angry deity who can be pacified only by a sacrifice. In such circumstances, he may offer a vegetable surrogate or donate an animal to the deity, but then let it go without killing it. Such procedures are probably more common now than in the past. Yet it is certainly not unknown, anywhere in India, for the Brahman to accept that a real animal sacrifice is imperative and to ask a low-caste person to perform it on his behalf. As Pocock (1973: 66) observes in discussing the situation in Gujarat, the Brahman will probably not even witness the sacrifice and he will definitely not eat the cooked meat afterwards. This resolution of the Brahman's difficulty, rather than revealing hypocrisy, reflects the critical importance of the values of nonviolence for his status. The Brahman, perhaps dangerously ill, recognizes that sacrifice is demanded by some deities under certain circumstances. He thereby accepts that this violent ritual, despite its inferiority to vegetarian worship, is indispensable, as is the low-caste man who actually kills the animal.

The same kind of thinking is revealed by an exchange that Pocock had with a rather conservative Gujarati Brahman in the 1960s. Pocock pressed the Brahman on the subject of animal sacrifice, asking whether it was not violent and therefore bad. "Of course it's *hinsa* [violence]," replied the Brahman, who specialized in conducting house and village foundation sacrifices, although he was never actually present when a low-caste officiant killed the animal. "So what? You can't have a foundation ceremony without a blood sacrifice, it's essential and that's that" (ibid.: 72–73). In both these cases—propitiation of angry deities responsible for disease and foundation rituals—it is recognized that sacrifice is necessary. But that does not make it any less polluting, so that it is incumbent on Brahmans not to degrade themselves by actual participation in the ritual. The behavior of these Brahmans is neither hypocritical nor in fact paradoxical; it is actually a self-consistent expression of the complementary, hierarchical logic of caste, which depends on a division of labor between pure Brahmans and impure lower castes. Under the influence of reformist attitudes, however, things change. Animal sacrifice is no longer merely an inferior ritual, for it is now morally wrong and the Brahmans we have just discussed are condemned as hypocrites.

Yet that is not the end of the story. As we have seen, there are many deities who are thought to want blood sacrifice, but the logic of reformism insists that these deities must also accept only vegetarian offerings. The deities, too, have to be reformed. Among many Hindus, this causes the profound misgivings that underlie the typical assertion by Chandi's devotees in Cuttack that the goddess must still be offered animal sacrifice, despite their own dislike of the ritual. There is a widespread belief among ordinary people that deities denied the sacrifices they want will wreak terrible revenge. Nonetheless, if such worries are put to one side, deities can be reformed or alternatively abandoned because they still accept animal sacrifice. As Pocock shows, abandonment has been common in modern Gujarat, where reformist teaching has combined with the impact of powerful Vaishnava devotionalist movements, which are also vigorously opposed to animal sacrifice. Large numbers of Gujaratis have joined the Vaishnava movements and, as a result, there has been a marked decline in the popularity of village goddesses, who are ritually linked with Shiva, and in the extent of sacrificial offerings made to them. The "ritual symbiosis" (ibid.: 94), which tied the sacrificial worship of the goddesses and Shiva to the purely vegetarian worship of Vishnu and his forms, has come close to collapse.

The pace of change in Gujarat has been unusually rapid. Elsewhere deities have been reformed or abandoned on a lesser scale. Especially where Tantrism is influential, pressure to reform fierce deities like Kali is relatively slight, although even in eastern India, particularly when Vaishnava devotionalism is also a powerful force, hostility to sacrifice is apparent. Still, the Gujarati material certainly does exemplify a development that is widespread throughout modern India, even if it is proceeding more slowly elsewhere. The decline of animal sacrifice, and the attempted reform or abandonment of deities thought to want it, undermine complementary hierarchical relationships between high and low deities, insofar as they are shaped by the deities' putative rejection or acceptance of sacrifice. Reformist pressure tends to make all gods and goddesses the same; they must all be vegetarians who never get blood sacrifices. They must, in other words, all be converted into superior "Sanskritic" deities, so that divinity—by a new path—is made uniform and substantial, rather than variable and relational.

There is a saying in the *Ramayana* that "whatever food a man eats the same is the food to be offered to his deities" (Kane 1968–77, 2: 733). The reformist corollary must be that if all deities are vegetarian, so too are all Hindus. Something akin to this idea lies behind the contemporary belief, so often voiced, that all good Hindus are vegetarians, a message assiduously promoted by Mahatma Gandhi, who raised his Vaishya caste's dietary code to a universal moral imperative. Caste inequality is then eradicated by making all Hindus pure and superior according to a mainly Brahmanical code that is, in this respect, also shared by Vaishyas. Of course, elevation by this means also requires all Hindus to give up animal sacrifice and the consumption of meat that follows. The logic is pervasive and socioreligious reform in Hindu India is almost always a double-edged sword, which tends to reinforce superior values precisely as it seeks to undermine superiority itself.

THE LIMITS ON RELIGIOUS REFORMISM

Commenting on the admission of Harijans into the public temples of Vishnu and Shiva, particularly in Tamilnadu, Dumont acutely observes that their entry meant that "the purity of the high castes and their very idea of worship and god is jeopardized: so the only solution is the forcible reform of the Untouchables, so that they would cease to be abettors of impurity" (1970a: 231). Because animal sacrifice is, in Tamilnadu, associated with the low castes and hence—though incorrectly in fact—most firmly associated with the lowest of all, reforming the Harijans requires the abolition of sacrifice. This, argues Dumont, is one crucial reason why, in 1950, shortly after independence, a law was passed to ban animal sacrifice in or near temples within Madras state, which then covered much of present-day Andhra Pradesh, Karnataka, and Kerala, as well as

Tamilnadu. At that time, Madras had a Congress party government, in which educated, urban Brahmans with typically reformist persuasions enjoyed very considerable influence. In fact, the law has always been a virtual dead letter and similar laws have not been passed in other Indian states. Nor have laws specifically prohibiting buffalo sacrifice been placed on any Indian statute-book, although it is commonly thought that buffaloes are protected by the ambiguous wording of several state laws prohibiting cow slaughter. Yet the very currency of the belief that buffalo sacrifice is banned is significant testimony to the widespread assumption that the modern Indian state, the powerful child of reformist nationalism, is hostile to animal sacrifice. The ritual is seen to have lost its legitimacy at the highest political level, despite the fact that it is still practised widely, albeit on a reduced scale, and is still thought to be called for by many gods and goddesses.

I will close this chapter with an episode in the recent history of Chellattamman's temple in Madurai. I heard about it from one of the non-Brahman priests at the temple, and although his story has not been corroborated by other witnesses, this is irrelevant to the point it makes.

The Chellattamman temple is under the control of the Minakshi temple's government administration. In 1977, during the period of emergency rule, when political and civil rights were suspended by the Indian government, the head of the administration, the executive officer, had complete supervisory responsibility for the two temples' affairs. The officer was a Brahman, of a distinctly orthodox cast of mind. According to the priest, he decided that animal sacrifice should cease at Chellattamman's temple and that her names should be recited during worship in Sanskrit, the language of ritual for the great deities, instead of Tamil. He probably did make the first ruling, although the second seems bizarre. All the same, the priest insisted that these decisions were made and said that during the period when sacrifice was banned, Chellattamman came to him in a dream to protest. When the priest awoke the next morning, his waist-cloth was stained with blood, which he took as a sign of her feelings, and animal sacrifice was then resumed as soon as possible. At the start of the goddess's annual festival, a few days before she visits Sundareshwara, a Brahman has to come from the Minakshi temple to take part in one ritual, which involves reciting Chellattamman's names. In 1977, the executive officer, who was present, ordered the Brahman to chant the names in Sanskrit. He started to do so, but then became tongue-tied and could not continue. The officer became agitated and the priests told him that it was Chellattamman's doing; the Brahman gesticulated to them to complete her names in Tamil and when they had done this, he regained his power of speech. That was the first and last time that anyone tried to praise Chellattamman in Sanskrit.

In this story—which is quite typical of its genre, as a similar case involving the prohibition of buffalo sacrifice shows (Hiltebeitel 1985: 181–82)—we see limits to a reformist Brahman's ability to impose his standards. The men who resisted him believed that the goddess herself was intervening to support their efforts to grant her desires. Chellattamman's rights and those of her priests were asserted against the pressure exerted by Brahmanical reformism, personified by the politically powerful executive officer. A blow for sacrificial village goddesses and non-Brahmans was struck.

But for this small victory against reformism there has been a price to pay. The goddess got her blood sacrifice and vernacular liturgy, but these—as the priest himself knows—are inferior religious practices by reference to Brahmanical and reformist standards. The non-Brahman priest has helped to reconstruct Chellattamman as inferior to Minakshi and Sundareshwara, and he has also reconstructed his own socioreligious inferiority in relation to the Brahmans offering purely vegetarian worship in nearby Minakshi's temple. Brahmanical reformism has been halted and the non-Brahmans' point of view has been vigorously reasserted, but since Chellattamman remains the subordinate goddess who guards the temple of Sundareshwara and his consort, she and her priests—by insisting on their right to sacrifice animals—reconfirm the principle of hierarchical inequality itself. The failure of reformism, no less than its success, reinforces the superior value attached to nonviolent worship, deities who reject blood sacrifice, and the people who participate in rituals for them.

Chapter 5

RITUALS OF KINGSHIP

ON THE EVE of independence in 1947, there were 565 kingdoms or "princely states" in the Indian subcontinent, which were not under direct British rule. Within a year or two all of them had disappeared for ever. Some princely states—such as Hyderabad, ruled by a Muslim, and Mysore, Travancore, Kashmir, and Baroda, ruled by Hindus—were large and populous, but many others covered only a few square miles. After independence, all the states (with the partial exception of Kashmir) were constitutionally incorporated into either India or Pakistan, although in India nearly three hundred former kings kept their titles and privy purses until 1971. Throughout the area that was British India, where the majority of the subcontinent's population lived, all the old kingdoms had already been dissolved by the imperial power, so that no Indian king has ruled for well over a century. Moreover, across much of northern India, the British displaced Muslim kings and no Hindu has reigned for half a millennium. The one exception within the region is Nepal, which is still constitutionally a Hindu monarchy, but in the contemporary secular republic of India itself, Hindu kingdoms have completely vanished.

Despite this history, kingship retains a central importance in Hinduism and Indian society. In the traditional Hindu worldview, as expounded most clearly in textual sources, kingship is seen as a vital institution; a society without a king is unviable and anarchic. It is true that the texts portray kings as violent destroyers, as well as preservers of peace. Nonetheless, all sources agree that the king's first responsibility is to protect his kingdom and subjects, by guaranteeing their safety, prosperity, and well-being. But these depend upon preserving order in the kingdom in the widest sense, so that, for example, the king is responsible for maintaining the hierarchical caste system within his realm; he must protect the privileges of Brahmans and the rights of all the different castes, confirm their relative rank, and uphold the authority of caste courts. Order in the kingdom, moreover, is ultimately continuous with order in the universe; the kingdom is correspondingly conceptualized as a microcosm of the universe and ideally their boundaries coincide. To put it differently, the order of the kingdom is itself part of the sociocosmic order or *dharma*, and it is ultimately preserved by king and deity together, rather than by the king alone. Consistent with this formulation, kingship is also the axis of the divine world, whose ruler in many myths is Indra, king of the gods.

Despite considerable empirical variation, the general relationship between human kings and deities has commonly been understood, at least in recent centuries, in two parallel ways. Either the king is himself a form or incarnation of the tutelary state deity, normally a form of Vishnu, Shiva, or the goddess (but not Indra) enshrined in the capital's principal temple, or he is the regent or prime minister (dewan) of the state deity. In Hindu polytheistic logic, however, the difference between these expressions is slight. The king, in exercising the power and authority of the state deity, inevitably shares in the latter's divinity, even though he can also be distinguished as a man from the deity with whom he jointly rules. This double relationship between king and deity is vital, as we shall see below.

Parenthetically, it is worth observing that because the claim to divinity is unremarkable for Hindus, the king's divinity does not in itself mark him out from innumerable other people, in the last analysis potentially everyone. Hindu "divine kingship"—to use that rather misleading phrase—is therefore very different from its counterpart in societies in which rulers enjoy a divinity unique to themselves. A corollary, of course, is that in the Hindu world a multiplicity of divine kings poses no difficulty in principle, whatever problems it may cause in the shape of political instability.

There are many reasons why kingship still matters to Hindus, despite the extinction of Hindu kingdoms in contemporary India. One important factor lies in the royalty of the deities—particularly Vishnu, but also Shiva and the goddess, who can all be represented as monarchs, notably in the temples. The disappearance of Hindu kingdoms as political entities has not been enough to undermine the royalty of deities or, more generally, the significance of kingship as a socioreligious institution. Thus, for example, independent India chose as its national emblem the capital of a column erected by the Buddhist emperor Ashoka, who unified the country in the third century B.C. More significantly, the notion that the ideal state is Rama's kingdom, the *Ram-rajya*, retains its force even in the Indian republic, although by the late 1980s, the Bharatiya Janata party had turned "*Ram-rajya*" into an aggressive slogan of Hindu communalist "fundamentalism." Irrespective of the BJP, however, the *Ram-rajya* notion implies that Rama's role as a perfect king remains central to his representation. The story of Rama's kingship is probably known by more Hindus today than at any time during the two millennia since the *Ramayana*'s composition, because the epic was serialized at length on Indian television in 1987–88. Each weekly episode attracted a vast audience, exceeding that for any other program. Apart from its religious appeal, the televised *Ramayana*'s political message about good government seems to have been readily understood by commentators and is unlikely to have been missed by millions of viewers, although it may have encouraged support for Hindu fundamentalism as well. Ironically, though, in keeping alive the idea of divine sovereignty, the state-controlled television network has probably contributed a very great deal.

THE NAVARATRI FESTIVAL

In this chapter, I shall look at the ritual representation of kingship, especially the relationship between human king and royal deity, in a more traditional and now largely historical form. My principal topic will be royal celebration of the autumnal Navaratri ("Nine nights") festival, which is often described as *the* festival (*utsava*) of kings and Kshatriyas. Although numerous other rituals and festivals were also important in Hindu kingdoms, Navaratri eclipsed any other single event as the most prominent ritual of kingship across India.

Navaratri (or Durga Puja), as I have mentioned before, commemorates Durga's glorious victory over the buffalo-demon Mahishasura and his army. According to a famous myth, Mahishasura is the king of the demons (*asura*), who represent the forces of ignorance and chaos. With his demonic army, Mahishasura has defeated the gods in battle, but because of a boon granted to him, the gods cannot destroy him. So the task falls to the goddess, who is created and armed by the gods, and finally kills Mahishasura by cutting off his buffalo-head.

Sculptured images of Durga as the slayer of Mahishasura abound in temples of the goddess and Shiva; many of them are artistic masterpieces and some are centuries old. But for the majority of contemporary Hindus, the buffalo-demon's death is probably most vividly depicted in popular colored prints. A typical one, by the prolific Bombay artist B. G. Sharma, shows Durga clad in a red sari and mounted on a golden lion. She has eighteen arms with which she carries the various weapons given by the gods, and her leading right hand wields the sword that has just severed the buffalo's head from its body. In the picture, there are also two identical demons; each is a swarthy, muscular man with a jagged scimitar and vampirish teeth, whose eyes and long red tongue seem to pop out from his face in fear. These demons are Mahishasura himself, who has emerged from the buffalo's body in his true guise after its head was severed. The goddess grasps one demon in two of her left hands, and the lion's teeth and claws are sunk in the other demon's throat, from which blood spurts all over his chest. The most striking feature of the picture, though, is that astride the fierce lion sits a fair, serene goddess, with a twinkle in her eyes and a smile on her lips. She is young and beautiful, and calmly, almost dispassionately, happy in her murderous victory over the demon whose reign of terror has ended in blood at her feet.

King Mahishasura's mythical reign started when he threw the defeated gods out of heaven and forced them to live on earth oppressed by the demons. In other words, he turned the cosmic order upside down, specifically by usurping the throne of Indra. Durga's victory enables the gods to regain their kingdom and so restore the universal *dharma* predicated on rule by a rightful king. It is this theme in the myth that is so vital to royal celebrations of Navaratri. (For other groups of Hindus, this is not always so. Their Navaratri festivals sometimes make no reference to the myth of Durga's battle.)

The "Nine nights" of Navaratri are immediately followed, on the tenth day, by the festival of Vijayadashami ("Victory tenth") or Dasara (Dashahara; "Ten days"), although the entire festival of Navaratri plus the tenth day is often called Dasara. To complicate matters further, another festival known as the Ram Lila ("Rama's play") overlaps with Navaratri, and is actually the more popular event in much of the Hindi-speaking area of north India. Vijayadashami is the climax of the Ram Lila and the tenth-day festival primarily celebrates the victory of Rama, king of Ayodhya, over Ravana, demon king of Lanka, who abducted Sita after his fellow demons had suffered defeat at Rama's hands. Sometimes, though, Vijayadashami is treated as an additional commemoration of Durga's victory, which occurs on the eighth day of Navaratri. Since Vijayadashami, as part of the Ram Lila, is about a divine king's defeat of a demonic king, there is an obvious and significant convergence between Durga's and Rama's festivals.

The timing of Navaratri is crucial, but to explain it I must introduce a little material on the Hindu ritual calendar. Almost all major, pan-Indian festivals are fixed by the lunar calendar that prevails in most of the country. Synodical lunar months, ending on full-moon or new-moon day, are divided into thirty lunar days. The period of fifteen lunar days ending on full moon (while the moon waxes) is known as the "bright fortnight," while that ending on new moon (while the moon wanes) is the "dark fortnight." Navaratri is held on the first nine lunar days of the bright fortnight of *ashwina* (September–October). The technical features of the Hindu calendrical system (outlined in the appendix) are irrelevant here; what matters is the religious significance of time as it pertains to the date of the Navaratri festival. Two factors are especially noteworthy: the idea of Vishnu's four-month sleep, and the year's division into auspicious and inauspicious halves.

Throughout northern India, Vishnu is said to fall asleep on the eleventh day of the bright fortnight of *ashadha* (June–July) and to wake up on the corresponding day in *karttika* (October–November). The idea of Vishnu's sleep is ancient, although its rationale is rather obscure and numerous explanations have been advanced. However, it is relevant that it starts at more or less the same time as the south-west monsoon breaks over northern India. Until all-weather roads and railways were constructed, communications were severely disrupted for approximately three months during the monsoon. In particular, warfare normally ceased because armies could not march easily. Clearly, there is a connection between cessation of movement across the land during the rainy season and Vishnu's dormancy.

Whatever the reasons given for Vishnu's sleep, its overall significance is plain enough. When the great god who preserves the world withdraws from it for four months, a time of danger is heralded, when demons and other malevolent forces can become more active. Sometimes, Brahma and Shiva are said to fall asleep at other times of the year, but in north Indian popular Hinduism all deities are often said to go to sleep with Vishnu during the monsoon and early autumn, thus exacerbating the world's vulnerability at this time. It is consistent with this notion that Mahishasura and his demon army are able to gather strength to overthrow the gods just before *ashwina*, approximately one month before Vishnu reawakens.

The second factor pertains to the auspicious (*shubha*) and inauspicious (*ashubha*) halves of the year. The relative auspiciousness of temporal periods is multiply and complexly determined, but one crucial variable is the alternation of light and dark periods, the former being auspicious relative to the latter. These periods particularly include day and night, the bright and dark fortnights of the lunar month, and the yearly division into the *uttarayana* ("northern path") and *dakshinayana* ("southern path"), which I shall now briefly explain.

Although the lunar calendar is prevalent in India, Hindus also divide the year into twelve solar months. A solar month is the period in which the sun, in its apparent annual orbit round the earth, moves through one zodiacal house. Each house is identified by the same constellation as in western astronomy, but in the Hindu system solstices and equinoxes coincide with four of the transitions between months, when the sun moves from one house to another. The six solar months stretching from the winter to summer solstices, when the sun appears to move north and days lengthen, is the auspicious *uttarayana*. The other six months, when the sun moves south and days shorten, is the inauspicious *dakshinayana*. Moreover, because one human year equals one divine day, the *uttarayana* is the deities' daytime and the *dakshinayana* their night-time. The winter solstice is then sunrise, the spring equinox midday, the summer solstice sunset, and the autumn equinox midnight.

In northern India, the binary division of the year is not accorded much significance. It is far more important in the south, especially in Tamilnadu and Kerala, where a solar calendar is used instead of a lunar calendar as in most of the rest of India. Conversely, in the south, the notion of Vishnu's sleep is given hardly any weight. The south-west monsoon mostly falls within both the *dakshinayana* and the period of Vishnu's dormancy, but it is also material that in Tamilnadu, where the majority of the annual precipitation is brought by the north-east monsoon between October and December, the rainy season still occurs within the *dakshinayana*. Most important of all, though, Navaratri occurs close to the autumn equinox, the gods' midnight and the middle of the dark half of the year. One critical feature of inauspicious, dark periods is that they are preferred by demons, who are most active then, so that Navaratri once again occurs at the right time for Mahishasura to gather his forces.

In relation to both the mainly northern idea of Vishnu's sleep and the mainly southern idea of the year's binary division, Navaratri therefore falls at a predominantly inauspicious time, when the gods are inactive or weakened and the demons are at the height of their power. But from this reversal of order and good fortune finally comes Durga's victory, and out of the chaos engendered by the demons—as well as the blood and gore of a terrible battle—a new universal order, presided over by the gods under their king, is created and established. The goddess's slaying of the buffalo-demon signals the end of demonic supremacy. In this glorious victory and its aftermath, the recreation of a kingly order, Hindu monarchs participate by celebrating royal Navaratri. I shall now describe these celebrations in two major Hindu kingdoms of the past, Mewar and Mysore, for which we have fairly detailed accounts of Navaratri as it used to be conducted.

NAVARATRI IN MEWAR

Our information on Navaratri in Mewar comes mainly from the vast compendium of Rajasthani history and custom written by James Tod, a British political agent, who first went to the state in 1818. Much of Tod's writing is infused by his romantic belief in royal Rajasthan's golden past, but his account of Navaratri in Mewar is fairly prosaic.

In the early nineteenth century, Mewar, whose capital was Udaipur, was still one of the most powerful Hindu princely states in India, as well as one of the most ancient. Mewar also assumed preeminence among the Rajasthani kingdoms, partly because of its legendary history. The greatest moments in that history took place at the fortress of Chitor, three times besieged by Muslim armies. On each occasion—in 1303, 1535, and 1567—it is said that the women inside the fortress either went out to attack the Muslims or committed mass suicide by walking into a fire, before all the men rode into battle, dressed in yellow wedding robes, to die fighting against impossible odds. Among the thousands who perished in the holocaust of 1567 were 1,700 men and women of the Mewar royal clan. Their illustrious and honorable death is recalled to this day as the true symbol of royal, Rajput courage in the face of the enemy.

The kings of Mewar were styled Maharana, a variant of Maharaja, "great king." Their Rajput dynasty—traditionally regarded as the senior branch of the *suryavamsha*, the solar line of kings—claimed descent from Rama. But despite the link to Rama and the popularity of Vaishnavism in the region (focused on Krishna's famous temple at Nathdwara that lay within Mewar) the dynasty's tutelary deity was Eklinga, a form of Shiva at the temple at Eklingji, a village near Udaipur. As Tod repeatedly remarks, the king was held to be Eklinga's viceregent and a common title of the Maharana was "Dewan of Eklinga" (1914: 173, 181–82, 184). In addition to Eklinga, various other deities were regarded as tutelary clan deities of the royal dynasty and in Mewar, as in other kingdoms, the identity of all these deities and the relationships among them are not entirely clear. In particular, how far a royal clan deity would protect the kingdom, as opposed to just the king and his clan, appears to have varied in ways that are poorly understood. In Mewar, though, Eklinga was or had become the state deity, as well as a royal clan deity, and he had the supreme place. Eklinga, together with his dewan the king, were the true sovereigns of Mewar.

In Mewar, many annual festivals were marked by the king, and elements of Navaratri recurred at other times of year. Nevertheless, the autumnal Navaratri was by far the most elaborate royal festival, although its antiquity and origins are unclear. I shall now describe it as it was in the early nineteenth century by summarizing Tod's account (ibid.: 464–68). Afterwards, I shall refer to Madeleine Biardeau's description of the festival in the more recent past (1989b: 305–6), as well as to information collected in Udaipur by Adrian C. Mayer. Their data clarify some obscurities in Tod's account, but most of the apparent discrepancies are probably the result of later alterations to the festival.

Tod says that Navaratri in Mewar was "sacred to the god of war," Shiva, but in fact the goddess, rather than Shiva, was the principal deity of the festival. On its first day, the state sword was taken in procession from the palace's hall of arms to the Raj Jogi, chief of a monastic order of militant Shaiva ascetics. He was waiting with other ascetics of his order beside a temple near a city gate, dedicated to Devi, "*the* goddess" according to Tod, but not otherwise identified. The Raj Jogi put the sword before the image of the goddess. Tod says (1914: 472) that the state sword was a double-edged scimitar believed to have been made by Vishwakarma, the divine blacksmith and architect of the universe.

Later on the first day, the king and his retinue went to the palace stables, where a buffalo was sacrificed "in honour of the war-horse," and then to Devi's temple where a special seat (*gaddi*) had now been carried.

The king sat on this seat beside the Raj Jogi, performed "homage" to the sword, and afterwards returned to the palace. Tod gives "homage" as a translation of *puja*, "worship"; he probably means that the king worshiped the sword at this time, although his account does not make this entirely clear. The term *gaddi* denotes the mattress on which a Hindu king sits, and often more specifically a dynastic throne (Mayer 1985: 206–10). But it can also refer to any seat for the ruler, as in the above case, and in Mewar (exceptionally) no permanent dynastic throne existed.

On the morning of the second day, the king and his retinue went to the parade ground, where a buffalo was sacrificed and another was later killed beside one of the city's gates. In the evening, the king proceeded to the temple of the goddess Amba Mata, where several buffaloes and goats were killed. The morning procession to the parade ground, followed by a buffalo sacrifice, occurred daily until the eighth day inclusive (the day of Mahishasura's death), except that no sacrifice was performed on the sixth day after the procession. In the afternoon of the third day, buffaloes and rams were sacrificed to the goddess Harshid Mata. On the fourth day, the king worshiped the sword and the Raj Jogi's standard at Devi's temple. He also offered homage to the Raj Jogi and then sacrificed a buffalo to Devi by piercing it with an arrow fired from his place on a portable seat. After the morning sacrifice of the fifth day, an elephant fight was staged and a buffalo and ram were offered to the goddess Ashapurna. On the next day there were yet more sacrifices to Devi, before the king visited the chief of the Kanphata order of Shaiva ascetics. Further sacrifices to Devi occurred on the seventh day and the royal horses were bathed in the lake. In the evening, a sacred fire was kindled, a buffalo and ram were killed for Devi, and the Jogis were fed. The day closed with a visit to an ascetic's hermitage by the king accompanied by the Mewar chiefs, the king's vassals who were all in attendance at Udaipur during Navaratri. The *homa* ritual, when sacrificial oblations are made into a fire, was held in the palace on the eighth day and later the king paid a visit to another celebrated ascetic living in a nearby village.

There was no morning procession on the ninth day. Instead the horses of the king and chiefs were bathed in the lake, before receiving the homage of their riders. The king presented gifts to his master of the horse, the equerries, and grooms. In the afternoon, a procession went to Mount Matachil, a hill overlooking the city, to bring the sword (presumably taken there earlier from Devi's temple) back to the palace, where it was accepted by the king from the Raj Jogi's hands. He and his ascetics were given gifts, homage was rendered to the elephants and horses, and the sword, shield, and spear were worshiped inside the palace.

The tenth day, Dasara, was celebrated as the day on which Rama began his victorious expedition to Lanka to conquer Ravana; it "is consequently deemed by the Rajpoot a fortunate day for warlike enterprise"

(Tod 1914: 467). In the afternoon the king, his chiefs, and their retainers went to the parade ground, where they worshiped the *kaijri* tree and set free a blue jay (sacred to Rama). They then left the ground to the sound of gunfire. The Dasara celebrations continued in Mewar on the next day as well, when they started with a great procession toward Mount Matachil. The king reviewed his troops "amidst discharges of cannons, tilting, and display of horsemanship. The spectacle is imposing even in the decline of this house" (ibid.: 467). The entire city appears to have been decorated and the king, reposing in a tent, received from all present their *"nuzzurs"* (*nazar*; *najar*), the ceremonial presents offered to a king as an act of homage and allegiance. The glorious history of the Mewar dynasty was recounted and celebrated, and at the end of the day the king brought the whole festival to a close by presenting gifts to his chiefs.

Let me now turn briefly to the data from Biardeau (1989b: 305–6) and Mayer. According to both of them, in more recent times anyway, the state sword was kept throughout the Navaratri festival by the Shaiva ascetics, identified as Naths by Biardeau. Furthermore, Mayer tells me that the sword remained in a special hut and received a daily goat sacrifice; it was also the weapon believed to have been used by the Mewar king to recapture Chitor from the Muslims in 1313, a decade after the first great siege of the fortress. Biardeau's description of the sacrifices suggests that the festival eventually became more focused, because all of them were made to Ambamataji (Amba Mata), whose royal temple lies at the edge of the city. She also states that the king took part in a buffalo sacrifice on the first day; another buffalo sacrifice occurred on the eighth day, with goat sacrifices on the remaining days. Nowadays, though, goats or a vegetable surrogate have replaced buffaloes completely. The *homa* ritual, according to Biardeau, actually began on the second day and lasted until the tenth. She provides further details about the end of the festival, notably that an image of a royal goddess brought from the palace accompanied the king to the parade ground, and indicates that in the more recent past the tenth day was the last. Despite a decline in the scale of sacrifice and a reduction in the festival's length, however, Navaratri remained the most spectacular ritual expression of the Maharana's sovereignty in Mewar.

Dasara in Mysore

The grand festival celebrated by the Maharaja of Mysore in his capital, Mysore city, has always been known as Dasara. It was observed in the 1930s by C. Hayavadana Rao, and I shall mainly refer to his description, although there is information about the more recent past from Biardeau and Mayer.

The Mysore kingdom emerged as an independent polity out of the ruins of the great fifteenth- to sixteenth-century Hindu empire of Vijayanagara, and was its most direct successor regime. For part of the eighteenth century, Mysore was ruled by Muslims, but after the British defeat of Tipu Sultan, the kingdom was restored to Hindu rulers in 1799. As a royal festival, Navaratri (or Mahanavami, "Great ninth") grew into an enormous spectacle of sacrifices, processions, and other pageants in the Vijayanagara capital, which awed the Portuguese and other foreigners who witnessed it. The Vijayanagara festival was probably the prototype of all royal Navaratris in south India, and the festival begun by the Mysore king around 1650 (Wilks 1869: 32–33) was certainly modeled on it. In the early nineteenth century, according to Mark Wilks, it was again being "kept with a creditable degree of splendour." To the best of my knowledge, it has been celebrated continually since then, although Dasara is now held on a much reduced scale, and the great city processions and court assemblies of preindependence days no longer take place. If traced back to Vijayanagara, Mysore's Dasara is around five hundred years old, but we cannot assume that it and other royal festivals are even more ancient, merely because they develop mythical and ritual themes of still greater antiquity.

The tutelary deity of the Mysore royal dynasty was the goddess Chamundeshwari, whose shrine lies inside the royal palace, inaccessible to the public. Partly for this reason, Chamundeshwari appears to have been less forcefully identified as the Mysore kingdom's tutelary deity than, say, Eklinga in Mewar, although her role in the Dasara festival shows that she did assume the state deity's function. Chamundeshwari as Chamundi also has a prominent public temple on Chamundi Hill near the city, where the Dasara festival was simultaneously held (Biardeau 1989b: 309). Chamundeshwari and Chamundi are forms of Durga, slayer of Mahishasura, and in local legend Mysore is the site of the buffalo-demon's death (Rao 1936: 73–74). At the same time, however, the Mysore royal regalia were associated with Indra as well as Chamundeshwari. The king's throne contained the goddess's power, but when worshiped it was also referred to as Indra's throne; to Indra too were assigned the state horse, elephant, and carriage, the state weapons, and the state cow (ibid.: 6–7).

According to Rao (ibid.: 142–48), on the initial day, after preparatory rituals for Chamundeshwari at her shrine inside the palace, the first important event was worship of the royal throne in the Durbar Hall, where the court assemblies took place. The king then mounted the throne and the state sword was placed beside him. Gifts from monasteries, temples, and selected Brahman priests were given to the king, before the state's prime minister (the dewan), other officials, and prominent citizens offered homage in the form of ceremonial presents. Those attending the assembly marched past the king in order and were given flowers by him, before he retired into the palace to attend the rituals held for Chamundeshwari, which continued without a break for all nine days of Navaratri proper. The state sword was also worshiped daily inside the palace on all nine days. During the evening of the first day, another court assembly was held, and from the second to the eighth days, an assembly was held every evening in the Durbar Hall. On the ninth day, the state arms, elephant, and horse were worshiped and a fire sacrifice was held for Chamundeshwari. After this was over, the king removed the thread that he had tied on his wrist on the first day. This action marked the end of his vow to perform the goddess's rituals, as well as the close of Navaratri itself.

On the morning of the tenth day, Dasara itself, the state arms were worshiped before being taken in a procession headed by the king to the Banni Mandap, a hall set up on the parade ground. The king returned to his palace and in the afternoon another longer and more elaborate procession, now including the princes as well as the king seated on an elephant, set off through the city for the Banni Mandap. The procession was led by a magnificent array of camels and elephants, and the various state regiments, as a Mysore princess later recalled (Allen and Dwivedi 1984: 282–83). On the parade ground, the king reviewed his troops and worshiped the *shami* tree beside the Banni Mandap, heard the palace genealogy read, and distributed consecrated leaves from the tree to the state officials. With the state arms, he then returned to the palace, held a final court assembly, and retired, to bring Dasara to its close.

Biardeau describes Dasara in Mysore during modern times, and some of the details she provides plainly fill gaps in Rao's account from half a century ago. According to Biardeau, the state sword was kept in Chamundeshwari's shrine and her worship on the first day could not actually begin until the throne had been worshiped. On the eighth day, there was special worship for Chamundeshwari to celebrate her defeat of the buffalo-demon. On the ninth day, after worship of the arms and the fire sacrifice for Chamundeshwari, the king went to Chamundi Hill to worship Chamundi and to the nearby shrine at Uttamahalli, where the presiding goddess is Chamundi's younger sister and inferior complementary partner. Through these visits, the two exterior goddesses were incorporated into royal Dasara, a testimony to the significance of the complementary relationship between the goddesses at the center and the boundary. On the tenth day, in addition to the events described by Rao, Biardeau reports that the king used his sword to sever a branch of the *shami* tree, which was later laid at Chamundeshwari's feet in the palace shrine with the weapon (1989b: 308–11).

At the Vijayanagara Navaratri, animal sacrifice was conducted on a massive scale, as we know from contemporary reports by foreign visitors

(Rao 1936: app. 3, Paes' account [c. 1520]; cf. Stein 1980: 385–92). There were no buffalo or other animal sacrifices in Mysore's Dasara in the 1930s, although they had taken place much earlier and probably stopped during the nineteenth century; it was then that the Chamundi Hill temple came under direct royal control following the king's appointment of Brahman priests responsible for introducing "vegetarian" worship and ending animal sacrifice there (Goswami and Morab 1975: 9–11). Nevertheless, according to Mayer, on the ninth day of the festival, even in recent times, the king sliced a pumpkin in half before red powder was sprinkled over it, and then watched four men fight until at least one of them was bleeding. Cutting the pumpkin is plainly a surrogate animal sacrifice, just as the bleeding man is a kind of surrogate human sacrifice. In addition, Biardeau draws attention to the displacement of sacrificial ritual from the center in the city; on the tenth day of Chamundi's festival on the hill, a sliced, reddened pumpkin was dropped into the sacrificial fire, and animal sacrifices were offered to the goddess of Uttamahalli on another occasion (1989b: 311, 312–13, 316–17).

THE WORSHIP OF THE GODDESS

Navaratri in Mewar and Dasara in Mysore were complex events, and I shall focus on five specific aspects important for our theme. These are the worship of and sacrifices to the goddesses during Navaratri proper (i.e., the first nine days); the rituals for the state sword and the worship of elephants, horses, and weapons; Rama and Dasara (the tenth day); the celebration of warfare at Dasara; and finally, the court assemblies.

In Mysore, Dasara unambiguously focused on the worship of Chamundeshwari, the slayer of Mahishasura, to make a patent connection between the festival and the classical Navaratri myth. Nevertheless, the texts in praise of the goddess recited during the Mysore festival do not appear to have included the *Devimahatmya* (Biardeau 1989b: 309), the most famous classical myth of Durga's victory. Biardeau's research shows that it would be wrong to take the *Devimahatmya* (or other comparable texts) as a kind of script for royal Navaratri celebrations. Rather, there is a common core of symbolic themes, particularly focused on the goddess and her sacrifices, which are developed at both ritual and mythical levels, but not by any predetermined connection between them. That common core was as evident in Mewar's Navaratri as Mysore's Dasara, despite the absence of any goddess specifically identified as the slayer of Mahishasura in Mewar.

The king was, in the first place, the patron of the rituals. He assumed the classical role of *yajamana*, the patron and beneficiary of the Vedic sacrifice, who was ideally the king. In the terminology of Henri Hubert and Marcel Mauss's seminal study of sacrifice (1964), the king was the *sacrifiant* as opposed to the *sacrificateur*, the priest who actually performs the ritual. In Mewar, the king was literally the patron of the sacrifice; in Mysore, the king took an equivalent role in the nonviolent worship conducted there. At the simplest level, therefore, the festivals reiterated the durable relationship between the goddesses and their principal worshipers, the respective kings who presided over the rituals.

A clear symbol of this relationship was the thread worn by the king of Mysore to proclaim his vow to complete the Navaratri rituals, an aspect also emphasized in Carol A. Breckenridge's discussion (1978: 87) of Navaratri in late nineteenth-century Ramnad, a petty kingdom in southern Tamilnadu. The rituals also symbolically identified each king with the victorious goddess herself. Thus for example, the thread worn by the Mysore king, which is meant to protect him in addition to signifying his vow, can also be interpreted as a sign that he himself joined the goddess in her campaign. The king's identification with Chamundeshwari was again displayed when he donated flowers to the people assembled before him, for each flower had been placed at the goddess's feet while the king, seated on the throne, was "in communion" with her (Rao 1936: 147–48).

In Mewar, where animal sacrifice was so important, the identification of king and goddess was equally transparent. All sacrifices to the goddesses—both buffaloes and other animals—were obviously made in the king's name; he actually presided over them on some days and even killed the buffalo himself on the fourth day. The king was the sacrificial patron and once the executioner too. By the symbolic logic of sacrifice, the buffalo must be seen as a substitute for him (and his subjects). Nevertheless, because every buffalo sacrifice at Navaratri symbolically reenacts the killing of the buffalo-demon by the goddess, these sacrifices plainly joined the Mewar king to the victorious goddess as well.

In several ways, Navaratri identified the kings of Mewar and Mysore with the goddess and made them participants in her victory over Mahishasura. But in the myth, as we know, Durga's triumph allows the gods to regain their kingdom, reinstall their own king on his throne, and reestablish the proper order of the universe. The rituals bear a parallel message and Navaratri also showed the Mewar and Mysore kings as restorers, alongside the goddess, of the rightful order that is predicated on the royal authority of the gods. Furthermore, the festivals commemorated the reestablishment of a divine sovereignty in which the human kings themselves respectively shared as regents of Eklinga (Shiva), the state deity of Mewar whose restoration followed from the goddess's victory, or Chamundeshwari functioning as the state deity of Mysore who has brought about her own restoration. In brief, through the victory enacted at Navaratri, the order of the Mewar and Mysore kingdoms was recreated in the likeness of the order of the universe.

Like the myth of Durga "sacrificing" Mahishasura by decapitating him in battle, a Navaratri festival that incorporates animal sacrifice—especially buffalo sacrifice—exemplifies the ancient idea that this rite, an act of destruction, is an act of creation as well. Indeed, sacrifice is the means by which the universal order predicated on kingship is brought about. In Mewar, the sacrificial theme was patent, and we also know that there was extensive sacrificial slaughter in medieval Vijayanagara. In modern times, however, there has been strong reformist pressure against animal sacrifice, and this has had as much impact on kings as ordinary people. In Mewar, goats are still killed, but buffaloes no longer are; in Mysore animals are not killed at all. But even in Mysore—as the bisected, reddened pumpkin shows—sacrifice did not completely disappear, and the sacrificial theme at the heart of Navaratri, so bloodily expressed in early nineteenth-century Mewar, still survived in muted but obvious form in twentieth-century Mysore.

THE STATE SWORD AND THE MACHINERY OF WAR

The state sword of Mewar, according to Tod, was delivered to a Shaiva ascetic, who gave it to Devi on the first day of the festival. The ascetic returned the sword to the king on the ninth day. Alternatively, as Biardeau and Mayer indicate, the sword was kept by Shaiva ascetics throughout the festival. In any event, it appears to have been retained by Devi, or by ascetics on behalf of Shiva, for all nine days of Navaratri. In Mysore, the state sword, identified as Indra's, was placed beside the king on his throne on the first day and worshiped inside the palace on all nine days, but it was normally kept within Chamundeshwari's shrine. In the two kingdoms, the sword therefore appears to have been transferred in opposite directions. In Mewar, the king put his sword into divine custody during the festival, so that it could be kept by or given to the goddess for use in her battle with the demons. After her victory, the king got his sword back. In Mysore, by contrast, Chamundeshwari ostensibly relinquished her sword during the period of battle to the king. In fact, though, both sword rituals surely conveyed an almost identical message: a further identification between king and goddess, who were allies wielding the same weapon in the same cosmic war.

A fuller discussion of the state sword would have to extend to other royal insignia, as well as to the throne, but the available evidence is not detailed enough to do this. We know from Mayer (1985: 206–10) that the throne is consistently treated as a symbol of the kingdom itself and is believed to contain the powers of one or more deities, typically forms of the goddess, sometimes in conjunction with the royal clan and state deities. When the king sits on his throne, he is united with the deities within it and from their power (*shakti*) he draws part of his own. This formula clearly applies to Mysore, but for Mewar, which exceptionally had no permanent throne, further discussion is precluded by insufficient data. The source of a king's power and its legitimation as royal authority are large topics, and comparative evidence shows that there was a great deal of variation over time and space. Invariably, though, the transfer of the state sword (often with other insignia) served to demonstrate the delegation of power and authority from deity to king, whether the king took the sword from the deity's image himself (as in Mysore), was handed it by ascetics (as in Mewar), or received it from court Brahmans or other representatives of the deities (as in other kingdoms). In all cases, though, a ritual of legitimation seems to have been an intrinsic part of royal Navaratri festivals.

From the sword, we can move easily to the machinery of war. Both the elephant and horse are animals emblematic of kingship, particularly in its martial aspect. The elephant is the preeminent mount of Indra and the traditional Hindu king, and it was extensively used in war in early India. Much more effective on the battlefield, however, is the horse, the animal consistently associated with warfare and a vital symbol of military kingship. Worship of elephants and horses, together with the weapons of war, appears to have been universal at royal Navaratris and it was generally held on the ninth day—in many parts of India the day of *ayudha puja*, "weapon worship"—although it was often repeated or occurred instead on the tenth day. The significance of the ritual is plain to see. The military animals and arms, like the state sword, are imbued with divine power; their worship associates them with the weapons given to the goddess for her battle. The king's armies are thereby identified with hers and they participate in her victory. Moreover, they will enjoy victories as glorious as the goddess's after Navaratri, which was traditionally regarded as the start of a new campaigning season, following the end of the south-west monsoon when military activity was practically impossible.

Rama and Dasara

It will now be clear that Navaratri's conventional association with kings, Kshatriyas, and warfare is well attested and was emphatically displayed in the Mewar and Mysore festivals. Yet it is Dasara on the Victory tenth, not Navaratri, that specifically commemorates victory. The goddess's slaying of Mahishasura can be commemorated on the tenth day—sometimes to reaffirm the events of the eighth day and sometimes as the actual day of her victory—but Dasara is more widely linked with Rama. Often, it celebrates Rama's conquest of Ravana, which was gained by favor of the goddess. Rama's victory is therefore aligned with the goddess's—or anticipated by hers—and Ravana, like Mahishasura, was a demon king who benefited from a divine boon. Ravana's defeat therefore reiterates the same fundamental theme as Navaratri: the restoration of the socio-cosmic order predicated on kingship.

In classical mythology, however, Dasara marks the start of Rama's campaign against Ravana, as it did in the Mewar ritual, with victory coming only six months later, at the time of his birthday during the spring Navaratri. The review of troops, a central part of royal Dasara festivals, clearly signaled the preparation for a successful expedition like Rama's. Retrospectively, we can therefore interpret the worship of the machinery of war during the whole festival as a ritual to identify the king's armies with Rama's, as well as the goddess's.

Worship of the *shami* or *vanni* (*banni*) tree (probably *Prosopis spicigera*), as performed in Mysore, is a very common feature of Dasara. The Mewar *kaijri* tree was almost certainly equivalent to the *shami*. Worship of the *shami* tree has complex classical motifs, but one pertains to Rama's worship of it, intended "to restore to his weapons the fire which the monsoon water had taken away" (Biardeau 1984: 7). The link between worship of the tree and the power of weaponry is widely recognized. The king's processional march to the tree was sometimes specifically called a march to the battlefield. In sum, the Dasara rituals herald a new military campaign like Rama's.

At the same time, for this is the Victory tenth, the success of the new campaign is already anticipated and celebrated. The rituals admit no possibility of defeat, as the recitation of the glories of the Mewar dynasty showed. Commemorating the start of Rama's expedition was not, in ritual terms, inconsistent with celebrating his (and the goddess's) victory.

At this point, let me remind the reader that Dasara, instead of being connected to Navaratri, can also form part of the Ram Lila, in which case it always celebrates Rama's victory. His destruction of Ravana is typically commemorated by burning a large effigy of the demon on Dasara day. In Jaipur in Rajasthan, like Mewar, royal Navaratri was a major festival, but simultaneously and separately a Ram Lila was held on a smaller scale (Biardeau 1989b: 308). This reflects Jaipur's proximity to the fairly clearly delimited, Hindi-speaking area of north India, where the Ram Lila displaces Navaratri as the more prominent and popular festival.

Often but not always, the Ram Lila is a pageant lasting several days, at which Rama's story is told and acted out, culminating in Ravana's death on the pyre. One of the longest and most elaborate of these pageants is held in Benares, or more exactly at Ramnagar, the site of the Benares king's palace on the other bank of the river Ganges. The version of Rama's story always used in the pageants is the *Ramcharitmanas*, a Hindi recension of the *Ramayana* by Tulsidas (1532–1623), the devotionalist poet who is believed to have started the Ram Lila in Benares. In fact, most of the modern Ram Lila dates from much more recently, and it largely attained its final, present-day form in the late nineteenth century. The Hindu kings of Benares began to wrest their independence from Muslim overlordship in the mid-eighteenth century, and their preoccupation with the popular tradition of Rama "reflected among other things their need to cultivate an explicitly Hindu symbol of royal legitimacy" (Lutgendorf 1989: 41), marking them off from Muslim rulers. By the time that they had extended the Ram Lila to a month-long pageant in the early nineteenth century, the Benares kings were free of the Muslims, but real political power had now passed to the British; "the symbols used to legitimate authority can serve equally well to compensate for its loss" (ibid.: 42).

The royal Ram Lila in Benares is organized on a huge scale. Richard Schechner (1985: chap. 4) provides a detailed account of its celebration in the 1970s, which I summarize here. During the month that the festival lasts, the entire *Ramcharitmanas* is chanted and its key scenes are enacted by men and boys personifying Rama and the other main protagonists, both male and female. The most important section covers the story from Ravana's birth to the restoration of Rama's rule and his coronation. The recitation of this section is heard throughout by the king of Benares—still treated as the Maharaja despite the official loss of his throne—who sponsors the entire performance (although he does not meet all the costs). At the Ram Lila, writes Schechner,

> the maharaja of Benares is most vividly and demonstrably a king. It is [then], more than at any other time, that he rides on his elephant, or in his 1928 Cadillac; that he is accompanied by troops and a military marching band; that he shows himself again and again as a king to assembled thousands who chant an homage to the king of the city of Shiva that corresponds neatly to the homage this Shaivite king gives to Rama, Vishnu incarnate. (Ibid.: 158)

The king of Benares is the regent or form of Shiva as ruler of the city, and is hailed as such throughout the Ram Lila, but his association with Rama is also plain, especially at the climax of the festival.

On Dasara day, the royal weapons are displayed and worshiped in the fort and afterwards, in a magnificent procession of elephants, the king leaves his fort, goes down the main street of Ramnagar, and reaches the place that is Lanka in the Ram Lila arena. It is at the very edge of the arena and before returning to his fort, the king goes just outside the arena—a gesture to symbolize his possession of the whole territory beyond. But the king does not actually see Ravana's ritual defeat, because—as he told Schechner—he thinks that "It is not right for one king to watch the death of another" (ibid.: 169). A couple of days later, when Rama returns to Ayodhya to be crowned, "the whole of Ramnagar becomes Ayodhya," whose streets Rama traverses on an elephant; Rama is then welcomed at the fort by the king of Benares, who offers him and his family a sumptuous meal (ibid.: 183). As Schechner observes, "the maharaja and Rama are mirror images of each other, the twin heroes of the Ramnagar Ramlila" (ibid.: 190), and their relationship—between the Maharaja as Shiva and the god Rama as a king (ibid.: 191)—is the axis of the ritual drama. The interplay between Shiva's regent and Rama gives the Ram Lila a special coloring: the king is Shiva as the counterpart to Rama, but he is also Rama, because on Dasara and afterwards he is shown to participate in Rama's victory and restoration to the throne. Hence, like Navaratri in Mewar and Dasara in Mysore, the Benares Ram Lila—although without any sacrifices—is an equally dramatic ritual display of the relationship between king and deity, and of the annual restoration of the sociocosmic order.

To complete this section, let me briefly comment on Divali or Dipavali, the "Row of lights" festival. After Navaratri and the Ram Lila, this is the most widely celebrated festival in most of India and it usually lasts two days, or a little longer. Divali's characteristic feature is the lamps that are lit in the middle of the dark night preceding new moon in *karttika* (October–November).

Divali is a celebration of auspicious light dispelling the blackness of a moonless night. The lamps are identified with Lakshmi, goddess of good fortune and wealth, and her annual visitation is one of the most popular rationales for Divali, which often includes special worship for the goddess. Here we can see an opposition with and sequential development from Navaratri, despite the lack of any explicit link between the two festivals. At Navaratri, a fierce goddess, most closely associated with Shiva, waged war against the demons; her victory ushered in a new period of order and prosperity, a quality with which auspicious Lakshmi, consort of Vishnu, is specially identified. Lakshmi's appearance at Divali also anticipates her husband's awakening from his four-month sleep, which occurs twelve days later. But probably the most widely told story of Divali is that it celebrates Rama's triumphant return with Sita to his capital city of Ayodhya, where he was welcomed by the lamps. In this version, a connection with Navaratri and the Ram Lila is more obvious. Unmarried Durga has been displaced by Sita, the ideal Hindu wife reunited with Rama, and the victory over demon kings gained at the earlier festivals has now, at last, resulted in complete restoration of the deities' sovereignty. Rama, the model king, is again on his throne

and demonic power has been liquidated. Divali is the crowning celebration of the order that emerged out of disorder at Navaratri and the
Ram Lila.

THE CELEBRATION OF WARFARE AT DASARA

To return now to Dasara: as I have already explained, the ideal Hindu
kingdom is coextensive with India, the world, and the universe, and every
Hindu king should strive to expand his kingdom's boundaries to the ut-
termost frontier. This ideal, which necessitates expansive conquest, is
evoked in the classical rite of "crossing the limit" (Biardeau 1989b: 302),
which forms part of the *shami*-tree ritual. In Mewar, it was represented
most specifically by the release of the blue jay, which represents Rama's
departure for war (ibid.: 306), and more generally by the king's procession to Mount Matachil; in Benares, the equivalent rite was enacted when
the king's procession crossed the edge of the Ram Lila arena. In Mysore,
the rite of "crossing the limit" was apparently absent from the Banni
Mandap rituals, and Biardeau therefore argues that the *shami*-tree ritual
signified peace rather than war (ibid.: 311, 317). But for the tenth-day
events in Mysore taken as a whole, this interpretation is implausible,
given the display of military might on the parade ground.

At Dasara in some south Indian kingdoms, another ritual was held. In
the little kingdom of Ramnad, the ruler rode on the state elephant, with
guns blazing, to a ground where he shot arrows in different directions to
symbolize his conquest of the world (Breckenridge 1978: 86). A similar
arrow-shooting ritual took place in the large kingdom of Travancore (Pillai 1940: 574–75). In these arrow-shooting rituals, the king was shown to
be a hunter as well as a warrior. Yet another kind of Dasara ritual was
held in the little state of Dewas Senior (western Madhya Pradesh). There,
according to E. M. Forster (1983: 134–36), the king and his retinue
"drove out a couple of miles against the enemy in landaus, planted a
victory-tree [presumably the *shami* or an equivalent], and drove back
again," although the tiny state had already been immodestly declared to
extend from Lahore to Poona to Bengal.

Comical though that may sound, the Dewas ritual had classical prece-
dents, and according to Forster (although Tod does not mention it), the
king of Mewar asserted his sovereignty over the whole of India at Dasara,
perhaps when the dynasty's history was recounted. Our modern image of
expansionist warfare, which is rightly colored by the chaos, death, and
destruction that it brings in its wake, has ancient Hindu parallels. Moreover, because all killing is impure and violates the ascetic-Brahmanical
ideal of nonviolence, a warring king and his soldiers are inevitably tainted

by sin and pollution. Nevertheless, it is the king's duty to make war to expand his kingdom, principally by forcing other rulers to submit to his suzerainty, rather than by annexing their territories as such. Because it brings the kingdom closer to its ideal form, military expansionism is a harbinger of prosperity for the realm, which engenders a more perfect order, not the opposite. Furthermore, because war is classically conceptualized as sacrifice—just like Durga's onslaught on Mahishasura and his demonic army—military confrontation can be seen as a religiously sanctioned act necessary for the sustainment of the world. Consistent with this, to fall in battle is to die a glorious hero who is likely to be deified. Thus warfare itself is a reiteration of the idea that an ordered cosmos is created by sacrificial destruction.

In the Hindu tradition, the king achieves his expansionist and sacrificial ends through a universal victory over all quarters—the *digvijaya* or "victory of the directions"—and a ceremonial *digvijaya* is prescribed as an essential ritual to be celebrated regularly by Hindu kings. It is this victory that is most patently symbolized by the south Indian ritual of shooting arrows in different directions. In every royal Navaratri and Dasara festival, however, war and victory are prominent themes, and all the martial celebrations on the tenth day have to be understood in a double sense. They reiterate the entire festival's central theme of recreating and restoring *dharma* in the kingdom and the universe, but the battles won and yet to be won are not only over demonic enemies. They are also over other kings, the potential foes to be faced during the new campaigning season inaugurated at this time.

THE COURT ASSEMBLY

The court assembly or durbar (*darbar*) was a more prominent and regulated feature of Dasara in Mysore than of Navaratri in Mewar. This may be because our description of Mysore dates from a century after that of Mewar, by which time the great Delhi Durbars held by the imperial government in 1903 and 1911 would have made an impact, especially in a well-administered state like Mysore. In any case, I begin with Mysore, where a court assembly in the Durbar Hall of the palace was held every day during Dasara. At the assembly, gifts were made to the king as acts of homage by religious institutions and Brahmans, followed by the dewan (the prime minister and highest-ranking official), and then others. The order of precedence, as we shall see, is significant. In turn, the king on his throne gave flowers taken from the feet of Chamundeshwari; these too were distributed in order of rank. The flowers, of course, were a form of *prasada* from the goddess. The importance attached to the king's contact with the throne and its divine power at a festival durbar comes out clearly in Mayer's account (1985: 209) of several rulers' own reflections on this event.

In Mewar, only one full court assembly was held, on the final eleventh day in the tent, not the palace. Tod states that "all present" offered homage with gifts, but he gives no details. He does refer to other gifts given by the king to his chiefs at the palace afterwards. All the chiefs, locally powerful vassals of the king, were required to attend the court at Udaipur during the Navaratri festival (Tod 1914: 171).

Court assemblies, as in Mysore and Mewar, were an essential part of Navaratri and Dasara in practically all Hindu kingdoms. They were also held at other festivals and on special occasions, such as the king's birthday. The "modern" durbar, which originated in the court of the Mughal emperors, had been widely adopted·by both Hindu and Muslim kings by the eighteenth century. In all durbars there were clear rules of hierarchical precedence, but the relationship between the deities and the king and his subjects was, of course, symbolically displayed only in Hindu assemblies.

Let us first consider precedence, always crucially important. As a nobleman who attended the court assemblies held at Udaipur in Mewar's final years explained, "Everybody had a seat at the darbar according to their status. It was first, second, third, fourth on the right, all with fixed seats on the floor, then on the left and then at the back of the gadi [king's seat]" (Allen and Dwivedi 1984: 217). The arrangements could easily multiply in complexity. Nor were chiefs, noblemen, officials, and prominent citizens the only attenders, for at some durbars (as in Dewas Senior) the village headmen also had to come to pay homage from the back of the hall at the Dasara court assembly (Mayer 1960: 96). Hence at assemblies there was a public display of the hierarchical structure of the kingdom, at which everyone of rank was ideally present. In Bernard S. Cohn's words, "The spatial order of a durbar fixed, created and represented relationships with the ruler. The closer to the person of the ruler or his representative one stood, the higher one's status" (1983: 169).

At the assembly, those present offered homage and received in return honorific gifts. Cohn argues that this exchange was a ritual act of incorporation, for in the Indian conception of kingship, "rulers not only outranked everyone but could also encompass those they ruled" (ibid.: 173), from conquered vassal kings to the common people. Such acts of incorporation were common to all Indian durbars, but they took a distinctive form in Hindu states, owing to the king's double relationship with the state deity.

Often—but not, as it happens, in Mewar—the king sat on his dynastic throne at the court assembly and was linked with the deity (or deities) within it, whom he had already worshiped. The deity primarily identified with the throne was not necessarily the state or royal clan deity, but that is not very important, for otherwise differentiated deities can easily be merged together, so that they are all divine protectors of the king and kingdom. Moreover, whichever deities were said to be powerfully present in the seat or throne at the assembly, the ritual act of incorporation always linked subjects to the king and the deities conjointly, rather than to the king alone. But this, of course, was done within a hierarchical structure, whose apex was defined by the supreme position of the deities, particularly the state deity, and the latter's first worshiper and highest-ranking subject, the king. At one level, therefore, the state deity-cum-king was displayed as a sovereign unity, so that the human king participated in the deity's royal divinity. At another level and simultaneously, the state deity was displayed as the supreme ruler who had delegated authority to his separate, inferior regent, the human king. The court assemblies therefore provided an exemplary illustration of the king's double relationship with the state deity, whereby he was both a form of the deity and the latter's human representative on earth.

The court assembly also gave shape to a hierarchical structure of relationships, focused on the deities and king, which was an ideal image of the complete order of human society within the kingdom, as well as of its solidary link to the universe over which the great deities are sovereign. The assembly displayed and reconstituted the kingdom's internal order, which was the inseparable complement of its external order as principally determined by the prosecution of war, the theme so prominent in much of the rest of the festival. Hence throughout royal Navaratri and Dasara, and almost equally dramatically at the Ram Lila, there was a constant and central theme: the recreation and representation of a unitary socio-cosmic order around the axis of sovereign authority, personified in the king who was inseparably bound to the deities of his realm. And at the same time, kingship was portrayed as a vital component of the relationship between the deities and humanity within an ordered, harmonious, and prosperous world.

For Hindus living in the secular republic of contemporary India, these themes have lost remarkably little of their old importance, even though constitutional democracy has now become fairly well established. Kingship has survived the extinction of the maharajas' kingdoms. Despite the dangers recently posed by fundamentalist manipulation of the *Ram-rajya* notion, the ideal democratic state can still be likened to Rama's realm, recaptured by its legitimate ruler after Durga had killed Mahishasura during Navaratri.

Chapter 6

RITUALS OF THE VILLAGE

THERE ARE about half a million villages in India and four-fifths of the population lives in them. In most of the country, villages are named, nucleated settlements, each consisting of a cluster of houses and other buildings, which are often arranged in streets, blocks, or quarters mainly inhabited by particular caste groupings. Village populations range between several hundred and a few thousand. At the village center there is commonly an open space, flanked by the settlement's main temple, other public buildings (such as a school and a village council office), and shops. Many villages also have outlying satellite hamlets. Each village is surrounded by fields—mainly owned and worked by members of that village—which separate it from neighboring settlements. These fields and the site of habitation constitute the village's territory, which usually has recognized boundaries dividing it from the territories of other villages, although the boundaries may be ill-defined and do not necessarily coincide with lines drawn on the map by administrators.

The term "village" translates Sanskrit *grama* and its vernacular variants (as in *gramadevata*, "village deity") as well as a host of other words, whose precise meaning varies considerably. The nature of the Indian village has been debated at length in a large anthropological and historical literature. In general though, notwithstanding the existence of internal divisions and external links to other settlements, villages are normally recognized as significant social units, which are defined and constituted by relationships among villagers themselves, their local deities, and the land on which they live. There should always be harmony between the deities and the population and territory that they protect and rule over, as well as compatibility between the people and their land, whose qualities are ingested by eating food grown in village fields and drinking water drawn from village wells. Harmony and compatibility are usually thought to be greatest when people live in their ancestral villages, but often of course they do not. Because the elements that define a village community vary subtly from place to place, Indians readily speak of their own village's "customs" and insist—however true it is in fact—that they differ from those found elsewhere.

Both within and between regions, there is considerable variation in village social structures as defined, for example, by relationships between local castes and subcastes, or kin groups and affinal networks, among landholders, tenants, laborers, and artisans, or the headman, other local magnates, and ordinary people. Moreover, especially in Kerala, deltaic Bengal, and the Himalayan foothills, the settlement pattern is non-nucleated and houses are scattered across the countryside singly or in very small clusters. Because village structures in these regions tend to be sharply differentiated from elsewhere in India, I shall omit them from my discussion.

Despite all this variation, villages are still generally recognized as local communities, rather than places in which people merely happen to live and work. For the majority of Indians, including many urban migrants, the village where they were born and brought up or have lived for a long time is home in the full sense of that word. Village rituals are one manifestation of the social significance of the local community, and in much of India the unity or solidarity of the community is most strikingly expressed in the celebration of village festivals. Sometimes a few villages join together to hold a festival; sometimes festivals are held by sections of villages, rather than the whole unit; in non-nucleated villages, such festivals are not held or take a different shape. Moreover, in addition to village festivals, villagers take part in many other kinds of ritual activity that are mainly the concern of, say, families or kin groups.

In this chapter, though, I shall focus on village festivals themselves, specifically on those which are *collective*, because they are explicitly intended to benefit the whole village, even if some villagers do not actually participate. Through comparative analysis, I shall uncover a pattern of regional variation (depicted on map), which it may be helpful to outline in advance. In south India—particularly Tamilnadu, southern Karnataka, and southern and coastal Andhra Pradesh—the principal annual ritual in many villages is the temple festival of a tutelary deity, normally the village goddess. In north India, especially the Hindi-speaking regions, similar temple festivals are rare and the collective village festivals are mainly Navaratri (and/or Dasara) and Holi, although in some places there are no collective festivals at all. In central India—the Deccan plateau of northern Karnataka and Andhra Pradesh, and Maharashtra—the pattern is a combination of southern temple festivals and northern celebrations of Navaratri and Holi.

The myth of Navaratri and its timing in the autumn have already been discussed in chapter 5. Holi, a popular festival in northern and central India that is not celebrated in the south, falls on the first day of the dark fortnight of *chaitra* (March–April), but it normally starts on the previous day, full moon in *phalguna* (February–March). It is usually said to take its name from Holika, a mythical demoness who tried to burn her brother (or nephew) Prahlada, a devotee of Vishnu. But Vishnu intervened to save Prahlada and Holika perished instead. In the bonfires lit on the eve of

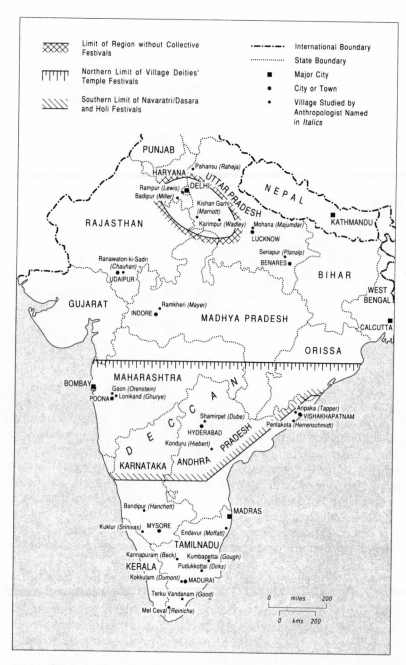

PUNJAB

HARYANA
Pahansu *(Raheja)*
Rampur *(Lewis)* DELHI
Badipur *(Miller)*
UTTAR PRADESH
Kishan Garhi *(Marriott)*
Karimpur *(Wadley)*
Mohana *(Majumdar)*
LUCKNOW
NEPAL
KATHMANDU

RAJASTHAN

Ranawaton-ki-Sadri *(Chauhan)*
UDAIPUR
Senapur *(Planalp)*
BENARES
BIHAR
WEST BENGAL

GUJARAT
Ramkheri *(Mayer)*
INDORE
MADHYA PRADESH
ORISSA
CALCUTTA

BOMBAY
MAHARASHTRA
Gaon *(Orenstein)*
POONA
Lonikand *(Ghurye)*
D E C C A N
Shamirpet *(Dube)*
HYDERABAD
Konduru *(Hiebert)*
Aripaka *(Tapper)*
VISHAKHAPATNAM
Pentakota *(Herrenschmidt)*
ANDHRA PRADESH

KARNATAKA
ANDHRA

Bandipur *(Hanchett)*
MADRAS
Kuklur *(Srinivas)* MYSORE
Endavur *(Moffatt)*
TAMILNADU
Kannapuram *(Beck)* Kumbapettai *(Gough)*
KERALA
Pudukkottai *(Dirks)*
Kokkulam *(Dumont)* MADURAI
Terku Vandanam *(Good)*
Mel Ceval *(Reiniche)*

0   miles   200
0   kms   200

Regional Distribution of Collective Village Festivals in India

Holi, Holika's cremation is reenacted, although sometimes other evil beings are said to be burnt and—as with other festivals—many different rationales are given for the whole event.

Holi is also famous as a kind of Hindu saturnalia, when ordinary social mores are ignored as otherwise sober citizens celebrate by drenching each other in colored water or paint, hurling obscenities, and consuming quantities of hashish. The most evocative description of Holi in north India comes from McKim Marriott (1968a), who studied Kishan Garhi village in western Uttar Pradesh. In Kishan Garhi, people claim that Krishna first taught them how to celebrate Holi as a "feast of love" and they do so with passionate exuberance. But they revel according to a precise scheme in which all social norms are reversed: "Each riotous act at Holi implied some opposite, positive rule or fact of everyday social organization in the village" (ibid.: 210). Rich, high-caste farmers find their shins beaten by their laborers' wives; respectable Brahman elders are chased by untouchable latrine-sweepers; a notoriously mean moneylender hears his death announced in parodic song by an ascetic; the anthropologist who asks too many questions is "made to dance in the streets, fluting like Lord Krishna, with a garland of old shoes around his neck" (ibid.: 212). Throughout Kishan Garhi, then, humiliation is piled upon those who rule the roost for the rest of the year.

It is a wonderful scene that Marriott describes, but in most villages the jollity of Holi is not so close to the bone and licensed rebellion is fairly carefully restrained; high-caste landlords may be teased by female relatives, but not chased and abused by untouchable menials. Moreover, later in the day, the antics should always stop, so that order is restored and more conventional celebrations—such as worship of domestic deities and a collective meal—can take their place. Even so, throughout north and central India, temporary reversal is always a central theme in Holi. Moreover, although the north Indian New Year does not officially begin until a fortnight later, Holi can undoubtedly be understood as a new year festival too, at which the old year is symbolically destroyed in the fire to give way to a marginal period of reversal and chaos, before the normal order of things is restored.

SOUTH INDIAN TEMPLE FESTIVALS: A COORG CASE

Now I turn to the comparative ethnography of collective village festivals that will be surveyed in this chapter, and I begin in the south. Although there are several studies of village temple festivals in Tamilnadu, I shall take my principal illustrative example from M. N. Srinivas's monograph on the Coorgs, partly because he directly addresses the problem of village unity.

In Coorg (now in southern Karnataka), the high-ranking, non-Brahman Coorgs, who consider themselves Kshatriyas, form the largest single caste and the main landholding group. They are, in Srinivas's later phrase (1969: 18), the "dominant caste" enjoying preponderant political and economic power at the local level. Coorgs have significant relationships, especially at festivals, with Brahmans, the low-ranking Panikas, the semi-untouchable Medas, and the untouchable Poleyas. The Brahmans act as the Coorgs' priests and at many village deities' temples in Coorg, Brahmans regularly officiate, although they withdraw when animal sacrifices are made. The Panikas play their most important role in Coorg ancestor worship, when they act as oracles of the dead ancestors. The Poleyas (formerly agrestic serfs of the Coorgs) play a major role in some festivals and, with the Medas, usually act as musicians at them. Each village deity's temple has a high-caste headman, generally a Coorg, and a festival is organized by the temple headman in collaboration with the village headman, who also belongs to a high-caste family (Srinivas 1965: 37–43, 181, 185).

In 1941, Srinivas observed the festival celebrated for the single goddess Kundat Bhadrakali of Kuklur village and I draw on his account (ibid.: 187–203), retaining the present tense. The festival lasts for twelve days and occurs during May–June. On the first day, Kuklur villagers gather at Bhadrakali's temple. An oracle, a Coorg man possessed by the goddess, allocates to the various Coorg patrilineal joint families their customary duties at the festival. These duties, which define a "thorough and minute" division of labor, as well as each family's contribution to the festival costs, are clearly laid down. None of these duties belongs to the Brahman temple priest. An elder of the temple headman's family administers the vows to the villagers, who must observe various restrictions on their conduct until the evening of the tenth. For example, they cannot slaughter an animal, break an egg or a coconut, or produce alcoholic drink, and people suffering from the pollution of birth, death, or menstruation are normally not allowed to participate in the festival.

There is relatively little activity during the festival until the eighth and ninth days; the climax is reached on the tenth day. Then, in the afternoon, the villagers go in procession to Bhadrakali's temple, led by Poleya oracles who face the Coorg Bhadrakali oracle and accompanied by bullocks carrying offerings of rice. When the rest of the procession enters the temple, the Poleyas stop outside before a platform bearing images of the "Poleyas' deities"; the latter are distinct from and subordinate to Bhadrakali and are normally worshiped only by Poleyas. The Brahman priest conducts worship inside the temple shrine, while the Bhadrakali oracle, standing behind the shrine, answers questions from anxious devotees who want the goddess's advice. Meanwhile, the Poleya oracles, possessed by their own Poleya deities, are in the temple courtyard and may exorcise evil spirits from people. Their possession ends when the Bhadrakali oracle's does, and offerings are then made to the goddess, before the afternoon's proceedings close with the priest offering food to the devotees.

In the evening, the villagers gather at a threshing yard. Coorg men dance to the music of the Medas and Poleyas, and the animals to be sacrificed are herded together. These include one "village goat" and two "village fowls," offered by the villagers collectively, as well as many sheep, goats, and fowls presented by individuals. A Panika dancer makes a bamboo image of Bhadrakali; he then worships it and kills a chicken, which is cooked in a huge fire burning nearby and offered to the image. Some time later, the Bhadrakali oracle rushes into the threshing yard, stamps on the fire with his bare feet, and touches the goddess's bamboo image, a signal to the Panika to place it on his head. The oracle dashes away to the temple and dances before Bhadrakali's shrine. Three Poleya oracles possessed by the Poleyas' deities have also been waiting in the yard and two of them now run around, while the third groans and writhes on the ground. He stops when the Bhadrakali oracle leaves the yard.

The villagers, driving the votive animals along, then accompany the Panika carrying the goddess's image to the temple. The procession is led by the Poleya oracles who face the rest of the crowd. The Poleyas stay outside the temple, while the other people enter and go round the shrine in a procession headed by the village goat. Now the Bhadrakali oracle dances vigorously before the goddess's shrine, but he does not enter it; only the Brahman priest, as always, can go inside. When the oracle stops dancing, he announces how many of the animals may be sacrificed to the Poleyas' deities in exchange for chickens donated by the Poleyas the day before. The oracle then starts to gash his head with two swords until it is soaked in blood; the Poleya oracles follow suit. This gashing is known as "human sacrifice." When he has finished, the Bhadrakali oracle again answers people's questions, orders the Panika to remove the bamboo image from his head, and drinks consecrated water given to him by the Brahman priest. The priest begs the oracle (goddess) to pardon lapses by the villagers and to leave without causing anyone harm. The oracle then demands that the festival be properly conducted before his possession ceases. The priest closes the shrine door and departs—as do women, children, and many men—before the sacrifices begin. The Panika actually kills the animals: first the village fowls and goat are decapitated, and then the remainder. He takes the heads of the village goat and every fowl as his perquisite. The village goat is killed at the edge of the temple courtyard facing Bhadrakali's shrine and the other goats are killed nearby; fowls and sheep are slaughtered outside the temple. When all the animals are dead, the villagers fall silent for a while to allow the deity to consume their essence in peace. The headless village goat is tied to a tree and left until the twelfth day; the rest of the carcasses are taken to people's homes. The animals offered to the Poleyas' deities are sacrificed separately, presumably by Poleyas themselves.

On the next morning, a Coorg cleanses the temple courtyard of blood-stains; the Brahman priest then purifies the temple. On the final day, the priest performs an elaborate purification ritual in front of the assembled villagers, and the festival accounts are checked before fees are paid to the priests, oracles, cooks, and musicians who took part in the festival. The village goat's carcass is cut down from the tree and cooked with the village fowls to form the heart of a huge meal for all male villagers except the vegetarian Brahmans.

The Division of Ritual Labor

Bhadrakali's festival in Kuklur, despite many distinctive elements, is typical of its kind in south India in a number of important respects. To bring these out clearly, I shall divide my discussion of the festival into three sections, which examine the division of ritual labor, the position of the untouchable Harijans, and the question of sovereignty at the local level. Although I shall draw on Srinivas's analysis, much of my argument depends on later research into other, comparable south Indian festivals, and this will allow the Coorg festival to be situated in a wider regional context.

A Coorg village deity is sometimes the tutelary deity of two or three villages, whose members cooperate at its annual festival (Srinivas 1965: 177–78). In that case, the community concerned is a grouping of villages, rather than only one, but that does not significantly alter the festival's structure. According to Srinivas, in a festival like Bhadrakali's in Kuklur, the unity of the village is particularly expressed by the restrictions that villagers, especially those with ritual duties, observe for its duration. At the assembly on the first day, adult males of all castes publicly accept the ban on killing animals, participation by polluted people, and so on. During some Coorg festivals, the polluted are completely excluded from the village. All such restrictions are partly designed to maintain the settlement's purity and they show, argues Srinivas, that the village is being marked off from others, that each person recognizes a responsibility to the entire village, and that "the unity of the village is projected to the 'mystical' plane and is supported by ritual sanctions" (ibid.: 201).

But this argument looks mainly to the unity of the village as defined in opposition to other settlements. Srinivas merely mentions the need for cooperation among different castes within the village (ibid.: 187, 191), which is actually crucial to Bhadrakali's festival. The key element is the division of ritual labor among the temple and village headmen, personnel of different castes, and the Coorg families, who all have vital and diverse roles in the festival. In fact, in Kuklur, not every resident caste seems to be allocated festival duties and to that extent the division of labor is incomplete. Overall, though, it is through the division of ritual labor that an "organic solidarity," to employ Durkheim's classic phrase, is generated among the various castes and families within the village, as focused on and organized by the headmen. This solidarity has two dimensions: a relatively egalitarian solidarity among the Coorg families and a hierarchical solidarity among the different castes. The festival expresses both the solidarity of the dominant caste and, simultaneously, the unity of the whole village to which the dominant caste belongs. The hierarchical, intercaste solidarity of the village is not undermined by the more egalitarian solidarity of the dominant caste, but is instead built around it.

Other ethnographies show that a comparable division of ritual labor is found at village deities' annual festivals throughout the south, although considerable variation does exist. For example, the relative emphasis given to the solidarity of the dominant caste as opposed to the village (or a set of resident castes) varies from place to place. In Kuklur, the Coorgs' solidarity is relatively strongly stressed in relation to that of the whole village. In Kannapuram in Coimbatore District, Tamilnadu, there is a sharp division between "right-hand" and "left-hand" castes, and the dominant Kavuntar (Goundar) caste belongs to the right-hand section. At the annual temple festival of the village goddess Mariyamman, no left-hand caste has any ritual role, but "each and every locally resident sub-caste of the right division has a ritual duty to perform" (Beck 1972: 118). In Kannapuram, therefore, the Kavuntars' solidarity is subsumed by that of the entire right division, whose members stress their "tradition of brotherhood" (ibid.: 120), while the left division is excluded. Thus the unity of a major section of the village, rather than the whole settlement, is ritually expressed at the festival, although that in turn is consistent with the fact that the village is a far more significant social unit for right-hand than left-hand castes. Quite different is the annual festival in Terku Vandanam in Tirunelveli District. There, "every ritual specialist, craftsman, village servant or official has some particular part to play," which includes special roles for the village officers who are (or were) the former ruler's local representatives (Good 1985: 149–50). In Terku Vandanam, however, no caste is really dominant, and the stress is correspondingly placed on the solidarity of the whole village. These three cases alone show considerable variation, but everywhere in the southern region, the significance for village unity of the division of ritual labor, especially among castes, emerges from the ethnographic evidence.

In addition to the division of ritual labor, the financing of festivals is important. The costs of the Kuklur festival are met by precisely specified contributions from Coorg families, who also make regular payments to the headman of the temple for its upkeep. Between the Coorgs, the division of contributions parallels the division of duties, although members of other castes participating in the festival are not contributors, but recipients of fees for their services (Srinivas 1965: 186, 198). Hence the Coorgs are the sponsors and patrons of the event. This might suggest—were we to follow Louis Dumont's advice (1986: 351) to the letter—that Bhadrakali's festival really belongs to the dominant Coorg caste that pays for it, rather than the village as a whole. But that is not so, because Bhadrakali is plainly conceptualized as a tutelary deity of Kuklur, rather than the Coorgs alone. Her festival is celebrated for the settlement's benefit, as is particularly shown by the principal sacrificial offerings, the village goat and village fowls, which are "subscribed for by the entire village" (Srinivas 1965: 194). That the Coorgs meet most of the expenses reflects their leading role, but the offerings demonstrate that the Kuklur festival is celebrated by and for the whole village community, rather than just the dominant caste.

How festivals are paid for, though, does vary considerably from place to place. At one extreme is Terku Vandanam, where an equal levy is applied to all local households (Good 1985: 149), consistent with the absence of any dominant caste. At the other extreme is Kumbapettai, a Brahman-dominated village in Thanjavur District, whose festival (in the early 1950s) was mainly funded by fines extracted from lower-caste offenders by the Brahmans (Gough 1960: 38). Variations of this kind reflect the relative power and wealth of the dominant caste, if there is one. Even when there is no levy on every household, a festival can still be intended to benefit an entire village.

Sometimes the system of sponsorship found at major urban temples is also employed in village deities' festivals, notably in Pudukkottai District (Dirks 1987: 293–97). In this system, a festival is divided into segments—conventionally defined as the right to bring the deity's image to a hall—which are paid for by the hall-owners. Each day of a ten-day festival, for instance, might be sponsored by the headman, a particular set of families, or a caste. Once again, the festival can be designed to benefit the whole settlement even if some groups do not act as sponsors of any segment.

Finally, I should note that at village festivals offerings are normally presented to the deity, and *prasada* (and honors) received from it, in a sequence that reflects a headman's leading position and, after him, the rank order of other officials, families, or castes. But not infrequently (as I mentioned in chap. 3), disputes over precedence break out, and these can even lead to the foundation of separate temples and festivals, so that any potential village unity is wrecked by factionalism, as in the cases described by Brenda E. F. Beck (1972: 196–202) and Nicholas B. Dirks (1987: 368–70). In such circumstances, unity is at best reestablished in the separated smaller settlements, which each hold their own festivals, whereas once they joined together.

The Position of the Harijans

A crucial restriction on the village's organic solidarity is revealed by the untouchable Harijans' role in local festivals. In Coorg, an assembly like the one on the first day of Bhadrakali's festival in Kuklur occurs on other occasions too. At the harvest festival assembly, which is presumably typical, the village headman addresses the Poleyas as "the one who stays outside [the village]" (Srinivas 1965: 202). Simultaneously including and excluding the Poleya outsiders is a constant feature of Coorg festivals. At one village festival, Poleyas are forbidden to show themselves to high-caste villagers (ibid.: 62, 116), but more usually, as at Bhadrakali's festival, the Poleyas (with the slightly less degraded Medas) must participate in the indispensable role of musicians. They are included in the community as worshipers of Bhadrakali, because they partake of the meat from the village goat and fowls, although they do appear to eat separately (ibid.: 198, 203). At the same time, though, Poleyas are worshiping their own deities outside Bhadrakali's temple, which they are forbidden to enter. Poleyas collect no share of the animals sacrificed to Bhadrakali by individual high-caste people and they keep the animals sacrificed to their deities exclusively for themselves, although the latter animals were given to the Poleyas by the Coorgs in exchange for chickens.

Hence in some contexts, the Poleyas join with the rest of the villagers, the community of Bhadrakali's worshipers, but in other contexts, they are excluded and left to worship their own deities, who are subordinate to the goddess. According to Srinivas, "the position of the Poleyas varies from festival to festival," although overall the "exclusion-aspect" predominates (ibid.: 200). In fact, Srinivas's analysis is rather equivocal. About the harvest festival, for example, he writes that "Every caste in the village co-operates during the harvest festival of Coorgs." But he goes on: "It is the harvest festival of the *Coorgs* alone, and not, for instance, of the Medas or Poleyas." Yet the latter two castes have to participate as musicians and they eat at a harvest-festival meal called "village harmony," even though they sit apart from the Coorgs and others (ibid.: 61–62).

To some extent, there is also a corresponding partial exclusion of the Brahman priests, who take no part in sacrifices to Bhadrakali and do not eat meat at festival meals. But their position is very different from the Harijans' and is primarily explained by the distance from the violent sacrifice that vegetarian Brahmans must maintain to preserve their purity.

The conclusion to be drawn from Srinivas's material, I believe, is that the village's unity, as ritually expressed at a festival, is predominantly a unity of Coorgs and other high-caste people, which leaves out untouchable Poleyas (and semi-untouchable Medas). However, the Poleyas' position as simultaneously included and excluded at festivals raises wider questions that I must now explore.

Since Srinivas wrote about the Coorgs, research has shown that Harijans consistently occupy an ambiguous position at south Indian village deities' festivals. Harijans are widely required to attend as musicians (or in other roles, such as sacrificial slaughterers) and are therefore firmly included in the division of ritual labor. On the other hand, they are rarely incorporated as coequal worshipers of the village deity. Alongside the latter's festival, Harijans generally hold another for their own deity, who is an inferior subordinate of the village deity. Thus the village community—despite its already unegalitarian character—partially excludes the untouchable castes and places them, so to speak, in a lower tier. This is consistent with the Harijans' ambiguous position in the caste system as a whole, for they are both rejected from it as "outcastes" and included by it because their economic and ritual services are required to sustain the system (Deliège 1988: 117).

Partially excluding Harijans from the village community is also more specifically consistent with the assumption that they are not really members of the village, because they "stay outside" it. In south India, Harijans often live in their own colonies or hamlets outside the main settlement inhabited by the higher castes. Thus in Tamilnadu, the Harijan colony or *cheri* is normally separate from the main settlement or *ur*, "village," and the *ur*—to which Harijans do not belong—is distinguished from the *gramam* (*kiramam*; also normally translated as "village"), which generally includes the *cheri* as well (Moffatt 1979: chap. 3; cf. Daniel 1984: chap. 2). In some places, like Endavur village in Chingleput District described by Michael Moffatt, the position is complicated by the existence of separate tutelary deities for the *ur* and *gramam*. Nevertheless, the general pattern is that although Harijans must be incorporated into the complementary relationships of caste, which are manifested in the division of ritual labor at a village festival, the social unit protected by a village deity more or less sharply excludes them. In contrast, it does not exclude Brahmans, who are always members of the *ur*, even when they do not actively participate in a festival involving blood sacrifice.

The unity of the south Indian village is, in an important sense, ritually predicated on the Harijans' exclusion. In her discussion of a village goddess's festival, Beck remarks that Harijans "are often thought to be 'demon-like', locally, because of their low status, generally black skins, and (presumed) sexual prowess" (1981: 125). This stereotype is widely reinforced by the assumption that untouchables are associated with demons and evil spirits, with whom they are supposed to be able to mediate, and all these beings are commonly said to live outside the village. It is true that Harijans can also be called upon to invoke powerful spirits dwelling in the forest, so that they are not linked only to malevolent supernaturals. But whether their role as mediators is evaluated positively or negatively, there is a clear symbolic opposition between, on the one hand, polluted Harijans and evil and wild spirits, who belong to the uncultivated exterior and forested regions beyond the village, and, on the other hand, the pure higher castes and the village deity, who inhabit the civilized center that is the village proper.

In constituting village unity at a temple festival, therefore, the division of ritual labor requires Harijans to participate. In that way, the hierarchical design of the village community is forcefully displayed. Harijans must also be present as symbolic denizens of the exterior in opposition to which the village is represented as a civilized center. From the latter perspective, Harijans are included precisely so that they can be portrayed as excluded, and the ambiguity of their role is intrinsic to the ritualization of village unity.

Plainly, village festivals also reconstruct the social degradation of Harijans in relation to their "civilized," higher-caste neighbors. Not surprisingly, in recent years Harijans and other low castes have quite often refused to take part in village festivals that "reflected their servitude," as has happened in Kumbapettai and other Thanjavur villages since the late 1960s (Gough 1989: 349). The very fact that Harijans are increasingly asserting their right to stay away from collective village festivals is telling evidence about the power of these rituals to construct a hierarchical image of the village community and the higher castes' privileged place within it.

SOVEREIGNTY AND VILLAGE TEMPLE FESTIVALS

To open this discussion of sovereignty at the local level, I start with a well-established conclusion of comparative ethnography. As Dumont puts it, the Indian village is "a reduced version" of the kingdom and "there is a homology between the function of dominance at village level and the royal function at the level of a larger territory: the dominant caste reproduces the royal function at village level" (1970a: 160, 162). The king's counterpart in the village is the headman, who normally belongs to the dominant caste and is its senior representative. In some regions headmen were confirmed in their office or appointed by royal authority. In fact, not all villages have truly dominant castes enjoying preponderant politicoeconomic power and, where they do exist, their power can vary considerably. Furthermore, the term "headman" is a loose one, because authority within the village is often shared or disputed by a number of men and does not carry identical responsibilities everywhere. But despite these qualifications, Dumont does identify a crucial aspect of the relationship between the kingdom and the village, which is fundamental to the following argument.

At the Coorg festival, the village headman, in collaboration with the temple headman, organizes the event. However, the leading ritual role is taken by the Coorg oracle possessed by the goddess, who issues instructions on the conduct of the festival and presides over the sacrifice of the village goat and fowls, although a Panika actually kills them. Among different festivals in different south Indian localities, there is considerable variation in the village headman's rights and responsibilities, as well as the manner in which they are shared with or delegated to others. Consistently, however, headmen or other people acting in their stead publicly preside over festivals, especially when major sacrifices are being offered. In Mel Ceval in Tirunelveli District, the first goat sacrificed to the village goddess Muppidariyamman at her festival is given by the president of the panchayat (local council), the modern equivalent of the traditional headman, "in the name of the village." Mel Ceval affords a particularly clear-cut case, but Marie-Louise Reiniche's argument that the panchayat president assumes the royal function of the *yajamana*, patron of the Vedic sacrifice, and "acts as the representative par excellence of the socioreligious totality of the village" (1979: 157) has wider validity. Most crucially, the headman, as patron of the sacrifice offered to a tutelary deity of the village, acts as a local-level equivalent of the king.

To proceed further, I have to look at the connection between village temple festivals and Navaratri. In the vast majority of south Indian villages (although not all), the principal tutelary deity is a goddess (or a set of goddesses) without any male consort. Her annual festival, in which animal sacrifice is the climax, usually occurs during the hot season, between March and June. As we saw in the preceding chapter, the autumnal Navaratri is (or was) held by kings to commemorate Durga's victory over Mahishasura, the buffalo-demon, as symbolically reenacted in a buffalo sacrifice. Buffalo sacrifice is restricted to goddesses and so important is royal Navaratri that it serves as a kind of paradigm, by reference to which all festivals involving buffalo sacrifice tend to represent a goddess as a multiform of Durga, the slayer of Mahishasura.

Yet the connection between south Indian village goddesses' festivals and Navaratri is rarely explicit on either ritual or mythical planes, as Madeleine Biardeau (1989b) repeatedly shows. Local legends that "explain" festivals in which buffalo or animal sacrifice is (or was) the climax infrequently refer to the *Devimahatmya*, the classical myth of Durga and Mahishasura, and other myths about buffaloes and buffalo-demons are usually more pertinent. Moreover, although buffaloes were the favorite offering to goddesses in much of Karnataka, Andhra Pradesh, and northern Tamilnadu, they were never widely killed in the rest of the Tamil country, where goats or other smaller animals have generally been offered instead. Today, of course, buffalo sacrifice is rare everywhere, although it does occasionally occur (Hiltebeitel 1985).

Nevertheless, as Biardeau (1989b) also demonstrates at length, rituals for the goddess in south India form a unified set of systematic transformations of each other, which crosses, in particular, the boundary between zones where buffalo sacrifice was either prevalent or rare. Furthermore, a mythicoritual complex focused on the goddess and buffalo sacrifice, which integrates a series of important structural relationships, is actually pan-Indian and ancient, since the complex was already extant in the *Mahabharata*; even the goddesses' cult in contemporary southern villages, argues Biardeau (ibid.: 239), could have developed from the epic through a succession of stages. Although the latter claim is controversial, Biardeau is certainly right to stress the permanence and centrality of the link between the goddess and buffalo sacrifice, which underpins all village goddesses' festivals across south India—even when buffaloes are replaced by other sacrificial victims. Calendrically, this link is manifested by equivalence between hot-season festivals for village goddesses and the autumnal Navaratri (ibid.: 280–81, 328–29). Alf Hiltebeitel (1988: 45) is probably correct to argue that the lesser spring Navaratri, retaining the main features of its autumnal counterpart, provides a key model for the village goddesses' festivals.

In her festival, which represents a kind of temporally displaced Navaratri, a tutelary village goddess—perhaps most explicitly in Andhra Pradesh, where buffalo sacrifice was prevalent—is "the exact analogue" of the goddess worshiped by kings at Vijayadashami, and "the ritual replica" of the goddess of the *Devimahatmya* (Biardeau 1989b: 103). More generally, alongside other local deities, the village goddess protects the settlement over which she is sovereign like the royal goddess, in conjunction with the state deity, protects her kingdom. As we have already seen, a village headman assumes the royal function at the local level, so that he presides as patron over sacrifices to the village goddess at her annual festival like the king presides over sacrifices to the royal goddess at Navaratri. Very emphatically therefore, albeit in a "reduced version," sovereignty is symbolically central in village goddesses' festivals just as it is—in a grander and more explicit display—in royal Navaratri. Correspondingly, too, the village is ritually represented as a miniature kingdom recreated through sacrifice. The hierarchical solidarity of the village community constructed at the goddesses' festivals, like the structure of the realm displayed at the court assembly during royal Navaratri, is an ideal representation of ordered human society. This social order is built around the joint sovereignty of the goddess and the "royal" village headman, and is itself constitutive of the universal sociocosmic order.

Crossing some of the same ground as myself in carefully analyzing ethnographic data from Pentakota village in Vishakhapatnam District, coastal Andhra Pradesh, Olivier Herrenschmidt concludes that the concept of village unity is misconceived for various reasons, notably because the several village goddesses' "kingdoms" are not one and the same for all villagers (1989: 165–66; chaps. 4–5 *passim*). The background to Herrenschmidt's argument is Dumont's contention that the village is not in fact a fundamental sociological unit in India. I leave this controversy to one side because Herrenschmidt plainly overstates his case, at least in relation to evidence from south India as a whole. Of course, in all settlements there are many rituals besides the main goddess's annual festival, and we certainly cannot assume that all local people share the same religious outlook. Yet the overall structure of annual temple festivals for south Indian village goddesses is remarkably uniform and they do consistently represent the village as a hierarchically ordered unity in the likeness of a kingdom. For that reason among others, the concept of village unity is not a misconstruction.

In this section, I have shown that a central theme in south Indian villages' collective festivals, as in royal Navaratri and Dasara, is the recreation through sacrifice of the sociocosmic order predicated upon kingship. But finally, a variation in emphasis has to be noted. Biardeau (1989b: 329–30) highlights the contrast between the permanency of villages and the historical fragility of Hindu kingdoms, which she relates to her observation that the goddess worshiped at Navaratri protects the royal clan, not the kingdom itself. But her argument discounts the significance of state deities and it is, I think, more relevant that a village goddess's festival almost always underscores the boundaries around a settlement, because it is celebrated for a tutelary deity who protects her own particular population and territory. In contrast, royal Navaratri and Dasara festivals emphasize the expansiveness of the kingdom, ideally coextensive with India, the world, and the universe. The sovereign domain of a village goddess is represented as localized, whereas a state deity's is ideally universal. But the difference is one of degree, and south Indian village festivals show that the concept of kingship is fundamental, even in a rural settlement far removed from the magnificence of a royal capital.

FESTIVALS IN CENTRAL INDIA

In central India on the Deccan plateau, annual temple festivals for village goddesses are also held, although on a smaller scale than in the south. In this region, Navaratri or Dasara and Holi are celebrated as collective village festivals as well, as they are in much of north India. The clearest ethnographic example of this intermediate pattern, combining character-istically northern and southern festivals, comes from Shamirpet near Hyderabad, described by S. C. Dube.

The festivals of two tutelary village goddesses, Pochamma and Mai-samma, "are observed by the village as a whole" (Dube 1955: 111). Pochamma's festival lasts one day and is held annually in *shravana* (July–August), rather later than the southern hot-season festivals; Mai-samma's lasts three days and is not held every year (ibid.: 111–16). Both events are celebrated at the goddesses' temples and resemble the southern festivals described above. At both, especially Maisamma's, there is a systematic division of ritual labor among the resident castes. At Pochamma's festival, the procession of villagers to the temple is led by the hereditary headman, a member of the dominant Reddi caste (ibid.: 45, 72). All castes in the village take part in making offerings to the god-dess, which are presented to her in order of caste rank. At both festivals, the animals sacrificed include goats and sheep offered by the Golla shep-herd caste on behalf of the entire village. The untouchable Madigas par-ticipate as drummers. During Pochamma's festival, however, Madigas also make offerings to their own Pochamma at her separate shrine. Al-though the Shamirpet festivals are shorter and simpler than their equiva-lents farther south and east, they are clearly of the same kind, because their structure—particularly the division of ritual labor and the role of the headman—is very similar, as too is the ambiguous participation of the Harijans.

As well as these goddesses' festivals, there are just two other events in the annual festival round that bring Shamirpet villagers together. These are Dasara, celebrated on the tenth day after Navaratri (actually observed in Shamirpet by a women's festival for a local goddess), and Holi (ibid.: 103–4, 107–8, 113–14). Dasara is observed by individual families, but also collectively. A Brahman priest worships the headman's ancestral weapons and a flag is hoisted on the village's central flagpost, where peo-ple gather on hearing the Madigas' drumming. A procession, led by the Brahman, the headman, and the village elders, goes to a shrine at which the Brahman worships Durga and some leaves of the *shami* tree. This ritual and the weapon worship plainly replicate a feature of royal Dasara festivals. Then the villagers snatch the leaves and give them away. Part-ners of equal status exchange a few leaves with each other before embrac-ing; but between partners of unequal status, the superior donates some leaves to the inferior, who responds by touching the former's feet or the ground beside them. But despite the many unequal exchanges, "people are expected to forget their quarrels of the last year, and to meet each other in a spirit of friendship" (ibid.: 104). Although ethnographic evi-dence is scanty, the snatching and exchange of leaves, a kind of mock combat, is probably a custom confined to villages in the central region (cf. Hiebert 1971: 151, for Konduru, another village near Hyderabad).

Holi in Shamirpet is marked, as elsewhere, by a huge bonfire, to which people come with offerings. The headman of the Kummari potters' caste makes the offerings to the fire on behalf of all, except the Brahmans and high-ranking Komtis, for whom a Brahman officiates. On the second day of the festival, the main activity is indulgence in the licence typical of Holi: hurling mud and dirt at people, exchanging insults and singing obscene melodies, and throwing colored powders and water at each other. Although most villagers participate in Holi, it is less truly collective than the goddesses' festivals and Dasara because, in particular, the offerings are not from the village as a unit and the village headman has no leading role. Compared with Shamirpet, information on Konduru is slight, although the two villages' festivals appear to share common features (Hiebert 1971: 134, 150–55, 178).

The data from Maharashtra are also scanty, which is unfortunate because there is definite if slight evidence that the state is, as in other respects, a transitional zone between north and south (Biardeau 1984: 8–9). G. S. Ghurye's study of Lonikand (1960) and Henry Orenstein's of Gaon (1965)—both villages near Poona (Pune)—reveal a broadly similar picture, although there certainly are differences. In Lonikand, the village's principal collective temple festival is for the god Mhasoba (the deified buffalo-demon), who serves as a tutelary deity for the settlement, although he is particularly linked to the Mali gardeners' caste. Considerable numbers of goats are sacrificed for the god, an important village deity in Maharashtra who is often the local goddess's subordinate guardian as well. Additionally, at Dasara Mhasoba is taken in procession, accompanied by all the men of Lonikand, to a place beyond its boundaries, where a *shami* tree is planted. The tree is worshiped by the hereditary headman and afterwards, as the procession returns, some of its leaves are placed in every village temple. Finally, the men give leaves to their relatives, friends, and neighbors. At Holi, the main event is the village bonfire, lit by the headman in front of the Maruti (Hanuman) temple, although interestingly he lights it with fire taken from the separate bonfire of the untouchable Mahars (Ghurye 1960: 49–51, 60–61, 65–66). In Gaon, the principal annual festival is for Mariai, the smallpox goddess, and it is primarily concerned with protection of the village as a whole. The people of Gaon also celebrate Dasara, which involves a "mock raiding party" and an exchange of leaves, and Holi, whose high point is the bonfire (Orenstein 1965: 199–202). Both Ghurye and Orenstein imply that there are other festivals in the two villages that are at least partially collective, but neither author is precise. Orenstein says, for example, that Dasara, Holi, and other festivals "helped to produce community integration" (ibid.: 202), but it is unclear whether they are genuinely collective celebrations of or for the village as a whole.

Somewhere in the northern Deccan, across an imprecise dividing line, annual temple festivals of the southern type cease to be celebrated. I need not analyze the central Indian goddesses' festivals to repeat results already set out for the south, and the "northern" festivals also observed in the region will be discussed later.

FESTIVALS IN NORTH INDIA

From north India—mainly Uttar Pradesh and Madhya Pradesh—there are several detailed ethnographic accounts of village ritual, but the places described are scattered across this vast region. That may be why there seems to be more divergence in the pattern of village festivals in the north than the south, although there might be greater consistency within northern subregions that is not revealed by available ethnography. Still, there is a definite division between villages with collective festivals and those without. I shall begin by looking briefly at collective festivals in four villages.

The first is Ramkheri in Madhya Pradesh, which was introduced in chapter 2. In Ramkheri, there are no annual festivals for the village deities—Shakti Mata, Hanuman Kherapati, and the rest—at their temples or shrines. According to Adrian C. Mayer, although Navaratri, Divali, and Holi are also times for observances by individual families and kin groups, they are "the major annual occasions for village gatherings. Almost the whole village assembles in one place; and the headman and other village officials act on behalf of the entire population" (1960: 110). Navaratri and Holi, but less so Divali, are also explicitly "concerned with general village welfare" (ibid.: 106).

Rajputs are the dominant caste in Ramkheri and its three headmen are all Rajputs. In the past, when Ramkheri had a landlord belonging to the Dewas Senior royal family, he "sponsored the major village festivals." At Dasara, all village headmen reaffirmed their links to the state by attending the king's court (ibid.: 96). In Ramkheri itself, the headmen's main duties occur on the final day of Navaratri (ibid.: 100–103), when various rituals are performed, including goat sacrifice at the shrines of Shakti Mata, Hanuman Kherapati, and another goddess. The goat meat is later distributed to all village households. In the course of these rituals, the headmen go to all the shrines in Ramkheri accompanied by the "village servants," who follow their caste occupations as barbers, potters, drummers, and so on; most of these men also have specified duties at village festivals. Although the majority of villagers do not accompany the headmen on their round,

Mayer insists that this "does not alter the fact that the rites are done on behalf of the whole village, and are made at both public shrines and those which may 'belong' to a single unilineal descent group" (ibid.: 101). At Holi, there is the usual ritual at the bonfires (two in Ramkheri), as well as licensed horseplay on the second day. The first "government fire" used to be sponsored by the royal landlord, but now it and the second "village fire" are paid for by the headmen. Their leading role is also marked by the right to light the bonfires (ibid.: 106–8).

Festivals in Ranawaton-ki-Sadri, a Rajput-dominated village in the Udaipur region of Rajasthan described by Brij Raj Chauhan (1967: 104–6, 183–202, 230), have some marked similarities with those in Ramkheri. In Ranawaton-ki-Sadri, there is no annual festival for any of the principal village deities: Lal Mata, the main tutelary goddess, Bhaderiyaji, the main god, or the Devi who is the settlement's founder deity. According to Chauhan, "the most significant festival for the village" is Navaratri, at which most villagers participate. At Navaratri, the village deities are worshiped. On the ninth day the headman inaugurates the sacrifices offered to five of them, starting with Lal Mata and ending with Bhaderiyaji; goats and sheep, but occasionally a buffalo, are killed. The headman belongs to a Rajput clan, related to the Mewar royal family, which granted the village to his ancestors, and the animals are purchased with contributions from villagers on behalf of the whole community. A collective emphasis is also evident at Holi, when the fire is lit by a village official and offerings are made to it by all male residents who have married during the previous year.

The third village, described by D. N. Majumdar, is Mohana, near Lucknow in Uttar Pradesh, where Thakurs are the dominant caste. Bhooian (Bhuiyan)—who is usually a god, but appears to be a goddess in Mohana—has a general protective function and twice a year special worship for her is "organised on a grand scale and all the villagers participate in it." This ritual is held on the initiative of the village panchayat (council) head or another prominent Thakur, who arranges for a collection to be made from each village household (1958: 247–48, 251). Bhooian's worship closely resembles Bhumiya's in Pahansu, a Gujar-dominated village in northwestern Uttar Pradesh, in which most resident castes have prescribed roles in a ritual performed for the village's protection and well-being (Raheja 1988a: 20). In its principal objective and the division of ritual labor, the Pahansu ritual—and probably Mohana's as well—obviously resembles south Indian festivals for tutelary village goddesses, although the latter are far more elaborate. From available ethnography, however, it is unclear how common periodic rituals for the village deity are in north Indian villages, although they certainly do not exist everywhere.

According to Majumdar, Mohana's most important annual festival is Holi. The main event is the bonfire, attended by all villagers except those debarred for ritual reasons. The fire is lit by a man appointed by the village priest. On the next day, the custom of throwing colored water is observed, but mostly in a restrained manner, for people do not try to dye members of higher castes (Majumdar 1958: 260–63). Holi also brings together Thakurs of Mohana and ten other villages, who all claim common descent (ibid.: 8, 22–23). Krishna's birthday in *bhadrapada* (August–September) is also important in Mohana, and is paid for by a subscription levied on all villagers and collected by senior Thakurs. Villagers assemble in front of a swing bearing Krishna's image to sing his praise. The swing is first erected at a Thakur home and then taken to all houses, except those of the untouchable Chamars and three other very low-ranking castes (ibid.: 270–71). During Divali, there is a ritual in which men of every caste take burning maize stalks across the boundary of the village to cleanse it of evil (ibid.: 275–76). Otherwise, no other festival popular in Mohana is concerned with the benefit of the whole community.

Finally, a paragraph on Senapur, near Benares in Uttar Pradesh, which was studied by Jack M. Planalp. There, especially for Thakurs who form the dominant caste, the high point of the festival year is the Ram Lila, when Rama's story is acted out in a twelve-day pageant, with the climax on Dasara. The Thakurs formerly recognized the authority of the king of Benares and claim Rama as a clan ancestor. Organization of the pageant used to be in the hands of a Thakur man who was accepted as the village headman. He was responsible for collecting contributions from all Thakurs and shopkeepers, and he arranged the supply of labor from different castes for an event that is "ideally a cooperative endeavor." By the 1940s, shortly before Planalp's fieldwork, factionalism among the Thakurs had led to the need for improvised arrangements each year (1956: 8, 308–11). Divali is also popular in Senapur, but "there are no formal community-wide activities" (ibid.: 328). At Holi, there used to be "a high level of community enthusiasm and participation" at the bonfire, but this was largely destroyed by a factional split within the village (ibid.: 372–73), an all too common occurrence throughout the country.

Northern and Southern Festivals Compared

This is the appropriate place to draw a comparison between north and south Indian collective festivals. As we have seen, temple festivals in south Indian villages are typically elaborate ritual sequences lasting several days, which focus directly on the settlement's principal tutelary deity, normally a goddess, and celebrate her link with the people and territory she protects and rules over. In the north, even when a village deity or deities are worshiped at a festival like Navaratri, the rituals are less clearly focused and the relationship between the settlement and its divine protectors is more weakly and diffusely expressed.

The division of ritual labor is a very distinctive element in southern festivals, and there is a comparable division at events like Navaratri and Holi in both central and north Indian villages. For example, in Ramkheri, the village servants' various duties at festivals are laid down, and in some other villages too, specific ritual tasks are assigned to people of particular castes. Yet in general, the division of ritual labor is less elaborate in the north than the south. Even Gloria G. Raheja's information from Pahansu, which is not echoed in other ethnographies, testifies to nothing as complex as the division of ritual labor at Bhadrakali's festival in Kuklur, which typifies the southern pattern. As a result, even when northern collective festivals do display an interdependent structure of caste relationships (or elements of one), they do so less fully than their southern counterparts, so that the hierarchical solidarity of the village community is constructed in a less dramatic form.

In the north, too, the partial exclusion of Harijans is reported and there are some vivid examples, such as the failure to take Krishna's swing to Chamar homes in Mohana. But in northern villages, it is more a matter of marginality than ambiguity, which is consistent with the rarity of completely separate Harijan colonies outside the south. The complex design that requires Harijans to be included, so that they can simultaneously be represented as partially excluded—vital to the ritual construction of village unity in the south—is scarcely visible in any northern festival.

Finally, let us consider the question of local-level sovereignty in northern festivals. In Ramkheri and Ranawaton-ki-Sadri, Navaratri is the most important collective festival and their headmen play vital roles, particularly because they preside over sacrifices to the village deities. In both villages, too, the headmen were formerly connected with the respective kings of Dewas Senior and Mewar, who presided as sacrificial patrons at their royal Navaratri festivals—grander in Mewar and humbler in Dewas. Navaratri in Ramkheri and Ranawaton-ki-Sadri are clearly small-scale versions of their royal counterparts, at which the headmen assume the king's function at the village level. In Shamirpet, Dasara rather than Navaratri is celebrated, but one key element is the headman's worship of his weapons and the *shami*-tree ritual. These rituals, like similar ones in Lonikand and Gaon, plainly show how local Dasara festivals imitate the royal event. A similar conclusion holds for Senapur, whose unofficial Thakur headman organized the Ram Lila pageant like a miniature version of the grand Ram Lila held by the king of Benares, about twenty-five miles away.

Thus in each of the above villages, the principal collective festival is, more or less patently, a small-scale replica of the royal festivals discussed in the previous chapter. In each locality, moreover, the headman takes on a royal role at the village level. There are therefore obvious parallels with south Indian temple festivals; like them, the northern festivals—most sharply in Ramkheri and Ranawaton-ki-Sadri—ritually express the village deities' sovereignty and, more generally, portray the hierarchical solidarity of the village community as continuous with a wider universal order predicated on kingship. Once again, though, the northern festivals do so less emphatically, because they are not as elaborate or clearly focused as those in the south.

In Mohana, on the other hand, Dasara is a relatively minor event and the Ram Lila is not held (Majumdar 1958: 272–73). Without better ethnographic coverage, we cannot tell whether Mohana is exceptional, but in any case Holi is its principal collective festival. The celebration of Holi, ignored in the south, is a distinguishing feature of the northern pattern; it is commonly a collective festival, if normally not the most important one, throughout north and central India. As we saw earlier in this chapter, Holi is in part a new year festival at which the old year is consumed in the flames, before order is reestablished after a marginal period of social reversal and anarchy. In fact, in Mohana, as in most villages, Holi's licensed horseplay is circumscribed by the rules of caste and seniority, so that reversal and anarchy are strictly controlled. Nonetheless, the collective celebration of Holi—which may be led by the village headman, as in Ramkheri—is yet another kind of ritual recreation of hierarchical solidarity out of chaos. In this crucial respect, Holi mirrors Navaratri (Dasara, Ram Lila), even though it lacks any ostensible connection with kingship, sacrifice, or warfare. But it is certainly significant that the same pair of festivals, Navaratri and Holi, close to the autumn and spring equinoxes, respectively, consistently recur as the two principal occasions for ritually constructing hierarchical village unity in the north Indian pattern. To claim that Holi is a "royal" festival as well would undoubtedly be wrong. Yet there are real parallels between Holi and Navaratri, and the expression of village unity at collective festivals, however transformed, is never entirely divorced from the idea that it is built around the deities' sovereignty.

VILLAGES WITHOUT COLLECTIVE FESTIVALS

Finally, I turn to villages with no collective festivals at all. As is common with negative findings, assessing the evidence can be difficult, since an author's failure to mention an event does not prove its absence. There are, however, at least four ethnographic accounts that definitely show that no collective village festivals are held. Because the data are being quoted only to support a negative finding, I shall summarize the four cases very briefly.

The first is the Jat-dominated village of Rampur, near Delhi, described by Oscar Lewis. Rampur's annual festivals tend to be mainly family concerns observed by women (1958: 237–38), which appears to be common in this region. Navaratri is a good example and at it there is no collective village-wide participation (ibid.: 215–17). At Holi, there is a village bonfire, but Lewis says nothing about any ritual expression of village unity, and most of the licensed horseplay is confined to familial groupings (ibid.: 229–33). From his detailed account of the annual cycle (ibid.: chap. 6), we can confidently conclude that Rampur has no collective village festival.

In Kishan Garhi in western Uttar Pradesh, which is dominated by Jats and Brahmans (although the former were the original village landlords), the picture is not very different. According to Marriott, "Social relationships concerned with religion in Kishan Garhi are fragmented to an extreme point." There is no temple for the whole village and most festivals are observed separately by individual families (1969: 175). The brief outline of Navaratri (ibid.: 200–201) shows that it closely resembles the event in Rampur. Unlike Rampur and many other places, Kishan Garhi's Holi festival is a truly saturnalian occasion, when insults and humiliations are traded across the whole village. Once again, though, there is no real expression of village solidarity at this festival (Marriott 1968a).

Badipur is a village in Haryana where Jats are the largest and most powerful caste, although they do not enjoy decisive dominance. Badipur's religious life, according to D. B. Miller, is much the same as in Rampur and Kishan Garhi, and his list of local festivals suggests that none of them brings together the whole community (1975: 50–52). In describing Holi, Miller (1973) remarks on Badipur's lack of unity and shows how the licensed rebelliousness, much less widespread than in Kishan Garhi, mainly consists of mock battles among people in separate neighborhoods within the village.

In Karimpur in western Uttar Pradesh, there are some slight variations. In the 1920s, Karimpur was studied by William H. Wiser, who investigated the hereditary ties between patrons (*jajman*), mostly from the dominant Brahman and Kacchi farmer castes, and their mainly lower-caste clients (*kamin*) (Wiser 1969). Four decades later, reports Susan S. Wadley (1975: 21), many of the old patron-client relationships had broken down, but at Divali the "complete circle of *jajman-kamin* ties," even "old or almost nonexistent" ones, is recognized through the distribution of food by patrons to clients (ibid.: 169). A similar custom is observed at Holi, when there is also extensive visiting and each man should go to every house in the settlement. On the second day, there is fairly restrained throwing of colors. The visiting custom does indicate a limited measure of village unity, and the gifts from patrons to clients—of which a bare residue also survives at the Tij festival in Rampur (Lewis 1958: 207)—are at least evidence of a network of interhousehold ties. In the 1960s, Karimpur acquired three new temples; one is open to all villagers, but it is seldom visited and has little significance for the settlement as a whole (Wiser and Wiser 1971: 257–58). In some years, men in Karimpur worship the goddess to rid the entire community of illness (Wadley 1975: 165), but otherwise there is no collective festival for the whole village. Karimpur has three separate Holi bonfires, which partly reflects the strength of two well-established Brahman factions and a third one dominated by Kacchis (ibid.: 172–74, 179).

The four villages just described are all fairly close to Delhi, although Pahansu (Raheja 1988a), which has a collective ritual for its village deity, is also quite near the capital city. Further, Karimpur does have some minimal collective rituals and factional fission is the immediate reason for its three Holi fires. Hence we cannot conclude that villages without any collective festivals are necessarily typical in western Uttar Pradesh and the Delhi region, and without more data the geographical distribution of such villages cannot be accurately mapped. On the other hand, the villages near Delhi that lack collective festivals obviously differ from the others described in this chapter, and some discussion of this fact is required.

Collective festivals, I have argued, ritually express village unity. One could imagine a case in which the solidarity projected as an ideal in a collective festival was a mere mirage, because fragmentation and dissension prevailed in all other spheres of village life. In fact, Srinivas's discussion of Coorg villages (1965: 60–65), Mayer's of Ramkheri (1960: 132–47), and most other ethnographies quoted in this chapter, show that a web of social relationships within the village, as well as relative separation from other settlements, do form the basis for a real degree of communal unity, albeit one qualified by internal divisions and external linkages. And yet, even in a village without collective festivals, the picture hardly differs. Of Kishan Garhi, Marriott writes: "Viewed as a society, as an economy, as a church, or as a polity, this little community has no close coherence or well-bounded physical locus" (1969: 175). Nonetheless, the village still "has a definable structure" and "is conceptually a vivid entity" (ibid.: 176) as expressed, for instance, by the ubiquitous north Indian notion that it is a fictional kin group (ibid.: 177–78). There is little here to suggest that village unity, along any dimension, is significantly weaker in Kishan Garhi, which has no collective festivals, than it is in, say, Ramkheri.

However, Kishan Garhi (ibid.: 175)—like Rampur (Lewis 1958: chap. 4), Badipur (D. B. Miller 1975: 116–19), and Karimpur (Wadley 1975: 19–21)—is characterized by persistent factional division within the leading castes. Factionalism may be more endemic in western Uttar Pradesh and the Delhi area than elsewhere, and this could explain why some villages in that region have no collective festivals. Yet it is by no means certain that factionalism is abnormally severe in this corner of India— even if Lewis's Rampur monograph (1958: chap. 4) does contain the first major study of the phenomenon—and collective festivals can survive factionalism anyway, as Mohana demonstrates (Majumdar 1958: 21–26, 86–92). Conceivably, a particular combination of interrelated factors— such as chronic factionalism, the dynamics of leadership within dominant castes and their constituent kin groups, and distinctive forms of "joint-village" land tenure—might account for the absence of collective festivals in some north Indian villages. But if this is so, the critical combination remains obscure.

Perhaps more relevant is that none of the four villages near Delhi has been part of or close to a Hindu kingdom for many centuries. The case of Shamirpet, whose headman was officially confirmed in office by the former Muslim government of Hyderabad, shows that the religion of the state need not affect his role at Hindu festivals. However, the great Mughal empire ruled from Delhi and Agra, especially under Aurangzeb in the second half of the seventeenth century, became vigorously Islamic in its policies, whereas Hyderabad, one of the empire's successor states, was generally accommodating toward its Hindu subjects. In the Delhi region, therefore, the distinctive symbols of Hindu kingship, as displayed in royal rituals, may have been more fully extinguished than almost anywhere else in India. If this hypothesis is valid, the idea of the headman as a Hindu king in miniature could have lost its vitality, at least among castes lacking self-consciously royal traditions like the Gujars of Pahansu (Raheja 1988a: 1–3, 21–23). Without a royal headman, collective village festivals make no social and cultural sense, and that may be one major reason for their absence in some villages near Delhi.

KINGSHIP AND THE VILLAGE

In conclusion, I return to the villages with collective festivals. These, as we have seen, take alternative forms: annual temple festivals for a tutelary deity, normally the village goddess, in the southern pattern, and Navaratri (or Dasara or the Ram Lila) and Holi in the northern pattern. Why this difference exists is puzzling, but I start with the fact that southern festivals do indeed take place at temples.

The landscape of south India is covered with built stone temples and many villages contain several, including the one dedicated to the principal village deity. In north Indian villages, temples are much less common and are usually cruder buildings, if they exist at all. In medieval south India, argues Burton Stein (1980: 24), "kings were essentially ritual figures." The growth of "ritual kingship" from the sixth century on was closely associated with the construction of temples, not only in royal capitals and towns, but also in rural settlements. This in turn stimulated new and more complicated temple-centered forms of ritual, including elaborate festivals. During the eleventh and twelfth centuries, when the Chola Empire based in Thanjavur was at its height, and especially after the rise of the Vijayanagara Empire from the late fourteenth century, the building of large temples continued apace and their rituals grew more and more spectacular.

The process was furthered in Vijayanagara's successor regimes, such as the Nayaka kingdom of Madurai (sixteenth to eighteenth centuries). Even in a small kingdom like Pudukkottai (founded in the late seventeenth century), temple-based religion played a prominent part in the institution of kingship, so that the state contained many local temples supported by royal grants (Dirks 1987: chap. 4). In his analysis of Pudukkottai, Dirks particularly focuses on temple "shares" and "honors." Yet "Service to the temple was in many respects structurally equivalent to service to the village community" (ibid.: 121). This statement, made when discussing land grants, also holds good for service to the temple and its deity given in the form of ritual labor at village temple festivals throughout south India, because the division of ritual labor, as we have seen, is ideally consonant with the wider division of labor by caste and office in the settlement as a whole. More generally, historical work by Dirks, Stein, and others gives us good reason to think that the intertwined history of kingship and temples in south India is one decisive reason for the prominence in southern villages of collective temple festivals in which sovereignty is a central theme. In the north, however, especially in the Hindi-speaking region—partly because of Muslim power and partly for other reasons—temple-centered ritual kingship never developed on the scale found in the south from the medieval era on.

Plainly, this is an incomplete argument. It neither explains why southern collective festivals are typically celebrated in the hot season for village goddesses, nor why Navaratri, the great royal festival of Vijayanagara and its Hindu successor states, did not become a major autumnal festival at village goddess temples in the south. Nor yet does it explain why northern collective festivals actually are mainly celebrations of Navaratri (Dasara, Ram Lila) and Holi. Some tentative, partial answers to these difficult questions can be found in the literature, notably Biardeau

(1989b: 143, 299–305), but since their evaluation would demand a long digression, I shall leave them aside.

Let me close instead with a few general remarks. My analysis of the differences between southern and northern collective festivals shows that the ritual expression and construction of an ideal, hierarchical village unity are more emphatically displayed in the south. This cannot be plausibly explained by regional variations in village social and cultural organization, and southern villages are not in reality any more integrated than those in the north. Rather, the north-south contrast is an indirect product of the historical development of ritual kingship and temple-centered Hinduism in the south. Hence the force with which the village community's hierarchical solidarity is ritually constituted in south India has to be understood in relation to Hindu kingship at the state level. In recent years, historians in particular have shown anthropologists how local political and economic systems have responded over time to the downward pressure exerted by greater polities. Strong, centralized kingdoms, for example, could extract more land revenue from villages than weak ones, and that had a significant impact on the power of village magnates, the wealth of dominant castes, or the degree of stratification within the local community. My analysis in this chapter suggests that the state's impact on the village was crucial in the religious domain as well.

More generally, we have seen that through the ritual construction of an ideal of village unity in collective festivals, the Indian village is represented as a miniature Hindu kingdom. Thus the concept and institution of kingship play a vital role, even in villages that are now far removed in time and space from royal power and authority. In the preceding chapter, I explored some of the reasons why kingship remains so pivotal for Hindus in modern India, despite the constitutional extinction of the maharajas. Now we can see that the festivals celebrated in villages, more or less forcefully, also help to keep kingship alive by reaffirming its importance for the relationship between deities and people within an ordered world.

Chapter 7

DEVOTIONALIST MOVEMENTS

THE *GITAGOVINDA* is a dramatic lyrical poem in Sanskrit, composed during the twelfth century by Jayadeva, who is believed to have been born into a Bengali Brahman family. The poem celebrates the love between Krishna—the beautiful, blue-skinned flute-player—and Radha—his delightful favorite among the cowherdesses (*gopi*)—by tracing its course from their first encounter when the god danced with all the girls in the forest, through the anguish and jealousy caused by Krishna's inconstancy, to the bliss of their final union. In the twenty-first of its twenty-four songs, Radha (also addressed as Padmavati and Shri, i.e., Lakshmi) is called to satisfy the longing of Krishna/Madhava (also Mura's enemy) for her:

Revel in wild luxury on the sweet thicket floor!
Your laughing face begs ardently for his love.
   Radha, enter Madhava's intimate world!

Revel in a thick bed of red petals plucked as offerings!
Strings of pearls are quivering on your rounded breasts.
   Radha, enter Madhava's intimate world!

Revel in a bright retreat heaped with flowers!
Your tender body is flowering.
   Radha, enter Madhava's intimate world!

Revel in the fragrant chill of gusting sandal-forest winds!
Your sensual singing captures the mood of love.
   Radha, enter Madhava's intimate world!

Revel where swarming bees drunk on honey buzz soft tones!
Your emotion is rich in the mood of love.
   Radha, enter Madhava's intimate world!

Revel where cries of flocking cuckoos sweetly sound!
Your teeth glow like seeds of ripe pomegranate.
   Radha, enter Madhava's intimate world!

Revel in tangles of new shoots growing on creeping vines!
Your voluptuous hips have languished too long.
   Radha, enter Madhava's intimate world!

Consecrate your joyful union with Padmavati!
Enemy of Mura, grant a hundred holy blessings
While poet-king Jayadeva is singing!
  Radha, enter Madhava's intimate world!

> Bearing you in his mind so long
> Has wearied him, inflamed with love.
> He longs to drink your sweet berry lips' nectar.
> Ornament his body with yours now!
> He worships your lotus feet—a slave bought
> With Shri's flashing glance. Why are you afraid?
>   (B. S. Miller 1977: 118–19 [diacritics omitted])

This song exemplifies the *Gitagovinda*'s open eroticism, in which "intense earthly passion" is used "to express the complexities of divine and human love" (ibid.: ix). Radha first emerged as Krishna's true lover in the *Gitagovinda*, and in the centuries since its composition, the intense passion of their love has captured the Hindu imagination.

DEVOTIONALISM AND ITS PLACE IN HINDUISM

Devotionalism is the form of Hinduism in which devotion (*bhakti*) to the deity is accorded the greatest value. Such devotion is archetypally a personal emotion felt toward a particular chosen deity. Devotionalism is not always characterized by eroticism; nor is the erotic mood in Hinduism confined to its devotionalist stream. But for many Hindus, Radha is the perfect devotee of god and her sexual love for Krishna is the perfect expression of devotion. In the *Gitagovinda*, notes Barbara S. Miller,

> Radha is neither a wife nor a worshipping rustic playmate. She is an intense, solitary, proud female who complements and reflects the mood of Krishna's passion. She is Krishna's partner in a secret and exclusive love, contrasted in the poem with the circular *rasa* dance Krishna performs with the entire group of cowherdesses. (Ibid.: 26 [diacritics omitted])

In the tradition that has grown up around Radha and Krishna, their love is normally understood to be "secret" because, in part, it is adulterous. Radha (like the other young women) left her husband when called to dance by Krishna's seductive flute. Moreover, since Radha belongs to the low caste of cowherds and Krishna, although reared by cowherds, was born a Kshatriya prince, their affair is ambiguously cross-caste as well. And their love remains secret, erotic, and not publicly sealed by marriage, because marriage in Hindu society is an arranged union subject to rules of caste endogamy, and inseparable from social and economic rights and responsibilities that would compromise Radha and Krishna's unconstrained passion. Furthermore, marriage implies the husband's authority over his wife, and the wife's adoration of her husband as a god, upon whose feet she lays her head. But Radha does not always do that; as the last verse of the *Gitagovinda*'s twenty-first song says, Krishna worships Radha's feet and earlier—in a couplet of the nineteenth song (ibid.: 113) said to have been written by Krishna himself (ibid.: 3–4)—he had entreated her to place her foot upon his head. Thus Krishna is Radha's lord, but she is also his, and their love denies the inequality of marriage, conventionally symbolized by Lakshmi faithfully worshiping at the feet of her husband Vishnu. Because Radha is also the perfect devotee, however, worshipers of Krishna whose love matches hers can potentially attain equality with their god as well and even bind him with their love. So in devotionalism the deity can come to need the devotees' love, so that the apparent subversion of hierarchical Hindu norms—already displayed by Radha and Krishna's secret love—proceeds still further.

Devotionalism, then, looks like a revolutionary negation of Hinduism itself, and this indeed is how it is sometimes portrayed. In proclaiming that a loving and submissive personal devotion to god has the highest value, *bhakti* is elevated above contemplative knowledge (*jnana*) and action (*karma*), including ritual action; *bhakti* is the path that brings a person closest to the divine presence and leads most surely to liberation (*moksha*) from the cycle of rebirth, commonly portrayed in devotionalism as entry into heaven to rest eternally at the deity's feet. The Vedic knowledge monopolized by Brahmans and the meditative wisdom of ascetic renouncers, as well as the rituals performed by priests, are worthless compared with true devotion. Moreover, true devotion can be felt by anyone—male or female, high or low, rich or poor, learned or illiterate—without renouncing the world, so that the male Brahmans' claim to privileged access to the divine and to potential liberation through renunciation is subverted. According to a common devotionalist formula, true Brahmanhood is achieved by devotion to god, not given by birth.

Nothing in this picture of devotionalism is wrong, but it is one-sided. For example, the Virashaiva (Lingayat) poets, who wrote in Kannada between the tenth and twelfth centuries about their total devotion to Shiva, did protest; classical belief systems, social customs and superstitions, image worship, the caste system, Vedic sacrifice, and animal sacrifice to village deities were all "fiercely questioned and ridiculed" (Ramanujan 1973: 30). On the other hand, their predecessors, the Tamil poets who extolled devotion to either Vishnu or Shiva between the seventh and tenth centuries—and first brought devotionalism into being as a distinctive religious movement—manifested little explicit hostility to Brahman supremacy and traditional ritual. Moreover, Hindus have rarely inferred any clear social message from devotionalism; inasmuch as devotionalism expresses opposition to, say, the caste system, it is generally criticism of caste privilege within religious circles alone. Not until the rise of modern social and religious reformism does the devotionalist ethic come to be widely interpreted as a charter for egalitarianism in society as a whole. In fact, for most of its history and in most of its guises, devotionalism's accommodation to institutionalized inequality has been one of its most significant features, as we shall see in more detail below. All in all, the spread of devotionalist Hinduism owes as much to permeation by hierarchical values, as it does to resistance against them.

Devotionalism is not a kind of Hindu "Protestantism" giving rise to dissenting sects outside mainstream Hinduism. There is, of course, no centralized Hindu church for any such sects to oppose, but more important, the very development of popular theistic Hinduism has been decisively shaped since medieval times by devotionalist beliefs, attitudes, and practices. The latter exist throughout the popular religion at all levels, and virtually every ritual of worship or sacrifice performed for the deities is or may be an expression of devotion, to a greater or lesser extent. On the plane of abstract ideas, the fundamental premise that personal devotion to god is supreme is antithetical to much in Hindu religion and society, but devotionalism is nevertheless a vital, constitutive part of popular Hinduism and a stream that runs all through it. So too, Radha and Krishna's secret love subverts conventional Hindu morality, divine or human, but it also definitively shapes their personalities within the religion, and represents for Hindus one influential model of the ideal relationship between the deities and humanity.

THE RADHA-KRISHNA *BHAJANAS* OF MADRAS

Throughout India, in homes and temples, by rivers or on pilgrimages, one of the most common kinds of devotionalist worship is collective singing of hymns (*bhajana, kirtana*). Many hymns are poems, sung to a musical refrain, which were composed by medieval poets belonging to devotionalist movements in different regions of India. The *Gitagovinda* is often sung in this fashion, particularly in Bengal and Orissa, where it is performed before Jagannatha in his great temple at Puri, but it is also popular in many other parts of India and in Nepal (B. S. Miller 1977: x–xii). When Hindus sing the *Gitagovinda* or other poems about Radha and Krishna, they typically imagine themselves either as Radha addressing Krishna or as her friends encouraging her to love the god. Thus in a Gujarati village, it is common to come across "a group of grizzled and burly Patidar farmers singing of themselves as lovesick shepherdesses." But the subtler implications of assuming a female role to worship Krishna in song trouble nobody and, equally important, none of the poems' true content normally has any practical impact because, as David F. Pocock says (1973: 105), "I never heard anybody suggest that the ritual and caste-transcending message of the *bhajan* should be put into practice." This is a simple but crucial reason why the ostensibly subversive story of Radha and Krishna has not had the revolutionary impact that one might naively expect.

But that, of course, is not the whole story and I shall now look at an ethnographic case described by Milton Singer (1968; 1972: chap. 6). This example is atypical, but it is particularly revealing about how devotionalist worship of Krishna can actually be profoundly supportive of inequality.

The principal activity of Radha-Krishna associations in the south Indian metropolis of Madras is hymn-singing sessions, known by extension as *bhajana*s. Various types of *bhajana* exist, the most important being weekly, monthly, and annual. The core group at a weekly session is a set of neighbors, who belong to one or two households and join with relatives and friends resident nearby. Many such groups do not last long, but those that become established and expand beyond the small neighborhood group are often responsible for organizing the larger monthly and annual events. Singer studied Radha-Krishna devotees living in the Mylapore suburb of Madras. The majority of groups have a mainly middle-class membership, with Smartha Brahmans predominating. Smartha Brahmans, or Aiyars, form the larger of the two great divisions of the Tamil Brahman caste and are often called Shaivas, in opposition to the other division, the Vaishnava Aiyangars. In fact, Smarthas never worship Shiva only, whereas Aiyangars tend to worship Vishnu exclusively, but Smarthas certainly have no established tradition of devotional ritual for Vishnu or, more specifically, Krishna.

A weekly hymn-singing session, lasting a few hours, has a leader, as all *bhajana*s do, and an active core of male devotees, but it is also attended by women and children who sit at the side of the room. Women sometimes organize sessions themselves, but this is uncommon. A weekly *bhajana* begins with the recitation of stanzas in praise of an array of deities and prominent "saints," the poets who are believed to have founded different devotionalist movements or orders since medieval times; the stanzas are followed by a set of songs from the entire canon of Krishnaite devotionalism, and then worship, *puja*, is performed before pictures of Radha and Krishna. After worship, the saints are again praised and there is a long period of hymn singing—first, a song from the *Gitagovinda* and then a series of hymns by various saints in different languages. The *bhajana* closes with more stanzas praising the deities, especially Krishna, and the distribution of food offered during the worship as *prasada*.

A monthly *bhajana* lasts a whole night and includes many hymns and stanzas from the weekly event. Its special feature is songs about the cowherdesses and Krishna, which are dramatized by singing and dancing around a lamp imbued with the god's power. The active male devotees enact the story of Krishna's dalliance in the forest and imagine themselves as girls in his presence, as represented by the lamp. After singing and dancing, each devotee prostrates himself before his fellows, rolls around the lamp to take the dust from their feet, and is then embraced by all other devotees. More hymns close the session and Krishna's power is transferred from the lamp back to his picture.

At an annual *bhajana* the marriage of Radha and Krishna is celebrated. It is an elaborate and well attended event, sometimes closing a ten-day festival of hymn-singing sessions. The wedding mainly follows the standard south Indian Brahman pattern, with male devotees acting out much of the ritual. However, devotionalist songs are added, notably the twenty-second song from the *Gitagovinda*, which ends as follows:

> Her eyes transgressed their bounds—
> Straining to reach beyond her ears,
> They fell on him with trembling pupils.
> When Radha's eyes met her lover,
> Heavy tears of joy
> Fell like streaming sweat.
>
> She neared the edge of his bed,
> Masking her smile by pretending to scratch
> As her friends swarmed outside—
> When she saw her lover's face
> Graced by arrows of Love,
> Even Radha's modesty left in shame.
>
> (B. S. Miller 1977: 121 [diacritics omitted])

The bride and groom attend the wedding in their form as pictures and metal images, and the ritual is conducted before these. Following the wedding, Radha and Krishna are put to bed with lullabies and a curtain is drawn to give them privacy; the twenty-first song from the *Gitagovinda* is sung. After an interval, more songs awaken the bride and groom. Worship is then performed, and food and presents are distributed to devotees, as well as to others in attendance and the poor (Singer 1972: 205–17).

As Singer says, the predilection of Mylapore's middle class for an ostensibly egalitarian and emotional style of religiosity, as well as the Smarthas' dominance of the Radha-Krishna associations, presents an apparent puzzle for which he advances several related solutions (ibid.: 225–29). Devotionalism, Singer suggests, is an "easier path to salvation" for urban, middle-class professionals, whose English education and partly westernized ways have made traditional forms of Hinduism—such as regular domestic and temple worship, or meditation and scriptural study—uncongenial and impractical. It is true that many urbanites throughout India claim that it is hard to continue traditional religious practices in the city. However, Madras Brahmans still hold domestic rituals, attend temples, go on pilgrimages, and visit monasteries (ibid.: 190), none of which suggests that they are significantly less involved in mainstream Hinduism than Tamil Brahmans elsewhere, in smaller towns or villages. Participation in the Radha-Krishna associations has therefore not displaced other styles of religiosity to any marked extent.

In relation to Smartha dominance of the associations, Singer notes that Brahmans in Tamilnadu, especially since independence, have been targets of the state's powerful anti-Brahman political movement. To some extent, by joining a devotionalist movement with a more popular and ecumenical outlook, Smartha and other Brahmans are able to reduce the divisiveness of caste and sectarian differences, so that the "multilingual, multicaste, and multisect *bhajana*" has "an integrative function" (ibid.: 229). But this argument is largely undermined by Singer's evidence that in reality *bhajana* congregations draw in few participants from outside the circle of Brahmans and middle-class professionals, so that they could hardly enhance a sense of ecumenical fellowship with the non-Brahmans who do not come.

The "integrative function" of the *bhajana* associations works, I suggest, in another direction. Similar associations of middle-class Tamils with majority Brahman membership also exist in Delhi. There, according to Andrea M. Singh (1976: 138), "They represent a major avenue for Brahmins in a heterogeneous urban setting to maintain their religious beliefs and practices, and some semblance of ritual purity and superiority." In a socially heterogeneous city, where no stable, local caste structure exists to uphold Brahman prerogatives, the associations help to define and maintain social boundaries, and hence promote an internal solidarity among people whose own identity is perceived to be at risk. By the same token, the associations also serve as means to preserve and reinforce Brahmanical status, at least in their members' eyes, and not to promote cross-caste equality (ibid.: 119–20, 149). In Madras, unlike Delhi, Smartha Brahmans are not immigrants in a distant city. Yet the characteristically urban problem of social boundaries arises in a very similar form. We can therefore conclude that membership of Madras *bhajana* associations is predominantly Brahman and middle-class because that is actually the wish, albeit unvoiced, of the participants. Hence the associations' integrative function has practically nothing to do with reducing social divisiveness, for it is mainly about the self-definition of a preeminently

Brahmanical, professional middle class in the urban milieu. The associations do not stand against the anti-Brahman movement, but against sections of society outside the Brahmanical middle class.

This brings us to the question of egalitarianism in the Radha-Krishna associations. Mylapore is one of Madras's smartest suburbs and most, if not all, of the people attending the *bhajana*s would employ domestic servants, but they are obviously not invited to come. Also, as we have seen, only men are normally active devotees; women and children are spectators from the side. Class and gender inequalities are therefore entrenched at hymn-singing sessions. The silence of Singer's informants about those who are excluded is itself eloquent, and when the ideal of equality is explicitly voiced, it has "little to do with democratic ideology and more to do with *noblesse oblige*" (Singer 1972: 230). This is wonderfully illustrated by one informant—ironically an active worker in the Congress party—who suggested that the democratizing effect of the *bhajana* consists "in the improvement of non-Brahmin speech, attitudes, and behavior that comes from association with Brahmins" (ibid.: 229). When they are apparently demonstrating equality by prostrating round the lamp, taking dust from each others' feet, and mutually embracing, they are—say some devotees—offering respect only to the aspect of divine Krishna present in everyone of them, not to their fellow devotees as such. Other devotees feel that human equality is manifested around the lamp because all are then equal before god. Yet this state never lasts afterwards (ibid.: 230–32). All this evidence reinforces the conclusion that one salient function of the associations in Mylapore is to express Brahmanical middle-class status, and they are definitely not "ritual dramatizations of the ideals of social equality" (ibid.: 239), as Singer supposes.

Lastly, let us look at the associations' most elaborate ritual, Radha and Krishna's wedding at an annual *bhajana*. The idea that Radha is Krishna's wife is current in some Vaishnava devotionalist thinking, but it does not seem to have influenced the Madras associations directly. They take their cue from the myth of the cowherdesses, and devotees openly seek to identify themselves with the girls who are the god's lovers. As we have seen, the *Gitagovinda* songs most prominent at the wedding patently celebrate Radha's sexual love for Krishna, and the lullabies sung when the couple are put to bed make an odd accompaniment to the twenty-first song. But it is the wedding ritual itself that effects the most dramatic transformation, because it changes Radha and Krishna's secret love affair into publicly approved, conventional wedlock. Radha and Krishna, joined in matrimony by south Indian Brahman ritual, can then be portrayed as the ideal Brahman wife and husband: a hierarchical pairing symbolized at *bhajana*s by the wives sitting at the side when their menfolk imitate Radha and her female friends.

In the final analysis, what takes place in Madras is a sort of Brahman-bourgeois *bhakti*, in which the potentially subversive elements of Krishnaite devotionalism lose their cutting edge. Instead, the devotionalist religion of the *bhajana* associations expresses the status and collective identity in the city of their Brahman and middle-class male participants. None of this makes the latters' devotion to Krishna meaningless or inauthentic; nor does it diminish their commitment to a style of worship that certainly does contrast with the emotional self-control and bodily restraint normally practiced by Tamil Brahmans. There are also no grounds for doubting the sincerity of the men who search, like Radha, for union with their chosen god. Sociologically, however, the Madras associations are particularly revealing, because they clearly show how personal devotion to god in *bhakti* ritual can be molded by the caste, class, and gender inequalities of Indian society, so that it takes a form consistent with the participants' social position. Acting out the role of Radha—who has become more like a Brahman wife than a low-caste girl whose feet caress her lover's head—allows middle-class Brahman men to express and reconstruct their own presumed superiority in Madras society.

THE RAMANANDI ORDER

> Monkey, boatman, bear, bird or demon,
>   whichever one you cared for,
> Master, that very one
>   at once became of service;
> The afflicted, orphaned, filthy,
>   wretched, whoever came for refuge,
> Each one you made your own,
>   —such is your kindly nature;
>
> My name was Tulsi, though
>   I was ugly as the hemp-plant,
> I styled myself Das—your slave,
>   and you accepted such a great imposter;
> There is none other master
>   so worthy—son of Dashrath,
> Nor God compassionate,—you alone
>   care for the shame of those who are yours.
>
> (Jordens 1975a: 276 [diacritics omitted])

These are the words addressed to Rama in the *Kavitavali* (Allchin's translation) by Tulsidas (1532–1623), author of the *Ramcharitmanas*, and they epitomize the idea of devotion as love between servant and master.

In this style of *bhakti*, characteristic of Ramaite devotionalism, the mood differs completely from Krishnaite devotionalism in which the perfect devotee is Radha.

One of the most important (and intensively studied) aspects of the development of devotionalism is the emergence of its orders, each traditionally said to have been founded by a "saint," generally known by a conventional title like guru or swami, or more specifically by *sant*. According to received history, the first major saint in the Hindi-speaking region of northern India was Ramananda, who founded the Ramanandi order of Rama's devotees in the fifteenth century. The teachings of Tulsidas, who is believed to have been one of its members, are the main source of the order's theology.

To describe devotionalist movements like the Ramanandis, the term "order" is preferable to the more common term "sect," because devotionalist orders are mostly unlike the dissenting sects opposed to an orthodox church with which writers on Christianity are familiar (van der Veer 1988: 66–70). Both "order" and "sect" roughly translate *sampradaya*, although the Indian word primarily refers to the "tradition" of a movement, rather than the movement itself. Sociologically, the Hindu order is a voluntary association that recruits individual members who affiliate themselves with a personal guru or preceptor already belonging to it.

As Richard Burghart explains (1978b: 125), a candidate for any Hindu order is initiated by receiving the ideally secret ritual formula or *mantra* of the order's deity, who is Rama for Ramanandis. The person who bestows the formula on an initiate is his guru, who in turn received the formula from his guru, and so on back to the order's founder, who had also received it from his guru; from him we eventually reach the beginning when the deity himself first divulged the formula. Structurally, therefore, the order is defined by guru-disciple (*shishya*) links and it is perpetuated by initiating new members, not ascriptively—like a caste—by the birth of children to members. Hence an order can be entirely composed of celibate ascetics, as the Ramanandi order is, although it need not be; many orders do recruit married householders. Even then the latters' children must in principle be initiated to become members, although this is often a mere formality, so that the order effectively reproduces itself like a caste.

The guru is always recognized as superior by disciples whom he initiates, and they conventionally greet him by prostrating at his feet. Hierarchical inequality is therefore embedded within the structure of all devotionalist orders, which can never be fully egalitarian.

The majority of saints who founded devotionalist orders were ascetic renouncers, and even in those that recruit married householders, the order's head and leading gurus are normally ascetics, although there are exceptions such as the Pushti Marga (which I briefly discuss in the next section). The prominence of ascetics among the founders and leaders of orders demonstrates clearly that devotionalism is not a dissenting branch of Hinduism. True, devotionalism ideally enables everyone to achieve closeness to god and liberation from rebirth without renouncing the world, so that householders within caste society, irrespective of their station, can aspire to the renouncer's goals. But rather than belittling the objective of the ascetic renouncer, devotionalism universalizes it, although it generally does so under the inspiration, teaching, and leadership of genuine renouncers, whose exalted position within Hinduism is thereby further consolidated.

In the sixteenth and seventeenth centuries, the Ramanandi order recruited Hindus of both sexes and all castes, including untouchables, and probably some Muslims too. Hence it was exceptionally diverse and this is linked with historical uncertainty about Ramananda himself (Burghart 1978b). Numerous legends of his life have circulated, each explaining in rather different ways his role and relationship with his own guru, who is said to have belonged to the south Indian Shri-Vaishnava order. This order was founded by Ramanuja (died 1137), the great philosophical systematizer of Vaishnava devotionalism in the Tamil country, from whom most Vaishnava gurus claim pupillary descent. Reflecting his disparate life-stories, many "Ramanandas" have been postulated and probably, argues Burghart, a historical Ramananda, founder of the sect, never existed at all. Not until the early part of the twentieth century did a clear-cut spiritual genealogy of guru-disciple links emerge, so that Ramananda's followers "finally affirmed their sectarian independence" and "solved the problem of their history" (ibid.: 133). Peter van der Veer, who has also studied the Ramanandis, points out (1988: 87) that even to speak of specific "foundation" by an individual saint is probably misleading for all older orders, which actually evolved gradually over the centuries. Practically all the information on older orders comes from literature produced by their own members, and all of it is partly mythological, hagiographical, or written to support a particular point of view. That every source insists on a named founder reflects the importance of pupillary descent from an original guru in the Hindu conception of a religious order, but it tells us virtually nothing about the real beginnings.

On the other hand, an order's self-representation, of which its history is a pivotal part, always reflects its need to situate itself in the wider world, not least because it must attract the patronage of the laity and especially, in the past, the kings. Particularly crucial for that self-representation is the order's attitude toward caste hierarchy, as well as its theological outlook. Let us now consider these issues in relation to the Ramanandis in India today. I shall draw on the work of Burghart, who studied Ramanandis in Janakpur in the eastern Tarai of Nepal close to the Bihar border, and van der Veer, who studied them in Ayodhya in Uttar Pradesh. According to legend, Janakpur is Sita's birthplace and the site of her marriage to Rama; Ayodhya is Rama's birthplace and the capital of his kingdom.

The core of the Ramanandi order is a body of ideally celibate, ascetic renouncers, and in principle it recruits from all castes. Today, however, its membership is almost entirely restricted to men. There are a few Ramanandi "nuns" living in communities in Ayodhya, as well as a tiny number of individual Ramanandi female ascetics in centers like Benares, but they are completely marginal figures who are ignored or criticized by the majority of the order's male members (Ojha 1981; van der Veer 1989: 462–63). On recruitment, ascetic initiates take new names. The renouncers forming the core of the order are "supported by a relatively unorganized group of lay disciples," who are also initiated by Ramanandi ascetics of their choice, but do not take new names. Lay disciples do not become celibate and this most clearly marks the laity apart from the core group (van der Veer 1988: 71–74). Lay Ramanandis, and indeed others who are never initiated, are vital to the ascetics, not least because they support the latter economically and make offerings in their temples; even itinerant ascetics often survive by attracting lay supporters (ibid.: 109). Succor from the laity is, of course, invaluable for all ascetic orders, particularly for those without endowed property or other sources of wealth. I should also note that few lay supporters of the Ramanandis (or any other movement) pursue only the religious observances stipulated by the order, so that it is rare for any devotionalist order to be exclusive, in the sense that all its members are solely committed to its doctrine, practice, or leadership.

To return to the Ramanandi ascetics themselves: in their own eyes, according to Burghart, they renounce the transient, material world within which the Hindu is condemned to perpetual rebirth. In order to escape rebirth and "to attain the unconditioned state of eternity," Ramanandis believe that "the individual must become desireless and this necessitates that he undertake a vow of celibacy and leave his family" (Burghart 1983a: 643). But Ramanandis do not, as such, renounce the social world and ignore or oppose the rules of caste. They claim that the mind and body are formed by a person's caste. Because the soul dwells in mind and body until death, caste rules of commensality must be observed within the order. However, because for Ramanandis caste is a matter of minds and bodies, not of social organization, they do not see themselves as members of mundane caste society. On initiation, they abandon performance of their customary caste duties, "for they now claim to be in the service of Lord Ram, not of other men" (ibid.: 644).

Even though they are all renouncers, some Ramanandis emphasize devotion as the path to salvation, whereas others emphasize renunciation itself, although neither section actually denies the value of the other's path. Devotionalist Ramanandis assume the role of Rama's loving servants and mostly live sedentarily in local hermitages and temples; they regard themselves as belonging to a higher grade of ascetic than those committed to the path of renunciation. The latter, who call themselves *tyagi*, literally "renouncer," disagree; they may lead either a sedentary or an itinerant existence, but they go almost naked and smear ash on their bodies, so that they assume the guise of Shiva the great ascetic and resemble the members of Shaiva ascetic orders. This is just one typical instance of how the symbols, values, and doctrines of any one Hindu order tend to be partly borrowed from others, for no order is normally insulated from external influence. Renunciatory Ramanandis refer to devotionalists as "wearers of garments," implying that their renunciation of the world is incomplete, so that as a group they are inferior. In addition, among the renouncers there is a group of "great renouncers," who are invariably wanderers. Since wandering is a clear sign of renunciation and total rejection of the householder's settled life, great renouncers (and all itinerants) claim superiority over sedentary Ramanandis, who remain closer to householders living in mundane society (ibid.: 645–48).

Van der Veer's portrait of the Ramanandis differs in some respects from Burghart's. In Ayodhya, Ramanandi ascetics are divided into three sections: *tyagis*, *nagas*, and *rasiks* (van der Veer 1988: chap. 3). *Tyagis*, as we have seen, are the true renouncers; many, however, are settled in Ayodhya, although wandering is highly esteemed by them. *Nagas* are the so-called fighting ascetics, who emerged out of the larger section of *tyagis*. In the past, armed ascetic bands—who profited greatly from the trading networks they controlled—were a prominent force on the north Indian scene, and although this is no longer so, *nagas* still make up a discrete section of Ayodhya's Ramanandi population. Van der Veer's evidence about the *tyagis* (together with the *nagas*) generally corresponds with Burghart's, and the most interesting variations concern the *rasiks* (ibid.: 159–72).

The *rasiks* pursue the path of "sweet devotion" and I shall refer to them simply as "devotionalists." They form the largest section of Ayodhya's Ramanandis and are entirely sedentary, living in temple-based institutions presided over by an "abbot" who normally owns the temple. The abbot is guru to others resident in his temple and there is a strong emphasis on his worship; in one large temple, a portrait of its founder-guru has even replaced the deities' images. Besides guru-worship, which seems to be an extreme development among Ramanandis, the service of Rama and Sita in the temple is the distinctive feature of *rasik* devotion, which is directed to the divine couple, rather than wholly or primarily to Rama alone as it is by other Ramanandis. In Ramanandi teaching in general, reflecting the writings of Tulsidas, religious servitude is the dominant mood and the idiom is moralistic and unerotic (ibid.: 80–82). Devotionalists, however, have reinterpreted the relationship between Rama and Sita in erotic terms and seek to identify themselves with Sita's female friends, assisting in the love-play of the divine couple. To this end, Rama's most devoted servant Hanuman, normally the paragon of masculine strength, is bizarrely recast as the leading girlfriend. Male devotionalists dress as women during temple worship. Undoubtedly, in another illustration of the Ramanandi order's openness to influence from other movements, this style of worship reflects the impact of Krishnaite eroticism on the normally moralistic devotion to Rama, although transvestite costumes are unusual, even among the most dedicated aspirants to the station of Radha and the cowherdesses.

Among Ramanandi devotionalists, the ideal of celibacy is also weakened to the limit and many enjoy sexual relationships or contract de facto marriages. This may partly reflect the influence of other Vaishnava orders that recruit householders as well as ascetics, but it is also consistent with the devotionalists' overall outlook. After all, these men do not worship only Rama, let alone an ascetic god, but Rama and Sita as a married couple, and they do so in an explicitly sexual idiom.

For devotionalists caste retains considerable significance. In their temples, abbots are always Brahman Ramanandis, priests come only from the "twice-born" higher castes classified as belonging to the first three *varnas*, and members of those castes alone can enter the inner shrines. Thus caste restrictions in Ramanandi temples scarcely differ from those in ordinary Brahmanical ones. Indeed, as a general rule, caste is still a principle of social organization, not just a matter of personal mind and body, among devotionalist Ramanandis. As van der Veer shows, the sedentary life, especially when combined with temple worship, is logically connected with the importance of caste within the order, notably for its devotionalist section; in his words, "The ascriptive caste identity forces itself upon sadhus [ascetics] who live near the watchful householders. Caste plays a role, not only within the order but also in the order's relations with laymen" (ibid.: 179).

Van der Veer suggests that the pressures exerted on Ramanandis by caste ideology grew around the turn of the nineteenth century, when castes tended to become more sharply defined, closed groups in this part of north India. But it is also relevant that Ayodhya is an ancient town within the former kingdom of Awadh (Oudh), which Ramanandis have come to dominate only since the eighteenth century (ibid.: 34–41). Janakpur, near the margins of north Indian Hindu society, was effectively founded by Ramanandis during that century in a relatively unpopulated area (Burghart 1978c). Although Awadh was a Muslim state, its rulers collaborated with Hindus and the impact of caste society on Ramanandis was probably always stronger in Ayodhya than Janakpur. That difference appears to account for much of the variable significance of caste among Ramanandis, as reported by Burghart and van der Veer.

In the scholarly literature, it is often suggested that in the long term an order or sect is transformed into a caste, which has a recognized rank in the local hierarchy and reproduces itself only through the birth of children to its members. The Lingayat or Virashaiva order in Karnataka is frequently cited as a clear example of this process. In fact, as Nicholas J. Bradford's work (1985) among contemporary Lingayats shows, the order's internal structure is not identical to that of ordinary castes of householders, but in any case the Ramanandis' history—like that of many other major devotionalist orders—plainly shows that an order need not become a caste at all.

Equally clearly, though, the data show that the Ramanandi order is not just a loose voluntary association, in which the guru-disciple link defines the only salient asymmetry of rank. The order displays a complex internal structure that is partly determined by its relationship with the caste society of householders. Within the order, there is a division between its two main sections—renouncers and devotionalists—although a common identity as Ramanandis devoted to Rama's service is still acknowledged and no formal schism has occurred. Nonetheless, each section claims superiority over the other, and "great renouncers" assert their primacy within the renunciatory section. Further, among renouncers, caste is a relatively unimportant matter, but for devotionalists, especially the temple-dwelling *rasik*s in Ayodhya whose celibacy is most nearly compromised, it has much the same weight as in the wider society. Consequently, the Ramanandis most attached to the devotionalist path and *bhakti*'s promise of universal salvation—and least impressed by the renouncers' elitist claims—are the ones who discriminate by caste in their temples, where they act out their devotion to Rama and Sita, and the ones most preoccupied by caste ranking within their fold. The devotionalists, who are probably doctrinally closer than the renouncers to Tulsidas's teaching, are the Ramanandis who actually depart further from his adoration of Rama as the lord willing to accept the "afflicted, orphaned, filthy, wretched" as his own. Like Krishna's lovers, Rama's slaves remain unequal in society and in their visible proximity to god.

THE SWAMINARAYAN ORDER

I take refuge in Swaminarayan.

I give over to Swaminayaran my mind, body, wealth and the sins of previous births.

The first of these *mantra*s is received by ascetics on initiation into the Swaminarayan order, and the second has to be chanted by lay members during their initiation (Williams 1984: 97, 136). The two *mantra*s are reworkings of an earlier formula—in which a devotee takes refuge in Lord Krishna and gives over his body, mind, and wealth to the god—that is recited on initiation into the Vallabhacharya order, also known as the Pushti Marga ("path of grace") (Monier-Williams 1974: 137).

The Pushti Marga order, which I briefly describe now, was founded by Vallabha (1479–1531), the leading medieval saint of Krishnaite devotionalism in western India, who exceptionally was not an ascetic renouncer. His younger son, Vitthalnatha, had seven sons and gave each of them an image of Krishna; the one held in highest esteem represents Krishna as Shri Nathji and is installed in the temple at Nathdwara in Rajasthan, the order's principal ritual center. Among Pushti Margis, the images are commonly said to be fully forms of Krishna himself—not merely containers of his power—so that they actually have a sensory response to the offerings and services made during worship (P. J. Bennett 1983: 170–75; 1990: 200–204; Lynch 1988: 189–90). Krishna is mainly worshiped as a boy, and although his romance with Radha and the cowherdesses is a prominent theme much weight is placed on the devotees' maternal love for their childish god, so that his dependence on them is strongly emphasized. Pushti Marga worship also develops very fully the homely aspect of *puja* to which I referred in chapter 3, for in its "jollity"—as Pocock (1973: 114) describes it—the devotee is almost a parent playing with a son at home.

Members of the Pushti Marga say that their own temples are actually the residences of the *goswami*s or "maharajas." The *goswami*s are the descendants, both genealogical and spiritual, of Vitthalnatha's seven sons and they, of course, are also householders, not ascetics. Pushti Marga doctrine regards the *goswami*s, who constitute the order's leadership, as bodily incarnations of Krishna (like Vallabha and Vitthalnatha themselves), and it is to these men as Krishna that devotees dedicate their bodies, minds, and wealth. In 1862, in a notorious libel case heard in the Bombay High Court, it was alleged that the Pushti Marga maharajas exploited their position to obtain sexual gratification from female devotees; the order survived the scandal, although it is still a sensitive topic for members (ibid.: 117). Today, the Pushti Marga is popular and influential in western India, and most of its members live in Gujarat, Rajasthan, and metropolitan Bombay.

The Swaminarayan order did not, as so often claimed, grow up as a reaction to degeneracy among the followers of Vallabha (Williams 1984: 21), and it inherited much from its predecessor. But whereas the initiate into the Pushti Marga still seeks refuge in Krishna, and pledges mind, body, and wealth to Krishna before his incarnation in the *goswami*, the Swaminarayan initiate addresses Swaminarayan himself. This change, as we shall see, is a significant one.

In discussing the Swaminarayan order, I mainly draw on the work of Raymond B. Williams (1984) and David F. Pocock (1973). Sahajanand Swami was born in 1781 and, unlike Ramananda, he certainly was the historical founder of his order. After becoming a wandering renouncer in his youth, Sahajanand joined a group of ascetics in Gujarat headed by one Ramananda (unconnected with the Ramanandis), who claimed spiritual descent from Ramanuja, the south Indian Vaishnava philosopher. Around 1802, Sahajanand succeeded Ramananda as head, although this split the group. Those staying with Sahajanand—himself in the line of descent from Ramanuja—became the original members of the Satsang ("society of the true") or Swaminarayan order. Until the death in 1830 of the founder, now called Swaminarayan, the order grew rapidly, with some two thousand ascetics being initiated. Swaminarayan and his ascetic followers carried out organized preaching tours in the towns and villages of Gujarat, spreading a message that combined Vaishnava devotionalism, puritanical ethical precepts, and severe criticism of animal sacrifice, female infanticide, immolation of widows, and other objectionable customs, which reflected the impact of early reformist thinking on the movement. Swaminarayan also supervised the construction of six large temples, the first in Ahmadabad, central Gujarat's major city (Williams 1984: 8–23).

At first, Swaminarayan administered the new order with the help of his ascetic disciples, but he then appointed householder devotees as administrators, eventually initiating and installing two male members of his family in the position of *acharya* (a near synonym of guru). The *acharya*s were given chief responsibility for administering the order, which was divided into two territorial dioceses. They looked after the temples and their assets, oversaw the welfare of the ascetics, and initiated new members, both ordinary householders who undergo a simple initiation (which mainly consists of reciting the *mantra* quoted above) and ascetics (who take a higher initiation). The *acharya*s, however, were not ascetics and succession to their office runs in the male line of descent. Thus in the Swaminarayan order, like the Pushti Marga, householders do assume the mantle of leadership, although the influence of the ascetics, who often attract their own lay followers, has tended to grow in recent times (ibid.: 25–42).

In 1906, the Swaminarayan order suffered its greatest (but not its first or last) schism, when an ascetic called Yagnapurushdas departed with a few others. Yagnapurushdas disputed the *acharyas*' authority, claiming instead that Swaminarayan had appointed Gunatitanand, one of his close followers, as his successor; from Gunatitanand, Yagnapurushdas traced his pupillary descent. His new group was called the Akshar Purushottam Sanstha and its principal doctrinal innovation was Yagnapurushdas's teaching about the "abode of god" (*akshara*). In other respects, the teaching of the "new school," as Williams aptly calls it, differed little from the "old school." The head of the Sanstha is the spiritual descendant of Yagnapurushdas and is an ascetic. The new school was and is one of the fastest growing orders in contemporary Hinduism, not only in India but also among the many Gujaratis resident overseas (ibid.: 44–55).

To see why the Swaminarayan order has been so successful, and with what results, let us look at some aspects of its organization. Although householders occupy leading positions, the order's core is mainly made up of celibate male ascetics; in the old school, there is also a declining group of female ascetics (ibid.: 100–101). In the old school, male ascetics belong to three ranked classes: initiates from the Brahman, non-Brahman twice-born, and Shudra castes. Harijans, it is claimed, never come forward as initiates. In the new school, the first two classes previously formed only one class, and the distinctions between it and the Shudra class were relatively slight, but in 1981 the Sanstha's leader abolished all caste distinctions among ascetics, except in relation to Harijans (ibid.: 92–94). The ascetics have various duties, particularly priesthood in the order's temples, religious study, and touring the region to preach and collect funds (ibid.: 97–99).

Lay members of the order are expected to commit themselves to its basic moral precepts, some of which explicitly reaffirm caste duties and observances (ibid.: 147). However, it is probably significant that the precepts "allow for, and even encourage, the acquisition and sober use of worldly possessions" (ibid.: 140) by householder devotees, and members "boast that followers of Swaminarayan have a reputation for honesty in business which attracts new business" (ibid.: 141; cf. Pocock 1973: 153). It is difficult to evaluate the connection between economic enterprise and membership of the order without more detailed data on the occupations of lay members, who certainly do include many agriculturalists, industrial workers, and others not engaged in business. Yet it cannot be coincidental that the Swaminarayan order flourishes in a region that has long been a major center of business and trade, both inside India and abroad, where Gujaratis have been continually active as merchants for many centuries. In general terms, the evidence clearly upholds Max Weber's conclusions about the Vaishnava devotionalist "propensities" of the Hindu "commercial stratum" (1978: 48; cf. 1967: 306–18).

In relation to caste, as already suggested, the Swaminarayan order was and is predominantly conservative. Caste divisions are scarcely effaced by membership of the order and Harijans were formerly excluded from Swaminarayan temples. All in all, especially given the ranking of ascetics, caste hierarchy seems to play a greater role in the Swaminarayan order than the Ramanandi, despite Swaminarayan's typical teaching that caste is really a matter of the person's body (Pocock 1973: 147–48; Williams 1984: 147–49). As Pocock explains, the order's conservative attitude has probably contributed to its indubitable success in attracting followers, owing to the paradoxical need to transmit its universalist message in a style that "accommodates the language and values of caste" (1973: 95). At the same time, the order's teaching tends to be unusually exclusive and dogmatic. In particular, it insists upon rigorous vegetarianism and utterly condemns animal sacrifice.

The abandonment of animal sacrifice, and the decline in worship of village goddesses offered it, have been unusually extensive in Gujarat, where Vaishnava devotionalist movements have been powerful vehicles for disseminating modern reformist hostility to sacrifice. The Swaminarayan order has been particularly powerful, and one reason seems to be its exceptional success among the laity. Since its foundation, the order, despite schisms, has been highly efficient in spreading its message. Throughout large parts of Gujarat, Swaminarayan temples are ubiquitous in villages as well as urban areas, and the order also runs schools, colleges, clinics, and libraries. As mentioned above, regular preaching tours have always been carried out by ascetics and money has been collected systematically, especially through the ideal tithe of 10 percent of a devotee's income (5 percent for the poor) that is a feature unique to this order (Williams 1984: 141). Let me give one illustration of the organizational efficiency of the Akshar Purushottam Sanstha, more dynamic than the old school; between 1971 and 1980, its leader is said to have gone to 4,297 towns and villages, visited over 67,000 devotees' homes, consecrated images in seventy-seven new temples, and undertaken three foreign tours (ibid.: 91–92). Both Williams and Pocock show that the Swaminarayan order has won a "grass-roots," lay commitment, particularly from Gujaratis, which is almost certainly unsurpassed—in numbers, dedication, or financial support—by any other devotionalist movement.

Yet from the beginning, the Swaminarayan order, through its reformist moral attitudes toward vegetarianism and animal sacrifice, combined with its conservative adherence to caste norms, has also strongly reinforced Brahmanical mores in Gujarat—even if the latter are actually identified with Vaishya (and Jain) merchant communities as much as Brahmans themselves. Thus Swaminarayan devotionalism is not merely permeated by hierarchical values; it is a powerful and partially modernized organizational expression of them. The order demonstrates very clearly how *bhakti* can be accommodated to institutionalized inequality in Hinduism and Indian society.

THE SAINT AS GOD IN DEVOTIONALIST ORDERS

The Swaminarayan order, as we have seen, has its roots in Krishnaite devotionalism. In general, however, as the initiation *mantras* imply, "most followers believe that Swaminarayan is the single, complete manifestation of Narayana [Vishnu] or the supreme person [Purushottam], and, as such, is superior in power and efficacy to all other manifestations of god, including Rama and Krishna" (Williams 1984: 67). Thus in the order's temples, "Swaminarayan is the focus of the ritual of the fellowship; Krishna, though always present, takes a subordinate position" (ibid.: 83). Swaminarayan, it is said, was god himself and his human form did not diminish his divinity. In the new school, the claim is extended to assert that Swaminarayan is eternally manifest in his "perfect devotee," so that he is also an "abode of god." Gunatitanand was the first perfect devotee, but through the line of succession his status has been assumed by subsequent heads of the Akshar Purushottam Sanstha. Each perfect devotee "is the perfect servant of god, and, as such, he is totally filled with god and therefore worthy of reverence and worship" (ibid.: 75). To summarize the difference, the old school has it that "Swaminarayan is present in the images . . . and in the sacred scriptures which he left," whereas for the new school, "he is primarily present in the person of the guru and also in the images and sacred scriptures" (ibid.: 80–81). In the new school's temples, Gunatitanand's image or picture stands alongside Swaminarayan's in the central position, with his successors (including the current head) at one side; Radha and Krishna are relegated to another shrine (ibid.: 75, 84).

No doubt, as Pocock (1973: 141) remarks, an ordinary member of the order knows little of its theology. Yet in his report of a visit to a major temple dedicated to Vishnu as Lakshminarayana and founded by Swaminarayan himself, it is clear that the devotee accompanying Pocock assumed that Swaminarayan was the focal object of devotion (ibid.: 124), which is precisely the kernel of the order's theology. Thus Swaminarayan, not Vishnu or Krishna, is the order's principal deity. During his lifetime, Swaminarayan was apparently regarded as fully divine by many of his followers (Williams 1984: 65), but for members of the old school today the divine personage has, of course, long been dead. In the new school, on the other hand, the living guru, the current head of the Sanstha, is perceived as divine, as an "abode of god," although he does not claim this on his own behalf (ibid.: 81–82). The new school's doctrine, however, represents a further transformation, whereby a living human being, rather than a dead one, is the leading god (cf. Pocock 1973: 160–63). Within the Swaminarayan order, this difference in attitude toward the divinity of a living person is plainly diacritical.

To place these transformations in context, I shall briefly consider the nature of devotionalist deities and saints. Devotionalism is often described as a monotheistic tendency within Hinduism in the sense that one chosen deity, such as Rama or Krishna, is revered to the virtual exclusion of all others. Devotionalism therefore reconstructs the polytheistic pantheon by elevating a single god (or occasionally goddess), so that others— notably Vishnu, Shiva, and Devi, the goddess—are either identified with him, relegated to the company of his subordinate forms, or simply ignored. Thus, for example, in the *Gitagovinda*, Krishna assumes many of the epithets and associated characteristics otherwise attributed to Vishnu, and is himself praised in the first song through Vishnu's ten incarnations—with Balarama, his elder brother, substituting for Krishna himself (B. S. Miller 1977: 70–71). Vishnu now is Krishna, the supreme god, and Shiva—mentioned only in passing—almost vanishes into insignificance. Radha likewise takes over many of Lakshmi's epithets and characteristics, and other forms of the goddess are unmentioned, although Radha's independent presence clearly qualifies the tendency toward monotheism, because she and Krishna keep their separate identities. In general terms, parallel processes occur for Rama, or other deities such as Shiva, when they become supreme in devotionalist movements.

In these movements, however, the saints' divinity is also important. As we know, the idea that a human being can be a deity or deity's form is universal in Hinduism, but saints, virtually by definition, are always regarded as divine personages by their followers (or even themselves), either when alive or after death. A saint, in Weber's terms (1978: 439), is a "prophet," "a purely individual bearer of charisma," because, despite his spiritual descent from earlier gurus, he displays his divinity and the divine power within himself through his personal qualities and achievements: holy countenance, sublime poetry, inspired teaching, unimpeachable morality, ecstatic visions, extraordinary miracles. Plainly, though, what his followers see, retail, and later elaborate in hagiography is ultimately more important than a saint's real life in constituting his divinity.

Let us now look briefly at some comparative examples. Bengali Vaishnavas worship Chaitanya (1486–1533), the preeminent founder saint of

Krishnaite devotionalism in Bengal, whose image stands in several temples in the town of Nabadwip (Navadvip), his legendary birthplace. Chaitanya is variously revered as the founder of the Gaudiya Vaishnava devotionalist order, as an incarnation of Krishna, as Krishna himself, as Krishna's perfect devotee Radha, and as the combined Radha-Krishna (Morinis 1984: 134–36). Hence Chaitanya is adored as divine, but his exalted status does not displace Krishna from his supremacy. Nabadwip is the Bengali Vaishnavas' most sacred site because the supreme god appeared there, as Chaitanya (ibid.: 122–23). The *goswami*s, who claim descent from close associates of Chaitanya, are the Gaudiya Vaishnava leaders and most of them are not ascetics. They initiate new members and in Nabadwip they are also temple priests (ibid.: 139–45).

In the Pushti Marga, Vallabha and Vitthalnatha are revered much like Chaitanya among the Gaudiya Vaishnavas, although Pushti Marga *goswami*s are identified far more directly than their Gaudiya counterparts as living incarnations of Krishna. Nonetheless, Pushti Marga *goswami*s are perceived as forms of Krishna, who also guard him in his image form in their temples. When devotees worship these men, they do so in order to worship Krishna the god. In one devotionalist Ramanandi temple in Ayodhya, Rama and his wife have been relegated and their images replaced by a guru's picture, but among the majority of Ramanandis, the idea that Ramananda himself was a form of Rama is relatively undeveloped, and Rama (and Sita) unequivocally remain their supreme deities.

A more modern comparison is provided by the Radhasoami movement, which emerged in northwestern India in the early nineteenth century within the devotionalist milieu, although its teaching extols a Supreme Being (*radhaswami*, unconnected with Radha) that is not identified with any specific Hindu deity. The Radhasoami movement has divided many times and one section, the Agra-based Soami Bagh, was studied in Delhi by Lawrence A. Babb (1987). At its religious meetings, devotees bow before a piece of paper on which the footprints of the Soami Bagh's last recognized saint-guru (who died in 1949) are imprinted. Food is also displayed before the paper to be eaten later as the *prasada* of the gurus, "who—although not physically present—symbolically preside over these and similar ceremonies, and are visible in the form of prominently displayed pictures" (ibid.: 62). For these Radhasoamis, the guru is identified as the Supreme Being and is seen as such by enlightened devotees. That the guru cannot now be physically present does not hinder them, since he need not be there to preside over their assemblies. Visions (*darshana*) of their vanished gurus "are greatly valued as signs of grace" by Radhasoamis; at death every true devotee has a vision of his guru (ibid.: 76). Hence for Soami Bagh Radhasoamis, the fact that the last guru is dead does not diminish his presence in the here-and-now, and the distinction between living and dead gurus, so important in the Swaminarayan order, is irrelevant.

What do these attitudes toward the divinity of saints and gurus, living and dead, show? In orders like the Gaudiya Vaishnava or Pushti Marga, the divinized founder saints are worshiped as incarnations of the supreme deity. Even a living Pushti Marga leader is worshiped only because he is a form of Krishna, so that worship is addressed to him as Krishna, as the initiation *mantra* indicates. Krishna, therefore, is not displaced from his phenomenal priority. Among most Ramanandis—given the lesser emphasis on the founder's divinity—Rama's supremacy is still more assured. In the Swaminarayan order, by contrast, there has been been "a reordering of divine beings," in Williams' words (1984: 67), and a divinized human being has displaced the deities, as he also has in the Radhasoami movement. A further reconstruction of the pantheon has occurred, so that a god like Krishna, who was elevated to supremacy by earlier devotionalism, is relegated to become a form of the saint, the supreme deity. Now the neophyte gives over his mind, body, and wealth to his guru as Swaminarayan, not Krishna, and Swaminarayan's divinity is further magnified by his proclaimed capacity to take and cancel human sins as well. When, as in the new school, the fully divine saint lives on, because he is in turn present in his living successor who is god as well, it is only another short step in the same logical progression and yet it also reveals a subtle change.

Devotionalism makes the goals of proximity to the divine and liberation from rebirth accessible to everyone through complete devotion to god. When a saint displaces other deities, however, he becomes the means to devotionalism's ends because he is actually living in the world as god to be worshiped. Moreover, because he is alive and visible, uncertainty about god is dispelled, even though this living god patently possesses human characteristics, mortality included. If a saint's divine presence on earth disappears with his death, his later followers cannot enjoy such certainty about god. For devotees like those belonging to the Swaminarayan new school, no deprivation of this kind occurs. Their guru's sentient existence means that the supreme god can be perpetually seen and adored in the here and now, and this is the changed premise that underlies all worship of living saints whose proclaimed godhead survives death.

THE MODERN "GOD-MEN"

The developments we have just traced in devotionalist movements, which allow the pantheon to be reconstructed and the saint to emerge as god alive on earth, reach their apogee in the phenomenon commonly called—for want of a better phrase—the cult of the "god-man." The first salient

characteristic of god-men, whose prophetic charisma is completely individual, is that their divinity is virtually asserted de novo, without any
systematic attempt to validate the claim by tracing spiritual descent from
a predecessor. This is a clear break from the tradition of older devotionalist orders, for even the head of the Swaminarayan new school ultimately
stands in the line of pupillary succession from Ramanuja, although the
Radhasoami movement (Soami Bagh section) does provide a precedent
for the god-men, because in its teaching the founder "was spiritually autonomous . . . and neither had nor needed a master" (Babb 1987: 20).

The most famous and popular god-man today is Sathya Sai Baba.
Everywhere in India, alongside the popular colored prints of different
deities hanging in homes and shrines, one is likely to see the instantly
recognizable picture of Sai Baba. It shows him, writes Deborah A. Swallow, as "a dark man in an ochre robe, with a round face, crowned with a
mass of black hair"; particularly striking are his "expressive face and
piercing eyes."

> In real life Sathya Sai Baba seems slighter than his representations suggest but
> more dramatic: he moves quietly but swiftly and tends to turn up unexpectedly
> and suddenly. His quick, flexible movements of hand and face contrast with
> periods of absolute immobility when he stares at a spellbound devotee. A fasci-
> nating man, even to non-believers, he is able to hold huge audiences in suspense
> by his continual change of pace—a mood heightened by the expectation that at
> any time he might perform some miracle. (Swallow 1982: 125)

The miracles are the key; as Babb says (1987: 178), they "are crucial
and central to [his] cult." Although sometimes downplayed by apologists
talking to skeptics, there is no doubt that faith in Sai Baba is inextricably
bound up with credence in his miracle-working powers. The range of his
miracles, as attested to by his devotees, is extensive. There are heart-
warming stories, like the one about a skeptical father-to-be praying to Sai
Baba, who then secured the live birth of his baby when the doctors said
that it would be still-born (ibid.: 181–82). And there are crazy yarns, like
the one about the American who tried to photograph Sai Baba with an
empty camera and was immediately given film by the god-man, together
with a cash receipt from the store in an American town where he had
magically flown to make the purchase (Swallow 1982: 130). Most consistently, however, Sai Baba materializes white ash (*vibhuti*)—itself containing wondrous power—from both his person and at a distance, so that it
flows from his pictures on the walls of a New Delhi house, home to a
family of wealthy south Indian Brahmans (Babb 1987: 180).

Sathya Sai Baba was born as Sathya Narayana Raju into a non-
Brahman agricultural caste in an Andhra Pradesh village in 1926. In his
teenage years, after some kind of epileptic or mental crisis, he claimed to

be a reincarnation of a Maharashtrian saint, Sai Baba of Shirdi, whose name he assumed. He attracted a nucleus of followers and by the 1940s, he was well-known in Maharashtra. In the 1950s, he traveled widely across India and his following steadily grew. In 1963, he announced that he was Shiva. By then, the real person at the center of the movement had largely vanished behind the public personality created by himself and his followers, and garnished in numerous hagiographies.

About the event in 1963, the hagiographical accounts say that Sai Baba had a series of seizures and went into a coma lasting several days (Swallow 1982: 129–30, 136–37). Then he was taken into the main hall of his ashram, the center where he resides, and he cured himself. He also declared that he was Shiva:

> This is a sacred day. I am Siva Sakti, born into the gotra [clan] of Bharadwaj [an ancient Brahman sage], according to a boon won by that sage from Siva and Sakti. Sakti herself was born in that gotra of the sage as Sai Baba of Shirdi; Siva and Sakti have incarnated as Myself in his gotra now; Siva will alone incarnate as the third Sai in the same gotra in Mysore state. (Cited in ibid.: 136)

This declaration legitimates Sai Baba as the descendant of a Brahman sage, but it also makes it plain that he has no guru, unlike earlier devotionalist saints. Without mediation, Sai Baba is simply and fully Shiva in his form as united with Shakti, and he is the second of three successive manifestations, the first being Sai Baba of Shirdi. Announcing the third also precludes any claim by a disciple to be his successor as the movement's leader. As Shiva alive on earth, Sai Baba appositely produces an endless supply of the ash that is the god's sacred emblem.

The connection between Sai Baba and devotionalism is clarified by Swallow's comment that he "offers his devotees . . . the traditional *bhakti* resolution to their problems; the chance of salvation while continuing to carry out their worldly duties, if they offer him devotion" (1982: 157). Particularly interesting, though, is that according to both Swallow (ibid.: 152–53) and Babb (1987: 6, 177–78), who worked in Orissa and Delhi, respectively, Sai Baba's following is predominantly drawn from the urban middle class. Exactly the same is true in Sri Lanka, where Sai Baba has also acquired a growing following among the Buddhist urban middle class, who mold him to their religion by claiming that he is a Buddhist god—an incarnation of Maitreya, the next Buddha—or even a Buddha already (Gombrich and Obeyesekere 1988: 53–55). In explaining Sai Baba's appeal to the Indian urban middle class, Swallow says that these people, mainly of high-caste background, feel threatened by a social environment that they can no longer control as once they did, or believe they did. A similar argument is advanced by Sudhir Kakar about Mata Nirmala Devi (Mataji), a "goddess-woman" whose cult is a "steady per-former," although it lags far behind "established enterprises of the first rank," like Sai Baba's (1983: 191–92). Mataji, who is famous as a healer credited with many miraculous cures, also mainly attracts the "newly urbanized, emerging middle classes." Her followers, contends Kakar, typify a general phenomenon, for "this transitional sector of the popula-tion, living in India's towns and metropolitan areas, is the natural reser-voir of the cults" (ibid.: 214), which provide the socially and psychologi-cally uprooted with a new sense of group identity.

To this line of argument, which generally applies to Sri Lanka's urban middle class as well, Babb also adds the suggestion that Sai Baba promises a kind of "re-enchantment of the world" (1987: 200) or, in Richard Gombrich and Gananath Obeyesekere's blunter phrasing, a "remystifica-tion of the world" (1988: 54). In this new world, miracles really happen and are seen to happen by people whose education and urban sophistica-tion make them distrust invisible forces with no scientific credibility. But there is a sociological aspect to miracles as well. A magical, miraculous world need not be renounced as meaningless and this is attractive to peo-ple who are prospering in it; thus miracles indirectly validate the urban middle class's relatively comfortable place within society. Sathya Sai Baba, a deity alive in the here and now, promises by his miracles immedi-ate proximity to god and salvation as well as a sense of justification to men and women who perceive themselves as both well-off and insecure in a rapidly changing and potentially alienating world.

It is important to Sai Baba's appeal as a god-man for the modern age that his divinity does not depend on legitimation through succession from an ancient line of precedent saints and gurus. In that respect, he is di-vorced from Hinduism's (or Buddhism's) medieval past, which is un-attractively anachronistic to so many of his followers. In many ways, however, Sai Baba is still a traditional figure who draws heavily on well-established mythical, ritual, and doctrinal elements within popular Hin-duism. He has a large number of western followers, but they remain a minority and the really innovatory modernists are arguably the god-men who have concentrated their efforts on attracting foreign devotees. Ac-cording to Gita Mehta—in her merciless but penetrating satirical report, *Karma Cola*—a magazine correspondent was told by one modern god-man that "My followers have no time. So I give them instant salvation" (1981: 107). On internal evidence, the speaker was probably the no-torious Bhagwan Rajneesh of Poona (who died in 1990). While he no doubt oversimplified, the remark makes good marketing sense. A self-proclaimed god probably has to supply instant salvation if he wants to attract devotees who see themselves as insecure in another continent and can, if dissatisfied, fly back as quickly as they came.

Sathya Sai Baba and similar god-men or god-women, I conclude, represent Hinduism's latest transformation of divinity, which stems from a devotionalist reordering of the deities consonant with some of the perceived religious needs of modern India's urban middle class (and a section of western society as well). Nevertheless, the tentative character of my argument, as applied to India itself, must be stressed. Despite the size of the god-men's movements, only a minority of the middle class are their disciples, and sound evidence on the religion of the urban working class is all too thin. Moreover, not all Indian urbanites are individualists who have lost their moorings in a society felt to be changing too fast. As we have seen, the middle-class south Indians who join the Radha-Krishna associations in Madras express in their gatherings a new kind of social identity, which tends to reassert their elite status, rather than their anomic rootlessness. Furthermore, a very large proportion of the urban population continues to practice traditional forms of popular Hinduism, both as members of older devotionalist orders and as ordinary worshipers in temples and at home. Despite their popularity, it is unlikely that miracle-working god-men represent the religion's future for most Hindus, although they certainly illustrate one way in which devotionalism, as a stream within Hinduism, adapts to contemporary change in the structure of Indian society.

Chapter 8

DEVOTIONALISM, GODDESSES, AND WOMEN

THE TAMIL solar month of *margali*, from mid-December to mid-January, is the last month in the inauspicious, dark half of the year, the *dakshinayana*. It is said to be the month of pain and suffering, and evil spirits are especially prevalent, particularly in the period just before dawn. Partly for this reason, it is good to express devotion toward the deities in the early hours, and *margali* is also the month that is, more than any other, given over to devotionalist worship in Tamilnadu.

In the city of Madurai, throughout *margali*, all the temples open at about four o'clock in the morning, an hour or two earlier than usual. Most of them are equipped with loudspeakers, which broadcast popular religious music at deafening volume, so that almost everyone—whether they live in the warren of houses in the old city center, the slums at its edge, or the spacious suburbs farther out—is woken up well before dawn for thirty days in succession. For many people, *margali* is therefore tiresome, but the older, pre-electronic custom of singing devotionalist hymns, *bhajanas*, in the very early morning also continues in both temples and homes. In homes, hymn singing is the special preserve of women and girls, and two particular works are favored. One is the *Tiruppavai* ("Sacred lady"), written by Andal, the only woman among the twelve saints of medieval Tamil Vaishnavism, and the other is the *Tiruvembavai* ("Our sacred lady") in conjunction with the *Tiruppalliyelucci* ("Sacred rising from bed"), which were written by Manikkavasagar, one of the four principal saints of Tamil Shaivism in the same period—the seventh to tenth centuries during which devotionalist Hinduism first began to flourish in south India. Andal's hymn and the two by Manikkavasagar each have a total of thirty verses, one to be sung each morning. The hymns about the "sacred lady" both describe the early-morning worship, for Krishna and Shiva respectively, that girls perform as part of a vow that may win them godlike husbands. A prominent theme in *margali*, therefore, is a young woman's search for a perfect husband, although no wedding can actually be held until the inauspicious month is over (Logan 1980: 308–9, 319–21).

On the first morning of *margali*, there is a constant stream of people flowing to Madurai's temples through the chilly darkness, and in the great Minakshi temple the crowd is vast. They come to watch the first period of daily worship, when Minakshi and Sundareshwara are woken in the bedchamber shrine, because *darshana*, a vision of the deities, is especially auspicious at the very beginning of the month. When the worship ends, part of the *prasada* distributed to devotees is milk, and the crush of people hoping to receive a sip is so great that the police have to force them into orderly queues. By dawn, around twenty thousand devotees will have been to the Minakshi temple on this first morning.

To describe all the ritual, so strongly inspired by *bhakti*, that occurs in Madurai during December and January would be impossible. Instead, I shall concentrate on three festivals held in the Minakshi temple, two for Minakshi herself and one for Manikkavasagar. Because the timing of these and other festivals is important—and their names may be confusing—tables 2 and 3 will serve as an aid to memory; more detailed information on timing is provided below when relevant. Through analysis of the three temple festivals—an intensive approach that contrasts with the wider perspective of the previous chapter—I shall show how devotionalism is firmly embedded within the ritual complex of Tamil Hinduism and gives special prominence to goddesses and women.

The Anointment of the Goddess Minakshi and Her Golden Swing

The most elaborate of the three festivals, which is celebrated for Minakshi, is an exceptionally charming one, which lasts nine days and is known as Ennai Kappu, "Anointment or bathing with oil." Fixed like most Tamil temple festivals by a *nakshatra* ("star") within a solar month, Ennai Kappu begins ten days before the day in *margali* on which *ardra nakshatra* is current. In *margali*, *ardra nakshatra* always coincides with full moon, or the day next to it. (For more information on solar months and *nakshatra*s, see the appendix.)

By a curious chance, the great Sanskritist M. Monier-Williams happened on Ennai Kappu—which he refers to as Tailotsava, "Oil festival"—when he visited Madurai in the 1870s, and his description (1974: 442–43) shows that it had not changed much by 1976, when I saw it, although the processions had declined in grandeur. Despite his deep knowledge of Hinduism, this festival provoked in Monier-Williams one of his evangelical outbursts. "No sight I witnessed in India made me more sick at heart than this," he wrote; it was a "sad example" of the idolatry "enslaving" the Hindu masses and "disfiguring" the country "with hideous images and practices unsanctioned even by their own most ancient sacred works"—presumably a reference to the Vedas (cf. ibid.: 18). Hideousness is a matter of taste, but Monier-Williams certainly let his prejudices get the better of him in Madurai, because the Ennai Kappu festival—firmly set in a devotionalist milieu—is actually a distillation

TABLE 2
Select List of Festivals in Madurai in *Margali* and Other Months

Month	Minakshi Temple	Vishnu Temples	Hindu Homes
chittirai (April–May)	Chittirai (Minakshi-Sundareshwara)		
ani (June–July)	Unjal (Minakshi-Sundareshwara) Uttiram (Nataraja) Manikkavasagar's *nakshatra*		
adi (July–August)	Mulaikkottu (Minakshi) Puram (Minakshi)	Puram (Bhudevi)	Adipperukku
purattasi (September–October)	Navaratri (Minakshi)		
aippasi (October–November)	Kolatta (Minakshi) Puram (Minakshi)		
margali (December–January)	Ennai Kappu (Minakshi) Ponnunjal (Minakshi) Ashtami Pradakshina (Minakshi-Sundareshwara) Tiruvembavai (Manikkavasagar and Nataraja) Tiruvadirai (Manikkavasagar and Nataraja)	Attitaya Vaikuntha *ekadashi*	Tiruvadirai
tai (January–February)			Pongal

TABLE 3
Dates of Festivals in *Margali*, 1988–1989

December	Karttigai/ Margali	Special Days[a]	Minakshi Temple Festivals	Vishnu Temple Festivals
9	24	1st bright fortnight		Attiyaya
10	25			
11	26			
12	27			
13	28			
14	29		Ennai Kappu Tiruvembavai	
15	30			
16	1	1st *margali*		
17	2			
18	3			
19	4	11th bright fortnight		Vaikuntha *ekadashi*
20	5			
21	6			
22	7	Full moon	Ponnunjal	
23	8	1st dark fortnight, *ardra* star	Tiruvadirai[b]	
24	9			
25	10			
26	11			
27	12			
28	13			
29	14			
30	15			
31	16	8th dark fortnight	Ashtami Pradakshina	

[a]Full moon and *ardra* star may fall on the same day, not proximate days as in 1988. Full moon can occur on any date in the solar month of *margali*; hence in 1988, the festivals began in the preceding month (*karttigai*), but in other years they may occur entirely within *margali* or end in the following month (*tai*). In an occasional year, owing to peculiar astronomical phenomena, festivals may be displaced from their normal timings.

[b]Hindu days begin at sunrise; the bathing ritual for Nataraja began before dawn on 7th *margali* (i.e., early morning on 23 December) and the Tiruvadirai procession occurred just after sunrise on 8th *margali*. Ponnunjal was held in the evening of 8th *margali*.

of a host of pan-Hindu sacred themes and not a disfiguring travesty at all.

The core of the festival is quickly described, for most of the rituals are performed identically each day. In the evening, the movable festival image of Minakshi is taken in procession to the end of a large hall, the Pudu Mandapam ("New Hall") close to the main temple buildings. After completing the preparatory rituals, the musicians start to play and one of the Minakshi temple's Brahman priests waves an oil lamp, followed by a camphor-flame lamp, before the image. Another priest then shows the goddess a mirror; washes her face; offers her a drink of water; cleans her teeth; offers another drink; offers her areca nut and betel leaves to chew, together with a spittoon; offers another drink and then the mirror again. (In India, areca and betel—*tambula*—are politely offered to guests on all manner of occasions, especially auspicious ones.) The first priest waves the same two lamps. The second priest returns to offer more areca and betel, and another drink. He then removes the garlands from the image and spreads out Minakshi's wig of hair; he rubs oil over the hair; trims it with scissors; combs it; and shows the mirror once more. The lamps are waved again; the dressing of the hair is repeated; the lamps are waved yet again; and the dressing is repeated a second time, after more areca, betel, and water have been offered. The first priest closes with the same two lamps. The image is then screened to be bathed and decorated, before the goddess, now wearing a crown, is shown a more elaborate display of lamps, culminating with a camphor flame.

Minakshi's image is then carried round the hall in procession and set down before a statue of the illustrious, seventeenth-century king of Madurai, Tirumala Nayaka, who was responsible for building much of the Minakshi temple, including the New Hall. The king is still regarded as the sponsor of the festival, which he is believed to have started, and a plate of coconuts and plantains is placed in the statue's hands, as if he were offering them to the goddess. Next, the image is returned to the end of the hall and offered food behind a screen, before a final display of lamps. The camphor flame is brought out for devotees to cup their hands over it, and the priests distribute sacred ash to them.

On the first seven days of the festival, Minakshi then returns directly to the temple. On the eighth, however, after the ritual in the hall, Minakshi is taken in procession round the city streets riding in a *goratha*, a "cow-car," actually an elaborate chariot drawn by bullocks. This is the longest procession of the festival. On the final day, her image is taken to the New Hall in the morning to remain there all day. After the evening ritual, she goes in procession through the city streets reclining in a golden palanquin. A palanquin is used for the final night's procession in several Minakshi temple festivals and it is designed to allow the goddess to rest after the rigors of a long and busy event.

On the evening of the next day, the day of *ardra* star, there is another festival for Minakshi, which has to be treated as a prolongation of Ennai Kappu. This second festival is known as Ponnunjal, "Golden swing," and takes place in a hall inside the temple. The swing used is not gilded, but it is decorated and on it sits Minakshi's image. In front of the swing are two silver vessels, one containing unhusked paddy and the other raw rice, as well as a brass grinding stone with cylinder. Alongside the swing are various items, including a winnowing fan. Beside the vessels and stone is a tray holding five bowls of sand. Just outside the hall stands a movable image of the saint Manikkavasagar.

The usual rituals preparatory to worship are carried out, but in addition five women come to drop seeds of the "nine grains" on the bowls of sand. These grains are planted at the start of many festivals, and in a longer event their germination is taken as a sign that the festival has been a success. The priest begins the ritual by holding up the vessel of paddy in front of Minakshi. He then walks round the swing led by a temple servant, who continually pours a stream of water into the priest's right hand. The priest next waves a censer of incense and an oil lamp before the image. He repeats the same sequence with the vessel of rice and the grinding cylinder. Several plates of areca nut, betel leaves, and sandalpaste are then offered to the goddess, before being distributed to a series of temple officials, and this sequence is completed by offering her the winnowing fan, which is afterwards given to a specific ritual officiant in the temple. Throughout this ritual no music is played.

Now the priest comes out of the hall to stand before the image of Manikkavasagar, whom he quickly worships. Two of the temple's non-Brahman devotional singers sing the saint's *Tiruvembavai* hymn. The priest returns inside the hall to start the swing rocking and different hymns are sung before Minakshi. A piper plays a special tune to accompany the movement of the swing. Finally, the priest offers food to the goddess and waves a series of lamps and a camphor candelabra before her. Afterwards, Minakshi's image joins Sundareshwara's Somaskanda image in a procession around the temple's outer precincts, so that she is then reunited with her husband after being alone since the start of Ennai Kappu.

MINAKSHI'S HAIR AND HER BEAUTIFICATION

The Ennai Kappu ritual's principal purpose is exactly what it appears to be: an elaborate and respectful beautification of Minakshi, focused on the dressing of her hair. The ritual is intended to make the goddess sexually attractive, as two aspects of the hairdressing plainly indicate. First, anointing the hair with oil is a normal part of a south Indian woman's beauty routine. In Madurai most women do it on Fridays, the day sacred to the goddess. Widows, however, may not oil their hair, because these personifications of inauspiciousness should not try to make themselves sexually attractive. Instead, widows should adopt the guise of ascetics, unadorned by long hair, jewelry, colored clothing, or a red forehead mark. Only unmarried girls and *sumangalis*, "auspicious women" who are married to living husbands, may make themselves attractive to the opposite sex.

Second, a Hindu woman's hair, although uncut, should always be fastened (usually in a pigtail). Obviously, it has to be loosened to be dressed, but loose hair is itself a symbol of female sexuality, especially unconstrained sexuality, so that when Minakshi's hair is spread out before the public gaze, it openly draws attention to her erotic powers. (It will be recalled from chapter 3 that the bathing and decoration rituals of Minakshi's worship are normally done behind a screen.) Moreover, as we saw in chapter 2, sexual arousal is a "hot" state according to Hindu notions of ritual temperature, and applying oil to the hair is itself considered as heating. Thus Minakshi's anointment at the festival directly heats her and is consistent with celebrating and enhancing her sexual attractiveness.

Hair is a polyvalent symbol. A Hindu woman's loose hair can indirectly signal a state of bodily pollution, especially menstrual pollution. When menstruating, high-caste Hindu women traditionally neither wash nor dress their hair, and only after the bath ending the four-day period can they bind it again properly. Further—in an extension of the idea of unrestrained sexuality—loose, dishevelled hair also symbolizes a more general state of dissolution, wildness, and violence, as in the iconographic portrayal of Kali, "the exemplary goddess of the dishevelled hair" (Hiltebeitel 1981: 206). However, Minakshi's hair has none of these connotations at the Ennai Kappu festival. When polluted, a woman should never oil her hair and Minakshi's hair is being dressed, not left dishevelled like Kali's. At Ennai Kappu, Minakshi appears as a beautiful, charming goddess; she is not polluted and she has none of wild Kali's ugliness.

MINAKSHI'S RELATIONSHIP WITH SUNDARESHWARA

Minakshi, of course, is being made desirable to Sundareshwara, but to understand how and why, Ennai Kappu must be seen in a wider context. A dominant theme in much of the Minakshi temple's ritual cycle is the relationship between the goddess and Sundareshwara. Despite variations in detail, Minakshi is consistently portrayed either as oscillating between separation from and unity with her husband, or as progressing from an unmarried to a married state. This fluctuating relationship between Minakshi and Sundareshwara is a specific ritual example of the goddess's transformation between light and dark forms, as discussed in chapter 2. To exercise her powers fully, Minakshi must be an autonomous goddess unconstrained by a superior husband, but in that state she is potentially dangerous. Were she to remain apart from her consort for too long, her cool, pacific character would be destroyed. A goddess's hazardous powers are checked, as we have seen, by marital unity to a god, which is represented in the Minakshi temple as the prime condition. Thus we find that Minakshi's progress toward marital unity is a prominent theme in several of her festivals.

Minakshi's state during a festival is clearly indicated by the images that are used. If she is single, her festival image either stands alone or is accompanied (as in most processions) only by Vinayaka (Ganesha), who leads the way, and Chandeshwara, a form of Shiva who always brings up the rear. If she is married and united with her husband, Minakshi is also accompanied by Sundareshwara's Somaskanda image and often, in addition to Vinayaka and Chandeshwara, by a separate image of their son Subrahmanya (Skanda) as well. At Ennai Kappu, as already mentioned, only Minakshi's image is used; Sundareshwara and Subrahmanya join her after the golden swing ritual.

Besides Ennai Kappu, three other important festivals are celebrated for Minakshi alone: Adi Mulaikkottu (whose name is arcane) in *adi* (July–August), which is her principal annual festival and lasts ten days; Navaratri ("Nine nights") in *purattasi* (September–October, although it is actually fixed by the lunar calendar, as explained in chapter 5), which lasts nine lunar days; and Kolatta ("Stick dancing") in *aippasi* (October–November), six days in length. Before discussing these events, let me note that Ennai Kappu, like every festival in the Minakshi temple, is woven into the temple's complete cycle of rituals; they in turn are linked to rituals in other temples, as well as homes, in Madurai, Tamilnadu, and all of India. To interpret Ennai Kappu fully, I would have to tease out a mass of overlapping connections. Because that task is impossible within one chapter, I shall have to be selective and sometimes cursory.

At the Kolatta festival—the most similar to Ennai Kappu—Minakshi is portrayed as a young girl performing a bucolic dance with sticks (*kolattam*), but on the festival's penultimate night the oil anointment ritual, exactly as in Ennai Kappu, is done for her. Afterwards, she goes in procession in the "cow-car"; this is the only other occasion (besides Ennai Kappu) on which this vehicle is used. The symbolism of the cow-car is not entirely clear, but one clue lies in its traction, which resembles the humble bullock-cart. Thus the car suggests that Minakshi is like an ordinary country girl, as she plainly is in the Kolatta festival, and this is consistent with the emphasis on Minakshi's unalloyed feminine charm, so characteristic of both Ennai Kappu and Kolatta. On the final night of Kolatta,

Minakshi joins Sundareshwara (and Subrahmanya) in another procession, and does not perform the girls' dance.

In sharp contrast to the mood of Ennai Kappu (and Kolatta), the Adi Mulaikkottu festival celebrates the ascetic austerities practiced by Minakshi. At the end, her image is not anointed with oil, but with sandal-paste, which cools the goddess heated by her asceticism. This festival does not close with a procession in which Sundareshwara joins Minakshi, and her unmarried state is represented as uniquely prolonged, because the next important festival celebrated for both of them occurs only a month later.

In none of the three festivals is there any explicit ritual reference to the Sanskrit myths of Shiva and Parvati. Yet in Ennai Kappu and Adi Mulaikkottu (although less so in Kolatta), the central theme of those myths—Parvati's dual attempt to win Shiva by seducing him with either her voluptuous beauty or her asexual ascetic powers (O'Flaherty 1973: 151–55)—is patently important. Thus the contrast between the Ennai Kappu and Adi Mulaikkottu festivals resonates with a classical, pan-Hindu portrayal of the relationship between Shiva and his consort.

There is a similar contrast between Navaratri and the Chittirai festival, held in *chittirai* (April–May). Chittirai is the temple's greatest annual festival and its climax is the wedding of Minakshi and Sundareshwara. The sequence of events at Navaratri and Chittirai is briefly as follows. On the eighth night of Navaratri, Minakshi—represented as Devi, *the* goddess—kills the buffalo-demon Mahishasura. On the ninth, she worships the *linga* of Shiva as the god's devotee. On the next day, the "victory tenth," a procession of Minakshi with Sundareshwara and Subrahmanya is held, and the god and goddess are now fully reunited as husband and wife. According to mythology (and the understanding of people in Madurai), the buffalo-demon is Shiva's devotee or even, in some Tamil recensions of the myth, a form of the god himself. At the Chittirai festival, Minakshi is crowned as the Pandyan queen of Madurai on the eighth day, defeated by Shiva in battle on the ninth, and married to him as Sundareshwara on the tenth. Unlike the myth, which tells of Minakshi's surrender when Shiva came to the battlefield, the festival ritual on the ninth day shows him as her conqueror. Hence at Navaratri, Minakshi wins her divine husband after a battle in which she kills his devotee (or even Shiva himself), whereas at Chittirai, she does so after defeat at his hands. This contrast between Navaratri and Chittirai, as defined by the violent manner in which Minakshi gains her husband, corresponds to an equivalent contrast prominent in Tamil temple myths about the goddess as a murderous warrior-bride (Shulman 1980: 176–92).

If Navaratri and Chittirai are now set alongside Ennai Kappu and Adi Mulaikkottu, we can see that in all four (and also, less clearly, in Kolatta) how Minakshi wins her husband is a central theme. She does so by four different means, arranged as two pairs of complementary opposites: seduction through beauty or asceticism, and battling to victory or defeat. As variations on this theme, all the festivals are transformations of each other, so that Minakshi's seduction of Sundareshwara at Ennai Kappu derives much of its dramatic ritual force from its contrasting relationship with the other festivals.

The pattern of transformation among these festivals is also significantly related to their timing. All four festivals celebrated for Minakshi alone—Adi Mulaikkottu, Navaratri, Kolatta, and Ennai Kappu—occur in the inauspicious half of the year, the *dakshinayana*. Further, Adi Mulaikkottu and Ennai Kappu respectively fall in the first and last months of the *dakshinayana*; *adi* (July–August) is the most inauspicious month in the whole Tamil year and *margali* is second only to it. In neither month should auspicious rites of passage, such as marriages, be held, but in *adi* Hindus are unwilling to change residences or start any new enterprise at all, believing that to do so would almost certainly cause serious problems. Like *margali* but even more so, *adi* is a month when evil spirits are abroad. Thus Minakshi, when apart from Sundareshwara, is specially associated with inauspicious months, and her longest and most elaborate festival is actually Mulaikkottu in *adi*.

Adi is not only the most inauspicious month; it is also very firmly linked with goddesses—especially dark single goddesses—throughout Tamil popular Hinduism. It is therefore logical that Minakshi should remain alone for so long during and after the Mulaikkottu festival, and that it should show her augmenting her autonomous and potentially dangerous ascetic powers. *Margali*, although inauspicious, closes the inauspicious half of the year, the deities' night-time, and heralds the arrival of the auspicious six months (*uttarayana*) that begin on the winter solstice, the first day of the next month, *tai* (January–February). This is the day of Pongal, probably the most popular of all Tamil domestic festivals, when sweet boiled rice (*pongal*) is cooked and offered to the sun. The threatening, ascetic Minakshi of *adi*, who brings the night, is therefore counterbalanced by the attractive, erotic Minakshi of *margali*, who heralds the dawn. Ennai Kappu promises happiness to come when the sun rises on the deities.

The Fertility of Minakshi and the Soil

In the Ponnunjal festival, until the procession immediately following it, Minakshi is still a single goddess, who retains the characteristics she showed during Ennai Kappu. The Ponnunjal festival has three rather different aspects, which I shall treat separately: the first is the ritual of the vessels and grinder, the core of the festival; the second is the significance of the swing; and the third has to do with Manikkavasagar.

The ritual at Ponnunjal is identical in all important particulars to one performed at two other festivals, known as Puram, except that in the latter Minakshi's image is placed near her main shrine and does not rest on a swing. The one-day Puram festivals are held in *adi* (July–August) and *aippasi* (October–November), on the *nakshatra* called *puram* in Tamil. Officiants in the Minakshi temple say that the Purams celebrate the goddess's first menstruation, and although this is never given as the reason for Ponnunjal, its close similarity to the Purams requires us to consider them together.

The five women who sow the seeds of the nine grains must be *sumangalis*, auspicious married women whose husbands are alive. (At most temple festivals, male priests sow the seeds.) In Tamil culture, the status of *sumangali* is particularly emphasized as the ideal for a woman. All females, as we know, have power (*shakti*), but in most contexts the most powerful female is not the unmarried girl, but the wife who can best bring prosperity and well-being like auspicious Lakshmi, Vishnu's consort. The presence of *sumangalis* clearly identifies the Ponnunjal ritual as one concerned with female power and auspiciousness. It is crucial to the Puram rituals that paddy, raw rice, and the grinder represent three basic stages through which rice, the most important foodstuff for Tamils both nutritionally and symbolically, must pass: from the seed planted in the fields, which is also the harvested paddy, via the husked raw rice, to its culinary preparation as symbolized by the grinder. The grinder is also a key symbol of marriage, because at one point in the Hindu wedding ritual, the bride puts her foot on a grinding stone to seal her commitment to marital domesticity. Because Puram celebrates Minakshi's first menstruation, however, the ritual most plainly links the growth and preparation of rice to the advent of her sexual maturity. In other words, the goddess's fertility and agricultural fertility are ritually equated.

When the priest walks round the image, the procedure is known as *dishti suttudal*, "cleaning the evil eye," and it is intended to protect the ritual or Minakshi herself from this noxious force. This element of danger and protection against it account for the unusual absence of musical accompaniment at this ritual. At her first menstruation, Minakshi, like all girls is in a dangerous state of transition and liable to attract the attention of jealous, malevolent beings, including those with the evil eye, an ubiquitous menace requiring frequent counter-measures. The significance of the winnowing fan was rather obscure to my informants: some said that it transfers the *dosha*, "taint" or "sin," of menstruation to the officiant who receives it, but others insisted that the taint is otherwise removed or, because a goddess rather than an ordinary girl is involved, there is no taint anyway. It is obvious that the fan further reinforces the symbolic association between agricultural and sexual fertility. Moreover, because the fan is used to separate grain from chaff, it is a logical symbol of separation in general, and particularly of the separation out of polluting and inauspicious elements that can then be cast away. As such, the fan is itself an auspicious symbol (Hanchett 1988: 141–43; Raheja 1988a: 123–24). However, the temple officiant who takes the fan away also removes the object used to get rid of the pollution and inauspiciousness of menstruation, insofar as *dosha* is implicitly incurred by Minakshi. By the end of the ritual, therefore, the auspiciousness of Minakshi's first menstruation, the promise of her sexual fertility, has been ensured.

Puram festivals, especially the one in *adi*, are held for most temple goddesses in the region, including Vishnu's second wife Bhudevi. The symbolic identification between agricultural fertility and the goddesses' sexual fertility made by Puram in *adi* is reinforced in several ways. For example, in July, after the first rain from the south-west monsoon has fallen on the mountains to the west of Tamilnadu, the rivers running through the plains rise. The rushing waters of the Kaveri—the "southern Ganges" and south India's most sacred river—are said to turn red as the goddess of the river menstruates. Her bleeding ends on the eighteenth day of *adi* (at the beginning of August), when a major domestic festival is celebrated by Tamil women. It is known as Adipperukku, "*adi* overflowing," a reference to the river and, by extension, to the goddess's menstrual flow. Hence Puram and Adipperukku together identify the goddesses as the divinized earth and rivers—Bhudevi and Ganga, respectively—and equate the fertility of agriculture, dependent on good soil and plentiful water, with that of sexually mature goddesses.

Ponnunjal, like Ennai Kappu, lacks any real link with the agricultural cycle, so that a central part of the ritual is apparently meaningless. Because the Ponnunjal and Puram rituals are virtually identical, however, they must be similarly interpreted. Thus the Ponnunjal festival of the golden swing, despite its timing, gives renewed ritual expression to the goddesses' association with soil and water, and reiterates the equation between Minakshi's fertility and agricultural fertility made most appositely in *adi*, when the inauspicious half of the year begins.

THE ROMANTIC SWING

The second aspect of Ponnunjal is the swing. Four other rituals in the Minakshi temple involve a swing. First, every night, at the last period of daily worship, images of Minakshi and Sundareshwara are taken to the bedchamber shrine, so that the god and goddess can be together as lovers at night after being apart during the day. Although the images are actually placed on a couch, the piper plays the same "swing song" heard at the Ponnunjal festival. Second, on every Friday evening the temple's weekly "swing festival" is held; images of Minakshi and Sundareshwara are put on a swing, which is rocked, and they are worshiped there. The third occasion is a ten-day swing festival during *ani* (June–July), Ani Unjal, when the divine couple's images are placed on a decorated swing each evening. While the swing is rocked, devotional songs are sung, and a piper and flautist play. Finally, immediately before the wedding of Minakshi and Sundareshwara during the Chittirai festival, their images rest on a swing for a short time and are entertained by a song. This ritual is also performed for the bride and groom at a Tamil Brahman wedding.

The swing as a favorite repose for lovers is a conventional Hindu motif, and all four rituals in the Minakshi temple are expressions of it. The swing is particularly associated with Krishna, who sits on it with Radha or his wives, and an annual swing festival is often a major event at Krishna's temples throughout India. But the swing also figures frequently in many other romantic ritual contexts, and swing festivals are common in many different deities' temples in Tamilnadu and elsewhere.

At Ponnunjal, however, Minakshi swings alone. Nevertheless, so transparent is the swing motif that we must infer a romantic connotation, and the most plausible interpretation is that Minakshi is anticipating the union with Sundareshwara that will shortly follow and end her period apart from him during Ennai Kappu. The connection is admittedly rather remote, but the Ponnunjal swing ritual is reminiscent of the north Indian custom of swinging at the start of the rainy season, a period traditionally associated in the north with a woman's longing for her absent husband. Hence the swing is not only the favorite seat of Hindu lovers, but also of women separated from their menfolk. This plainly fits the theme in Minakshi's golden swing festival, whose romantic mood is at one with the goddess's beautification in the Ennai Kappu festival.

MANIKKAVASAGAR'S FESTIVAL

The third aspect of Ponnunjal is its connection with Manikkavasagar. Manikkavasagar's own ten-day festival ends on *ardra* star day in *margali*, so that it is concurrent with Minakshi's Ennai Kappu and Ponnunjal festivals. The festival is named after the *Tiruvembavai* ("Our sacred lady"), the seventh in the saint's collection of hymns in praise of Shiva entitled *Tiruvasagam* ("Sacred utterances"). During the festival's ten days, the *Tiruvembavai* replaces the hymns, selected from the works of Manikkavasagar and other devotionalist saints, which are sung as part of daily worship throughout the rest of the year.

The salient events of the Tiruvembavai festival are as follows. On the first evening, an image of Manikkavasagar is placed in an antechamber of Sundareshwara's main shrine, facing the latter and close to an image of Velliyambalam Nataraja, Shiva as lord of the dance on a "silver stage." The temple's devotional singers then sing the *Tiruvembavai* as if the saint were singing it to the gods. On the next eight days, in the early morning, the image of Manikkavasagar is taken before a different image of Nataraja in the "hundred-pillar" hall, where the singers again sing the *Tiruvembavai*, before the saint goes in procession around the temple. On the evening of the tenth day, the *Tiruvembavai* is sung for the last time in front of Manikkavasagar standing near Minakshi. After her swing has begun to move, the *Tiruvembavai* gives way to the hymns sung during the rest of the year, and from this large selection come the next hymns for Minakshi.

The Tiruvadirai festival also falls on *ardra* star day, the end of Tiruvembavai. (*Tiruvadirai* is the Tamil form of *ardra*.) In the first important ritual of Tiruvadirai, held in the late evening, three immovable images of Nataraja—Velliyambalam, "hundred-pillar" hall, and "thousand-pillar" hall—are anointed with a special oil. A few hours later, around three o'clock in the morning, comes the festival's climax: an elaborate bathing ritual (*abhisheka*) for the movable images of Velliyambalam Nataraja, his consort, and Manikkavasagar, who all face Sundareshwara's main shrine, for a mirror in which Sundareshwara's *linga* is reflected, as well as for four other movable images of Nataraja and his consort in a nearby hall. The notable feature of this ritual is that it ends with copious amounts of liquid sandalpaste being poured over the images and the mirror. That oil is applied to immovable images, but sandalpaste to movable ones, matters little; it is far more crucial that at the beginning Nataraja alone is heated by oil, and at the end Nataraja and his consort, together with Manikkavasagar and Sundareshwara's *linga* in the mirror, are cooled by sandalpaste. I shall discuss the meaning of these bathing rituals below. Shortly after daybreak, a procession of all the movable images goes round the city streets, with Manikkavasagar facing the five Natarajas accompanied by their consorts. The sight of Nataraja at this auspicious time is known as *ardra darshana*, the vision at *ardra* star. Unless exceptional astronomical circumstances intervene, the Natarajas' procession closing the Tiruvadirai festival occurs on the morning preceding Ponnunjal and the end of the Tiruvembavai festival.

A major annual festival for Manikkavasagar in *margali* is celebrated in Shiva temples throughout southern Tamilnadu. However, in the Minakshi temple—during the god and goddess's swing festival in *ani* (June–

July)—Manikkavasagar has another shorter festival, close to one for Nataraja (Uttiram) that repeats the Tiruvadirai rituals on a lesser scale. In
both *margali* and *ani*, six months apart according to a typical pattern,
there are therefore swing festivals that coincide with festivals for Manikkavasagar and Nataraja.

DEVOTION, HEAVEN, AND THE WINNING OF A HUSBAND

In Tamilnadu, the worship of Vishnu and Shiva is thoroughly infused
with the ethos of devotionalism, and images of the medieval saints are
installed in all the larger temples. *Margali*, though, is undoubtedly the
month when devotionalism most completely and overtly dominates
Tamil popular Hinduism, and Manikkavasagar's festival is itself testimony to this fact.

In some respects, though, devotionalism is still more predominant during *margali* in Vishnu's temples, which hold twenty-day festivals for reciting the entire corpus of Vaishnava devotionalist poetry. The Attiyaya festival's name comes from the Tamil form of *adhyaya*, "(Vedic) scripture,"
because the corpus is the Vaishnavas' "Tamil Veda." The festival begins
on the first day of the bright lunar fortnight ending on *margali* full moon,
next to or coincident with *astra* star day, so that the Vaishnava festival
overlaps Manikkavasagar's. Half-way through the Attiyaya festival is the
eleventh day of the lunar fortnight, *vaikuntha* ("Vishnu's heaven") or
paramapada ("final release") *ekadashi*. All eleventh lunar days (*ekadashi*)
are sacred to Vishnu, but in Tamilnadu this particular eleventh is very
special and the god's temples are packed with devotees. On this one occasion in the year, the back door of each Vishnu temple is open all night, so
that devotees can walk through it to reach "Vishnu's heaven"—equated
with final release from the cycle of rebirth in devotionalist Vaishnavism—
and anyone dying at this time is popularly thought to go straight to
heaven (Logan 1980: 309–11). Hence the devotionalist promise of immediate access to god and salvation is very dramatically expressed in
Vishnu's temples.

In the Minakshi temple, there is yet another festival during *margali*,
Ashtami Pradakshina, which is held on the eighth lunar day (*ashtami*) of
the dark fortnight. The main event in this festival is a procession in which
the movable images of Minakshi and Sundareshwara, riding in tall decorated cars, are pulled by scores of devotees around the perimeter streets of
Madurai. Almost all major processions at the Minakshi temple consist of
a circumambulation (*pradakshina*) in the auspicious, clockwise direction
round the temple itself; the Ashtami Pradakshina procession is unusual
only because the route is so long. The festival is held to commemorate a
particular mythical incident. A Brahman caught a cow uprooting vegeta-

bles in his garden and he chased it round the perimeter streets and into the temple, where the cow disappeared into Sundareshwara's *linga*, a standard devotionalist image of transport to the god's heaven. The story implies that devotees who follow the cow's path may also go to Shiva's heaven, so that the Ashtami Pradakshina festival offers them a boon like the one granted to Vishnu's devotees on *vaikuntha ekadashi*.

Let me now turn to the worldly goal of finding a good husband. As I said at the beginning of this chapter, there is a popular belief that girls who sing Manikkavasagar's and Andal's hymns throughout *margali* can win husbands with the qualities of Shiva and Vishnu/Krishna. Manikkavasagar's own attitude toward women was ambivalent (Yocum 1982: 113–30). In his poetry, he often condemns women as seducers whose sexual allure entraps men, preventing them from pursuing their religious and social duties. But he is also—as one might surmise—fascinated by female beauty, and he uses almost identical erotic imagery to describe both the goddess who is Shiva's consort and women themselves. Moreover, the qualities of women are ideally possessed by all Shiva's devotees, who are "likened to females in love with him" (ibid.: 121) in the devotionalist idiom most famously associated with Radha and Krishna, although Manikkavasagar's *Tiruvasagam* is not as openly erotic as, say, Jayadeva's *Gitagovinda*. The *Tiruvembavai* sung during *margali*—in Manikkavasagar's temple festival and by women at home—is actually no more strongly concerned with female devotion to Shiva than much of the rest of his work, and it is apposite mainly because it describes early-morning worship. However, consistent with their central place in the month's rituals, the *Tiruvembavai*, together with Andal's Vaishnava *Tiruppavai*, clearly express the classic devotionalist concept of the devotee as a female lover.

Young women's hopes of winning a divine husband through devotion are further expressed in the Tiruvadirai festival held in homes on *ardra* star day. Among non-Brahmans in Madurai, the festival is not in fact very widely celebrated and when it is, it is normally regarded as an event for married women, who worship Shiva and Parvati for the welfare of their husbands and for a long, auspicious married life. Among Brahmans, however, Tiruvadirai is much more popular and is mainly celebrated by unmarried girls, who are said to worship Nataraja to win him as their husband. The festival particularly involves young girls, because traditionally—although never today—Brahman girls were married before puberty (Logan 1980: 323–25).

Minakshi, of course, is an attractive, single young woman in the Ennai Kappu festival. Although no ritual actually depicts it, she too presumably participates in the early-morning singing. Moreover, the *Tiruvembavai* hymn is sung to her at Ponnunjal, immediately before she starts to swing in anticipation of her union with Sundareshwara. Along one dimension, as we have already seen, the Ennai Kappu and Ponnunjal festivals fit into the temple's complete cycle of rituals, and owe much of their significance to connections with other festivals across the year. But along another dimension, the two festivals are part of all the devotionalist ritual activity taking place throughout Madurai and beyond during December and January. Minakshi, like so many other young women, is hoping to gain a godlike husband by her devotion. After all, as Manikkavasagar tells us, the perfectly beautiful goddess is also the perfect devotee, and in the end Minakshi will win Shiva for herself.

NATARAJA AND DIVINE SEDUCTION

To complete this discussion of the *margali* rituals, I must now turn to Nataraja, whose Tiruvadirai festival is widely celebrated in Shiva temples throughout Tamilnadu. Nataraja is the presiding deity in the great temple of Chidambaram, regarded by Tamils as preeminent among Shiva temples. The Chidambaram temple has numerous connections with the Minakshi temple, and the hierarchical relationship between them is neatly expressed by Nataraja's dance: on his left foot on a silver stage in Madurai and on his right foot on a "golden stage" (*ponnambalam*) in superior Chidambaram. A further link stems from the legendary career of Manikkavasagar, who was the Pandyan king's prime minister in Madurai before leaving his service to go to Chidambaram, where he devoted himself to his lord's worship and found religious fulfillment. Manikkavasagar's special devotion to Nataraja is the immediate reason for their joint participation in the Tiruvembavai and Tiruvadirai festivals.

The Chidambaram temple legend incorporates Shiva's famous "pineforest" myth. A popular version of this myth tells how Shiva left his wife to humble the sages' wives, who lived in the forest with their husbands and arrogantly believed that they had conquered the temptations of the flesh. Taking the guise of a naked beggar, Shiva seduced these women and thereby provoked a row with his own wife, who doubted the purity of his motives. Rituals to enact this "lovers' quarrel" between the god and his consort are regularly held in Shiva temples in Tamilnadu, including the Minakshi temple, where images of Nataraja and his consort then replace those of Sundareshwara and Minakshi—even though the latter are said to be quarreling. In these rituals, therefore, Nataraja's identity as Shiva the seducer of the sages' wives is reinforced.

The Tiruvadirai festival in the Minakshi temple in *margali* contains no overt reference to the lovers' quarrel, but so clearly is Nataraja identified with Shiva in the pine forest that an implicit allusion to his role as a seducer is inevitably there. Minakshi herself is not seen to celebrate Tiruvadirai, but her Ponnunjal festival also occurs on *ardra* star day and

Manikkavasagar attends it, so that he links the two festivals and hence Minakshi with Nataraja. Thus if Minakshi was trying to seduce Shiva during Ennai Kappu and sang to him through Manikkavasagar at Pon-nunjal, the Tiruvadirai ritual indirectly suggests that the god now has similar designs on her, even though Minakshi is a future bride, not like the wives in the pine-forest myth. It would be entirely consistent with Shiva's character, as revealed in his mythology, that he should respond to the goddess's advances by exercising his own seductive powers. In much the same way, the Brahman girls who worship Nataraja at the domestic Tiruvadirai festival also imply that they are open to seduction by the god, for they too know his mythological reputation.

The most straightforward interpretation of the Tiruvadirai bathing rituals in the Minakshi temple is that Nataraja is being heated before he begins his violent dance, which is performed to crush beneath his foot the black dwarf demon sent to attack Shiva by the enraged sages of the forest. At the end of the dance, his violent agitation is cooled by the sandalpaste poured over his images. But there is another, more germane line of interpretation open to us. In the Chidambaram legend, Nataraja also dances because he accepts a challenge from fierce Kali. He wins the contest to decide who is the better dancer and the now subdued goddess becomes his consort Bhadrakali. Bhadrakali's image in the Minakshi temple is not involved in the festivals under discussion. Nonetheless, the bathing rituals of Tiruvadirai can also be seen in the light of the contest with Kali. Before the dance, Nataraja alone is heated by oil. After it, when he has been united with his conquered bride, both of them are cooled by sandalpaste, as too are Sundareshwara himself (in the mirror) and Manikkavasagar, author of the hymns sung to win the god as a husband. Once more, Nataraja has won a wife and so too, it seems clear, Shiva as Sundareshwara has won Minakshi. But now, in yet another characteristic inversion, the goddess has been defeated in a contest instead of openly seduced, which in turn echoes Minakshi's defeat in battle before marriage to Sundareshwara in the Chittirai festival. It is entirely fitting and almost predictable that the interpretative path should have ended here, with divine marital union, because throughout the festivals of *margali* the archetypal devotionalist idiom of sexual love between men and women as a model for love between deity and devotee is fundamental.

DEVOTIONALISM, GODDESSES, AND WOMEN

As this chapter has shown, in Madurai during *margali* devotionalism is an integral part of ritual in the temples of Vishnu and Shiva, all of which are served by Brahman priests responsible for a mainly Sanskrit liturgy. Apart from the intensity of devotionalist expression during *margali*, this situation is not exceptional. Across India since medieval times, although especially thoroughly in Tamilnadu, *bhakti* has developed within the hierarchical, institutional frameworks of popular Hinduism, and has also shaped them. At the same time, rituals with a strongly devotionalist tenor are themselves linked with others of a rather different kind, in which alternative themes—such as the celebration of sexual and agricultural fertility during *adi*—are more in evidence. Devotionalism, as I stressed in the last chapter, is a constitutive part of popular Hinduism, but it is also a variable part that is not equally prominent in all places, times, and contexts.

More specifically, we have seen that the idea of winning a perfect, god-like husband is a striking feature of *margali* rituals in Madurai, most obviously in Minakshi's own Ennai Kappu festival. This feature highlights one vital aspect of popular Hindu devotionalism: devotion to the deities is inspired by the hope of worldly benefits (*bhukti*) while alive, as well as liberation (*mukti, moksha*) after death. Thus all notices erected in the Minakshi temple asking devotees to donate items for special worship, such as liquids for bathing Nataraja at Tiruvadirai, always promise donors the deities' "grace" (*arul* in Tamil), which is plainly understood to confer blessings in the here and now. These could be of many kinds, but the prospect of a good husband is always among them, albeit amplified during the devotionalist season of *margali*.

The concern with finding a good husband partly reflects the fundamental importance of marriage for women in India. Marriage confers full maturity on females and transforms girls into *sumangalis*, personifications of auspiciousness. Plainly, the rituals discussed above should be saying something about relationships between men and women, as well as between deities and devotees. Yet Minakshi's behavior as ritually portrayed in the Ennai Kappu festival patently contradicts conventional social norms. In India today, and even more so in the past, young women neither do nor should acquire husbands by displaying their feminine charms, and they are definitely not supposed to seduce prospective suitors, let alone lay themselves open to sexually active males in the image of Shiva/Nataraja. Among the vast majority of ordinary Indians, marriages were and are arranged by parents, so that their children, especially daughters, do not look for their own partners. Often a woman sees very little of her future husband before the wedding and sometimes she does not see him at all.

Of course, it could be argued that all rituals to win an ideal husband have to be understood against the background of arranged marriage. Then they would merely suggest that young women, like those who sing in the early morning and participate in the Tiruvadirai festival, are praying for ideal suitors to appear when prospective husbands are being sought through the usual channels. However, that suggestion simply does not ring true. Minakshi is presented as a beautiful but ordinary young woman in Ennai Kappu, and it and the other festivals of *margali*, with their patently erotic tone, do seem to hold out the prospect of a young woman independently attracting a husband to herself. In reality, neither freedom of this kind nor public displays of sexual attractiveness would be tolerated in a young woman belonging to a conventionally respectable family. Hence in the rituals celebrated in *margali*, the goddess Minakshi—and to some extent all young women—are represented as females who try to win husbands in defiance of social norms.

Particularly in south India, marriage, in conjunction with the female puberty rites celebrated in the region, can be seen as a ritual to control a girl's potentially dangerous sexuality—an aspect of her ritual power or *shakti*—in a manner analogous to the marriage of a goddess. However, a Tamil woman actually exercises her ritual power most completely when she is a *sumangali*, an auspicious wife with a living husband, to whom she is subordinate. The controlled, subordinate wife is generally idealized by women as well as men. As Holly B. Reynolds (1980: 56) says about Tamil women, they see any status other than that of an auspicious married woman as "lesser in power and lesser in being." On the whole, what applies to Tamil wives holds good for Hindu wives everywhere. Throughout India, the ideal Hindu woman is symbolized by auspicious Lakshmi who, as Vishnu's consort, is commonly represented as the perfect woman and wife, although there are many other goddesses who also exemplify the virtuous *pativrata*, "devoted to her husband." Prominent examples include Sita, who is absolutely faithful and obedient to Rama, the very model of a righteous husband, and Savitri, who was so devoted to her husband that she followed him into the underworld after his death and finally compelled Yama, god of death, to release him. More extremely, there is Parvati as Sati, the model for the virtuous wife who burns herself on her husband's funeral pyre. In all these cases and many more, the goddess who is a loving, faithful, and subordinate spouse is explicitly represented as the ideal Hindu woman. Often indeed, Minakshi herself is portrayed in this role, when she sits beside Sundareshwara with her son Skanda to complete the Shaiva "holy family."

The position of the married woman is more ambiguous in north India and Nepal. There, considerable stress is placed on a virgin girl's ritual purity, especially among the higher castes who practice hypergamous marriage, so that a daughter is given away in the "gift of the virgin" (*kanyadana*) to a higher-ranking family. A girl's purity is a precondition for worshiping her as a powerful goddess in the popular custom of *kumari puja* ("virgin worship"), whose most extraordinary manifestation is in Nepal. In several major Nepalese temples, little girls are installed as living goddesses to be worshiped until they are disqualified, normally when they begin to menstruate (Allen 1976). The deification of girls in the northern region is partly related to the eulogization of daughters (and sisters) in contrast to the ambivalence surrounding wives. Although a married woman still attains the pan-Indian ideal status of an auspicious wife, who is potentially a mother bearing sons to continue her husband's line, his family commonly treats her as a source of inferior blood and dangerous animosity, as Lynn Bennett's study (1983) of high-caste Nepali Hindus strikingly shows. In south India, where marriage is preferentially to a cross-cousin (or another close relative)—as well as in all communities without a strong hypergamous bias—the wife's position is less ambiguous and elaborate cults of virgin worship are rare.

Kumari puja often displays the influence of Tantrism and within Tantric circles, partially reflecting the unqualified supremacy of unmarried goddesses like Kali, women can enjoy unusually high status, at least in the religious context, as they apparently did in the Tantric Vaishnava-Sahajiya movement in Bengal (Dimock 1989: 96–102). Sometimes, too, the devotionalist premise that the ideal devotee is female allows the goddess to symbolize the autonomy and high status of women, as Radha does in some Bengali Vaishnava devotionalist movements (Wulff 1985). However, like Tantric ideas about the true status of women, this "feminist" style of devotionalism appears to be uncommon even in Bengal. Certainly, goddesses like Kali are rarely thought to exemplify the ideal woman among ordinary Hindus anywhere in India.

Between wifely light goddesses and single dark goddesses, there is therefore an asymmetry. The former, as perfect consorts, represent an ideal model for Hindu women, whereas the latter do not. It is important to see that this is not in itself problematic. People do not infer social norms from myths and rituals that show the deities acting in ways that would occasion moral disapproval within human society, because everyone knows that Hindu gods and goddesses are not always good. Similarly, when Minakshi in Ennai Kappu wins her husband by seducing him, she gives no moral lessons about how marriages between men and women should be made; after all, no one is expected to get married by practicing asceticism, going to war, or competing in dance contests. Minakshi, like other Hindu deities in many different settings, often does not act in conformity with moral and social norms, the *dharma* of society, but instead gives expression to a vision transcending the limits of the social order.

Some elements of that vision probably have their roots in unconscious fantasy. Thus Gananath Obeyesekere (1984: chaps. 10–11), employing a psychoanalytical framework, discusses the different types of Hindu goddesses in relation to unconscious fantasies engendered by the internal psychological dynamics of the Indian family. Obeyesekere's line of reasoning has some plausibility, although many of his generalizations are unsubstantiated. For example, his claim that fierce goddesses like Kali are expressions on the cultural level of the "infantile experience of the castrating mother" (ibid.: 444) owes more to Freudian theory about "projective systems" to channel "nuclear infantile experiences" (ibid.: 428) than it does to any sound data about Indian children. However, one of Obeyesekere's asides, where he comments that women disappointed by their husbands may find "loving surrogate male figures" in gods like Krishna (ibid.: 434–35), makes good sense and is relevant by extension to goddesses as well. Thus I would suggest, although I also lack firm evidence, that a goddess like Minakshi, especially as she appears in the Ennai Kappu festival, is a partial response to the fantasies of both her male and female devotees: for men, she is a loving surrogate female and an unattainable erotic object, and for women, she is an epitome of the free female sexuality forbidden by social norms. Quite simply, too, Minakshi—like deities such as Krishna—may manifest for all Hindus an image of personal romantic love that can only be dreamt about in a society with arranged marriage.

Lastly, let me return to the position of women in society. Minakshi's Ennai Kappu and Ponnunjal festivals, as well as other devotionalist rituals held in Madurai in the winter, dramatically express the very basic Hindu idea that women embody *shakti*, the ritual power personified as female. In doing so, they show women—in the image of autonomous goddesses—as far more powerful beings than their place in society normally allows. The limits placed on females by the social order are transcended, and on such powerful women, men significantly depend, in spite of their superior social status and authority over women. Symbolically, Minakshi is saying through ritual that the relationship between ordinary men and women is not as one-sided as it appears to be. Popular Hinduism, perhaps most evocatively and powerfully in some currents within its devotionalist stream, can always provide a counterpoint to the unegalitarian social norms and institutions that, in other settings, it so strongly reflects and legitimates.

Chapter 9

PILGRIMAGE

I N APRIL 1988, the Government of India's Ministry of External Affairs announced in the press that it would accept applications from citizens wishing to go on thirty-one-day pilgrimages to Mount Kailasa and Lake Manasarowar, at the foot of the mountain. Mount Kailasa, 22,000 feet high, lies in Tibet, under the authority of the Chinese government, and is virtually inaccessible to Indian nationals unless they go on officially organized annual pilgrimages. The ministry's announcement stated that all applicants would have to be medically examined to ensure that they were fit for trekking at high altitudes, and they would have to pay a fee of Rs 3,000, as well as US $380, a larger sum in foreign exchange, to the Chinese authorities.

It is unfortunate for Hindus that the peak on which Shiva prefers to meditate should lie in a foreign country. This particular diplomatic difficulty does not obstruct pilgrimages to other major centers. On the other hand, the fees are not beyond the reach of many of India's better-off citizens and government regulation of pilgrimage, as well as the imposition of health checks, is nothing new, although compulsory cholera vaccination is more usual at major pilgrimage sites. Moreover, the official arrangement of the pilgrimage to Mount Kailasa probably ensures that the relatively small groups that undertake it escape some of the other hazards and hardships commonly accompanying long-distance pilgrimage to major centers inside India. Before I consider these difficulties and their effect on the pilgrimage experience, let me look at Hindu pilgrimage in general terms to set the journey to Mount Kailasa in context.

PILGRIMAGE AND PILGRIMAGE CENTERS

Pilgrimage has always been a vital part of Hinduism, but never more so than in the modern era, as ever-increasing numbers of pilgrims set out on longer and longer journeys. In the early twentieth century, according to M. N. Srinivas, only a few inhabitants of Rampur village in Karnataka had heard of famous centers like Benares, and no more than a handful had been to them. Then "a pilgrimage to Banaras was regarded as a hazardous enterprise though much less so than in the nineteenth century when a pilgrim's successful return from it was a fortuitous accident"

(Srinivas 1976: 321). Today, the mass media and better education have improved ordinary people's knowledge about Hinduism's sacred centers and how to reach them. Pilgrimage has also become safer. Whatever the hazards faced by contemporary pilgrims, nowadays they rarely include uncontrollable cholera outbreaks in crowded centers, or attack by robbers and wild animals during journeys lasting for days or even weeks across wild terrain.

The most important factor in the expansion of pilgrimage has been improved communications, which has made long-distance travel quicker and cheaper. Communications began to improve markedly in the nineteenth century. In the 1840s, during the first phase of rapid railway construction in Britain, the directors of the East India Company were skeptical about the viability of railways in India. One objection raised was that the general preoccupation with caste purity rules would mean that too few people might use trains. J. C. Marshman, a missionary and newspaper editor, countered this argument by confirming with an association of traditionally minded Hindus in Bengal "that a pilgrim could travel by railway without losing the merit of pilgrimage" (O'Malley 1941: 238). The railways were built, and by around 1940, according to L.S.S. O'Malley, "thousands now flock to places of pilgrimage, where only hundreds or scores went in pre-railway days" (ibid.: 242). The railway companies themselves advertised to attract and encourage the pilgrim traffic; the nationalized Indian Railways do much the same today. During the last twenty or thirty years, there has also been a large increase in pilgrimage by road, and it is now common throughout India to see busloads of pilgrims, often unsophisticated villagers, arriving from far away states at all the major centers. Less numerous, but equally noticeable and naturally most welcome to priests and other people earning their livelihood from pilgrims, is the growing company of wealthy, urban middle-class travelers, both Indians and expatriates, who visit pilgrimage centers by air and in cars. For all classes of people, even when the religious purpose is uppermost, pilgrimage is commonly combined with ordinary tourism to monuments and museums, beaches and beauty spots, and a clear distinction between sacred and secular journeying is often impossible to draw.

Where are all these pilgrims going? Pilgrimage is classically a *tirtha-yatra*, a "pilgrimage, journey" (*yatra*) to a holy place, literally a "ford" or "crossing place" (*tirtha*). Some *tirtha*s are crossing places, such as the most celebrated of all pilgrimage sites, the city of Benares (Kashi) on the river Ganges (Eck 1983: 34). The Ganges itself is an object of pilgrimage, as are other rivers, such as the Godavari in Andhra Pradesh or the Kaveri in Tamilnadu, which are regarded as forms of the Ganges but do not attract so many pilgrims. The holy cities on the Ganges—especially Benares, Prayaga (Allahabad) at its confluence with the Yamuna and mythical Saraswati, and Hardwar on its upper reaches—are major pilgrimage centers, although for many Hindus Gaya, a city on a tributary of the Ganges in Bihar, is probably second only to Benares in importance.

Benares and Hardwar are always included in the classical list of seven holy cities, which is generally completed by Ayodhya (Rama's capital), Mathura (Krishna's birthplace), Kanchipuram (the "southern Benares" and the only one not in the north), Ujjain, and Dwarka (Krishna's capital). For Krishna's devotees, Mathura joins other nearby localities in Krishna's homeland in the Braj region of western Uttar Pradesh, such as Gokul, where he passed his infancy, and Brindavan (Vrindaban), where he danced with Radha and the cowherdesses. Brindavan, a favorite pilgrimage center, is particularly notable because it is imagined as a forest, not a true city, unlike so many other great centers. Allahabad preeminently, together with Hardwar, Ujjain, and Nasik, are also important destinations for pilgrims when the great triennial Kumbha Mela festivals are held. The main Kumbha Mela, held every twelve years in Allahabad, attracts vast numbers of pilgrims. In January 1989 an estimated 15 million arrived to bathe in the river. One of the seven cities, Dwarka, also takes its place among the four divine "abodes" (*dhama*), which stand at the compass points of the territory of Bharat (India): Badrinath in the Himalayas to the north and, on the coast, Puri in the east, Rameswaram in the south, and Dwarka in the west. For many Hindus, the ideal pilgrimage— although accomplished by only a few—is the journey round all four sites in the auspicious, clockwise direction, a circumambulation of India itself.

Besides Mount Kailasa, other peaks in the Himalayas are also pilgrimage centers, and so too are many lesser mountains and hills elsewhere in the country. In some mountain centers, a particular temple is the pilgrims' destination, such as Badrinath's Vishnu temple or nearby Kedarnath's Shiva temple. In countless other places too, the principal pilgrimage center is a specific temple and a few examples may be mentioned. Some temples (such as Kedarnath) stand where, in legend, Shiva's *linga* shone as a fiery, luminous column, and others (such as Kalighat in Calcutta) stand where parts of the goddess Sati's dismembered body fell to earth. Some are situated in famous holy cities, such as Vishwanatha's temple in Benares, and some are found in otherwise rather unimportant localities, such as the immensely popular and wealthy temple of Venkateshwara at Tirupati in Andhra Pradesh. All these centers, and many more, are "all-Indian" in the sense that Hindus everywhere would probably attest to their importance, even if they are unlikely to visit them. They are complemented by many other centers of predominantly regional significance, such as Ganesha's temples in Maharashtra or Murugan's in Tamilnadu, and even more of merely local appeal.

Elaborate typological schemes—partly built upon classical lists of the seven holy cities, four sites at the perimeter of India, and so on—have been developed by various writers to classify the disparate miscellany of Hindu pilgrimage centers according to the geographical range of their appeal, the special reasons for their sanctity, or the benefits gained by visiting them. Typological schemes are descriptively useful in organizing the material and Hindus themselves make classificatory distinctions of a similar kind. For example, different centers are generally visited for rather different purposes, and Rajasthani villagers even distinguish lexically between local pilgrimages (Rajasthani *jatra*) and long-distance pilgrimages to major centers (Hindi *yatra*), saying that the former are "frankly made to wangle boons from the lesser deities" while the latter are more "performed for their intrinsic worthiness and fruits are left 'in God's hands'" (Gold 1988a: 251). Nonetheless, such distinctions, although quite widely drawn by Hindus throughout India, provide no basis for a completely systematic, hierarchical classification of pilgrimage centers, as E. Alan Morinis convincingly shows by reviewing several typological schemes (1984: 233–38, 267–71). Nothing would be gained by essaying yet another classification.

The Symbolism of the Crossing Place and Center

As we have seen, the pilgrims' destination is a *tirtha*, literally a ford or crossing place, and many pilgrimage centers on riverside sites actually are crossing places. However, the term *tirtha* also implies a reference to the fetid river Vaitarani, which flows between the earth and the underworld ruled by Yama, god of death. After death, people must cross the Vaitarani with the help of a salvatory cow. The ritual to accomplish this, which is part of the mortuary sequence, is conducted at the side of a river, ideally the Ganges. By extension, the crossing after death is positively understood as liberation from rebirth (*moksha*), and this is the goal commonly proclaimed as attainable in pilgrimage centers, especially Benares and Gaya. Liberation, however, is not the only boon offered in such centers—even if it is classically the most exalted—and a visit to them, especially when it includes a bath in their sacred waters, is stereotypically said to produce great merit and efface all manner of heinous sins, as well as to bring health and wealth in this world.

If a *tirtha* is a crossing place between worlds for human beings after death, it is also a link between the divine and human worlds, and thus a place in which the deities appear on earth. At every pilgrimage center, therefore, the deities may be pervasively present. Mount Kailasa, for example, is where Shiva is most fully present on earth, so that a pilgrim who visits the peak attains the closest possible contact with the god. Every center's legend—as well as expatiating on the boons gained by visiting it—partly attributes the center's sanctity to a divine presence. This aspect is prominent in ordinary people's understanding, as Morinis's report on the views of Bengali pilgrims indicates: "Pilgrimage places, as sites where the divine has manifested itself, are therefore acknowledged as points on earth especially suited for approach to the deity, for here the invisible, transcendent deity has been 'proven' to be accessible" (1984: 280).

In the most general sense, therefore, a pilgrimage center is a crossing place between different worlds, as indeed it is in other religions besides Hinduism. As a link between worlds, the pilgrimage center is also conceptualized as an *axis mundi*, the central pivot of the cosmos, which is outside mundane space and time, even though it is a visible site on earth as well. Such a center, particularly a mountain site, may even be identified with the mythical Mount Meru rising at the central point of the cosmos. On Meru's summit sits the city of the gods and the Ganges falls from heaven directly above it, before finally flowing down to the earth (Dimmitt and van Buitenen 1978: 27–28).

In India, there are innumerable pilgrimage sites acknowledged as important crossing places and pivotal centers. All of them promise manifold benefits, transcendental and worldly, to their visitors, and each one's legend normally claims complete superiority over all other centers. Although it cannot be proven statistically, Kashi (Benares) probably enjoys the most widespread acclaim, but it is not a unique site for Hindus in any absolute sense. Other pilgrimage centers promise just as much as Kashi and their legends only partially distinguish them from that city, which is a single center from one perspective, but is also "said to embody all the *tirthas*" (Eck 1983: 39). Furthermore, there are numerous other Kashis throughout the land, so that the actual city in Uttar Pradesh is not the sole Kashi: "Not only are other *tirthas* said to be present in Kashi, but Kashi is present elsewhere" (ibid.: 40). This quality, as Diana L. Eck observes, is in evidence at every major pilgrimage center, but none is "duplicated and multiplied elsewhere in India . . . as widely as Kashi" (ibid.: 41).

Kashi's generally acknowledged preeminence thus depends on its quality as both all-inclusive and countlessly replicated, rather than on its incomparable singularity. The Minakshi temple in Madurai, for instance, contains three replicas of the Vishwanatha temple in Benares. Even though the Minakshi temple's legend naturally promises to the visitor every imaginable boon, the existence of the replicas testifies to the pan-Hindu primacy of Kashi and Shiva's temple there. On the other hand— and this is important too—nobody actually needs to go to Benares. A visit to the Minakshi temple can be a pilgrimage to the Vishwanatha temple too, just as worship of Sundareshwara there is also worship of the supreme god Shiva and all his forms. Because Kashi is everywhere, it can be visited everywhere. Exactly the same applies to every other pilgrimage center, albeit less pronouncedly for places without Kashi's esteemed status. In much the same way, we find that the inhabitants of Ghatiyali village in Rajasthan do not need to circumambulate India, because its four main deities' shrines are praised as the four sites at the country's compass points (Gold 1988a: 34).

This example from Rajasthan also illustrates how the logic of macrocosm and microcosm is relevant for understanding pilgrimage centers. In the end, any pilgrimage center, like any temple, can be homologized with the human body, so that a journey to the site is (or is like) a pilgrimage within oneself. The enlightened Hindu may then participate in pilgrimage without physically moving anywhere, just as the worshiper may revere a god or goddess within his own body conceived of as a temple. Because the pilgrimage center (and the body) can also be equated with the cosmos, such a center is simultaneously a microcosm of India, the world, and the universe. Hence the development of "sacred geography," in which the universe is mapped on to the site. In Benares, for example, the pilgrimage route around the city's perimeter is the circumference of the universe, whose center is alternatively represented by either the now ruined temple of Madhyameshwara, "Lord of the center" (whose place may be taken by the nearby Vishwanatha temple), or the main cremation ground beside the river, Manikarnika Ghat, where the cosmos is constantly recreated in the unceasing sacrifices performed on its funeral pyres.

Simultaneously, however, each pilgrimage center contributes to "sacred geography" in a second sense. Within any one area—such as Krishna's homeland of Braj, an entire cultural region such as the Tamil country, or even India itself—each center may be the site of a particular event, such as a deity's distinctive manifestation. All such sites are then related to each other as nodes of a spatial array mapping out a totality of divine events on to the land, so that the area itself is integrated by religious topography. Geography is then made in a sacred image by the pilgrimage centers.

The *tirtha* is therefore a crossing place, a pivotal center, a microcosm of the universe, and a node of an areal religious unity in a set of interrelated symbolic senses. Because the pilgrimage center is special or set apart as sacred, the traveler who approaches it becomes detached from ordinary mundane existence and the journey may equate with or substitute for renunciation. The idea that a Hindu pilgrim is a temporary renouncer is expounded in classical texts and is often, although not always, part of ordinary people's understanding as well. Thus in popular Hinduism, there is a powerful image of the ideal pilgrim as a renouncer who walks with only the bare necessities for subsistence, and it is generally acknowledged that pilgrimage on foot is more meritorious than by vehicular means. Indeed, some ascetics still embark on long journeys across India to pilgrimage centers without recourse to any form of transport but their legs.

Inasmuch as pilgrimage is the act of a renouncer, it is sometimes thought that it is better undertaken alone. However, many renouncers are actually organized into orders and—like the wandering Ramanandis who attend the Kumbha Mela—they often go on pilgrimages in groups. Among ordinary Hindus too, pilgrimages are sometimes made by individuals, sometimes by families or other small groups, and sometimes by larger companies of people. In choosing not to go alone, people partly express the devotionalist idea that pilgrimage replaces the lone ascetic's renunciation of the world. Devotionalism, as we shall see, strongly colors pilgrimage in popular Hinduism. In the anthropological study of pilgrimage, some of the most penetrating insights come from writers who have actively participated as members of relatively large groups. Three participatory studies—by Irawati Karve, E. Valentine Daniel, and Ann G. Gold—are exceptionally interesting and my discussion will mainly rely on them. These studies do not allow us to generalize about individual and family pilgrimages, but they do highlight the distinctive qualities of pilgrimage as a profoundly significant journey, in which the traveling can compare in importance with the destination.

ON THE ROAD IN MAHARASHTRA

Karve's essay (1988; first published in Marathi in 1951) describes her participation in the pilgrimage to Pandharpur, a town in southern Maharashtra, where the god Vithoba's principal temple is located. In Maharashtra, devotionalism began to flourish in the thirteenth century inspired by the writings of Jnaneshwara (1271–96; Dnyaneshwar to Marathis) and Namdev (1270–1350). Vithoba (or Vitthal) was already popular and was the god of the Varkari Panth ("pilgrims' path"), with which the two medieval saints were firmly connected, although Jnaneshwara is widely held to have founded it. During the seventeenth century, when the Maratha kingdom founded by Shivaji rose to power and Tukuram (1608–49), the Varkaris' favorite saint, flourished, the Varkari Panth became established as the most popular and influential devotionalist order in Maharashtra. Vithoba, a god famous for his lack of distinctive features, is usually identified as a form of Vishnu or Krishna, and he is central to Marathi devotionalism. The Varkari Panth—like the Pushti Marga—is a nonascetic order composed entirely of householders, and for its members and followers, the most important ritual expression of devotion to Vithoba is the pilgrimage to his shrine.

The pilgrimage is held on a large scale twice a year, but the principal event, in which Karve participated, occurs during the bright fortnight of *ashadha* (June–July). It is enormously popular and now attracts five or six hundred thousand people each year (Engblom 1987: 2), which undoubtedly makes it the greatest regional pilgrimage in India. As Karve explains (1988: 158), the event serves to define Maharashtra (except for the coastal strip) as "the land whose people go to Pandharpur for pilgrimage." Moreover, in a particular illustration of regional sacred geography, the Pandharpur pilgrimage combines with those to other major temples such as Khandoba's at Jejuri, near Poona, to form a significant component of the "religious traditions of the region [which] have contributed immeasurably to the Maharashtrian sense of cultural unity" (Courtright 1985: 204). Since the late nineteenth century, that unity has gained a greater political content, partly through the widespread worship of Ganesha, identified as a Maharashtrian regional god (ibid.: chap. 5).

As a totality, the Pandharpur pilgrimage consists of twenty to thirty separate processions, each one lasting fifteen days and starting from a place associated with the poet-saints of Marathi devotionalism. The various bodies of pilgrims converge on Pandharpur to arrive simultaneously at nearby Wakhari, from where they enter the town together on the eve of *ashadha* bright fortnight's eleventh lunar day (*ekadashi*), which is sacred to Vishnu. In each pilgrimage procession is carried a palanquin (*palkhi*) bearing silver models of a particular saint's sandals, which are revered and worshiped and symbolize the importance of the feet carrying the devotee to Pandharpur. Every procession is made up of "walking groups" (*dindi*), which have up to one hundred members linked by caste, local or family ties, or individual discipleship to the same guru. Each group has a fixed place within a procession's formation according to its seniority, with the oldest ones being closest to the palanquin. However, many unattached people join the processions as well. On the road, pilgrims chant the names of Vithoba, sing Marathi devotionalist hymns, stage religious dramas, listen to religious discourses, and otherwise express their devotion to the god. Karve joined the pilgrimage from Alandi (near Poona), where Jnaneshwara is believed to have voluntarily relinquished his life and achieved liberation. Since the procession from Alandi carries the palanquin of the Varkari Panth's legendary founder, it tends to attract the most followers (Engblom 1987: 15–22).

Karve wrote an intensely personal account, recording her own impressions of the journey, as well as her fellow pilgrims' attitudes and behavior. She described the persistence of caste divisions among the pilgrims, and angrily denounced them as inconsistent with devotionalism's egalitarian message. At least among the women, a partial fast is normally observed, together with other regulations about the timing and eating of meals, and these typify the ascetic and votive aspects characteristic of many Hindu pilgrimages. Naturally, fasting exacerbates the physical suffering experienced by walking daily for many hours on the road in the hot sun.

Complaints about aching feet are persistent and quarrels are far from rare, but nevertheless, says Karve, "The whole atmosphere was full of joy" (1988: 156) and "the pilgrims were intoxicated with happiness" (ibid.: 159).

Joy and happiness, though, coexisted with social divisions. In relation to caste and untouchability, the Varkari Panth has scarcely differed from many other devotionalist orders in its conservatism. In Karve's time, the Harijans' walking group was separate from the rest and in the lowliest position at the head of the procession, although since the 1970s Harijans have been successfully eradicating this indignity in each procession (Engblom 1987: 7). The Pandharpur temple, which has its own Brahman priests and is not actually controlled by the Varkaris, did not legally open its doors to Harijans until 1947 (Deleury 1960: 51). When Karve went on the pilgrimage, her group included Brahmans and Marathas, who form the region's dominant, non-Brahman landholding caste; they walked together but ate separately, and this appears to be usual. An incident over her fellow Brahman women's attitude toward water brought by a low-caste servant infuriated Karve, who railed against the persistence of such "outward pretenses" on a pilgrimage in which the hymns of untouchable saints are sung (1988: 154–56).

Since 1951, when Karve wrote about the journey she had recently made, an account of the Pandharpur pilgrimage in 1961 has appeared. *Palkhi* (1987), a book first published in 1964 by D. B. Mokashi, a noted Marathi "realist" novelist, is rather more detached and descriptive, and gives far more incidental detail about individual pilgrims and their daily activities, but it does not diminish the value of Karve's earlier article. Karve (and G. A. Deleury) are quoted in Victor Turner's influential essay on pilgrimages, where he argues that they are "liminal phenomena" that "exhibit in their social relations the quality of communitas" (1974: 166). "Communitas" is a state particularly generated in conditions of liminality, when a person is in a state of transition between normal social roles or statuses, and it is fully manifested as "a spontaneously generated relationship between leveled and equal total and individuated human beings, stripped of structural attributes" (ibid.: 202). In a state of communitas, people are fully and individually human, and they cease to play their socially ascribed roles. But the communitas of pilgrimage rarely achieves its full flowering, for "in long-established pilgrimages [communitas] becomes articulated in some measure with the environing social structure" (ibid.: 166–67), and "normative communitas" (ibid.: 169) prevails; "though pilgrimages strain in the direction of universal communitas, they are still ultimately bounded by the structure of the religious systems within which they are generated and persist" (ibid.: 205–6).

Since Turner first proposed his theory of pilgrimage as communitas (subsequently expanded and revised), it has been extensively criticized with evidence from many parts of the world, including India (Morinis 1984: 255–62, 273–74; van der Veer 1984; 1988: 58–60). Both the slipperiness of the communitas concept and the debatable evidence for its empirical manifestation have been comprehensively spelt out by many anthropologists, and I need not add to their number. But in relation to Pandharpur, it is worth making the obvious point that Turner, owing to his focus on pilgrimage as a cross-cultural phenomenon, fails to see that Karve describes yet another example of the inequality in Hindu devotionalist orders discussed in chapter 7, which could have included the Varkari Panth as a further illustration. Moreover, Karve's protest against caste divisions exemplifies well the modern reformist intellectual's appeal to egalitarian *bhakti* as a charter for social equality. As yet, though, this message has had relatively little impact on the mass of ordinary Hindus, for whom the religious joy created on the road to Pandharpur conveys no radical insights about social inequality.

In comparison with the journey, the arrival at Pandharpur is relatively unimportant, as Karve's anticlimactic conclusion implies (1988: 170). Once the palanquins have arrived, individual pilgrims should visit Vithoba's temple and stay in the town for five days, but many leave quickly and they all make their own way home. A small body of Varkaris take the palanquins back, but the great pilgrimage ends as soon as it reaches Pandharpur (Engblom 1987: 21–22). In emphasizing the journey itself, the pilgrims draw attention to their exceptional state, which clearly reflects partial, temporary renunciation of the mundane world, even though the devotionalist Varkari Panth, made up of householders, pays scant attention to the salvatory claims of ascetics.

Philip C. Engblom (ibid.: 27–28) argues that the Pandharpur pilgrimage is exceptional in India in its emphasis on the journey rather than the arrival at the pilgrimage center, but even if he is mainly correct there are comparable cases, such as the Pushti Marga pilgrimage to Krishna's homeland in Braj, described by Owen M. Lynch (1988). Sizable parties of Pushti Marga members—six thousand people in the group accompanied by Lynch—travel to the area before embarking on a forty-day, 160-mile circumambulation of Braj, which passes through the places where Krishna is believed to have spent his youth. The temples and other sacred sites visited are important and constitute the linked centers defining Braj's unity, but the circumambulatory journey itself is, for the Pushti Margis, the real expression of devotion to Krishna. Although the Pushti Marga is an order of householders, each pilgrim, before setting out, takes vows that are partly ascetic in character (for example, no cutting of the hair or beard, and no use of footwear). The long walk is also a hard one, lasting "for many miles over rocky soil treacherous with lurking thorns and under a burning, wearying tropical sun" (ibid.: 174). But plainly, too, the journey brings intense, emotional religious joy to the pilgrims who, in

Krishnaite fashion, identify themselves during the pilgrimage as cow-herdesses seeking union with their god, rather than renouncers of the world (ibid.: 175).

Both the Varkari Panth's pilgrimage to Pandharpur and the Pushti Margis' around Braj are themselves collective rituals expressing devotion to god. By going on them, pilgrims hope to come closer to their chosen deities, and perhaps win the promise of liberation after death, as well as boons in their lifetimes. Despite the problems inherent in his concept of communitas, Turner rightly draws attention to the fact that pilgrimage is a very special journey, in which the traveling itself is often vitally impor-tant for the participants, as is plainly so for those who walk to Pandhar-pur or round Braj.

UP THE MOUNTAIN IN KERALA

The pilgrimage to the temple of Aiyappan at Sabarimalai, high in the Western Ghats range on the Kerala side of the border with Tamilnadu, has long been popular with Malayalis, but since the 1950s its appeal has rapidly expanded among Tamils as well. Tens of thousands now go and in 1976, Daniel joined the pilgrimage with a group of people from the village near Tiruchchirappalli where he was doing fieldwork (Daniel 1984: 245–87).

In mythology, Aiyappan is the son of Shiva and Mohini, a female form of Vishnu. He has several temples in the mountains, from where he is said to protect Kerala from the east. In Kerala Aiyappan is also commonly present in village temples, playing a role similar to that of his alternative form Aiyanar/Shasta in Tamilnadu. In south India, there are also several other less popular deities with remote shrines and characteristics similar to Aiyappan's, such as Madeshwara in southern Karnataka (Srinivas 1976: 302–3).

At Sabarimalai, his principal temple, Aiyappan is represented as an unmarried god. For Tamils he is "the lord of celibacy par excellence" (Daniel 1984: 246), although he has consorts in some of his other temples and Malayalis in particular tend to stress his role as a hunter in the forest as well (Tarabout 1986: 85–88). The pilgrimage of Tamils to Sabarimalai occurs annually during *margali* (December–January) and preparations for it are unusually protracted. Only males, prepubertal girls, and post-menopausal women are allowed to participate, and the overwhelming majority of pilgrims are in fact men. Up to sixty days—but traditionally forty-one—before the start of the journey, prospective pilgrims begin to observe extensive restrictions, such as no sexual activity, no eating meat or eggs, and sleeping only on the floor. The men must wear only the traditional Tamil males' waist-cloth, but dyed black, dark blue, or ochre. All these rules and regulations closely resemble those imposed on ascetic renouncers, and during the period of preparation, "the pilgrim begins to be weaned away from society." Other people address the pilgrims only as "swami," "lord," and they in turn address everyone else as "Ayyappa Swami." "In other words, everybody became an Ayyappan for us," says Daniel (1984: 247). In some places, this collective identity is reinforced by nightly gatherings to sing hymns praising Aiyappan (Kjaerholm 1986: 132). On the eve of the pilgrimage, each man is initiated in his local temple, where he accepts a special bag containing the items to be offered to Aiyappan, and a miniature funeral is held. The pilgrim as a renouncer cuts his ties with the world and society by becoming dead to it. If pilgrims have a guru, he is a local man chosen informally (ibid.: 134), but Daniel's group had no such leader.

Daniel and his fellow pilgrims, as is usual today, traveled by road to the foot of Sabarimalai, from where they began the forty-seven-mile trek. They chose the longest and most tortuous trail, which is ideally preferred because Aiyappan himself took it, although most pilgrims opt for shorter paths of six or nineteen miles. It is most meritorious to complete the journey as quickly as possible and this was the aim of Daniel's party. The dramatic results are evocatively described by the ethnographer.

Daniel's horror at having to bathe in ritually pure waters contaminated by the excrement of thousands of other pilgrims was perhaps confined to himself; understandably, he did little to find out. But this form of unpleasantness seems to have been slight compared with the physical torture of the trek up the mountain. The pilgrim must walk barefoot, on an uneven and often stony path, up and down the hills on the way, and always under the southern sun, which even in December can be extremely hot. The pain, according to Daniel, was relentless. Everybody chanted the god's name all the while, but the agony continued to mount, so that many pilgrims said that although they still loved Aiyappan, "their predominant—if not sole—sensation was that of pain and that they did not (for the most part) know or care who was around them or what was said" (1984: 268). But for most sufferers (if not for the numbed ethnographer) the pain was said to disappear suddenly, to be replaced by love. "Yet the perfect pilgrim must not merely stop feeling pain, he must also stop feeling love" (ibid.: 274), and this is finally achieved at the shrine in the Sabarimalai temple, when each man breaks a coconut filled with clarified butter to pour over Aiyappan's image. In climbing the final step to the shrine and performing this action, every pilgrim expressed, albeit inarticulately, "the experience of having lost their identity and individuality, even if it had been only for a fleeting moment" (ibid.: 286). Merger with Aiyappan was ultimately accomplished.

Such union with the deity is, as we know, a fundamental goal in popular Hinduism, especially in its devotionalist stream. The love for Aiyappan that the pilgrims proclaim firmly belongs to the Tamil *bhakti* idiom; the hymns sung to the god are similar to other devotionalist hymns and it is significant that the pilgrimage takes place in *margali*, the month most completely identified with devotionalist worship in Tamil Hinduism. But central to that worship, as we saw in the previous chapter, is the image of the devotee as the god's lover or wife, and the hope of winning a godlike husband is a prominent theme in the hymns sung by women and girls at home. The pleasant, erotically tinged rituals in Madurai homes and temples contrast markedly with the pilgrimage to Sabarimalai, where union with the god is achieved through an arduous journey.

To explore the significance of this contrast, let us look at the hardship of the mountain trek, which is plainly a vital part of the religious experience. True, most pilgrims to Sabarimalai take a shorter route and many walk more slowly than Daniel and his fellows; other people who have been on the pilgrimage do not recall it as excruciating. Moreover, I am not entirely convinced that his pilgrims suffered so badly, for nearly all Tamils are used to walking on their hardened bare feet over burning, uneven ground. Nevertheless—however painful the journey really is—the arduousness of the pilgrimage, as well as the dangers of the forest in the shape of wild animals (once a serious threat), are themes that are central to its popular imagery. Severe suffering ought to be part of the pilgrimage to Sabarimalai, even if it actually is not.

The emphasis on physical hardship and danger is closely linked with other features, notably Aiyappan's celibacy, the rigor of the restrictions observed by pilgrims, the exclusion of menstruating women, the exceptional egalitarianism among pilgrims, and probably their social background. In the Tamil Aiyappan cult, the god's physical prowess is stressed, and this is directly linked to his celibacy and retention of semen, a source of strength according to traditional Hindu notions of physiology. Aiyappan is thus like Shiva, the chaste ascetic, who does not spill his semen; but he is unlike Shiva the seducer who, as Nataraja, is feted at Tiruvadirai in *margali*. Strict celibacy, a distinguishing characteristic of the ascetic, is enjoined upon the Sabarimalai pilgrims, whose renunciation—albeit temporary—is unusually elaborate for a pilgrimage attracting ordinary householders. Moreover, as one of Lars Kjaerholm's informants made clear (1986: 131), pilgrims must be celibate so that they can retain their semen and build up the strength needed for the hard journey, just like Aiyappan himself when he first traveled to Sabarimalai.

The identification of pilgrims as renouncers, as well as the shared observation of other restrictions, the universal mode of address as "lord," the collective singing, and the informality of the guru's leadership, are all instrumental in generating the rather exceptional egalitarianism found on the Sabarimalai pilgrimage (Daniel 1984: 250). Equality among pilgrims is not always complete; from one village, two separate parties of vegetarian high-caste and nonvegetarian low-caste pilgrims set off, and egalitarianism does not last after returning home (Kjaerholm 1986: 132–33). But certainly the separation of castes by walking groups on the Pandharpur pilgrimage has no equivalent on the way to Sabarimalai, and Aiyappan's pilgrims find a much greater equality among themselves than is usual in devotionalist movements. The prohibition on menstruating women is partly explained by the exceptionally strict rules of purity enforced on the journey and at Aiyappan's temple; any pilgrim breaking these rules is thought to risk death on the dangerous passage (Reiniche 1979: 37). Just as significantly, though, the prohibition debars females who are, actually or potentially, sexually active and this is consistent with the stress placed on the celibacy of both the god and his male pilgrims. However, the almost complete exclusion of women also means that one of the principal inequalities in society—between the sexes, and especially between husband and wife—is effaced within the pilgrims' bands. Eliminating this deep-rooted "natural" inequality is in turn conducive to unusual equality among all the male pilgrims.

The virtual absence of women also contributes to the distinctively masculine, physically tough style of religiosity that is so striking in the Sabarimalai pilgrimage, a kind of Hindu equivalent of "muscular Christianity." In generating this almost aggressively masculine style, the journey's physical hardship makes a signal contribution. In style and orientation, it means that the Sabarimalai pilgrimage is almost diametrically opposed to the devotionalist rituals, particularly those carried out by women, which are being held during December and January in homes and temples on the Tamilnadu plain. And the contrast between the devotee as male ascetic and female lover does, of course, reflect an opposition that is perennial within devotionalism (for example, in a very different guise, in the divisions between renouncers and devotionalists within the north Indian Ramanandi order).

Although detailed evidence on the social background of Sabarimalai pilgrims is inadequate, Daniel (1984: 250) reports that most of them belong to the urban middle class; Kjaerholm (1986: 132) says that they are mainly young or middle-aged men. These comments are consistent with my own and others' unsystematic observations. All this suggests that Aiyappan strikes the same kind of chord as Sathya Sai Baba and other modern gurus, albeit with a different response. Sai Baba, as we saw in chapter 7, promises miraculous solutions to the perceived problems of the urban middle class; Aiyappan and his pilgrimage offer a solution achieved by vigorous and rigorous masculinity in male peer groups,

which are predominantly found in towns and cities, but nonetheless reproduce themselves here in an antithesis of urban living in the forested
mountains. Such an interpretation is negatively supported by the scanty
evidence on Brahman attitudes. Brahmans do go to Sabarimalai—and
even their caste-minded bigots can lose a sense of superiority there, as
Daniel shows (1984: 271–72)—but they seem to be relatively underrepre-
sented. In my limited experience, the pilgrimage tends to be disparaged by
Brahmans, who expressly dislike its noisy manifestations of masculine
brotherhood. To their traditionally more restrained and cerebral style of
religiosity, Sabarimalai has little appeal; no doubt, even if unexpressed,
the pilgrimage's egalitarianism is unattractive too. But Brahmanical dis-
dain cuts little ice with most non-Brahmans in contemporary Tamilnadu,
and it cannot curtail the growing popularity of the Sabarimalai pilgrimage, in which the journey up the mountain is the true foundation of the
participants' devotional experience.

IN A BUS FROM RAJASTHAN

In her monograph on Rajasthani popular Hinduism, Gold describes a
variety of pilgrimages made by local people to nearby sites and to others
much farther away. The longest, and the one I shall discuss, was a month-
long tour made by bus to Gaya, Puri, and other centers in north India
(Gold 1988a: 213–98). Gold's is the first anthropological description of
this rapidly expanding form of motorized pilgrimage.

The pilgrimage party was made up of sixty-three adults (including
Gold) and four children—a dozen educated Brahmans from a small town
who were related to the bus driver, and the rest a mixed-caste group of
mainly uneducated rural people, mostly fairly elderly. As with most pilgrimages by bus from the region, the first stop was a Ganesha temple in
Rajasthan, where the god was prayed to for success along the way. Two
other places in the state were visited and then the party traveled to
Krishna's homeland to look at Brindavan, Mathura, and Gokul. From
there they went to Agra to see the Taj Mahal and the Red Fort. Next came
Prayaga (Allahabad) followed by Benares, where the pilgrims bathed and
"were taken on a whirlwind tour of central Kashi's most famed temples,"
leaving little but blurred impressions (ibid.: 280). Gaya, the first major
destination, was reached from Benares.

Many of the travelers were on the pilgrimage to deposit "flowers," the
bones and ashes of their deceased and cremated kinsfolk, in the Ganges'
tributary at Gaya and to perform the *shraddha* ritual of offerings (*pinda-
dana*) to the ancestors. Benares, "despite its fabulous reputation as giver
of release" (ibid.: 203), was not preferred over Gaya for these rituals,

which are carried out to honor deceased parents (or other kin). People guarantee their parents' liberation by placing their remains in the river, as well as discharge the traditional debt to the ancestors. Gaya is renowned as a great sacred center for these objectives in both the textual and popular traditions. Pilgrimages made in connection with death and ancestral rituals are, throughout India, widely seen as important or even obligatory by conscientious, traditionally minded Hindus. Unless they decide on a long journey to Gaya, the villagers studied by Gold usually make these pilgrimages to Hardwar, although Allahabad is sometimes chosen (ibid.: 203–13).

The Rajasthanis' bus arrived at Gaya during the dark lunar "fortnight of the ancestors" in *ashwina* (September–October), the preferred time for performing the rituals. This naturally meant that the town was crowded with pilgrims. All those on the bus were compulsorily immunized against cholera. They then had to confront the unsanitary filth littering the riverbank. On the first day in Gaya, everyone went to the river to bathe "in the shallow and very unappealing water" (ibid.: 219). Some of the "flower bearers" then placed bones and ashes on the river bottom, attended by beggar children eager to catch the coins emptied from the pouch containing them; one old pilgrim's pouch was grabbed by a child even before he could sink his relatives' remains. Despite a determination to complete the task for which they had come to Gaya, "there was a lot of uncomfortable talk . . . about the impropriety of placing one's forefathers in such a dirty place" (ibid.: 220). On the second day, elaborate offerings to the ancestors were made with the aid of pilgrimage priests (*panda*) who, as always, drove a hard bargain over their fees with the Rajasthanis. It proved to be a long and hot day's work and by the end disaffection was rife; almost all the pilgrims felt "that they had had more than enough; that they had paid an exorbitant price to suffer through a largely incomprehensible ritual which might or might not be effective in granting peace to the spirits of the dead" (ibid.: 227).

After Gaya the party went to Calcutta, a unfortunate port of call where the driver was harassed by the police because his vehicle was overloaded and the pilgrims were harassed by the Kalighat temple priests. From Calcutta they traveled to Puri, the journey's end point and a place to relax. For all the pilgrims, the highlight was their encounter with the sea, where they surrendered themselves to the waves "with remarkable abandon and togetherness" (ibid.: 282). For only a few was *darshana* of Jagannatha (Jagdish) in Puri's temple as profound or impressive as the Bay of Bengal, although the temple's famous food *prasada* did win favor and the pilgrims were generous when invited to give donations.

The bus then turned westward, to Ayodhya and Hardwar. In Hardwar, the ancestral rituals were performed by the pilgrims with their priests, albeit briefly because they had already been done at length in Gaya. All the pilgrims bought sealed pots of Ganges water, which they regarded as imperative. Via Delhi, Jaipur, and other places, the travelers finally reached Pushkar, the Rajasthani town where long-distance pilgrimages normally end, and eventually their home village. There they worshiped at the shrine of the goddess Pathvari Ma ("Path Mother"), who is a local form of Ganga and, as protector of pilgrims, is worshiped before and after all pilgrimages to submerge flowers in the river. The final closure of the pilgrimage comes when the Ganges water bought in Hardwar is drunk at a later ritual, the Celebration of Ganga.

As I implied, in Gaya most pilgrims openly wondered why they had come and their skepticism persisted back home. Indeed, many people, according to Gold, consistently doubt the merit of all pilgrimages to sink the remains of the dead, although they also insist that they must go and all those who can find the resources do so. Such apparent inconsistency is obviously difficult to interpret, although it is deeply rooted. As Age-hananda Bharati (1963: 144) notes, pious Hindus customarily go on pil-grimages and deem them meritorious, and yet also state that they are unimportant. Still, at the symbolic level, the whole event—the pilgrimage and Celebration of Ganga—can be understood as a "transformation from death to life, effected through the exchange of flowers for Ganges water." The rationale for the rest of the pilgrimage, where no obligation to deceased kin is involved, is, Gold concludes, "far less penetrable" (1988a: 260).

I am not convinced that this is true or, at least, that the reasons are less penetrable than for many other pilgrimages or rituals. In the first place, Rajasthani villagers, like others, go on long pilgrimages simply because they are an adventure. For most people on the bus to Gaya and Puri, it was the first time—and probably the last—that they saw the sights of north India and bathed in the sea. The pilgrims also had a lot of fun in their novel surroundings; they specially enjoyed telling stories about the gods and goddesses, and singing devotional songs, which made the bus journey an act of collective devotion, particularly for the women. More-over, the very description of the journey as a "*darshan* bus tour" partly answers Gold's question; an explicit purpose was precisely to have "many powerful *darshan*s of the gods" (ibid.: 263) by seeing the deities at some of their most celebrated sites, particularly Jagannatha in Puri, even if the Bay of Bengal did prove more impressive when the pilgrims actually arrived there. The songs on the bus and the hymn to Jagdish sung each evening patently belong to the Vaishnava devotionalist idiom. The hymn's final verse opens with the Vaishnava pledge: "My body, mind, and wealth are yours" (ibid.: 274). Thus the entire bus journey became a kind of devotionalist ritual comparable with the Pandharpur, Braj, and

Sabarimalai pilgrimages, so that union with god and liberation in the devotionalist idiom were indeed central to its purpose.

Yet, the bus tour was certainly not unmitigated pleasure or uplifting experience. Almost everyone worried endlessly about food, sanitation, seat allocation, and thieves. Many uncomfortable nights were passed beside petrol pumps and in stinking bus stands; the party was pestered by rapacious pilgrimage priests and all the other characters who make a living in India's major sacred centers. The Rajasthanis found this no more congenial than the anthropologist did, as one man's obscene denunciation of the Calcutta priests (ibid.: 275) aptly shows.

In asking her informants about the purpose of it all, Gold got many uninformative replies, but one consistent answer was that "giving away, using up, spending money" is "one firmly positive aspect of pilgrimage" (ibid.: 288). Despite its classical approbation, bathing in pilgrimage centers is widely regarded as rather futile. Liberal giving—especially to people, however unsavory, who are anonymous—is perceived as definitely meritorious; "here if anywhere was the potential for increasing chances of release in some distant future" (ibid.: 292). This outlook is consistent with the widely recognized merit of unreciprocated gift giving in classical and popular Hindu thought; the ideal gift is the one that is never returned (Parry 1986). Beyond this, though, there is also a vaguely articulated sense that the pilgrimage across the land externally corresponds to a pilgrimage within oneself, an idea dependent on the identification between body and cosmos. That sense, too, helps to explain why many of those who went on the bus from Rajasthan "felt at heart that it was their inner resolution to go and the outer hardship and expense endured as signs of that resolution which validated whatever fruits, gross or subtle, they did or did not hope to attain in this life or future lives" (Gold 1988a: 298).

In this interpretation, we see again the importance of the ascetic and votive aspects of Hindu pilgrimage, which combine with the age-old sense of obligation toward the ancestors and the spirit of devotionalism transparent in this *darshana* tour of sacred centers. Had they foreseen motor transport, the nineteenth-century Bengalis who confirmed that pilgrimage by rail was indeed meritorious would surely have said the same about pilgrimage by bus.

Conclusion

Unlike walking to or round Pandharpur, Braj, or Sabarimalai, traveling on a pilgrimage bus is not valued for its own sake. The Rajasthanis saw their activity in the sacred centers as far more important than the journey. The hardships on the bus tour were also very different from those on the pilgrimages described earlier. All the same, extremes of heat, cold, exhaustion, overcrowding, squalor, and extortion are typically part and parcel of almost every long-distance Hindu pilgrimage undertaken in company with many others. Such hardships are rarely sought out deliberately by pilgrims, but they are partially assimilated with ascetic austerities, so that they also contribute to the goals pursued by those who temporarily become or resemble renouncers.

Furthermore, in each pilgrimage discussed in this chapter, a central purpose—whether or not the sole one—is union with god, together with the pursuit of liberation after death and favors in this life, and that purpose is achieved in or through a journey that is itself a collective devotionalist ritual. The journey takes people away from their ordinary, domestic mundane life, and they join others who are not their day-to-day associates. Obviously, for the pilgrim traveling alone or with a handful of family members or friends, on a much shorter or more comfortable journey, none of this necessarily applies. And in principle, as we have seen, it is not even necessary to go anywhere to undertake a pilgrimage: Kashi is everywhere, including one's own body. But for most people, understandably, that idea does not match up to the actual experience of traveling, and strenuous long-distance pilgrimage in particular offers a kind of religious experience that is hard to find within the confines of a local community. Pilgrimage also generates a different kind of social experience; sometimes, as on the path to Sabarimalai, an unaccustomed equality develops, although often and probably more commonly, as on the road to Pandharpur, it does not. But even then pilgrimage requires people to dissolve or sustain their customary divisions of gender, kinship, caste, or class in relation to others with whom they are unfamiliar. Normal social boundaries do not merely persist in such circumstances, for they have to be actively reconstructed. That all this amounts to Turner's communitas is implausible, but pilgrimage in India certainly forces people to experience themselves in relation to others, and their deities, in ways that shake them out of their more stable local and daily routines.

Pilgrimage may also enhance the ordinary person's appreciation of Hindu cultural and religious unity. Commenting on the pilgrim villager's experience, David G. Mandelbaum writes: "He has seen a variety of customs and a diversity of peoples—yet all gathered for the same purpose, acting on the same assumptions and focussed on the same rites and symbols" (1970: 403). Mandelbaum also refers to ritual customs that underline this unity; for example, pilgrims who bathe in the sea at Rameswaram on the southern coast take away pots of sea-water to pour into the Ganges, and conversely pilgrims take pots of Ganges water to Shiva's temple at Rameswaram so that it can be poured over his *linga*. In fact, ethnographic evidence shows that pilgrims gathered at a center often do not share the same purpose, assumptions, and ritual focus posited by Mandelbaum, so that the pilgrimage experience may add little to any real sense of identity between them. Yet ritual customs like the two-way transport of water between Rameswaram and the Ganges are themselves means to link pilgrimage centers at opposite ends of India. These customs, albeit incompletely over such a vast area, do serve to integrate the country through a religious topography, and long-distance pilgrimage probably contributes something significant to the collective perception of unity among Hindus.

Moreover, as a special journey to a crossing-place and center where the deities' presence has an immediacy or accessibility absent at home, every Hindu pilgrimage has something in common with others, especially when they involve long-distance travel to major sites. Many pilgrimages are collective rituals carrying people closer to god through a physical movement, which explicitly symbolizes the devotees' progress toward unity with the divine. This, of course, is the goal pursued in worship and other rituals as well, particularly those imbued with the ethos of devotionalism. To climb Mount Kailasa—the actual mountain in the Himalayas—is to experience an approaching union with Shiva with a tangibility that could hardly be created by any other means. That tangibility of religious experience is crucial to the growing popularity of pilgrimage, as more and more Hindus take advantage of new opportunities to undertake long journeys to sacred centers that often used to be far too remote. At the very least, too, pilgrimage allows Hindus to sense the scale of the social and religious world to which they belong. In the lapidary English phrase of a pilgrim speaking to Olivier Herrenschmidt (1989: 64) as they sat together at the great Tirupati temple: "India, best gods."

Chapter 10

MISFORTUNE

I N TIMES of trouble, Hindus frequently turn to their gods and goddesses for help. Many acts of worship or sacrifice, at local temples or in far-flung pilgrimage centers, are made by victims of misfortune hoping to persuade the deities to release them and their families from illness, childlessness, poverty, or other kinds of human suffering. Much of this misfortune, it is generally believed, is caused by malevolent ghosts, evil spirits, witches, sorcerers, the evil eye, and other personified agencies, and much of it is caused by more impersonal mystical forces like the planets and other sources of inauspiciousness, as well as the effect of *karma*, which ensures that every misdeed will bear its "fruit" in subsequent suffering. In this chapter, I explore popular Hindu explanations of misfortune, and I begin with the role of the deities themselves.

DIVINE ANGER AND VIOLENCE

At the widest level, as we saw in chapter 2, the great gods Vishnu and Shiva command the universe and deploy their vast powers to sustain the sociocosmic order. In their form as monarchs, Vishnu and Shiva, as well as the goddess, protect their kingdoms; in their form as village and clan deities, they (and other little gods and goddesses) similarly protect local settlements and kin groups. Thus the deities act to uphold *dharma* throughout the universe and its constituent microcosms, and in so doing they protect human beings here on earth. The moral order that is *dharma*, and its divine sustainment, however, depend upon proper relationships between deities and the people who worship them, and also among people themselves. When these relationships are disturbed, the deities are justifiably angered and inflict misfortune on those responsible. The deities' anger is therefore a sanction against human misconduct and a significant dimension of their protective role.

In many cases, divine anger is provoked in relatively straightforward ways. For example, if someone accidentally or deliberately enters a temple when polluted or fails to perform a ritual properly, he or she may fall ill; if an illness is thought to have been caused in this way, the patient will seek a cure by making amends, usually by performing a reparatory ritual or making an offering to appease the offended deity.

Divine anger falls on groups as well as individuals, normally when the whole group or some of its members have offended its protective deity. Let me cite just one example relating to kin groups. Nayar joint families in Kerala are generally protected by deified ancestral spirits and a patron goddess. These deities are offended when their worship is neglected or badly performed, but they may also punish incest or other kinds of immorality within the family by killing the offender and sending misfortune to the whole group. Harm can also be inflicted on the group by the ancestral spirits so as to bring pressure on an irresponsible *karanavan*, the senior male head of the matrilineal joint family (*taravad*). In such a case, internal conflict can be brought into the open, for "a junior member might be possessed by [an ancestral] ghost and voice its threats to the *taravad* [which] added force to the complaints of young men who were cheated by their *karanavans*" (Gough 1976: 245). Although most Nayar joint families have now broken up, this example is fairly typical inasmuch as the tutelary clan deities of every joint family, lineage, or other kin group—which commonly include deified ancestors—tend to punish any disrespect shown to them by the group's members. Moreover, they also punish immorality and irresponsibility within the group, which are often linked to internal dispute and intrigue.

Tutelary village deities act in much the same way. In settlements struck by epidemic disease, drought, livestock deaths, or crop failure, the cause is often deemed to be neglect of the village deity, typically because its annual festival has not been held. The festival, of course, is then duly celebrated—with or without any subsequent amelioration. Allocating the blame for past neglect is frequently a lively source of conflict within a village. Sometimes the deity's anger is actually attributed to factional strife, as well as to breaches of the social and moral code by villagers, who may have broken caste or kinship rules. Hence the tutelary deity is likely to get angry if there is any breakdown of ordered unity within the settlement that it rules as a protective sovereign.

In principle, justified divine anger unleashed on human wrongdoers, whether individually or collectively, is a relatively clear-cut matter, even if in practice people often consider that their punishment is excessively harsh. Divine wrath does not always fall directly on the blameworthy, however, as the diseases sent by single village goddesses show. Epidemic disease—particularly smallpox until its elimination—is or was commonly assumed to be a punishment visited upon a community by its angry tutelary goddess. Yet the individual victims of smallpox typically included many innocent children. Moreover, the sickness was seen as possession by the hot goddess (the fever being a visible manifestation of her presence). The "treatment" was cooling worship of the patient, an image and form of the goddess, who was revered in the hope that she would leave.

That, of course, was more likely to occur if the whole community also took appropriate measures, like holding the annual festival that had been too long postponed. Nevertheless, individual sufferers from the disease sent by the goddess were often not being justifiably punished, at least for sins committed in this life. Nor were they true victims of divine wrath. Rather they were chosen by a goddess exercising her hot, dangerous power by possessing human beings.

The single goddesses who control diseases are not the only deities whose dangerous power can harm human beings, for the vast majority of little village deities can do so too. Many little deities are said to be former malevolent ghosts and spirits, and that is the main reason why they cause so much harm. All dark, single goddesses, as well as village gods who resemble them such as Bhairava, tend to be easily roused to anger and violence. Furthermore, all ferocious deities, irrespective of their ancestry, are closely linked with demons, malevolent ghosts, evil spirits, witches, and the like. Thus Bhairava and Kali are sometimes said to have cohorts of horrible allies, recruited from the ranks of ghosts and spirits, who bring them victims to assuage their thirst for blood. Hence the dividing line between angry, violent deities and other personified malevolent agencies is extremely fine, and a great deal of human suffering is laid at those deities' feet.

Moreover, it is not only the most ferocious deities who can harm human beings; any deity may call on a retinue of malevolent allies. This is especially true of Shiva, "Lord of the *bhuta*s," who stalks the cremation grounds to recruit his horde of *bhuta-preta*s, the collective term for malevolent ghosts and spirits. The damage wreaked by ghosts and spirits is partially contained by Shiva's supervision of them, but he can also order them to hit out, especially when he assumes the form of terrible Bhairava or angry Virabhadra. Consequently, when someone is victimized by a malevolent being, it might be working for a deity like Bhairava or Kali, but it could have been sent by great Shiva himself. Rather like a criminal boss whose public countenance is respectably benevolent, Shiva—or indeed any other deity—can always call on nasty henchmen who will maim and kill. As we shall see again, the gods and goddesses of popular Hinduism—even the greatest of them—are not always good and they are certainly not always kind.

I should also mention that in spite of their power all deities, even Vishnu and Shiva, are subject to the depredations of lesser malevolent beings. In temples, ritual precautions are taken to protect deities against harmful agencies. Protection is also afforded by subordinate guardian deities who, because they are mostly former demons or other malevolent beings, are mainly effective according to the rule that a thief is set to catch a thief. The deities are the enemies of malevolent beings and therefore find common cause with the human sufferers whom they help, but, as we have already seen, the deities are also closely associated with those beings, and the continuity between them will be a constant theme of this chapter.

GHOSTLY SPIRITS OF THE PREMATURELY DEAD

Throughout India, much human misfortune—particularly physical and mental illness, childlessness, and sometimes death—is attributed to the malevolent ghosts of people who met untimely "bad" deaths. This category includes those who died in childhood or youth, especially before marriage and the birth of sons, who can carry on the family line and perform their parents' funerary and ancestral rites. It also includes those who died by murder, suicide, accidental injury, snake-bite, and various diseases, as well as from pregnancy or childbirth, or at a very inauspicious time. The ghosts of people who met bad deaths or whose funerary rites were misperformed are unlikely to pass over to the world of the dead. Instead they remain in a state of limbo, half in this world, where they willfully harm the living. All such malevolent ghostly spirits (to combine interchangeable terms) belong to the assembly of *bhuta-preta*s, but it would be unrewardingly tedious to catalogue their numerous varieties. Instead, I shall introduce some particular spirits through two ethnographic case studies.

The first is about the pair of ghosts, known as *pattar* and *jhujhar(ji)*, who bring misfortune to people in the Rajasthani village of Ghatiyali. As is common throughout India, Ghatiyali villagers believe that their environment is populated by a host of different ghosts and spirits, many nameless and liable to "grab anyone who is so imprudent as to walk alone at night in uninhabited places" (Gold 1988a: 64). Besides the nameless ones, however, there is a sizable contingent of *pattar*s, normally said to be the undeparted spirits of unmarried people, typically children, and *jhujhar*s, the spirits of married people. Both kinds of ghost spring from human beings who died prematurely with strong, unfulfilled desires.

A *pattar* or *jhujhar* usually announces its presence by inflicting sickness, madness, or bad luck on living members of its former family, but since many other malevolent agencies do so as well, it is necessary to identify the ghostly spirit first. This can be done in various ways, but the commonest divinatory technique is to visit a little deity's shrine. "On the principle that it takes one to know one," deities "are able to reveal the names and wills of spirits of the dead who wish to become enshrined as deities in households" (ibid.: 70). Repeated consultations with one or several deities, through their diviner-priests, are often needed to identify

the troublesome ghostly spirit. Once this has been done, the spirit is enshrined and worshiped by its victim and members of the latter's family.
By deifying it the harmful spirit's power can be controlled and turned to
protective advantage by human beings. However, even deifying a cor-
rectly identified spirit may not solve the problem once and for all; for
example, someone starting a new venture may forget to approach the
spirit, which is then offended, so that "a new cycle of afflictions, consultations, and divinations" is needed. Or, because these ghostly deities "have
whims of their own," they "may cause troubles purely in order to gratify
such whims" (ibid.: 71).

People sometimes hope that ghostly spirits will eventually decide to
depart for good, so that they are "released . . . from their condition as
minor deities haunting the scenes of a past lifetime" (ibid.: 77). Alternatively, spirits may be persuaded to locate themselves somewhere else, especially if taken to the river Ganges. But, says Ann G. Gold, there is widespread skepticism about the efficacy of relocation, because spirits have a
habit of "jumping back," so that continual worship is the only sensible
solution for those still attached to their former homes. Then "it is imperative for the living to convince the spirits of the dead to continue to share
an interest in familial well-being" (ibid.: 78). This is vital because *pattar*s
and *jhujhar*s can "prevent or permit fertility" (ibid.: 79). Unhappy
ghosts, in other words, block the birth of children, especially sons, in
barely disguised revenge for their own untimely end.

Significantly, the "demands and treatment" of *pattar*s are like "those
of powerful, invisible children" (ibid.: 66). The adoration of deified *pattar*s (for instance, by worshiping them through songs) is partly intended
"to reassure them of continued love and care from the living" (ibid.: 75),
and thus to give them the quasi-parental attention missed because of premature death. Deified *jhujhar*s are worshiped more like other deities, but
neither they nor *pattar*s seem to be resented for causing afflictions; no one
blames them for behavior motivated by an understandably human reaction to death when unfulfilled.

Plainly, Ghatiyali's *pattar*s and *jhujhar*s illustrate the fluid distinction
among deities, human beings, and personified malevolent ghostly spirits
in popular Hinduism. They exemplify one path by which a dead person
can become a deity. Notice too that the spirit is originally identified by
another deity, speaking through its diviner-priest, and not by the latter
acting merely as a man with expertise. At one level, therefore, Ghatiyali
villagers who explain misfortune as affliction by ghostly spirits of the
prematurely dead ascribe it to potential or actual deities, with whom
other deities can most easily communicate. At another level, though, *pattar*s and *jhujhar*s are conceptualized as former family members with distinctively human characteristics, so that misfortune is imputed to anthropomorphic sources.

The second case study is about a cult, described by David M. Knipe, in the town of Rajahmundry in Andhra Pradesh, where the ghostly spirits of deceased infants and children are worshiped, either at home or in a local temple. But these deified spirits are also the focal figures in nocturnal processions for Virabhadra, a fierce form of Shiva. In classical mythology, Virabhadra was born from Shiva's rage, provoked by both his insulting exclusion from Daksha's sacrifice and the suicide of Parvati as Sati in shame at her father's action. Family groups take part in the processions. One member of each group carries on the head a tray from the domestic shrine bearing "ash-fruits" (*vibhuti-pandu*), small cones made of cowdung ash mixed with gum. There are normally three cones on a tray, representing the spirit of a child from the family who died recently or many years earlier. The processional marchers—especially women and most often young mothers—commonly become possessed; they "willingly risk their bodies as vehicles for the spirits, becoming agents who transmit to the family the immediate states of mind and wishes of their stranded kin" (1989: 127). As the possessed whirl around and fall screaming to the ground, attendant ritual specialists calm them down. Processions end at the riverside, where the last possessions occur. When all is quiet again, the ash-fruits are washed in the river, replaced on their trays, and offered worship. The trays are then taken home on an uneventful journey; control over the spirits has been reestablished.

As Knipe shows, the complex symbolism of the ash-fruits resonates with a range of pan-Hindu themes. But the central feature of the processions is that a child's deified spirit is recognized and worshiped as a *virabhadra*, a personification of rage and a form of the god Virabhadra. Sometimes, worship of the child-spirit becomes highly developed. For example, there is in Rajahmundry a lorry mechanic of the Golla (Shepherd) caste, who is in his fifties. When he was an infant, his elder brother (age five) died. The boys' mother established a shrine for her dead son; the mechanic later took over the worship. But then he became arbitrarily possessed by his brother's spirit, who demanded more attention. The possession states interfered with the mechanic's work, so he struck a bargain; he would worship the spirit daily if the latter agreed to possess him only at Mahashivaratri, "Great Shiva's night," the god's annual festival on the dark fourteenth of *phalguna* (February–March; *magha* in Andhra Pradesh), when the Virabhadra processions are commonly held for two successive nights. "And so the lorry mechanic has become the most celebrated ritualist in the [Virabhadra procession], dancing ecstatically for hours, his matted locks flying, a silver trident clutched in his hands. The brother has been satisfied with the dance, and life has been successful for the family" (ibid.: 140).

In his own mind, the mechanic when possessed "is his brother the virabhadra, the god Virabhadra, and transcendent Shiva" (ibid.: 140 [diacritics omitted]). He has progressively transformed the worship of his brother's spirit into worship of Shiva—his *linga* being represented by the ash-fruits—while the mechanic himself has adopted much of the lifestyle of a Brahmanical, ascetic Shaiva priest. The mechanic's elaborate worship is atypical, but it illustrates clearly a potential development inherent in the continuum between a living human being, a ghostly spirit of the dead, the latter's deified form, and a great deity like Virabhadra-Shiva. The mechanic has only realized the possibility that is always present when a ghost is controlled through deification.

As Knipe rightly says, the Virabhadra cult "is more than a statement about the death of a child: it is a review of Hindu eschatology" (ibid.: 144). Here, though, I shall focus on the premature death in relation to mystical explanations of misfortune. To identify a child's spirit as a *virabhadra* is patently to project on to the latter the child's anger about its early death. That anger, of course, is precisely why the spirit causes affliction and has to be controlled. Ghatiyali *pattar*s seem more frustrated than angry at their curtailed lives, but in both Ghatiyali and Rajahmundry, the dead children's spirits are thought to want to stay with their families by becoming enshrined and worshiped, and they make this clear by troubling their living relatives.

Sometimes, as reported from the Benares region, the spirits of dead children (*marva*) belong to the cohort of a more dangerous spirit, such as a *churail*. A *churail* is the ghostly spirit of a woman who was barren or died in pregnancy or childbirth. The *churail* jealously attacks other child-bearing women to kill their babies or unborn fetuses, whose spirits then join the *churail*'s cohort. When someone is afflicted by a *churail*'s childish spirit, the diviner often identifies an unknown infant who died in the family in an earlier generation. Then, of course, it is highly unlikely that anyone would see the spirit's malevolence as expressing a desire to return to the bosom of its living relatives.

When, however, as frequently happens in Ghatiyali and Rajahmundry, the ghosts of the prematurely dead spring from the sons and daughters of their victims, it is clear that the latters' worst misfortune was actually their own children's deaths. It takes little imagination to see that in reality the despair, anger, and guilt of the bereaved parents and other family members, rather than the child itself, are projected on to the enraged or frustrated spirit. Furthermore, the spirit's deification is plainly motivated in part by unwillingness to let the lost child go. As Knipe says, "the deceased child is not erased but remains a part of the family, the household, and the major events of its life" (ibid.: 142). Thus, for instance, in 1978 one young mother in Rajahmundry lost the youngest of her three children when he was eighteen months old. He possessed her the very day after his death, when she recognized him as a *virabhadra*. Seven years later, she was still worshiping him regularly (ibid.: 134). Similarly, in Ghatiyali, where the infant mortality rate is typically high, most women wear medallions enshrining *pattar*s round their necks; even very old women still wear them for infants lost many years earlier (Gold 1988a: 67, 77). People themselves insist that the children's spirits refuse to depart, but the psychological reality is that the bereaved, especially mothers, refuse to accept that they have lost their offspring, tantrums and all, for ever. Thus ghostly spirits of the prematurely dead, especially children, are one important explanation of misfortune occurring in their former families, but their lingering presence is simultaneously a response by the living to their tragic death. The spirits personify the grief that fellow spirits, along with other agencies, may also have caused.

Spirit Possession and Protest, Guilt, and Dispute

If despair, anger, and guilt are at the root of the survivors' affliction by their own children's spirits, different feelings often lie behind the imputation of misfortune to other kinds of malevolent ghostly spirits. Particularly common is animosity toward other people and—as in many societies—a lot of spirit affliction and possession can be understood as an oblique expression of protest by the victims. In this section, I shall explore this topic, but first I must look at spirit possession and its treatment in a little more detail.

Malevolent ghostly spirits almost always harm people by possessing them. They enter their victims to take control of their bodies and minds so that they fall ill, go mad, become unable to bear children, or find themselves thwarted at every turn. In all Indian languages, a distinction can be made between involuntary, "bad" possession by a malevolent being and voluntary, "good" possession by a deity (as experienced, for instance, by a diviner). Obviously, some forms of divine possession—for example, by a goddess of disease—are usually only euphemistically described in favorable terms. Nonetheless, if someone, for good or ill, is possessed by a deity, that person is then its form or image and may become an object of worship, like a feverish patient seized by the smallpox goddess.

Yet deities are not always treated respectfully and many capricious, bloody-minded little deities are induced to leave the people they have possessed by cajolery, taunting, or blatant bribery. For example, a deity speaking through its victim to the diviner may be promised a petty sacrificial offering or a bit of meat if it agrees to withdraw. Irritating deities of this kind, as well as many malevolent ghostly spirits whose ability to possess is seen as wholly undesirable, are commonly dealt with by exorcism. Worship and exorcism are, at first sight, diametrically opposed methods of coping with possessive affliction, but they can shade into each other, and successful exorcism of a spirit normally requires its subsequent relocation, often by enshrining it as a deity.

The symptom of possession by a noisome agency, be it deity or spirit, is often the misfortune itself, without any other visible signs. Sometimes, though, victims become hysterical or deranged, or enter trancelike states of dissociation, in which case the diagnosis of possession is strongly reinforced. If possession is not to be controlled by worship, exorcism is usually the prescribed cure.

Casting out malevolent ghostly spirits—the most common kind of exorcism—is normally accomplished by men who also act as diviners able to identify the spirits. Few exorcists are women. Many exorcists (Hindi *ojha*) specialize in the work, but many also work as priests in little deities' temples. An exorcist can succeed because he is voluntarily possessed by his own tutelary deity, typically a goddess or another little deity, who is more powerful than the spirit. The deity, working through the exorcist, converses with the spirit, speaking through its victim, and either persuades it to leave peacefully or drags it out forcibly. If this is done successfully, the victim should return to health and normality. A human exorcist, however, is not always necessary. Sometimes a deity can directly confront a malevolent possessing spirit. Victims of possession are often taken to temples in the hope that a vision of the powerful deities, present in their images, will drive out the frightened spirits.

Whether or not an exorcist is involved, exorcism is invariably a confrontation between a deity and a malevolent spirit (or lesser deity). Exorcism is deemed successful if the more powerful deity wins, so that its foe must capitulate and depart. In popular Hinduism, however, exorcism can never kill spirits, which must be dealt with by relocating them somewhere. Sometimes, a vanquished spirit is said to join the deity's cohort. Even if it stops troubling its original victim, it embarks on a second career as one of the deity's vicious henchmen, bringing illness and death to other people at the behest of its new lord. Alternatively, a spirit may be transformed or merged into one of the deity's subordinate guardian deities, so that it is now worshiped alongside its conqueror. A spirit, having been "seated" at an appropriate site and "released" from its ghostly state of limbo, may be independently enshrined and subsequently worshiped. Then the outcome of exorcism is deification by an agonistic route. Similar spirits—like Ghatiyali's *pattars* and *jhujhars*—achieve the same status more peacefully, because they are revered as soon as their possessing presence is diagnosed.

Deification of spirits, whether exorcised first or not, is the more usual end result when they are believed to spring from dead members of the victim's family or other kith and kin. To forestall further incidents of possession by the same spirits, their erstwhile victims must continue to

honor them as deities indefinitely. When spirits are identified as unconnected strangers, however, they are often abandoned after exorcism at a
suitable place, such as a cross-roads, so that they cannot find their way
back to their earlier victims. They are likely to grab anyone unlucky
enough to pass by, however.

None of these ways of coping with malevolent ghostly spirits is reck-
oned to be foolproof, and there is widespread doubt about the compe-
tence of diviners and exorcists, as well as about the efficacy of either relocating and enshrining spirits, or abandoning and confusing them. Spirits
have an uncanny ability to repossess their victims and, because none of
them can ever be exterminated, even by powerful deities, the risk of attack from old or new predators is always present.

During exorcism sessions, the possessing spirit is expected to explain,
more or less coherently, why it has seized its victim. One temple famous
for its exorcistic cures lies near Bharatpur in Rajasthan, where the presiding deity is the immensely strong Balaji (Hanuman). As Sudhir Kakar
observed, a spirit engaged in battle with Balaji or one of the temple's
other gods often speaks with vitriol.

> The torrent of aggressive abuse, especially when it is issuing out of the other-
> wise demure mouths of frail young girls and women, leaves little doubt that we
> are witnessing a convulsive release of pent-up aggression and a rare rebellion
> against the inhibiting norms and mores of a conservative Hindu society of
> which its gods are the most obvious representatives. (1983: 67)

This is a very common pattern. At many exorcisms in temples and during
sessions with diviner-exorcists the victims of possession pour out their
anger against society in general or their close associates in particular, in
a manner serving an obvious cathartic function.

When females are possessed, the spirit's words often make it plain to
all concerned that hostility is directed at dominating men, especially husbands whose sexual conduct is typically impugned. Indeed, it is widely
assumed that spirits who seize women enjoy an illicit sexual relationship
with them, so that they may talk through their victims not in anger, but
in the honeyed or erotic tones of lovers. In almost all cases of this sort,
people involved in the exorcism can see that the possessed woman is com-
plaining—indirectly but still forcefully—about her husband or other male
relatives. It is clear too, at least to an anthropologist with a knowledge of
comparative data, that women's possession episodes are also culturally
tolerated opportunities to complain about female inferiority and subordination within Indian society.

Much spirit possession is related to other forms of social inequality as
well, especially between high and low castes, and landlords and laborers.
Take, for example, the ghost of an untouchable Chamar (Leather-
worker), who has died bearing a grudge about his ill-treatment by some-

one of higher caste. Malevolent Chamar ghosts, thought to be common in the Benares region, afflict high-caste oppressors with *chamar dosh*, the "fault" or "sin" of the Chamar. These ghosts can be persuaded to depart only through the intercession of one of the Chamars' own deities, to whom offerings have to be made by a living Chamar, who naturally demands handsome recompense for his allegedly dangerous services (Parry n.d.). A similar example, from Kerala, is the ghost of an untouchable agricultural laborer, who either died after quarreling with the high-caste Nayars for whom he worked, or was actually killed by a Nayar. Such a ghost molests his antagonist's entire family and "demands regular sacrifices if misfortune is to be averted." These can be given only by men from the ghost's own caste, who must be paid for their services (Gough 1976: 258). Plainly, in both these and many similar cases, the ghostly spirit exacts revenge for mistreatment during its lifetime. Its appearance is also a protest, in mystical form, about high-caste exploitation, and an opportunity for the ghost's living caste fellows to extract some unaccustomed profit.

Yet spirit possession, it must be stressed, is not always a vehicle for protest against the high and mighty by the low and weak. It can work in the opposite direction as well. Thus, for example, affliction by *brahm*s, the ghosts of dead Brahmans, tends to reinforce Brahman claims to superiority, or at least to curtail contempt for them. Brahman ghosts occasionally attack Nayar families (ibid.: 259), but in some places, such as Benares, they are "one of the commonest sources of ghostly affliction" and "are probably one of the most dangerous," especially when the *brahm* is the ghost of a Brahman who fasted to death in revenge against his malefactor (Parry n.d.). Something akin to such a death once occurred in Daudpur village, near Benares. A Brahman priest lent money to his Thakur patron, who died, and his nephew refused to repay the loan. The Brahman protested in traditional fashion by letting his hair and nails grow long, like an unkempt ascetic approaching death, and by refusing to perform rituals for the Thakur family. Before dying, the Brahman told his grandson to bury his shorn hair and nail clippings, and to raise a shrine above the spot if his ghost began to trouble the Thakurs. After his death, the Thakur family was plagued by leprosy, attempted suicides, illnesses, and untimely deaths, which they attributed to the hostility of the *brahm*, now worshiped at his shrine by his grandson (Planalp 1956: 774–75). In this case, the Brahman had been a creditor without effective means of redress against a powerful Thakur family, but the devastating damage caused by his ghost exemplifies the great power of all *brahm*s, itself a product of the Brahmans' ritual superiority. Significantly, as Jonathan Parry observes, the more ritually fastidious was the Brahman in life, the more dangerous is his ghost afterwards.

Hence when misfortune is blamed on malevolent ghostly spirits, it can—depending on their identification—either subvert or reinforce claims to social superiority. Spirit possession and affliction are indirect means for women to rail against men, or untouchable laborers to take revenge against high-caste landlords. Many similar examples of ritual protest by inferiors against superiors are reported in the ethnographic literature. But in the light of the prominence in comparative anthropology of "religions of the oppressed," it is important to balance these cases by those in which injurious spirits ostensibly act in conformity with hierarchical norms.

On many occasions, social inequality as such is immaterial, because any ghost is liable to attack someone against whom it bears a grudge, such as a debtor. This is true whether the ghost springs from a Brahman creditor (as in Daudpur) or a carpenter, as in a Gujarati village where a carpenter's ghost possessed a man who had not paid him for building a house, so that the man went mad and destroyed his own home (Pocock 1973: 35). Clearly, the belief that a vengeful ghostly spirit is aiming at a particular individual partly depends on public knowledge about the latter's alleged offense, and such a ghost effectively acts as a mystical agency of retribution, reminding everyone about moral obligation to others. However, the afflicted may recognize their own wrongdoing (like the Daudpur Thakurs), so that they find vengeful ghosts returning to haunt and harm them. A guilty conscience greatly increases the likelihood of spirit possession.

Malevolent ghostly spirits can play a major role in disputes involving relatives as well. Parry (n.d.) describes several such cases, uncovered during a session held by a diviner-exorcist near Benares. Ghosts, it is widely believed, can be deliberately located on people, because they tend to cling to cloves or money, which can be slipped on to the clothes or into the house of an enemy, who then becomes possessed. Exorcists themselves can be hired for this black art. One family at the Benares session was plagued by three ghosts sent by agnatic kin with whom the family was engaged in a long-running property dispute. In a second case, a shopkeeper and his wife had lost a son, who died suddenly, and their daughter was continuously ill; the diviner revealed that the ghost of a powerful ascetic had been sent by the shopkeeper's aunt, who had inherited her parents' property but lost control of it to her nephew. In a third case, a family of four brothers complained that one of their daughters was possessed and made everyone's life a misery; the family turned out to be afflicted by eight separate ghosts and had an exceptionally complicated history. One major cause of trouble, though, was the daughter's possession by a *brahm*, deliberately sent by the family of one brother's wife, with whom relations were already severely strained.

Through an intelligent use of leading questions and his knowledge of likely patterns of dispute, the diviner, speaking with the voice of the tutelary deity possessing him, was almost always able to locate the source of affliction in ghosts sent by the victims' enemies. Misfortune was thus blamed, quite openly, on ghosts manipulated by other people. Usually, this was exactly what the diviner's clients wanted to hear, for they already knew his style of diagnosis before consulting him. His verdict gave them good cause to break off all social ties with their enemies, which was particularly valuable when the latter were relatives; there are strong moral sanctions in Indian society against total severance of kin and affinal relationships. Hence in these cases, which are typical of many, spirit possession is not understood as the work of a ghost acting on its own account; instead, its malevolence has been exploited by a living antagonist, whose expedient identification by the diviner is often the final twist in a dispute due to end in social rupture.

Although cases of misfortune caused by malevolent ghostly spirits vary considerably, they all share common features as well. In popular Hinduism, all spirits have both a human origin and potentially a divine apotheosis. These distinctive qualities are consistent with both the fluid continuity between divine and human beings characteristic of the religion, and the close association that exists between deities and harmful spirits. Thus the power of gods and goddesses is itself partly demonstrated through the power of ghostly spirits, who bring misfortune to the people from whom, after death, they can arise and then aspire to divinity.

All the material discussed above also shows that human misfortune can be blamed on personified malevolent agencies, which are either projections of the victims' own psychological state—notably their anger, despair, or guilt—or manifestations of strained and resented social relationships with others, whether or not these are systematically related to patterns of social inequality. Normally, of course, both psychological and social factors are involved and reciprocally influence each other. In these respects, spirit possession and affliction in popular Hinduism have much in common with comparable phenomena in many other societies across the world, where human suffering is also ascribed to personified mystical forces attacking victims in a pattern shaped by discernible psychological and social factors.

Malevolent People, Vulnerability, and Skepticism

People who meet bad deaths live on as malevolent ghostly spirits, but people who are still alive can cause exactly the same kinds of misfortune. The most important are sorcerers, witches, and those with the evil eye. I shall describe them briefly, before looking at the related issue of vulnerability to mystical sources of harm and skepticism about their reality.

The Hindu sorcerer is simply a magician working to evil ends. Magicians, almost always male, are known by many terms, but often by a vernacular form of the Sanskrit *mantravadin*, "*mantra* speaker," because they typically rely on *mantra*s or spells to do their work. These *mantra*s may produce their effect directly if, for example, they are chanted as spells to cause or cure illness, or they may operate in conjunction with charms, magical medicines, and ritual techniques. Frequently, though, a magician's *mantra*s enable him to control little deities or spirits, and these familiars actually do his work. Many magicians—typically belonging to low castes—also serve as diviners, exorcists, or little deities' priests, who use their magic to help victims of possession by ghostly spirits. Many other magicians—typically members of high castes—specialize in the work and advertise themselves as masters of Sanskrit *mantra*s derived from scripture. Magicians of all kinds sometimes work as sorcerers—even if they rarely admit it openly—and they may be employed by laypeople to harm their enemies. Those who think that they are victims of sorcery commonly engage other magicians to counter it, and the ensuing battle between black and white magicians will be won by the man with the more powerful magic.

The term "witch" translates numerous vernacular terms for women with the mystical power to harm. In Chhattisgarh, for example, a *tonhi* is allegedly indistinguishable from any other woman by day, but at night she has supernatural powers. She thirsts for her victims' blood and harms them by sending malevolent ghosts to possess them, by poisoning their food or water, or by causing attack from the evil eye. Witches are said to congregate in cemeteries or cremation grounds at night, where they dance naked for Kali or Bhairava, the fierce deities given some of the victims' blood. In detail, popular beliefs about witches vary a lot from place to place, but the notion that they destroy people by abstracting their blood or livers is extremely widespread. Living witches assume blame for misfortune much like *churail*s and other malevolent female ghosts, who are motivated by similar misanthropic sentiments and may ally themselves with witches. As Lawrence A. Babb rightly emphasizes in discussing Chhattisgarhi witches (1975: 203–6), the complex of beliefs surrounding both them and female ghosts is consonant with ideas about the dangerous power of hot single goddesses like Kali, whose ferocity is both stimulated and appeased by blood.

Everywhere in India, marginal women, such as lone widows, tend to attract suspicion as witches, although openly accusing named women of active witchcraft seems to be fairly rare. But there are exceptions; in

1951, in Sujarupa village in Rajasthan, an old widow was actually beaten to death because she was alleged to be a witch (*dakan*). G. Morris Carstairs, who studied this tragic episode, shows that the woman's murder was closely linked to a bitter inheritance dispute between her and some of her male relatives; one of her killers was a leader of the faction thwarted by the widow during the quarrel, although the accusation of witchcraft was widely voiced throughout Sujarupa (1983: 14–25, 41–42, 61–63). Despite the exceptional outcome of this case, the dead woman precisely filled the stereotype of a witch: an aggressive, bad-tempered old widow, who was thought to be consumed by the vengeful jealousy that also motivates *churails* and similar ghostly spirits.

Jealousy and envy lie behind the evil eye as well. The evil eye—commonly known as *najar* in north India and *dishti* in the south—is treated as a widespread menace throughout India, and the harm is caused, often unconsciously, by the gaze of envious people. All kinds of trouble can be brought by the evil eye, and any display of good health, splendor, or success is likely to attract it. There are innumerable rituals to ward off the evil eye or cure its effects, and many means of magical protection against it, which are particularly used to counteract the evil eye's notoriously harmful effect on vulnerable young children. Children, it is widely thought, can be killed by the evil eye, whereas it rarely harms adults so seriously. Many Indians carefully avoid fulsome praise of other people's bonny infants for fear of arousing suspicion about their own gaze, and children thought to be victims may be deliberately left unkempt, so that they do not attract envy.

The evil eye, as a manifestation of jealousy, is motivated by the same ill-sentiment as other anthropomorphic agencies of misfortune, living or dead, and embittered childless women (who might be witches anyway) are particularly suspected of deliberately trying to kill babies with their gaze. On the other hand, the evil eye is so commonplace that almost anyone might exercise it and it often serves as hardly more than an idiom for mild envy. Half-jokingly, therefore, a man might blame his friend's eye for causing a tear in an admired new shirt (Srinivas 1976: 280). Yet there is a definite tendency, as David F. Pocock (1973: 28) observes, for the evil eye to be most feared "from those with whom one is, in most other respects, equal, or has reason to expect to be." Social equals, who are nonetheless doing a bit worse than oneself, are the people whose envious eye may cause harm, and in this respect the evil eye serves as a brake on ostentatious flaunting of success and a reminder that others, even in one's own social group, are less fortunate in life. As Pocock also comments (ibid.: 32–33), however, there is definitely a feeling that the mean and vain, at least among adults, are probably most at risk. People who complain loudly about the evil eye tend to attract the contemptuous comment that their behavior toward others, rather than just the latters' envy, lays them open to attack. Hence to accuse people of the evil eye may be taken as a sign of one's own meanness and vanity.

This last point raises the question of vulnerability to mystical sources of misfortune. Young children are particularly endangered by the evil eye because they are naturally weak. Adults make themselves vulnerable by fear of others, as well as by lack of generosity and unjustified pride. Indeed, and this is crucial, any sort of weakness makes a person vulnerable to mystical harm. Thus, for example, Hindus in Chhattisgarh explain that weakness is particularly manifested by "light" people with fear and they are most vulnerable to predatory witches (Babb 1975: 207). Similar beliefs are reported from all over India and apply to all kinds of mystical misfortune, whether inflicted by angry or violent deities, malevolent ghostly spirits, sorcerers and witches, or the evil eye.

As we have seen, many personified agencies of misfortune can be partly understood in relation to the victim's own internal disposition. Hindus themselves often more or less openly recognize this, but their psychological insight that "it's all in the mind" may, of course, persuade them that no agency of misfortune has any reality outside the disturbed minds of the weak. Actually, complete skepticism is rare; hardly any Hindus deny the existence of angry, violent deities, and few aver that all ghosts, spirits, witches, and so on are imaginary. But doubt that the latter really are as numerous and powerful as many folk claim is fairly common. An aristocratic Rajput, talking to Carstairs (1957: 197), put forward a typical view when he simultaneously asserted that ghosts, witches, and their ilk mostly do not exist except in the minds of the uneducated, that those beings cannot harm anyone who worships god, and that "if you are a man with strong will-power, with a good spiritual rise, then you will not be afraid of them—they cannot do you any harm."

In general, it is usually higher-status, wealthier, and more educated men—like Carstairs's Rajput informant—who claim that devotion to and proper worship of powerful deities is by far the most effective means to prevent and deal with misfortune. It is the same men who tend to decry as ignorant superstition many beliefs about ghostly spirits and like agencies, as well as methods for their supposed control. Consistent with this pattern, the Benares Brahman priests studied by Parry (n.d.) are openly skeptical about the efficacy of rituals to relocate exorcised ghosts, which they perform on behalf of their more credulous clients.

Some contemporary skepticism about mystical misfortune has been stimulated by the impact of strongly theistic devotionalism and modern reformism, both hostile to what they condemn as superstition, as well as by the expansion of modern education and medicine. But the skepticism also has older roots and is partly the product of an unegalitarian society. In men's eyes—although not so uniformly in their own—women are weaker and therefore more vulnerable to mystical harm. Moreover, because childlessness in India is invariably blamed on women rather than their husbands, the "evidence" ostensibly shows that women really are more likely to be persistently victimized by agencies of misfortune. And because mothers tend to be more deeply affected by miscarriage and infant mortality than fathers, they are also more likely to give vent to their grief by displaying the symptoms of spirit possession. The evidence for women's "natural" susceptibility is further reinforced by the belief that malevolent spirits thirst for blood, so that they always seek out menstruating females. As a result—partly because they do not often deny these putative facts—women are also more prone to imagine that they really are victims of malevolent agencies, which in turn strengthens the male belief that females are more credulous. Ideologically, therefore, women's ostensibly greater vulnerability to mystical sources of misfortune is conjoined with their greater credulity.

A similar logic operates in relation to caste and other social inequalities. There is a widespread assumption among high-caste people that the low castes, especially Harijans, are in closest contact with troublesome little deities and malevolent spirits, partly because low-caste men often serve as little deities' priests and are well represented among the diviners and exorcists dealing with spirits. Moreover, the poor and uneducated, among whom the low castes are disproportionately represented, are also supposedly weaker in mental and spiritual terms, and this elitist prejudice is again not systematically contested by its victims. Consequently, by such ideological reasoning, the low castes, the poor, and the uneducated are stereotypically thought to be most vulnerable to malevolent agencies and most credulous about them.

It is true that the evil eye may beset the relatively successful within a social group. Nevertheless, in broad terms it is clear that higher-caste, wealthier, and more educated men—who are least likely to find themselves in desperate straits anyway—tend to voice more skepticism about mystical agencies of misfortune than the rest of the population. The same men tend to insist simultaneously that their own mental and spiritual strength protects them from any harmful forces that actually do exist. Convinced of their relative invulnerability, the skeptics thereby reinforce their own social superiority—in their own eyes and also to some extent in other people's. Furthermore, in an exemplary case of bodily symbolism, the skeptics' superiority is confirmed by their own proclaimed immunity to possessive seizure or invasion by other beings.

PLANETS AND INAUSPICIOUSNESS

Let me now turn away from personified agencies of misfortune to look at more impersonal sources. As the malevolent planet Saturn, Shani, orbits the earth, it takes about two-and-a-half years to pass through each of the twelve zodiacal houses. When Saturn is in a person's own house, as determined by the time of birth, he or she can anticipate two-and-a-half years of misery—or even seven-and-a-half, if the preceding and succeeding houses are counted in as well. Shrines containing images of Saturn and the other planets are found throughout India, and in Tamilnadu they stand in most large temples. On the day when Saturn moves from one house to another, as I have seen in the Minakshi temple, there are very large crowds at the planets' shrine as people wait to make their offerings to Saturn—half of them in thankful relief at surviving the last thirty months, and half of them in anxious prayer that they will survive the next thirty. At any one time, one-twelfth of the population is suffering Saturn's malignancy. Although few of them blame all their ills on the planet, most are likely to regard it as one significant factor. Saturn's depredations are not, however, confined to those who currently have it in their house. In some areas of India, such as Tamilnadu, planetary affliction or *grahadosha*, "fault of the planets," is one of the most common explanations for everyone's misfortune.

Although wholly malevolent, Saturn—like all the nine planets—is regarded by Hindus as a god, which explains why he is worshiped at his image exactly like other deities by people seeking to propitiate him. But those who believe that they are victims of Saturn—because they know he is in their house or because an astrologer has divined his influence—may also worship Hanuman to seek his aid. According to popular myth, Hanuman's immense physical strength has made him the only god ever to have worsted Saturn. From one angle, therefore, affliction by Saturn and the planets is like that caused by other harmful deities and is dealt with by similar means.

From another angle, however, there are real differences, for the planets can also be seen as impersonal causes of misfortune, which are unlike the deities and other personified agencies. Thus there is, as Judy F. Pugh (1983a: 136) puts it, "something autonomous and irrevocable about the power and movements of the heavenly bodies. . . . Very inauspicious celestial conjunctions are considered to be almost beyond the control of the gods." Of the heavenly bodies, Saturn itself is the most intractable, so that the two-and-a-half years when it is in one's house must in the end simply be lived through, as indeed must every inauspicious Saturday, since nobody wants to confirm the Tamil saying that "The Saturday corpse does not go alone."

The celestial or astronomical conjunctions referred to by Pugh do not turn only on Saturn, because there is an infinity of harmful astronomical conjunctions, as well as temporal and spatial ones. All are the source of inauspicious (*ashubha*) forces that are part of the natural order of things and cannot be averted, although conversely there is also an infinity of auspicious (*shubha*) conjunctions that can bring all manner of good fortune to those who take advantage of them.

Thus, for example, the heavenly configuration of planets at the moment of birth is a determinant of life chances—of a person's fate as "written on the forehead" and revealed in a horoscope. A horoscope may predict a long life of health and happiness. Unfortunate people are born under a conjunction spelling their early demise or that of any future spouse, and this is one reason why horoscopes must be scrutinized and compared before arranging a marriage. The prediction of a devastating horoscope can sometimes be forestalled (for example, by performing a reparatory ritual), but the affliction emanating from inauspicious configurations cannot be entirely eliminated.

The cyclical oscillation of auspiciousness and inauspiciousness is a quality of time itself. The probability that any venture will succeed is enhanced by starting at an auspicious time. Hardly anyone, for example, would hold a wedding without consulting an astrologer about the best timing. Conversely, there are many inauspicious times when it is foolhardy to start a major ritual or any other new project, such as laying the foundations of a building. Every day, for instance, there are two inauspicious periods governed by Rahu, a malevolent mythical planet, and a third governed by Yama, god of death. These daily periods are not necessarily taken very seriously, but many Hindus do avoid them when starting something really important, lest it should fail and bring misfortune. Very much the same applies to conjunctions between time and spatial movements or dimensions. Thus it is dangerous to travel in certain directions on certain days, or to live in houses incorrectly aligned in space. Much of the danger inherent in inauspicious conjunctions and times derives from the fact that harmful beings, such as ghostly spirits or witches, prefer them and are most active then. These personified agencies, of course, are subject to some degree of control, but the onset of conjunctive and temporal inauspiciousness itself is not, because it is an inevitable outcome of time's arrow within the physical world. From this point of view, time (*kala*) itself—which is also deified—"is the ultimate cause of everything that happens" (Madan 1987a: 69).

As a phenomenon emergent from the natural order, inauspiciousness is an impersonal force that cannot be blocked and it is easily conflated by latter-day astrologers with physical forces like gravity and magnetism (Pugh 1983a: 135). Nonetheless, its harmful impact can be either mitigated or exacerbated by human action in the light of information about its occurrence. Although completely accurate prediction is rarely easy, a lot of the misfortune produced by inauspiciousness may be blamed on people who fail to worship Saturn, discount the prognostications of horoscopes, start new ventures at the wrong time, or otherwise ignore its probable occurrence. Those who miscalculate inauspicious forces and build a house facing the wrong way, so that they suffer from childlessness (Raheja 1988a: 55–56), are therefore as foolish as those who ignore physical forces and are injured when their badly built house falls down. Of course, there is also plenty of scope for disagreement about predictions, which often reflects or masks some other quarrel. It is, for instance, a notorious commonplace in India that marriage negotiations are frequently broken off on the pretext that the bride and groom's horoscopes are incompatible, when the real argument is about the size of the dowry. In practice, therefore, even when impersonal inauspiciousness is thought to be a cause of misfortune, much of the responsibility may still be attributed to human culpability.

Significantly, inauspiciousness, although emergent from the natural order, is also commonly personified (for example, by widows or funeral priests who, so to speak, radiate inauspiciousness and can harm people who see them). Conversely, good fortune comes to those who see auspiciousness personified in a bride or an image of the goddess Lakshmi. Furthermore, some personifications of inauspiciousness are appropriate recipients for gifts given to remove it from oneself, and donation—as Gloria G. Raheja (1988a) shows most clearly—is one crucial means of dealing with inauspicious misfortune. For example, in northwestern India, Saturn's malignancy can be dealt with by transferring it in alms given to Dakhots and Vedpatras, who belong to degraded Brahman subcastes. But by accepting such gifts, the recipients put themselves at risk, particularly when the gifts are more specifically deemed to transfer sin as well. Thus inauspicious Mahabrahman funeral priests in Benares see themselves as largely unable to "digest" the sins of the deceased that they accept, and they face "the prospect of a lingering death from the rotting effects of leprosy, or even—in the case of certain particularly 'indigestible' kinds of offering—an immediate demise" (Parry 1980: 89). Taking on sin or malignancy through gifts therefore reinforces the inauspiciousness embodied in the recipients, who stand as glaring personifications of this impersonal cause of misfortune.

Inauspiciousness is a very broad category in popular Hinduism and it is easy to give it a spurious precision that oversimplifies the connotations of the term *ashubha* and its vernacular variants. These generally overlap with rather more specific terms for negative moral attributes such as *papa*, "sin," or *dosha*, "fault," although neither of those terms is straightforward either; thus the "fault of the planets" (*grahadosha*) refers to an impersonal planetary force, but it also refers to its effect, a defect in human beings productive of misfortune that can connote ritual pollution and moral failing as well. The partial overlap among concepts of impersonal inauspiciousness, physical or mental illness, ritual pollution, sin and immorality reflects the fact that in popular Hindu etiology natural phenomena can affect the whole human condition. As we have just seen, the Mahabrahman's inauspiciousness is closely connected with his absorption of human sins, which cause his physical body to rot, and the absorbed sins in turn reinforce his inauspiciousness, which may harm those who gaze upon him.

At this point, we could start to explore the whole field of Hindu medical anthropology, for all illnesses may be described, diagnosed, and treated by medical means, whether or not mystical causation is a factor as well. India has a wealth of traditional medical systems, such as classical Ayurveda and its popular variants, all of which continue to flourish alongside modern western medicine. A more complete account of misfortune would have to look at the interpenetration of mystical and medical approaches to illness, which cannot be strictly separated, but that task is beyond the scope of this book.

Instead, to give one final and striking example of the effect of natural phenomena on human beings, let me take the case of eclipses, predictable astronomical conjunctions that are said to be caused by the mythical planets Rahu and Ketu swallowing the sun and moon. Eclipses produce a state of inauspiciousness, which may be countered by worshiping the planets or donating gifts, but misfortune would still befall anyone who started a ritual or new venture, or even ate a meal, during their occurrence. However, eclipses also pollute people, who counteract the effect by bathing during them, as well as the deities' images, which calls for extra rituals of purification and appeasement before normal worship can be resumed. Thus the natural, inevitable occurrence of eclipses causes a general disturbance of the whole human and divine order, which demands appropriate ritual counteraction, although these astronomical events also just have to be lived through while they last.

It is not uncommon, at least in some circumstances, for Hindus to argue that every misfortune caused by divine or personified agencies is ultimately determined by natural phenomena—time itself or the inauspiciousness emergent from the natural order. Hence people who suffer at the hands of angry deities or malevolent ghosts or jealous witches do so because they are afflicted by impersonal forces or states that leave them open to attack. It is "in their stars" to be afflicted and although they can try to control injurious beings, they cannot change their own objective situation. Hence anyone born at an inauspicious astronomical conjunction can confidently expect to be victimized by ghosts, witches, and so on, and their depredations precisely confirm the dire predictions made when the birth horoscope was cast. According to this line of reasoning, harmful deities and other personified agencies are merely the vehicles through which impersonal forces affect people. Human fate, in the final analysis, is determined by the natural order.

But that is hardly ever the end of the story. Fate is understood in several different ways, and the idea that it is naturally determined is only one strand in popular Hindu discourse about misfortune. Particularly vital is fate's relationship with *karma*, to which I now turn.

KARMA

In its most elementary form, the famous theory of *karma* postulates that every action has its inevitable "fruit" or consequence, so that a person's condition is determined by good or bad deeds in this and previous lives. In Hinduism, *karma* is conceptually inseparable from *dharma*, understood as the moral code by which good and bad are evaluated, and *samsara*, the eternal cycle within which a person is successively reborn. *Karma* is also a crucial concept in Buddhism and Jainism—although it is not, of course, linked to the Hindu *dharma* in those two religions—and *karma*, in conjunction with *samsara*, is frequently identified as the definitive feature of Indic religions. According to W. Norman Brown (1970: 7–8), "the joint doctrine of *karma* and rebirth" was popularized over several centuries "until it was accepted as an axiom, and it continues to be so accepted in modern Hindu India." Brown's claim that *karma* is an axiom of contemporary Hinduism is basically correct, but the picture is complicated because there are variant concepts of *karma*, which interpenetrate other explanations of misfortune.

Let me begin by outlining the perspective of the scriptural texts, which do not advance one unified theory of *karma*. The most celebrated theory—especially influential among Hindu intellectuals—is the "orthodox," Brahmanical version elaborated in the monistic philosophy known as *advaita vedanta*. In this radically individualist version, *karma*—understood as the consequences of action—attaches exclusively to the actor and can never be transferred to another being, so that every individual must fully accept the fruits, fortunate or unfortunate, of all previous deeds, even if they were committed in earlier lives unknown to the living subject. Furthermore, the causal chain is inexorable, so that the consequences of action can never be deflected, even at the behest of the most powerful deities, and must be discharged later, probably in subsequent rebirths. The only escape, therefore, is to cease to act and to extinguish all desire by renouncing the world, in the hope that rebirth need not recur and final liberation (*moksha*) will be attained.

In the texts, however, there are also other ideas about *karma*. In the *Laws of Manu*, the most influential compendium of Brahmanical orthodoxy, there is a pervasive assumption that action always cumulatively leads to one or several rebirths. Nonetheless, alternative theories of *karma* are expounded and *Manu* does allow exceptions: not only can ascetics acting without desire escape the consequences, but individuals living in the world can also counteract or eliminate the effects of action by various means, such as knowing the Vedas whose "fire" burns the evil results, or performing penances and reparatory rites to expiate sin (Rocher 1980: 80–85).

More dramatically, in medieval Puranic mythology, especially when infused with devotionalism, the most powerful and eternally divine deities are often said to be outside the compass of *karma*, so that devotion to them can ensure that sin brings no subsequent misfortune. As Wendy Doniger O'Flaherty explains, "The Puranas abound in stories in which the unrepentant sinner, about to be dragged away by the minions of Yama, is saved at the last minute by the arrival of the chariot of the servants of the sectarian god, landing like the marines at the eleventh hour" (1980b: 27–28). In Puranic texts, moreover, *karma* is transferable because good and evil are; for example, "the chaste wife can release her husband from his sin" (ibid.: 29), and *karma* can flow "from living children to dead ancestors" or sometimes "from parents to children" (ibid.: 35). Hence the Brahmanical theory of *karma* as an iron law operating like an impersonal force, which condemns all individuals to reap the fruits of their own action without hope of remission, is contested within the textual tradition itself, especially under the influence of devotionalism.

I now turn to popular versions of *karma* theory and begin with the story of a fire which, in 1984, struck Karimpur village in Uttar Pradesh, killing six people and a dozen animals, and destroying or badly damaging twenty houses. All the victims were fairly well-off. One of the dead was a Brahman widow and nearly all the burnt houses belonged to Brahmans, who form the dominant landed caste in Karimpur. According to Susan S. Wadley and Bruce W. Derr (1989), who were living there at the time, the villagers concluded that the fire was the fruit of past misdeeds: a punishment for both the whole community and the individuals who fell victim to its erratic path of destruction.

Wadley and Derr show that the Karimpur villagers' theory of *karma* emphasizes retribution during this life; there is little attention to its connection with rebirth. The consensus of opinion was that blame for the fire rested primarily on the village's Brahman leaders, who had sinned and—

even worse—profited by "eating the earnings of sin" (ibid.: 139) through-out their lives. The fire broke out, many people claimed, because there had been "an overwhelming accumulation of sins" (ibid.: 141) in Karimpur; the fire was a community punishment. In part, though, this was because the fruits of the sins of some especially evil people had been visited on others, just as a boatload of passengers can all drown if one awful sinner is on board. *Karma*, in other words, is transferable from one person to others, although some villagers argued that, even in a collective disaster, no one who is completely blameless would suffer.

Moreover, despite the notion of community punishment, it was widely held that retribution in Karimpur was really directed at the households of sinners, an argument dependent on the premise that *karma* is particularly transferred within a residential kin group. True, some ostensibly dreadful sinners' households escaped the fire completely, but this was because of counterbalancing merit. For example, the household of three notoriously reprobate Brahman brothers escaped perhaps because their father had been a very good man; in any case, the net accumulation of sin and merit among present and past members of this household could not have been sufficiently negative. But, concluded public opinion, the known vices of gambling, lechery, drunkenness, and usury adequately explained the disaster visited on all the fire's victims, except for one seemingly blameless household whose loss probably was due to misdeeds in previous lives. Significantly, when discussing those who suffered in the fire, it was invariably assumed that the fruits of sin had normally been shared; only those who were actually killed had fully "eaten" the fruits of their own personal sins.

Karma as an explanation of the Karimpur fire did not completely over-shadow alternatives, such as the claim that Saturn caused the disaster, which occurred on a Saturday. However, any suggestion that malevolent ghosts or vengeful deities had caused it was strikingly absent. Against such agencies, human beings can take remedial measures. "But the Karimpur fire was over, the houses ruined and the dead gone. Human counteractions were no longer feasible or thinkable." The more imper-sonal, abstract, comprehensive explanation of *karma* was appropriate to the magnitude of the disaster, although even this explanation did involve Bhagwan, the remote supreme deity, "who started the fire after calculating village, lineage, household, family and individual *karma*s" (ibid.: 147), according to a totality of knowledge that he alone possesses.

In general, although detailed ethnographic evidence is admittedly sparse, ideas about *karma* held in Karimpur closely resemble those reported from elsewhere, such as Ghanyari village in Himachal Pradesh (Sharma 1973). In popular Hinduism, it seems clear, *karma* as an explanation of misfortune focuses on retribution for sins committed in this life as well as, if not more than, in previous lives; it is always premised, too, on the possibility of transfer and sharing, particularly within the kin group, although individuals do also pay for their own sins. Further, the consequences of sin are commonly held to be counterbalanced by merit acquired through good deeds, and the inexorability of *karma*'s causal chain is modified by the decisions of a deity who keeps the record of sin and merit. All these popular ideas about *karma*, I must stress, actually have close analogues in the textual tradition. The common assumption in anthropological literature that popular thinking deviates from *the* textual theory of *karma*—mistakenly identified with the radically individualist, Brahmanical version—is incorrect. Rather, a range of similar ideas about *karma* exist in both popular and textual Hinduism.

Major irreversible tragedies like the Karimpur fire are mercifully infrequent and for more common afflictions—as Wadley and Derr imply—*karma* is less widely invoked. As Babb observes (1983a: 168), in accounting for misfortune, *karma* "is by no means the usual way, or even a very important way, at least as far as certain everyday misfortunes are concerned." Instead, the explanations discussed above—which impute affliction to deities, personified malevolent agencies, the planets, and so on—are much more common, and it is certainly not unusual for *karma* to be mentioned only rarely. Why should this be so?

There are several answers to this question. In the first place, theories of *karma*, in explaining present condition by past conduct, seem to exclude the possibility of remedial measures, since what has been done cannot be undone. Actually, as we have seen, this is not always so, because devotionalist worship, expiatory ritual, or meritorious action may cancel past sins. Such measures, though, are always rather indeterminate. Partly because no one ever knows the full record of their own past conduct, it is impossible to make them more specifically effective. Thus the chain of *karma* cannot be completely broken. For divine or personified agencies of misfortune, or even impersonal forces like the planets, more exact diagnosis and more specific remedies are generally held to exist, so that these explanations tend to be more attractive because the victims (or their families) see some real hope of dealing pragmatically with their suffering.

The second answer, initially proposed for Buddhists by Gananath Obeyesekere, is that the theory of *karma* is "psychologically indeterminate" (1968: 21) because it leaves people in the dark about how their future is related to the past and present; after all, they do not know what they did in their former lives and therefore cannot know what tomorrow will bring—which may be disaster as some sin in an earlier existence catches up with them. In fact, partly because popular Hindu theories of *karma* tend to postulate retribution within this life, past lives are not a major preoccupation, and in general the psychological indeterminacy thesis is not so well supported by Hindu ethnographic evidence. Yet it does point us toward the question of psychological unacceptability: can I really be responsible for my present misfortune? It is noticeable, on the internal evidence, that the Karimpur informants quoted by Wadley and Derr seem to have escaped the fire. The lucky ones blamed the victims for their misfortune, but the victims themselves do not appear to have done so. Hence it is at least plausible—if hard to demonstrate convincingly with available evidence—that *karma*, insofar as it implies willful misconduct in the past, is likely to be acceptable as an explanation of misfortune only to victims guiltily willing to blame themselves. Such victims no doubt exist, but they are always likely to be a minority. Coupled with rebirth, the Brahmanical theory of *karma* may make the world into "a completely connected and self-contained cosmos of ethical retribution" (Weber 1978: 524), but even when modified by popular Hinduism and partially disconnected from the idea of rebirth, such rationality is intolerably cold comfort for ordinary people who see themselves (and those close to them) as innocent sufferers.

The next important point to make is that popular ideas about *karma*—however frequently they are invoked—can quite easily be merged with other, more specific explanations. Thus, for instance, in Ghanyari an angry deity took revenge on the sinful community so that the rains failed, and a malevolent ghost inflicted suffering on the children of an unpopular Brahman, because he had died with a burden of bad *karma* (Sharma 1973: 352–53). Moreover and more generally, all theories of *karma* are immune to contradiction by alternative explanations because, as people can and do argue, anyone who falls foul of another source of misfortune does so only because their accumulated load of *karma* makes them vulnerable—just as people in Karimpur were when the fire struck. Victimization by a particular agency of misfortune can therefore be interpreted as a specific instance of the general law of cause and effect, so that theories of *karma* are buttressed, rather than undermined, by alternative etiologies. Hence Babb (1983a) is undoubtedly right to insist that *karma* theory supplies a long-term, comprehensive framework of moral meaning within which specific misfortunes attributed to other causes are short-term occurrences.

Yet this long-term framework also means that *karma*—although conceptually predicated on a moral thesis about human conduct and its fruits—can closely resemble fate, as ultimately determined by the natural order and its impersonal forces. Paradoxically, the idea that everyone is ultimately responsible for their own fate can be turned on its head, so that *karma* appears as an uncontrollable, impersonal determinant of the human condition. When *karma*, acting like a law of nature, is seen in this way, its appeal as an explanation of misfortune to sufferers who want to take remedial action is plainly reduced still further, and this is a third reason why *karma* may not be mentioned.

But when all is said and done, the basic idea of *karma*—partly because it is immune to contradiction—is rarely denied altogether and it attracts little of the skepticism expressed about many other agencies of misfortune. There are some grounds for thinking that the *karma* concept holds more sway in north than south India (Moffatt 1979: 296–97), but it is also germane that skepticism about *karma* is probably greatest among the lower castes, where there is also least doubt about the reality of personified agencies of misfortune. Conversely, those most dismissive about the latter—especially high-caste, wealthy, educated men—are the people most inclined to assign a greater proportion of misfortune to *karma*, partly because it fills the void left by their skepticism about other causes. In other words, the probability that misfortune will be ascribed to *karma* tends to vary inversely with the probability that it will be blamed on other sources, especially the personified agencies whose reality is most commonly questioned.

There are also important sociological factors at work here. One is that *karma* theories equally explain good and bad fortune, and therefore appeal to those who are comfortably settled in the world, because they provide some ethical justification for it. Next, because skepticism about personified agencies of misfortune is closely tied to the belief that mental and spiritual strength are effective defenses against them, people in the higher social strata who assume that they are strong are inevitably reluctant to accept that any misfortune befalling them comes from those agencies. To ascribe suffering to *karma*, or other impersonal forces inherent in the natural order, avoids the need to wonder about one's own weakness and, at one remove, the grounds for asserting social superiority. Lastly, because the concept of *karma*—irrespective of its actual formulation—is invariably seen as scripturally validated, its very deployment is a discursive strategy to identify oneself with the socioreligious elite and to distance oneself from the allegedly superstitious lower orders. Like skepticism about personified agencies of misfortune, credence in the law of *karma* is the partial construct of an unegalitarian society. That in turn is yet another reason, the fourth, why large sections of the population—especially women, the low castes, the poor, and the uneducated—often do not explain their misfortune in terms of *karma*. In popular Hinduism, *karma* does not enjoy the currency that its fame might suggest.

KARMA, FATE, AND DIVINE PLAY

Fate, in effect, is a null explanation of misfortune—an expression of the idea that things just happen for no known, predictable reason, or because in our current degenerate epoch, the *kaliyuga*, nothing can be expected to go well. Fate is a basic concept in popular Hinduism and although it is sometimes marked out by distinctive terms—like the Muslims' word *kismet* widely used in north India—it is often equated with *karma*, taking the sense of an uncontrollable, impersonal force determining destiny in relation to past lives for which nobody can be held responsible. Although fate is uncontrollable, however, it is often said to be written on the forehead at birth in accordance with the balance of *karma* accumulated through previous existences. To that extent, everybody's preordained fate is ultimately determined by past conduct—even though no one knows how—so that popular theories of *karma*, despite partial detachment from the idea of rebirth, constantly tend to qualify the explanation of blind fate. Rarely, therefore, is fate as *karma* an absolutely null explanation of misfortune.

Yet as we have seen, what is written on the forehead can also be understood as the outcome of impersonal forces exerted by the planets. Then fate and misfortune are finally blamed on a natural order beyond any human or even divine control. This notion of fate does have some currency. Still there is a distinct reluctance in popular Hinduism to accept the idea of a physical universe that the deities cannot fully control, and in that sense the absolute nullity of fate is again qualified. After all, the planets and time itself are deified, and the same is actually or potentially true of all natural phenomena. Furthermore, the great deities' power over the universe is a basic assumption in popular Hinduism, so that even apparently uncontrollable human fate should ultimately be in the hands of the gods and goddesses. This may be because they alone know and control the balance of everyone's *karma*, but it can also depend on the notion of fate as divine providence.

While Hindu deities can evilly harm people, they also created the universe for their own amusement, for their "play" (*lila*). In their play—unfathomable to human beings—the deities shower unanticipated boons on people, even dreadful sinners; they also engage in crazy acts of destructiveness.

One forceful expression of this idea comes in the *Mahabharata* through the voice of the heroine, Draupadi. She likens god to a "puppeteer," who "hiding behind a disguise, assembling and breaking the creatures, plays with them as a child plays with its toys." The deities alone control everything that happens in the world, and although the righteous Yudhishthira denies it, insisting that "either man alone or man in concert with god is responsible for the occurrence of events," Draupadi's discourse expounds a Hindu verity that is widely echoed in popular religion. We are all, in her words, "wooden puppets who are 'propelled by the Lord' to their several destinies" (Long 1980: 46–47). Or, as one man succinctly told Parry in Benares, "It's all god's tamasha [show, circus]. Why do you go to the cinema? God wants some diversion too."

This man voiced a common judgment on the Hindu deities: they are capable not only of deliberately harming people as well as helping them, but they can also just play with them for their own delectation, so that anyone can be fated to become one of their toys. Imputing misfortune to fate as divine providence is often no more than a conventional idiom, as westerners might blame "bad luck," but sometimes it despairingly expresses anguished hatred of god after everything has been done to combat other likely causes of affliction. Divine play as a determinant of human fate can therefore vary greatly in significance between the trivially conventional and the desperately final. Human weakness, jealousy, and other negative dispositions are a source of so much misfortune, even when it is sent by a host of malevolent agencies, but there are many powerful, impersonal forces as well. Sometimes, though, people's helplessness as puppets seems to be the most potent, constant, and irremissible source of all, and it testifies yet again to the vast power of the Hindu gods and goddesses over the world and all its inhabitants.

Chapter 11

CONCLUSION

A T THE RISK of oversimplifying, let me open this concluding chapter by restating some of the most basic findings of this study of popular Hinduism and society in India. First and foremost, popular Hinduism is the religion of a multitude of gods and goddesses, whose principal attribute is their power. Divine power (*shakti*) is changeably manifested by different deities in different ways, but the fundamental reason why Hindu gods and goddesses are worshiped, offered sacrifices, and otherwise entreated or propitiated is because they have power over the world and its people. Popular Hinduism is polytheistic; its numerous gods and goddesses are consistently represented as distinct beings. At the same time different deities are often seen as alternative forms of a single deity, and in some contexts every Hindu will say that ultimately all gods and goddesses are one. Powerful deities differ from human beings, particularly because they are immortal. Yet they also share many similar qualities, and in numerous contexts men, women, and children are regarded as divine. One fundamental objective of worship or *puja*, the core ritual of popular Hinduism, is to achieve identity between deity and worshiper. In Hinduism, therefore, the likeness between divine and human beings is as critical as their unlikeness, and god is never distinguished by his quality of absolute otherness.

Hierarchical values and institutionalized inequality are at the heart of both Hinduism and Indian society. In general, as so many rituals show, deities are superior to human beings, who must accord them due deference and respect. Moreover, many rituals also reflect, legitimate, or construct inequality among members of human society. Nonetheless, rituals sometimes invert or deny relationships of inequality, and it is also important that the honorific respect shown to powerful, superior deities in ritual is often accompanied or even displaced by a display of loving devotion toward them. On the other hand, particularly when dealing with troublesome little deities and the malevolent spirits who merge into them, respect can give way to contempt. The main purpose of ritual for harmful beings is to make them leave people alone. The gods and goddesses of popular Hinduism are not consistently benevolent and they can wield their power to harm people, sometimes just for their own unfathomable amusement.

Looking back at this book, an aspect of its plan calls for comment. In chapter 2, I began where a study of popular theistic Hinduism must begin: with the principal gods and goddesses, and the relationships among them. In chapter 3, I looked at *puja* and in chapter 4 at sacrifice, specifically animal sacrifice or *bali*, the inferior complement of *puja*. In chapters 5 and 6, sacrifice remained a central theme, but I also investigated the important topic of kingship—in both the kingdom itself and the village—as well as the relationship between human kings and sovereign deities. Throughout chapters 7, 8, and 9, the principal connecting thread was devotionalism, the stream of Hinduism characterized by devotion (*bhakti*) to a personal deity. Because animal sacrifice is rarely an overt part of devotionalist Hinduism, whereas worship invariably is, these three chapters were more closely linked to chapter 3 than to chapters 4, 5, and 6. In chapter 10 on misfortune, we found elements of devotionalist worship, addressed to deified malevolent beings, as well as sacrificial propitiation of them.

The sequence of chapters roughly reflects the conventional contrast between sacrificial and devotionalist Hinduism, which partly derives from the religion's evolutionary development as revealed in textual sources. However, I never intended to suggest that popular Hinduism is divisible into early sacrificial and late devotionalist halves, because it certainly is not. Thus, for example, animal sacrifice is always complemented by *puja*—which itself can be understood as a transformation of the sacrificial rite. Moreover, devotion is often shown through sacrifice, even if Madeleine Biardeau's claim (1981: 100–101) that *bhakti* is found everywhere in the popular religion overcorrects received wisdom. Her work powerfully shows, however, that the relationship between sacrifice and devotion is fundamental in Hinduism, and it is certainly far more significant than their historical origins for a mainly structural, anthropological analysis of latter-day popular religion. I hope that the plan of this book, designed to present the material intelligibly, has not obscured the fundamental relationship between the two interpenetrating fields of sacrificial and devotionalist religion.

The reference to Biardeau allows for another brief observation. Throughout this book, I have drawn inspiration and insights from her and other major contributors to modern textual scholarship, and at the methodological level, I have shown how vital such scholarship can be for analyzing ethnographic evidence on popular Hinduism. Hence I completely disagree with one recent ethnographer's opinion that "orientalist" Indology is the bane of the anthropology of Hinduism (van der Veer 1988: 52–58). Nevertheless, as I insisted in chapter 1, ethnography must be the major source of evidence and the touchstone of interpretation for a study of popular Hinduism, and I have consistently tried to use textual scholarship to illuminate ethnography, not to overshadow it.

The ethnography of Indian society and its theoretical analysis have been the indispensable background for this study, frequently referred to explicitly and always present implicitly. Evidently, this book is not a contribution to Indian social theory as such, but it does have some implications for it. In the preceding chapters, the familiar figures of the Brahman and the untouchable Harijan, the king and the ascetic renouncer, have made their expected appearances. But it is notable too that the king has been particularly prominent, especially because of his role in sacrifice, and I have repeatedly stressed the pivotal importance of kingship, kings, and royal deities. In this respect, my analysis is consistent with recent anthropological, textual, and historical scholarship on India. Much of this work has sought to rescue the king from the sidelines, where he was persistently relegated by anthropologists too preoccupied empirically with local caste systems or theoretically with purity and the Brahman.

Yet I cannot go as far as Nicholas B. Dirks, who argues—against Louis Dumont in particular—that "kings were not inferior to Brahmans" in precolonial India and that "the prevalent ideology had not to do, at least primarily, with purity and pollution, but rather with royal authority and honor" (1987: 4, 7). In some contexts, kings undoubtedly occupied the preeminent place, but in others they were plainly classified as Kshatriyas ranked below Brahmans. Moreover, the hierarchical relationship between nonviolent worship and blood sacrifice, over which the martial king presides as patron, is one important expression of the supremacy of values identified with the Brahman and the ascetic renouncer. The king was and is crucial in Hinduism and Indian society, and he is not the secondary, secular figure portrayed by Dumont. Yet to elevate him as if he were consistently superior to the Brahman, and the renouncer with whom the latter is partially assimilated ideologically, is to replace one distortion by another. Brahmans, as I explained in chapter 1, are not always at the top, but they very often are and that fact has to be given due weight. A similar distortion, incidentally, is present in some recent attempts to argue, in Gloria G. Raheja's words (1988b: 519), that "hierarchy . . . is not the encompassing value of caste society"—a revisionist thesis lacking support from the mass of evidence on popular Hinduism, as much of this book has shown.

Another group that has been prominent throughout my study is, simply, the common people. Many of them are actually Brahmans, kinglike local headmen or ascetics belonging to devotionalist orders, but here I also have in mind the bulk of the population who occupy no prominent social or religious role. Criticism of an excessively Sanskritic, Brahmanical, or otherwise elitist perspective on Hinduism and Indian society has been both just and longstanding. As many anthropologists and historians have shown, the world does not necessarily look the same to all the common people: for instance to Brahmans and non-Brahmans, or men and women. Thus in the religious sphere, there is clear evidence that deities particularly favored by Brahmans, who are offered only vegetarian food and are worshiped in Sanskrit by Brahman priests, are disparaged by some low-caste Hindus, who see them as much weaker than other deities, such as village goddesses, who are offered animal sacrifice and praised in the vernacular by non-Brahmans. There are alternative voices in Hinduism and we must also remember that people at the foot of the social hierarchy, especially today, often deny their own putative inferiority. Furthermore, the socially and religiously inferior are never, under any circumstances, mere pawns in a process of social and cultural construction directed by their superiors.

Yet it would be false to claim that there is, except in limited cases, any genuine "religion of the oppressed" that has been ignored in the literature. In plenty of instances, especially when devotionalist influence is strong, religious belief and practice do not directly reflect or uphold wider social norms as shown, for example, by the celebration of female eroticism in the temple festivals discussed in chapter 8. But little of this constitutes subversive opposition to the social and religious system as a whole. Even when they are resisting elitist pressure to conform, as in the case of Chellattamman's priest discussed in chapter 4, lower social groups consistently tend to reconstruct their own socioreligious inferiority, precisely because their own beliefs and practices are perceived as distinct from those of higher groups. And conversely, when lower groups do adopt the beliefs and practices of higher groups—the process of Sanskritization, in M. N. Srinivas's terms—they again reconfirm the superiority of those who are being emulated. As this "double bind" shows, inequality is deeply entrenched in Hinduism and Indian society, at both ideological and institutional levels, despite the fact that the principle and practice of equality clearly have gained ground in contemporary India, particularly in the political, economic, and legal fields. In the face of this development, however, Hinduism itself tends to represent a predominantly conservative force, notwithstanding the contribution made by devotionalism to Indian egalitarianism.

Much of the above applies to inequality between the sexes, as well as to caste or class inequality, although I should stress that, in most sections of Indian society, gender inequality still attracts far less condemnation than caste inequality. Yet, as we saw in chapter 8 in particular, the position of women in popular Hinduism is not uniformly inferior, notably because all females share, to a greater or lesser extent, in *shakti*, divine power personified as feminine and embodied in goddesses. The ritual power of women, which partly depends on their symbolic identification with the goddesses, significantly contributes to women's self-esteem and the definition of their socioreligious role. It is true, of course, that ritual power rarely allows women to challenge men's dominance in the family or society as a whole, and many women see their power as something to be deployed primarily for the protection of husbands, brothers, and sons. Nonetheless, Hinduism and its spectacular goddesses do afford women a status and role that genuinely qualify their inferiority in other social domains.

The distinction between the religious beliefs and practices of higher as opposed to lower groups in society is commonly described as one between Sanskritic, great-tradition Hinduism and non-Sanskritic, little-tradition Hinduism. The latter distinction, I argued in chapter 1, is fundamentally the product of an indigenous ideological discourse of evaluation, current especially among the Brahmans and other high-status groups predisposed to emulate them. Particularly crucial in this discourse is the judgment that beliefs and practices deemed to conform closely to scriptural norms are superior to those that do not, so that, for example, vegetarian worship is represented as superior to animal sacrifice.

On the whole, the beliefs and practices of lower social groups are treated as valid for them by people from higher social groups; the relativistic principle that different sections of society have their own "elective affinity" for alternative religious styles is a pervasive one. Hence Brahmans, for instance, normally acknowledge the existence and power of deities predominantly worshiped by the low castes, but not by themselves. As we saw in chapter 10, however, the attitude toward personified agencies of misfortune such as malevolent ghostly spirits or witches tends to be rather different. Whether these agencies really exist and cause harm is quite often questioned, especially by high-caste, wealthy, and educated men. Indeed, some skeptics decry belief in all such sources of misfortune as mere superstition, and are inclined to appeal to the scripturally sanctioned concept of *karma* as the truest explanation of human suffering.

Superstition, though, is a concept that also readily comes to the lips of Hindus influenced by modern reformist thinking. For them, many demotic practices, notably animal sacrifice, must be condemned as superstitions that do not belong to "true," scriptural Hinduism. In reformism, the relativistic principle—and with it the structural complementarity between high and low—tends to be replaced by uniformity, by an insistence on the universal validity of superior doctrine and ritual, as supposedly expounded in Sanskrit scripture. On the ideological plane, this is one of the most far-reaching developments in contemporary popular Hinduism, even if its real effect has been fairly limited in most of the country. Thus the sacrifice of buffaloes—the ideal victim for goddesses—has dwindled away owing to reformist pressure, but sacrifice carried out with alternative offerings shows little sign of vanishing in the foreseeable future.

One significant legacy of modern reformism is the idea that Hinduism is a distinct religion or "ism" in its own right, possessing a body of doctrines and rituals that can be sharply separated from those of other religions, notably Islam and Christianity. As mentioned in chapter 4, religious reformism in the late nineteenth and early twentieth centuries developed in tandem with political nationalism, and the strengthening of separate Hindu and Muslim communal identities. In 1947, independence was accompanied by partition into the two states of India and Pakistan. Although India is a secular republic, officially neutral in its policy toward different religions, its population is overwhelmingly Hindu. The ghastly communal massacres during partition have never recurred on such a scale, but friction between the Hindu majority and the Muslim, and most recently Sikh, minorities has repeatedly erupted into violence.

Outbreaks of communal violence, in both the recent and more distant past, have hardly ever been caused by religious difference alone. Nevertheless, Hindu self-assertiveness has grown considerably since 1947 and it became more militant during the 1980s. The rather misleading terms, "fundamentalism," "revivalism," and "Neo-Hinduism," have all gained common currency among observers, and many influential Hindu spokesmen have become more strident in defending what they claim to be Hindu interests and eternal Hindu values. Even suttee, first prohibited in 1829, was openly defended during the late 1980s on the grounds that it was an authentic Hindu cultural and religious tradition. Fortunately, defenders of suttee have been vigorously criticized by other Hindus, and any large increase in the number of widows who still occasionally die on their husbands' funeral pyres is highly unlikely. Nonetheless, one significant result of the rise of Hindu fundamentalism has been a widening division within the Indian intelligentsia about the wisdom of the country's constitutional secularism; some continue to insist that it must be defended and made to work, while others, like T. N. Madan, argue that its failure and "the falsity of the hope of secularists" (1987b: 757) should be frankly recognized and a new approach developed.

Probably the most dramatic saga of modern Hindu fundamentalism concerns the long-running conflict over the Babri Masjid or "Babar mosque" in Ayodhya, which is said to stand over the site of Rama's birth, the Ramjanmabhumi. Friction between Hindus and Muslims over the mosque dates back to the mid-nineteenth century, if not earlier, but the first serious riots after independence occurred in 1949 when an image of Rama suddenly appeared in the mosque. Tension ebbed and flowed throughout the next thirty-five years, but since the mid-1980s it has risen sharply. In 1984, the fundamentalist organization known as the Vishwa Hindu Parishad (VHP) attempted to "liberate Lord Ram from his Muslim jail" (van der Veer 1987b: 291). In 1985, a court ruled that Hindus were entitled to worship in the disputed building, and this decision led to widespread agitation across India by both Hindus and Muslims.

In 1989, the Babri Masjid-Ramjanmabhumi dispute (as commentators evenly call it) entered a new phase. In November, at the time of the Indian general election, VHP members tried to start building Rama's temple with bricks brought to Ayodhya by thousands of Hindus from far and wide. Initially, they were allowed to do so by Rajiv Gandhi's Congress government, but then they were stopped. In the feverish atmosphere created by events in Ayodhya, hundreds of Muslims and many Hindus as well were killed in massacres, especially in Bihar. The communal flames were fanned by a host of politicians seeking electoral gain, and the Ayodhya crisis was a major factor in the Congress party's defeat at the polls.

A year later, the dispute erupted again. In October 1990, there were widespread violent protests in India against the decision of V. P. Singh's National Front government to implement the Mandal Commission report, which recommended an increase in the quota of jobs reserved for lower castes. At the same time, the Hindu fundamentalist Bharatiya Janata party (BJP) withdrew support from the coalition government, and openly joined forces with the VHP to mobilize volunteers, *kar-sevaks*, to go to "serve" in Ayodhya, where work on Rama's temple would be restarted. The police tried to prevent the volunteers from reaching the site; some did get there, but many more were arrested and an unknown number were killed by police fire. By the end of November, mainly owing to the Mandal and Ayodhya crises, V. P. Singh's government had fallen. Yet another attempt to start building Rama's temple was made in December, though trouble was largely avoided in Ayodhya itself, where an uneasy peace ensued. However, from October until December, several hundred people probably died in communal killings across India. Serious rioting broke out in numerous towns and cities in Uttar Pradesh, and in Hyderabad in Andhra Pradesh, and there were also countless smaller outbreaks, in both urban and rural areas, over a huge part of the country. The total number of deaths and injuries is impossible to estimate, but the violence between Hindus and Muslims provoked by the Ayodhya dispute in 1989 and 1990 was certainly the worst since partition.

In May–June 1991, another general election was held, which cost the lives of Rajiv Gandhi and many other people. The Babri Masjid-Ramjanmabhumi dispute and Hindu fundamentalism were central issues in the election, particularly in the aggressive and well-organized campaign of the BJP, whose share of the vote rose markedly in many parts of India. The BJP gained a majority of the parliamentary seats in Uttar Pradesh, Delhi, and Gujarat, and became the largest opposition party facing the new Congress government in parliament. In no previous general election had an anti-Muslim, Hindu fundamentalist party won so much popular support.

The Ayodhya conflict and the growth of Hindu fundamentalism in general have persuaded some commentators that the religion's future, and indeed India's own, is dark. We are witnessing, it is said, the unstoppable transformation of Hinduism into a violently aggressive creed—the final, baleful result of the reformist movement originally influenced by western currents of thought around the turn of the eighteenth century in Bengal. There can be no doubt that the rise of Hindu fundamentalism is a very threatening development, likely to cost more lives in the future. Yet we must keep it in proportion, and western writers in particular have a duty to do so. In recent years, especially since the transformation of the Soviet Union and the end of the cold war, it has been plain that communism may be replaced as the west's bogeyman by oriental fundamentalism—predominantly Islamic, but more plausibly terrifying with Hindu, Sikh, and Buddhist limbs as well. The original juggernaut, to which people blindly sacrificed themselves and others, grew from fevered orientalist misapprehensions about events at Jagannatha's temple in Orissa. None of us, by exaggerating the impact of fundamentalism, should misimagine Hinduism like a new juggernaut purportedly calling on the faithful to kill in its name.

By 1990, it was very clear that the Ayodhya dispute—like the Mandal Commission report—was being blatantly exploited by politicians, and ordinary people were well aware of this. Of course, such perspicacity by itself does little to heal the divide between either Hindus and Muslims, or high and low castes. Nevertheless, events in 1990 and 1991 demonstrated that the divisions among Hindus remain as politically important as those between Hindus and Muslims. Even in Uttar Pradesh, where the BJP was probably most successful in winning votes from all sections of Hindus by exploiting anti-Muslim sentiment, it gained more support among upper-caste urban than lower-caste rural voters, and least of all among Harijans. The BJP's electoral advance also owed much to purely political factors, such as its own very effective organization and the disarray of its opponents. Hence it would be a serious mistake to conclude that religious difference alone principally determines the course of communal conflict and political competition throughout India today.

Moreover, despite fundamentalism, the evidence at the time of writing (July 1991) suggests that the majority of Hindus in most regions of India are not aggressively assertive about their religion or even the supposed interests of their "community." They worship their gods and goddesses, offer sacrifices to them, celebrate festivals for them, sing devotional hymns to them, go on pilgrimages to their sacred sites, and ask them for help in times of trouble much as they have done in the past, largely unaffected by fundamentalist influences. For the most part, anthropologists who have studied the religion of ordinary Hindus in cities, towns, and villages during the 1980s have reported essentially the same phenomena as their predecessors over at least the last fifty years. And even when there has been significant change, fundamentalism has not necessarily been a factor, as illustrated by the rise in popularity of god-men or the expansion of long-distance pilgrimage. Hindu fundamentalism should plainly not be underestimated, but neither should its impact be exaggerated, not least because the religion generally remains more significant in relation to social inequality among Hindus, than it does to antagonism between them and adherents of other faiths.

In January 1991, BJP activists were touring north India with urns allegedly containing the ashes of *kar-sevak*s killed in Ayodhya. The urns came to several villages in Budaun district, about one hundred miles southeast of Delhi, where local people heard about the BJP's plan to defend the Hindu religion and nation. According to Inderjit Badhwar, a reporter from India's leading news magazine, the villagers remained skeptical, for they had heard politicians prate and promise too many times before. One Harijan acutely observed that the real problem still lay among Hindus themselves: "We can't even enter the temple in the village, so what does the Ram Mandir [temple] in Ayodhya mean to us?" And another man, speaking in the spirit of devotionalism, concluded that "Ram is supposed to dwell in our hearts, not in a temple. We don't need to learn about our *dharma* from politicians seeking votes" (*India Today*, 31 January 1991, p. 35).

The opinions of just two north Indian villagers prove nothing by themselves, and they may have altered during the general election campaign later in the year. Then Badhwar, reporting again from rural Uttar Pradesh, heard VHP leaders campaigning for the BJP by declaring that Indians were either believers in or opponents of Rama. The opponents—Muslims and other non-Hindus—were poisoning the land and had to be destroyed (*India Today*, 31 May 1991, p. 45). Such inflammatory oratory must have had some effect on its audience, at least at the time. Yet it is inconceivable that discrimination against Harijans, or devotionalist ideas about Rama in the heart, have suddenly been eradicated by fundamentalist pressures after so many centuries. Even the continuing conflict in Ayodhya and all that it epitomizes will probably leave the ordinary people's religion largely unchanged. That Hinduism is a timeless "eternal religion," the *sanatana dharma*, is a modern reformist myth, but the popular religion I have discussed in this book has old and deep roots. It is not about to disappear from the home and the world of most of India's Hindus.

Afterword

POPULAR HINDUISM AND HINDU NATIONALISM

ON 6 DECEMBER 1992, the ancient mosque in Ayodhya known as the Babri Masjid was torn down by a mob of militant Hindu activists determined to clear the site for a new temple to be built on top of the purported birthplace of Rama, the Ramjanmabhumi. At the time of writing in late 2003, the temple has still not been erected—although its carved stones and pillars are ready to be transported to the site—and controversy about it continues to be as divisive and dangerous as ever. The consequences of the mosque's demolition have deeply penetrated the body politic and it is now very clear that that fateful day in 1992 marked a dramatic turning point in the history of independent India.

During the 1990s, the rise of Hindu nationalism—by common consent, a more accurate label than "fundamentalism"—was one of the most important political developments in India, although equally significant in many regions was the growing power of the lower castes, the Other Backward Classes (OBCs), and the Dalits (or Harijans), the ex-untouchable Scheduled Castes (SCs). These political changes have been accompanied by economic liberalization, especially since 1991, when the Indian government embarked on a wholesale policy of economic reform that has particularly led to a sizable increase in urban, middle-class affluence and consumerism. In the 1990s, the Hindu nationalist Bharatiya Janata Party (BJP; "Indian People's Party") eclipsed the once hegemonic Congress party; after the 1996 general election, the BJP became the largest single party and after the elections in 1998 and more decisively in 1999, it was the leading party in the coalition governments ruling India. The BJP is closely linked with the powerful Rashtriya Swayamsevak Sangh (RSS; "National Volunteers' Association") and its allied organizations in the Sangh Parivar (or RSS "family"), such as the Vishwa Hindu Parishad (VHP; "World Hindu Federation") led by ascetics, gurus, and other holy men.

In his review article on *The Camphor Flame*, Jackie Assayag (1994: 145–46) asked how the rise of Hindu nationalism could fail to affect popular Hinduism and he dismissed as implausible my concluding claim that the Ayodhya dispute "will probably leave the ordinary people's religion largely unchanged" (p. 261). Replying to Assayag, I acknowledged that he was probably right, because the mosque's demolition (several months after the book's publication) and the serious Hindu-Muslim riots that ensued had almost certainly modified people's understanding of their own religion (Fuller 1994: 156). In 1994, of course, there was very little relevant evidence and even now it remains sparse. In particular, there is much less literature about Hindu nationalism's impact on ordinary people's religion than about the reworking of mythical and ritual themes by nationalism and its ideology of "Hindutva" ("Hinduness"), which equates India with an essentialized Hindu religion and culture. This Afterword, which partly reflects that imbalance in the material, is thematically organized by the deities themselves and I begin with Ganesha.

GANESHA AND THE CREATION OF NATIONALIST RITUALS

The historical roots of today's Hindu nationalism can be traced back much earlier, especially to the religious reform movements of the colonial period that were briefly discussed in chapter 4 (pp. 99–101). The first major attempt to create a politicized Hindu ritual was the invention of the public Ganesha Chaturthi yearly festival in Maharashtra in the 1890s by Bal Gangadhar Tilak—who was prominent in the "conservative," neotraditionalist wing of the Indian National Congress—and other Hindu leaders. Even for a discussion about contemporary change, it is useful to start with this festival, because it highlights several features that are still important today. Elaborate public festivals for Ganesha (Ganapati) had been held by Maratha princely states during the previous hundred years or so, and the god was especially popular among the Brahman political elite. By the late nineteenth century, however, Ganesha's annual festival was a mostly private, domestic event, even though people living in the same neighborhood commonly joined together in little processions to immerse the images in water afterward. In 1894, in the Brahman-dominated city of Pune (Poona), Tilak and his associates transformed the annual festival into a public event lasting several days, when large images of the god were on display until everybody joined together in one big immersion procession at the end. From the outset, the festival was intended as a manifestation of religious revivalism, as well as a means to mobilize the Hindu population against both the British and the Muslims. Within a few years, public Ganesha festivals had started in towns and cities across Maharashtra and elsewhere in the old Bombay Presidency, such as Surat (Gujarat) and Belgaum (Karnataka). In the early twentieth century, the festival's anti-British and anti-Muslim political message was explicit, although it was eventually regulated by the government. In Maharashtra after 1919, to quote Richard I. Cashman (1975: 93): "Although Ganesha was permitted to resume a political career, his political stock was never to reach the heights of the earlier period. . . . In the present-day celebration [circa 1966] politics plays a rather minor role."

After independence in 1947, as Cashman says, the festival became less and less political, although even in the 1970s, according to Paul B. Courtright, it brought "a heightened sense of unity among Hindus" and anxiety among Muslims "because of the aggressive mood some Hindus exhibit" (1985: 195). In the course of time, moreover, Ganesha's festival has become immensely popular across Maharashtra. In the big cities, hundreds of elaborate images are displayed in complex tableaux, and hundreds of thousands of people turn out for the immersion processions at the end. Even in Ahmadnagar, a medium-sized city, it took about eight hours for the images to move slightly over one mile in 1970 (ibid.: 196). In Mumbai (Bombay), where there were approximately 7,400 festival organization committees in 2000 (Kaur 2003: 60), vast crowds throng the city's Chowpatty beach to watch Ganesha's colorful images bob on the waves before sinking into the Arabian Sea. Since the late 1980s, Ganesha Chaturthi has again became more strongly politicized, especially as a vehicle for Hindu nationalism, so that in some respects it has come full circle in one hundred years, as Raminder Kaur (2003) shows. In Mumbai, around two-thirds of the festival committees are controlled by the Shiv Sena (ibid.: 167), but many images there and in other cities like Pune are still erected and immersed by devotees with no overt political affiliation, so that this "multifaceted" festival (ibid.: 18) is neither completely controlled by religious nationalists nor totally dominated by communal politics.

The Shiv Sena, as I should explain here, is the most powerful Hindu nationalist organization in Mumbai and elsewhere in Maharashtra. It is primarily a regionalist organization, which now stands for Maharashtrian, rather than all-Indian, Hindu nationalism, and its preeminent icon is Shivaji, the seventeenth-century warrior-king who founded the Maratha state and helped to destroy the Mughal empire. The Sena, whose name is normally taken to mean "Shivaji's army," also represents itself as a modernist movement born in India's most cosmopolitan city, as opposed to the traditionalist BJP, which allegedly expresses the values of old-fashioned Hindus in northern India. Between the Shiv Sena and the BJP, persistent tension and rivalry exist despite their shared commitment to Hindu nationalism.

Ganesha's festival exemplifies several important features. First, in this and all other cases, the new ritual created for political purposes is an adaptation of an already existing ritual, partly so that it can be represented as a natural continuation or extension of traditional practice. In Mumbai today, heated arguments go on about whether, for instance, novel images of Ganesha that portray him as another deity, or a politician, actor, or cricketer, are legitimately "traditional" (Kaur 2002: 82–

83); nonetheless, as all sides agree, they certainly should be. Indeed, every new ritual must be designed to exemplify sufficient continuity, simply because no "invented tradition" can be effective unless it is connected to extant traditions retaining some appeal and authority among people who might adopt it.

Second, the new ritual is a public, rather than a private, event, so that it can draw Hindus together in a display of collective action. As Tilak himself wrote in the 1890s: "Through this nationalist appeal, the worship of Ganapati spread from the family circle to the public square. The transition is noteworthy since . . . Hindu religious worship is largely a matter of individual or family worship. Congregational worship as that in Christianity or Islam is not common" (quoted in Jaffrelot 1994: 265). Of course, in most of India, collective festivals—for instance, for tutelary village deities—are common (chap. 6) and congregational worship—for instance, singing hymns together—is normal in devotionalist settings (chap. 7). Other examples could be added and all Hindus are certainly conversant with collective rituals. Nonetheless, many Hindus insist that they lack regular rituals to express and generate collective unity, unlike—so they imagine—Muslims who join together in Friday prayers or at Id, or Christians who do the same at Sunday services or Easter. A pointed response to this deficiency was the *maha-arti*, provocatively invented by the Shiv Sena in Mumbai in December 1992 during the riots following the demolition of the Ayodhya mosque. The *maha-arti* ("great worship" in this context), which was promoted by the Sena for about a year, transformed the act of private devotion into a large-scale, public ritual held outside temples as a deliberate counteraction to Muslims gathering in and outside mosques for Friday prayers (Hansen 2001: 121; K. Sharma 1995: 278–79, 283). The creation of public rituals, like the Ganesha festival in the 1890s or the *maha-arti* a century later, was and is a response to the Muslims' and Christians' supposedly greater unity. Moreover, these public rituals are designed not only to promote Hindu unity in the abstract, but also to display it physically through ubiquitous Hindu control over the streets and other public spaces.

A third feature is that because Hindu unity is the objective, the ritual or the deity on which it focuses must appeal to as many Hindus as possible, rather than to a minority only. Thus Tilak converted a festival mainly associated with Brahmans into one appealing to non-Brahmans as well. Yet polytheism and hierarchical differentiation within the religion are plainly inimical to Hindu unity at the symbolic level, in striking contrast with Islamic monotheism and its ideal of equality before God. A critical question, therefore, to which we return in this Afterword, is this: how can Hindu nationalists create unifying rituals that overcome the problems posed by their plenteous divine pantheon?

It is immediately clear that only the great deities whose general powers transcend local boundaries can potentially symbolize Hindu unity effectively. The little deities cannot do so because they are normally conceptualized as local gods and goddesses who mainly protect particular communities, such as villages, urban quarters, and kin groups. Among the great deities, Ganesha is a leading candidate, because he is or can be revered by all Hindus, and he is worshiped throughout India as the lord of beginnings and obstacles. Ganesha is prominent in both classical and vernacular Hindu mythology; he is worshiped in temples by Brahman priests with a Sanskritic liturgy, but he is also regularly worshiped by non-Brahman priests, as well as by ordinary people of all social strata. Small shrines for Ganesha are ubiquitous in urban and rural India, often guarding road junctions or wells, so that this pan-Indian god has local protective functions as well. Hence Ganesha is a powerful mediatory deity within the pantheon and that is clearly one reason why Tilak promoted his festival.

Ganesha—already prominent in Maharashtra in the nineteenth century—progressively emerged as "the patron deity of the Marathi-speaking people" (Courtright 1985: 251). In the eyes of Maharashtrian Hindu nationalists, their regional deity can readily expand his role to become a powerful symbol of pan-Indian Hindu unity. Developments in the south seem to justify their viewpoint, because in the mid-1980s, the Maharashtrian Ganesha festival was copied in Tamilnadu by the Hindu Munnani ("Hindu Front"), the state's leading Hindu nationalist organization, and its BJP and RSS allies. Vinayaka Chaturthi, as the god's festival is known in Tamilnadu, was always widely celebrated in homes and temples, but in earlier years, there were no public ceremonies and processions. In a suburb of Chennai (Madras) in 1983, a little group of Hindu activists installed an image of Vinayaka or Ganesha in a public place; a few days later, they took their image in procession for immersion in a temple tank. One year later, images were set up in several other localities, including Triplicane in the city center, and from this tiny beginning, the scale of public celebrations expanded fairly rapidly in Chennai. In 1990, for the first but not the last time, a procession of many tall images en route to immersion in the sea, which was accompanied by thousands of Hindus, led to a bloody riot with Muslims near a mosque in Triplicane. Vinayaka Chaturthi remains a major public festival in Chennai, but in the late 1980s and early 1990s its celebration spread across Tamilnadu, to both urban and rural areas.

Promoting Vinayaka Chaturthi throughout most parts of Tamilnadu—not only in towns and cities, but also in rural areas—has been a major achievement by the Hindu Munnani and its allies, although the festival is still small in scale compared with Maharashtra. Since the mid-1990s, the Tamilnadu festival has undergone a partial evolution and, in many places, it has become less overtly anti-Muslim or anti-Christian than it used to be. Especially in Chennai—apart from Triplicane, where confrontation by the mosque is itself an annual ritual—the festival has also become a religious-cum-cultural celebration that is less nakedly political, and many independent celebrations not organized by the Hindu nationalists have sprung up (Fuller 2001).

Hindu activists in Tamilnadu repeatedly told me, when I was studying Vinayaka Chaturthi in 1999 and 2000, that Ganesha was an effective symbol of Hindu unity for reasons like those discussed already; in particular, he bridges the gap between great and little deities. Furthermore, even Vaishnava Tamil Brahmans—who traditionally refuse to worship Shiva—will worship his son and, unlike Rama, who may be categorized as a "north Indian" god, Ganesha never offends Tamil regionalists. Murugan (Skanda) shares many mediating characteristics with his elder brother Ganesha, but Murugan cannot now stand for pan-Hindu nationalism, because he is the principal divine symbol of Non-Brahman, Dravidian, Tamil regionalism, which developed in opposition to Brahmanical, Sanskritic religion and culture, and to what Tamils tend to see as the Hindi-dominated Indian state. Almost by a process of elimination, Ganesha is the most suitable of all the deities in the Tamils' pantheon for the Hindu nationalists' cause.

Vinayaka's Tamil festival is interesting partly because the entire event was deliberately copied from Maharashtra, the first time (as far as I know) that such a strategy has been used to devise a political ritual. Over the same period, however, the Ganesha festivals in Gujarat and northern Karnataka became more politicized, provoking communal riots in Surat and other Gujarati towns in 1990 (Nandy et al. 1995: 109) and in Belgaum in 1991 and 1992 (Assayag 1995: 196–97). Similarly, the festival in Hyderabad, which also dates from the end of the nineteenth century, has greatly expanded and become more anti-Muslim (Deshpande 2003: 95). In Jaipur, Ganesha's festival declined after independence but has recently revived in a more politicized form, supported by the RSS and sponsored by Hindu merchants (with quiet support from Jains as well) (Laidlaw 1995: 281–82). There is some evidence that public festivals for Ganesha are now springing up elsewhere, such as northern Kerala (as I saw in 2003) and coastal Orissa (Herrenschmidt 2002: 100). Hence it is possible, though uncertain, that Ganesha is now emerging as a more prominent deity of Hindu nationalism across many different regions of India.

Yet it would be a mistake to assume that everyone who takes part in one of Ganesha's public festivals supports Hindu nationalism, as Kaur (2003) convincingly shows for Maharashtra. In Tamilnadu, too, numerous Hindus actively participating in Vinayaka Chaturthi insist that they have nothing to do with the Hindu Munnani and are strongly opposed to its political exploitation of religion. To give but one example from Madurai: a particularly attractive Vinayaka, made in Maharashtra instead of locally, has been set up in a street of jewelry shops in the city center since 1983. The cost of the image and the six-day festival is met by the city's Maharashtrian "friends' association" and a Chettiyar jewelers' association, neither with any link to the Munnani. The Maharashtrian bullion refiner who spoke to me in 1999 explained that he was strongly in favor of Hindus uniting together to celebrate Vinayaka's festival, but he also strongly objected to its politicization, which—he ironically argued—was a departure from Tilak's true teachings.

When I met the president of the Hindu Munnani's Madurai branch in 1999, he told me that Mumbai's Ganesha festival was extremely popular, not only among Hindu nationalist supporters, and that Chennai's was developing similarly; he hoped Madurai would follow suit. For this Munnani leader, like other Hindu activists in Tamilnadu, non-Munnani, "non-political" events are to be welcomed, because they can all be claimed as evidence of ever-increasing Hindu pride, assertiveness, self-consciousness, and unity as a "community" publicly joined together in worshiping their god—even though many participants in the festival actually see their own involvement as a non-political expression of devotion to Ganesha.

There is, in other words, a contested discourse surrounding the god's public festival, which does not mean the same to all the Hindus who are involved, let alone to those who are not. Certainly, in Tamilnadu as in Maharashtra earlier, Ganesha's public festival has now become a more important event in the Hindu calendar than it was in the past and this does represent a notable change in popular Hinduism. Moreover, the Hindu Munnani's promotion of Vinayaka Chaturthi has significantly helped to "normalize" Hindu nationalism within Tamilnadu, so that "Hindutva ideas may percolate into the commonsense of the people of Tamil Nadu" (Geetha and Jayanthi 1995: 265). Yet these developments are ambiguous: on the one hand, many Hindus celebrating the festival do not support the nationalist cause; on the other hand, they are publicly and collectively worshiping Ganesha, which definitely can be seen as a manifestation of Hindu unity by both the nationalists and their opponents.

RAMA AND AYODHYA

In spite of Ganesha's importance for the Hindu nationalist cause in Maharashtra, Tamilnadu, and elsewhere, Rama is the nationalists' preeminent deity and his birthplace in Ayodhya is the epicenter of their struggle. Rama is the hero of the *Ramayana*, which was televised in India in 1987–

88. Every weekly episode attracted a vast audience, which ensured that more people than ever before became familiar with the epic. Some Hindu nationalists claimed that the *Ramayana*'s serialization dramatically increased their support and Purnima Mankekar's interviews with Hindu viewers suggest that it helped "to consolidate their Hindu identity and . . . to naturalize the slippage between Hindu culture and Indian culture" (1999: 183). Yet she also shows that not everyone saw the same thing on the screen and Arvind Rajagopal concludes that the serial contained and projected multiple meanings, not a single message. He writes: "If the Ramayan phenomenon reinforced anything, it was not national identity so much as an immense national dis-identification, the sense of confirming what the nation was *not*, in the innumerable perceptions of millions of viewers." It was this "political problem or opportunity" (Rajagopal 2001: 150) that the Hindu nationalists successfully exploited.

Rama was the seventh incarnation of Vishnu. According to Valmiki's classical Sanskrit *Ramayana*, Rama was the first son of the king of Ayodhya, whose citizens loved him for his wisdom and compassion. But Rama was forced into exile, so that his half-brother Bharata became king, and he went to a forest hermitage with his wife Sita and another half-brother, Lakshmana. The demon-king Ravana tricked his way into the hermitage and abducted Sita. The immensely strong monkey-god, Hanuman, became Rama's fervent devotee and helped him to invade Lanka, where Rama killed Ravana. Rama and Sita returned in triumph to Ayodhya, but Sita was banished owing to rumors about her chastity and in a hermitage she raised twin sons. Eventually, Sita abandoned the world to return into the earth and a grieving Rama ascended to heaven.

Crucial in the *Ramayana*, like so much Hindu mythology, is the battle between deities and demons, which the deities must ultimately win, so that the proper sociocosmic order predicated on kingship can be restored throughout the universe and its earthly microcosm, in this case the Ayodhya kingdom. As I explained in chapter 2 in particular, deities and demons are eternally opposed, but they are also symbiotically linked; thus Ravana gained his power from Shiva, to whom he was utterly devoted, and Shiva granted Ravana liberation after Rama killed him. Another key feature is that the majority of Hindu deities are not truly moral exemplars, but Rama is exceptional; especially in Valmiki's *Ramayana* and Tulsidas's Hindi recension, the *Ramcharitmanas*, which was the main inspiration for the televised serial, Rama is mostly portrayed as an ideal king and husband, joined with Sita the ideal wife and Lakshmana the ideal brother.

Because Rama is a perfect king, "Rama's rule," or the *Ram-rajya*, has long signified an ideal of good government. For Hindu nationalists, this ideal means that India should be a Hindu state, in which Hindus are

devotees of the sacred land of Bharata (India) modeled on Rama's kingdom, not just citizens of a secular republic. Furthermore, Ravana and his
fellow demons are no longer identified primarily as Shiva's devotees; instead, they become figurative Muslims, foreigners who are completely
separate from Hindus and must ultimately be crushed by Hindu royal
power. When the equation between demons and Muslims first developed
historically is controversial but, in any case, in today's "Hindu history"
(Pandey 1995), the *Ramayana*'s mythical ambiguities, as well as the narrative diversity of its many recensions, become rigidified into a linear
chronology of rightful Hindu sovereignty battling demonic Muslim subversion. The characteristically serene figure of Rama also takes on a new
and often angrier appearance, as Anuradha Kapur (1993) shows. Thus in
many pictures produced by the VHP, two alternatives are available:
"Ram the warrior, fighting for his rights in a battle that signifies apoca-
lyptic upheaval, and Ram the king, embodiment of a golden age of Hindu
culture, source of stability and reassurance." In both guises, though,
Rama primarily "symbolizes martial prowess" (Basu et al. 1993: 62), so
that his portrayal closely resembles Shivaji's. The demolition of the Babri
Masjid built by the Muslim emperor Babur, once it has been replaced by
Rama's new temple, will finally end the long battle for supremacy between Hindus and Muslims on the very site where the Hindus' immacu-
late god-king was born.

   Given his modified attributes as a perfect and now martial king, Rama
is the most fitting patron deity for Hindu nationalism in the entire pantheon. Anthropologists writing about the Chinese pantheon commonly
refer to the "imperial metaphor," by which they mean that relationships
among Chinese deities are conceptualized with reference to the imperial,
bureaucratic hierarchy, so that the higher deities are "celestial bureau-
crats" (Sangren 1987: 138–39). Following this example, we may describe
Rama as the principal "celestial nationalist." Rama, though, has not been
portrayed only as a king. In the 1980s, another popular nationalist design
showed Rama as a baby imprisoned behind bars, thus coupling the demand for his liberation from his presumptively Muslim jailers with the
notion, more prominent in Krishna's cult, that the god needs maternal
protection. Giving Rama more than one face undoubtedly expanded his
appeal to a wider constituency of Hindus.

   Yet Rama could still not easily fulfill his role as a celestial nationalist
everywhere in India. The god's popularity is concentrated in the Hindi-
speaking northern region, where Tulsidas's *Ramcharitmanas* is a favorite
devotional text and the annual autumnal festival celebrating Rama's victory over Ravana—the Ram Lila—is a major event that displaces the
Navaratri festival celebrated in most of the rest of the country (pp. 120–
23). Historically, this region was also the Mughal empire's heartland and
its population still includes a large Muslim minority. As Alf Hiltebeitel

(1995: 218) suggested, "one could regard the recent Ramjanmabhumi agitation as an attempt to sponsor a multimedia pan-Indian *ram lila*"; especially to north Indians, the Ayodhya campaign was a recognizable, if radical, extension of the supposed struggle between Rama's forces of good and the demonic, Muslim forces of evil. I return to the Ram Lila shortly, but first I discuss some strategies used by the Hindu nationalists to widen support throughout India.

Although largely restricted to north India, one of the first VHP initiatives in the 1980s was the mass production and distribution of small stickers and badges depicting Rama and his future temple. Hindu households were also asked to fly saffron flags or paint the mantra *om* on their doors. By these means, adapted from mass marketing techniques, the VHP sought to give the impression that there was a spontaneous upsurge in popular nationalist support. The stickers in particular "swamped individuals in their ubiquity, contriving a sense of the irresistible tide of Hindutva" (Basu et al. 1993: 60).

A second effective strategy, also developed by the VHP in the 1980s, was the program to encourage Hindus everywhere to send special, consecrated bricks inscribed with Rama's name to Ayodhya, which would be used to build his temple. Actually, all sorts of probably unsuitable bricks were sent, but the program succeeded in keeping the Ayodhya campaign alive and spreading the nationalist message farther, while also permitting individuals to make and consecrate their bricks "as a small act of devotion to Rama, rather than an endorsement of the VHP" (Davis 1996: 41). Like independent, non-political celebrations of Ganesha's public festival, the brick program allowed Hindu nationalists to claim support even from people who may not really have been supporters at all. Conversely, it also enabled supporters to pursue their own aims; thus Brahmans displaced by non-Brahmans in rural Tamilnadu could give bricks to link themselves to a greater Hindu movement and regain some sense of their importance in the village and the world (D. P. Mines 2002: 73–75).

The third and most spectacular innovation was the invention of new forms of ritual procession as part of Hindu nationalism's "spatial strategies" (Deshpande 2003: chap. 4). The first VHP procession, known as the "sacrifice for unanimity" (*ekatmata yajna*), was held in 1983. It consisted of three major processions, crossing the whole of India from north to south and east to west, which intersected at Nagpur (home of the RSS) in the center of the country, as well as many more smaller processions that joined the major ones. By adapting the traditional idea of a long-distance pilgrimage that constitutes a "sacred geography" as discussed above (pp. 207–10), the VHP's procession was a powerfully resonant vehicle for attracting support and enacting a vision of a unified Hindu nation situated on a sacred land.

The most dramatic and explosive of all the nationalists' processions took place in 1990. This "chariot pilgrimage" (*rath yatra*) started in September from Somanatha, on the Gujarat coast, which is the site of a major Hindu temple dedicated to Krishna. For more than nine hundred years, the temple was repeatedly sacked by Muslims and rebuilt by Hindus. After independence, it was reconstructed as "a monument of the Hindu nation that has finally won its continuous struggle against 'foreign' oppression" (van der Veer 1994: 151). The procession of Rama's decorated chariot, which traversed eight states and about 6,000 miles, was scheduled to reach Ayodhya after thirty-five days, on the day when pilgrims come for the annual ritual circumambulation of the city. Labeled the "Hindu juggernaut" by the English-language press, this procession had an enormous impact, partly because it was headed by the BJP leader, L. K. Advani, who stood on the chariot and carried a bow like Rama himself. Advani was arrested in Bihar, but violence then flared in various places and in Ayodhya itself a (disputed) number of activists were killed by the police, which renewed the VHP's cult of heroic martyrdom. Although it actually started a few days early, the procession from Krishna's Somanatha to Rama's Ayodhya clearly replicated the royal military progress that simultaneously celebrates victory and starts a new season of warfare on Dasara, "Victory tenth," after the end of Navaratri (pp. 119–25). Conspicuous in the procession were young men belonging to the Sangh Parivar's militant youth organization, the Bajrang Dal, "Hanuman's army," who carried bows and tridents, and tried to give Advani both a sword and a vessel of their own blood to smear on his forehead as a *tilaka*. The 1990 procession seemed designed to show that Rama, accompanied by his army and young men willing to die, was now marching to Ayodhya to liberate it by force. In this event, the imagery of sacrifice, violence, and warfare played a vital part; I return to this point when discussing Durga below.

Since "Hanuman's army" has just been mentioned, let me briefly discuss Hanuman the monkey-god, Rama's most faithful devotee, who is famed in popular Hinduism for his gigantic physical strength and is widely worshiped as a divine "go-between who gets things done" (Lutgendorf 1994: 243). Hanuman has become more popular all over India in the last twenty or thirty years, and since the 1980s, very tall statues of him have been erected in many places. His strength, which makes him the wrestlers' patron deity, and his role as "Rama's strong-arm, who speaks eloquently but carries a big stick" (Lutgendorf 2002: 93), largely explain why militant young men are organized in "Hanuman's army." Yet the evidence overall suggests that the rise in Hanuman's popularity actually preceded the rise of contemporary Hindu nationalism and that increased competitiveness encouraged by economic liberalization has contributed more to his appeal than politicized religion.

Thus Hanuman is favored because he is both approachable and thought to be very effective in dealing with the vexations of society and the economy today, which all require the ability to fix snags or wield no-nonsense strength. The latter quality is mostly shared by the single goddess who embodies *shakti* (pp. 45–48) and in some regions, such as Tamilnadu and Kerala, the popularity of Durga and similar goddesses, as well as some other strong or fierce deities, has risen for much the same reason as Hanuman's over the same period (Osella and Osella 2000: 167–68; Tarabout 1997: 139–40).

To return to the VHP's processions: after 1990 and especially after the mosque's demolition in 1992, their impact declined and eventually the strategy of staging processions looked "more and more like [an] electoral stunt" (Deshpande 2003: 94). The fading appeal of newly created rituals is in fact a pervasive problem; for example, in Chennai by 2003, the Vinayaka Chaturthi festival had stopped growing in size and may have started to shrink, as some people began to lose interest. As Rajagopal (2001: 211) observes, the nationalists' media-driven strategy generates new cultural and political symbols whose "half-life" tends to be shorter than more traditional religious symbols. New symbols, unlike old ones, are prone to lose their impact as fashions change; as one teenage girl said to Rajagopal: "I am tired of Ram. I want a new name."

Boredom alone, however, is unlikely to cripple the Hindu nationalist movement. The various wings of the Sangh Parivar have shown themselves adept at continually creating new rituals and modifying old ones, and they have had a lot of success in promoting Hindutva ideology by these means. Yet their success is never total and the nationalist movement cannot exercise hegemonic control over the politico-religious domain, as two cases concerning the Ram Lila illustrate. The first, small example comes from Karimpur village in western Uttar Pradesh, where the Ram Lila was always organized by the dominant Brahman community. The festival was in decline during the 1980s, but it was revived in the early 1990s "with the rallying cry of 'Ram rajya' . . . as a political move" by the BJP. A few years later, a second Ram Lila was started by the middle-ranking Farmer caste, rivals of the Brahmans (Wadley 2000: 336). Whether both events carry the same political connotations is unclear, but Karimpur's two Ram Lilas—even if they both enact Rama's victory over demonic Muslims—now express inter-caste division among Hindus as well.

The second, more detailed example comes from the city of Kota, in Rajasthan, which lies on the edge of the region where the Ram Lila, rather than Navaratri, is the major autumnal festival. Norbert Peabody (1997) explains that Kota's principal Ram Lila used to be celebrated by its Rajput royal family and, before 1947, the king sometimes took

Rama's role in the play enacting Ravana's defeat; nowadays, the festival is jointly sponsored by the palace and the municipality, and the king sends a Rajput deputy in his stead. In the 1986 play, when Rama was about to fight Ravana, two men came forward to impersonate the god: the king's deputy and the local Congress Member of the Legislative Assembly (MLA) in Rajasthan. The MLA insisted that the rule of kings and landlords was over and that he was therefore entitled to play the part of Rama. In the end, the politician had to yield to the royal deputy, but he still managed to make his point by firing a second arrow at Ravana's effigy.

The MLA belonged to the Gujar caste, which is also a major landowning caste like the Rajputs. In the past, Gujars and Rajputs were closely allied, but now they tend to be rivals; Gujars have become relatively more prosperous, but Rajputs look down on them. Peabody explains that the MLA's intervention symbolically placed Rajputs—not Muslims—on the demonic side as feudal oppressors of Gujars and low-caste people, and portrayed them as reactionaries resisting the progressive Congress party. Indirectly, the MLA was also articulating opposition to the BJP, which Rajputs tend to support, although Rajputs have resisted Ravana's identification with Muslims, partly owing to their historic ties with the Mughals. On the other hand, the whole episode also reflected the BJP's success in establishing the Ram Lila as the critical site for political debate; this was so even though Rajputs tend not to interpret Rama's story as anti-Muslim and the MLA read it against the background of Rajput, rather than Mughal, domination, so that "temporarily, at least, [he] marginalized or bypassed the entire issue of the disputed mosque in Ayodhya" (Peabody 1997: 570). Thus when potentially "hegemonic forms"—such as those of Hindutva ideology—are extended into local contexts, they are reshaped by local political alignments and oppositions that can divert or undermine them. Kota's Ram Lila had been reconfigured by Hindu nationalism, so that it was no longer an ostensibly non-political celebration of royal tradition, but the fracas in 1986 meant that the nationalists' version of Rama's victory over Ravana never actually appeared on stage.

KRISHNA AND SHIVA

Rama's popularity, as we have seen, is concentrated in the Hindi-speaking region. Krishna, Vishnu's eighth incarnation, was and is more popular and prominent than Rama in the extreme west of Uttar Pradesh and throughout Rajasthan and Gujarat in particular.

Because Rama's restricted appeal is a major problem for the Hindu nationalists, the VHP, since the 1980s, has also been demanding the "liberation" of Krishna's purported birthsite in Mathura, the Krishnajanmabhumi, and Shiva's holiest temple, the Vishwanatha temple, in Benares (Kashi). In Mathura, the seventeenth-century Shahi mosque was built over the remains of a temple razed by Mughal armies that allegedly stood on the exact site where Krishna was born; in Benares, the Vishwanatha temple seen today is only part of a larger temple, also destroyed by Muslims, on whose ruins the Gyanvapi mosque was built. If the Mathura and Benares campaigns could generate as much momentum as Ayodhya's, a much larger constituency of Hindus could be brought into the nationalist fold. Partly for tactical reasons, BJP politicians have repeatedly stalled these two campaigns, but they also recognize that neither Krishna nor Shiva makes such a potent celestial nationalist as Rama.

In devotionalist Hinduism, especially in western India, Krishna is adored as a small boy who steals butter and plays tricks, and as a flute-playing youth who dances with the cowherdesses and is passionately in love with Radha. Krishna in these forms is plainly unsuitable as a symbol of nationalism but in fact, under the pressure of moralistic reform over several decades, the pastoral youth has been progressively eclipsed for many Hindus by the "epic" Krishna. This Krishna is a Yadava prince who killed his wicked, usurping uncle Kamsa, but above all he is the charioteer in the *Bhagavad Gita*, who urges Arjuna to do his duty on the battlefield in the great war between the Pandavas and Kauravas, which is the theme of the *Mahabharata* epic. Particularly by Gandhi, who extolled the *Gita*, the war was interpreted as a struggle between good and evil, but even by fanatics it could hardly be read as a struggle between Hindus and Muslims, because the wicked Kauravas were the Pandavas' cousins. Whereas Rama, a more unequivocally perfect king than Krishna, fought demonic enemies who can be transfigured as Muslims, Krishna killed his own uncle and went into fratricidal battle against his kinsmen, all of them Hindus. Significantly, the "discourses about the state" were more subtle and less conservative in the televised *Mahabharata* (1988–90) than in the preceding *Ramayana* (Mankekar 1999: 186).

Yet Krishna's representation has been affected by Hindu nationalism since the mid-1980s, although the most striking development for which we have detailed material is his emergence as the patron deity of the Yadavs, one of the most politically active and powerful OBC castes in north India. In Mathura since the late nineteenth century, as Lucia Michelutti shows, the low-ranking, cowherding Ahirs have turned themselves into Yadavs in a prototypical process of caste unification designed to raise their status. As part of this process, during the last fifty years, local lineage deities have been gradually replaced by Krishna, now identified as the tutelary deity of the whole Yadav community. This deity is the epic

Krishna, the warrior-king, not Krishna the cowherd who would remind Yadavs of their lowlier Ahir past. The epic Krishna has also been systematically distanced from the god who was the cowherdesses' lover or the husband of 16,000 queens. For Yadavs in Mathura today, as Michelutti was often bluntly told, "Krishna was a Yadav" and "We descend from Krishna-Vasudev" (2002: 222); Krishna is also a moral paragon and when Radha appears, she is his wife, not his mistress (ibid.: 287). Today, too, Krishna is portrayed as the consummate warrior-politician who was also "the first democratic political leader" (ibid.: 252). For Yadavs, especially political activists in the OBC-supported Samajwadi Party in Uttar Pradesh, led by Mulayam Singh Yadav, Krishna is the divine protagonist of backward-class politics, not Hindu nationalism.

As Michelutti explains, in spite of the Yadavs' political opposition to the BJP, Krishna's transformation into a warrior-king and democratic politician has clear parallels with Rama's emergence as the warrior-king of Hindu nationalism, and there has been an "incorporation of Hindu nationalist themes in the local Yadav narratives" (ibid.: 239). Thus, for example, in the contemporary iconography of Krishna the charioteer and Rama the martial king, there are many similar features that are indirectly reinforced by Krishna's development as a more conventionally moral god. Yadavs are a minority in Mathura, where the BJP actually dominates the political scene, but we have no ethnographic data about Krishna's portrayal among activists campaigning to "liberate" his birthplace. Nonetheless, Michelutti's study well illustrates both how Krishna has been recruited into contemporary backward-class politics—even if his transmutation into a royal pioneer of democracy and "affirmative action" is more convincing to Yadavs than members of other castes—and how this development has been influenced by Hindu nationalist themes more evident in Rama's persona. Furthermore, although the Yadavs' god is opposed to the BJP, many people in the Mathura region now insist, more than in the past, that Krishna and Rama are indeed the same god, so that the epic Krishna's convergence with Rama the nationalist, martial king is further reinforced.

Of the three "liberation" campaigns, Benares has generated the least momentum and one reason is probably that Shiva, of all the great deities, is hardest to convert into a convincing nationalist symbol. Especially in Benares, Shiva's own city, the god is associated with death and its conquest, and there, as in much of north India, he is primarily imagined as an awesome ascetic renouncer transcending the mundane world. This is not so everywhere; in his south Indian temples, for instance, Shiva is prominently represented as a husband and father, as well as an ascetic, and he is often a king as well. Shiva assumes similar roles, too, among the Maheshwari merchants of Jaipur and was actually transformed into their caste's patron deity during the twentieth century (Pache Huber 2002: 122–31). If Shiva can become a caste's patron deity, it is not inconceivable, I suggest, that he could become a celestial nationalist as well, but in fact the VHP appears to have made no serious effort to deploy Shiva in this role in Benares or elsewhere.

DURGA AND THE GODDESS

Outside the Hindi heartland, the goddess's autumnal festival—Navaratri, Durga Puja, or Dasara—is normally celebrated instead of the Ram Lila. Among Bengalis, Durga Puja is the year's greatest festival and the goddess, especially as Durga or Kali, is their most popular deity; Sita, incidentally, is often seen as the *Ramayana*'s true hero and Rama's treatment of her after their return to Ayodhya is judged priggish and supercilious. Indeed, in some Bengali versions of the epic, "Rama's actions are as problematic as his rule is suspect," which, it has been polemically suggested, may reflect the Bengalis' "cynicism about the possibility of truly beneficent rule" (Stewart and Dimock 2001: 264).

At first glance, Durga's victory over the demon-king Mahishasura seems to serve Hindu nationalist purposes as well as Rama's over Ravana. One significant obstacle, though, is that autonomous, violent forms of the goddess, such as Durga, cannot be represented as perfect wives or other ideal role models for Hindu women. Only exceptionally, too, are goddesses portrayed as rulers, who are normally male, so that they are not easily translatable into celestial nationalists. On the other hand, the goddess is equated with the country itself as Bharat Mata, "Mother India," whose cult "in combination with militant matriotism" (McKean 1996b: 279) has played a central role in the VHP's campaigns. A popular poster, seen in various formats all over the country, also shows a map of "Greater India" (incorporating Pakistan and Bangladesh) with Durga imposed upon it, standing triumphantly next to her lion and holding a saffron flag. Durga can indeed become a ferocious inspiration to defend the Hindu nation against demonic usurpers. Thus when the Ayodhya mosque was being demolished, one of the VHP's fieriest orators, the female ascetic Sadhvi Rithambhara, chanted this prayer over the loudspeakers (quoted in Nandy et al. 1995: 196):

> Let us together praise Mother Durga,
> Mother, your sons are calling you,
> Come down,
> We shall cut our heads off and offer them to you,
> Bring your drinking bowl and we will fill it with blood,

Listen to my pleas,
Fulfil my wishes,
Give me Ayodhya, give me Mathura, give me Kashi.

In this prayer, the theme of filial sacrifice to blood-drinking Durga is joined to the idea of a just war to seize Rama's birthsite and recapture his kingdom, which extends the traditional notion both that the god's victory over Ravana is won by favor of the goddess and that it is anticipated by her defeat of Mahishasura in a war that is also a sacrifice (pp. 119, 121). Rithambhara's oratorical imagery thereby situated the Ayodhya (and Mathura and Kashi) campaigns within the context of the goddess's sacrificial cult and made them resonate with the themes central in Navaratri as well as the Ram Lila, so that the struggle over Rama's temple could better appeal to the goddess's devotees in Bengal and elsewhere.

More generally, for Hindu nationalists, the legitimating symbolic source of violence is primarily the fierce goddess, especially Durga or Kali, even though Hanuman and sometimes Shiva may be invoked. Violence, real or imaginary, is an intrinsic part of militant Hindu nationalism. Surrounding many processions, for example, there is an atmosphere of potential violence—even if none actually breaks out—that is mostly generated by young men, with saffron scarves tied round their heads, who brandish tridents and sticks, whirl around in a kind of war-dance, and shout ferocious slogans. Violence is especially vital in the "method and ideology" of the Shiv Sena (Eckert 2003: chap. 5), which stresses the legitimacy of "Maharashtrian warriordom" and the "Hindutva construction of national defence" (ibid.: 148), and Sena activists consistently invoke Shivaji, as well as the goddess, to justify their violence. In processions in Maharashtra, a favorite slogan is "Jai Shivaji! Bharat Mata ki jai!", proclaiming victory to Shivaji and Mother India. In Vinayaka Chaturthi processions in Tamilnadu, a favorite is "Om Kali! Jai Kali! Bharat Mata ki jai!", which announces victory for Kali and Mother India; invoking violent Kali, say activists, inspires courage in them. The young men who make up most of the crowd in such processions are typically recruited from the ranks of the urban poor and form "a reservoir of street-smart muscle power" (Nandy et al. 1995: 97); they are led by a small number of senior officials, who dress in neat white clothes and behave with restraint, as if to separate themselves from the "rowdies" around them—just as Advani did on the 1990 chariot pilgrimage to Ayodhya. Otherwise, "respectable" men and all women are normally conspicuous by their absence from these processions.

Support for the Hindu nationalist cause can certainly be forfeited by violence on the streets. Nevertheless, violence or its threat—even though the leadership often claims to deplore it—is crucial to the militancy or "disciplined aggression," to quote a Bajrang Dal leader (ibid.: 97), that nationalist processions and other demonstrations are designed to project. Apart from Bal Thackeray, the Shiv Sena's supremo, it is Sadhvi Rithambhara, one of the Sangh Parivar's very few female leaders, who has most resoundingly advocated violence. As Tanika Sarkar comments, Rithambhara "embodies *shakti* . . . within herself. But she also calls Hindu men to action, to vengeance." In addition, she tells Hindu women that "they must produce sons who will kill Muslims" (2001: 424–25). Although Rithambhara is an exceptional figure, the nationalist movement includes various women's organizations, whose members are encouraged to assist a cause that generally reinforces gender inequality in the name of traditional Hindu values; Hindu women should be ideal wives like Sita, not independent like Durga. This paradox, which has been widely discussed, is well illustrated by the experience of members of the Durga Vahini ("Durga's army"), a VHP women's organization, who took part in processions during the Ayodhya campaign. As Amrita Basu (1998: 180) observes, these women experienced "self-affirmation through self-sacrifice, and . . . empowerment through public-sphere activism, which ultimately renewed their commitment to their domestic roles." But even for women who are not activists, nationalism can shape their religious belief and practice. V. Geetha and T. Y. Jayanthi point out that female involvement in public religious events, some of them invented to appeal to women specifically, enables women to see themselves as valued participants in "public and even political demonstrations of Hindu fervour and faith" (1995: 246); it also transforms the "Hindutva idea into a matter of great personal concern for 'ordinarily religious' Hindu women" (ibid.: 247). This transformation is another aspect of the "normalization" of Hindu nationalism referred to above, but it also conversely means that the idea is no longer controlled only by nationalist activists or ideologues, so that it can become subject to a variety of possible interpretations by ordinary women.

Let me close this section by referring to an extraordinary young woman whose death became famous partly because it was seized upon by Hindu nationalists. In Rajasthan in 1987, an eighteen-year-old Rajput, Roop Kanwar, immolated herself on her husband's funeral pyre (p. 23). Rajasthani Rajputs regard the *sati* tradition as primarily their own and shortly after Roop Kanwar's death, a "Committee for the Defence of Religion" was formed by educated Rajput men to defend the right to commemorate her *sati*. The Rajasthani branch of the BJP rallied to their cause, although the VHP was equivocal and the BJP's national leader, A. B. Vajpayee, denounced the glorification of *sati*. Crucial in this context, though, is that Roop Kanwar's death vitally contributed to the development of "Rajput Hindutva" (Jenkins 1998: 117), a version of nationalist ideology that enshrines Rajput honor, courage, and virtue—exemplified by *sati* and reverence for *sati matas* (divinized heroines who immolated themselves)—as the heart of Hindu tradition. Rajputs were lukewarm about the Ayodhya campaign in the 1980s, even in Kota where the Ram Lila was celebrated (Peabody 1997: 575), but many of them would and did support a movement that defended their right to commemorate *sati*. More than Rama, the apotheosized Roop Kanwar became the shining symbol of Hindu nationalism for Rajputs and many other Rajasthanis.

How this development affected the BJP in Rajasthan politically may be left aside. Unfortunately, in spite of a voluminous literature about Roop Kanwar's death, no sound ethnographic data exist about its impact on *sati mata* worship and popular Hinduism in Rajasthan, although Lindsey Harlan's monograph (1992) shows how Rajput women's understandings of *sati* are complex and changing, so that any modification would certainly not be a simple one. Anne Hardgrove (1999), however, has written about *sati* worship among the Calcutta Marwari business community, who trace their origin to Rajasthan. Marwaris and Rajputs do not conceptualize *sati* identically, and Marwaris definitely do not accept that only Rajput women can be genuine *sati*s. Marwaris control one of India's wealthiest temples, the Rani Sati temple in Jhunjhunu in the Shekhawati region north of Jaipur, which is the heartland of the cult. (According to legend, Rani Sati was a Marwari girl bride who, several centuries ago, burned herself to death by bursting into flames after her husband was killed.) After Roop Kanwar's death, the annual Rani Sati festival in Calcutta was banned and the temple in Jhunjhunu was closed. The Marwaris protested vigorously, but they also insisted that they were defending their traditional right to worship *sati mata*s and that they did not support the practice of *sati* itself today—a position that many Rajputs take as well. The controversy over the Marwaris' *sati* worship was plainly shaped by Hindu nationalist exploitation of Roop Kanwar's death. Nevertheless, as Hardgrove shows, for Marwari women and men themselves, *sati* worship and especially the public worship of Rani Sati allow them "to make a public statement about the internal values of the community" (1999: 747), which is and remains their own, consistent neither with the nationalists glorifying Roop Kanwar nor with the secularists who denounce them.

"SANSKRITIZATION" AND "JUNGLY" DEITIES

Unlike the great deities of the Hindu pantheon, the little local deities, as already mentioned, cannot be effective nationalist symbols. Yet their worshipers are obviously not ignored by the RSS, VHP, and other Sangh Parivar organizations, which have long been involved in a combination of social, educational, and religious programs among Dalit, tribal, and other marginal groups in order to promote Hindu unity and solidarity.

In many tribal communities, for example, the VHP runs welfare organizations, which often also try to convert tribal people—including the many Christians among them—to "recognizably respectable Hindutva forms of worship," so as "to replace existing beliefs and practices among tribals and ensure a homogenized version of religion" (Basu et al. 1993: 67). In effect, the VHP is promoting "Sanskritization," in M. N. Srinivas's original sense (1965: 30), whereby low-status castes, tribes, or other social groups, whose members are most likely to worship little deities, emulate the more prestigious Sanskritic religion of the Brahmans and higher castes.

Detailed ethnography about these activities remains thin. S. Anandhi, however, studied Dalits in Chennai slums and saw how high-caste RSS and Hindu Munnani activists spread their message effectively among Dalit men and women, partly by teaching them devotionalist hymns or introducing new festivals; many young men in particular were persuaded to participate in the Vinayaka Chaturthi festival from the late 1980s. Overall, she concludes, the militant organizations had considerable success in forging a collective "Hindu" identity among the Dalits (Anandhi 1995: 36–43). Christophe Jaffrelot (2002) reports on the RSS Sewa Bharti ("Service of India") and its educational and other activities among Dalits in Agra in the late 1990s, which included the promotion of major Hindu festivals mainly celebrated by the high castes. Especially striking is the Sewa Bharti's *kanya puja*, in which the organization's high-caste male officials revere young Dalit girls and wash their feet. All these activities, says Jaffrelot, are aimed at holding the Dalits within a "logic of Sanskritization" (ibid.: 335) and restricting the influence of the Bahujan Samaj Party (BSP), which commands widespread Dalit support in Uttar Pradesh. In practice, however, the Sewa Bharti is much more successful among the Valmikis (Bhangis), the impoverished sweeper caste, than among the Jatavs (Chamars), the more numerous and better-off leatherworkers, who mostly support the BSP and its egalitarian ideology.

Another account comes from Peggy Froerer, who did fieldwork in a remote village inhabited by both Hindus and Christians in Chhattisgarh. One day in 1998, four young men from the RSS turned up in the village to teach the local Hindus how to conduct Shiva's annual festival of Shivaratri properly. The villagers had never heard of this festival before, and one old woman lamented that "We didn't know about this city people's holiday. We have never celebrated it here in this village." She classified the visitors as "city folk," who had come to criticize the villagers' crude, "jungly" (*jangli*) Hinduism. Although most adults had already gone to their fields, the four men managed to drag a few women and children up a hill to a little Shiva shrine, where the RSS leader spoke about the festival and led a ritual to celebrate it (Froerer 2002: 30–35).

The reform of Shivaratri is a textbook example of Sanskritization and although this sudden initiative to reform backward Hinduism, as the local people interpreted it, may sound trivial, it was actually the first decisive step in RSS campaigning in the village. Within a year or two, the RSS had persuaded the Hindus that they should stand up for themselves against the large Christian minority and the Catholic priests who supported their flock. Longstanding land disputes and perennial complaints about Hindus wasting money on alcohol brewed by Christians soon started to be interpreted as instances of Hindu versus Christian ethnic conflict. These changes did not mean that all existing beliefs and practices were abandoned, that all Hindus united against all Christians, let alone that all Hindu drinkers stopped visiting Christian brewers. Yet the RSS initiative was primarily intended to turn "backward" villagers worshiping jungly deities into members of a united Hindu community and nation; divisions among them did not then vanish, but these Chhattisgarhi tribal Hindus became more self-consciously Hindu and in this important respect the RSS largely achieved its aims.

The RSS can also modify its tactics when Sanskritizing initiatives fall on stony ground. In another fairly remote village in southern Rajasthan inhabited by members of the Banjara community (an "ex-criminal" tribe), where Mandira Kalra was doing fieldwork, RSS activists first arrived in late 2001 to spread their message with fiery speeches and quotations from the *Ramayana*, but they made no impression on the local people and soon went away again. A few months later, after the killings of Muslims in Gujarat in early 2002, a second set of RSS activists arrived in the village. These young men, who dressed more like Banjaras than city-dwellers, delivered no Hindi speeches and had learned some Banjara dialect. They spent a lot of time conversing with the villagers, they talked about local Banjara deities instead of Rama, and they discussed local problems while emphasizing their strong support for the Banjara community. Unlike the first set of RSS activists, the second set quietly gained the villagers' trust and began to persuade them that in the glorious new world to be made by Hindu nationalism, Banjaras, as fellow Hindus, would find their rightful place. The eventual outcome is unpredictable, but at least some Banjaras became very impressed by their new, sympathetic RSS friends (Kalra n.d.).

SYNCRETIC DEITIES AND MUSLIM SAINTS

Another major objective of the Hindu nationalist movement is the "purification" of Hinduism by eradicating Muslim (and sometimes Christian) elements. The development of separate Hindu and Muslim communal identities and distinct religions is of course a long-term, historical process that has been proceeding unevenly since the colonial period or even earlier. Yet it has gathered pace since the 1980s and in latter-day "Hindu history," as we have seen, the Ayodhya dispute continues an ancient struggle between Hindus and Muslims, as if they always were and are two distinct religious groups.

In popular belief and practice, however, Hinduism and Islam (and other non-Hindu religions) are often intertwined. Muslim figures are common in popular Hinduism, so that, for example, in the goddess Draupadi's Tamil temples, one of her subordinate guardian deities is the Muslim Muttal Ravuttan (p. 92), whose stone icon sometimes turns into his own saint's tomb (Hiltebeitel 1989: 341). Hindu polytheism is particularly eclectic and there are also many mixed deities like Guga, who may be identified as both a Hindu hero and a Muslim saint (pp. 49–50). Moreover, Hindus throughout India often worship at Muslim saints' tombs and Muslims often worship in Hindu temples. As more research in this area is published—for example, Hiltebeitel's work (1999) on Draupadi among Rajputs, Muslims, and Dalits—the historical interpenetration of Hinduism and Islam in India becomes increasingly apparent. But to Hindu nationalists, as well as to Islamists whose numbers are growing in India as elsewhere, all religious mixture is abhorrent, because people should practice only their own religion. Or at least their own co-religionists should do so; even militant Hindus normally do not mind if Muslims worship in their holy places, and vice versa, because attendance by people from the other group can be interpreted as evidence of their own religion's tolerant superiority.

Dominique-Sila Khan (1997a; 1997b) describes a syncretic deity, Ramdev Pir, who is now becoming more Hinduized. Ramdev, who resembles Guga, is worshiped throughout Rajasthan; his principal temple is in Runicha (Ramdeora) between Jodhpur and Jaisalmer. Ramdev attracts devotees of all Hindu groups, as well as Muslims, Jains, and Sikhs, and he is also the god of a devotional order (sect) with Ismaili Islamic origins that is associated with the Meghval and other Dalit castes. For his Hindu devotees, Ramdev is a form of Krishna, but many features of his cult are unmistakably Islamic; for example, the Runicha temple looks like a Muslim cemetery and Ramdev's *samadhi*, his funerary monument, is not a Hindu structure but a typical Muslim tomb (1997b: 122). Ramdev can be described as a syncretic deity, although syncretism in India emerges out of acculturation (ibid.: 136) through which, as Assayag (1995: 10–13) argues, Hindus and Muslims absorb elements from each other's religions, but normally remain aware of their religious difference. This awareness need not amount to communal opposition, but even when Hindus and Muslims worship the same deities or participate in the same rituals, they usually have alternative methods or understandings. A clear and simple illustration in Ramdev's cult is the preserved footprint in one of his temples, which—say Hindus and Muslims respectively—was made by either Vishnu bestriding the world or the Prophet Muhammad (Khan 1997b: 130).

Even today, most devotees who flock to the Runicha temple do not query its religious identity, because they just want to make vows and offer thanks to their god. The priests of the Ramdev order are questioning its mixed character, however, and "the general tendency . . . is towards a progressive elimination of Islamic elements in the myths, rituals and terminology" (ibid.: 133). At Runicha, the temple's appearance is also changing and recently a warrior's face-mask has been hung on the tomb so that it looks more like a Hindu icon, for worshiping a Muslim tomb could embarrass some Hindu devotees, especially educated Brahmans, Rajputs, and merchants (ibid.: 136). In one of Ramdev's newest temples, the main image simply portrays him as Krishna, which may represent the future (ibid.: 137), and even though the Hinduizing process (and a converse Islamicizing separation from the cult) has been going on for many decades, current changes plainly flow with the Hindu nationalist tide.

As already mentioned, Hindus as well as Muslims worship at saints' tombs, and a good example comes from Assayag's detailed examination (1993; 1995; 2004) of mixed religion in northern Karnataka. At Yellamma's temple in Saundatti, the goddess's shrine is at the center of the site and outside it are her consort Jamadagni's shrine and the Muslim saint Bar-Shah's tomb. To most Hindus, the saint is a subsidiary figure in a tomb at the temple's exterior, but Muslims say that the goddess is Bar-Shah's servant, exploiting a standard Hindu motif about paired superior and inferior deities to make their point. Both Hindus and Muslims visit the tomb to gain access to the saint's power (Islamic *baraka*), although they worship in slightly different ways. Similarly, at several Hindu and Muslim festivals, numerous goats and cocks are sacrificed by both low-caste Hindus and Muslims, but Hindus behead them and Muslims cut their throats (Assayag 1993: 232–36). Yellamma's temple is controlled by members of the dominant Banajiga-Lingayat caste, who have managed to exclude Brahmans and untouchable Madigas from temple offices; in the 1970s, they eventually succeeded in expelling Muslims who had held hereditary positions in the temple (ibid.: 238–39). Action of this sort has been common in the region, and in 2002 the VHP started a clamorous campaign to "purify" and claim exclusive Hindu control of the famous Budangiri shrine in southern Karnataka, a joint Sufi Muslim and Hindu place of worship. In Saundatti, though, we see a contrast between worship by both Muslims and mainly low-caste Hindus at Bar-Shah's tomb, and increasingly monopolistic Banajiga-Lingayat high-caste control over Yellamma's temple. The temple's "purification" does not prevent mixed devotion at the tomb, but it testifies to the progressive creation of "facts on the ground" that supposedly prove that Hindus and Muslims are and should be separate.

Another campaign focused on a saint's tomb took place in Thane, north of Mumbai. For centuries, the tomb of Haji Malang on top of Malangadh Hill has attracted large numbers of pilgrims, both Hindu and Muslim. The saint's annual festival has long been managed by a Brahman family and many rituals at the festival are plainly Hindu in form. In 1988, Shiv Sena activists—inspired by the Ayodhya campaign—claimed that Haji Malang was actually a Muslim conqueror who had destroyed an ancient Hindu shrine and built a tomb on top of it. The Sena called for the "liberation of Malangadh" and for several years, during the festival, it led processions of Hindus to reclaim the site, which were accompanied by often violent demonstrations. Very many Hindus still worship at the tomb, but the Shiv Sena has succeeded in representing the site as definitively Muslim and has affected popular perceptions of what used to be a very typical Maharashtrian example of mixed devotion (Hansen 2001: 107–9).

Similar events, to give one last example, have occurred at Tirupparankundram, near Madurai, where Subrahmanya's great temple is built below a rocky hill. During the annual Karttigai festival in November–December, a big lamp is lit on top of the hill, which has two peaks. On one peak stands the Muslim tomb of Sikandar, which has always attracted Hindu and Muslim worshipers. In the Madurai region, Sikandar has been popularly conflated with both Skanda (Subrahmanya) and Iskandar, Alexander the Great, who may be seen as a Muslim precursor king (Bayly 1989: 108–9, 191–92, 210). In 1994, the Hindu Munnani demanded that the Karttigai lamp be lit next to the tomb, whose existence had supposedly displaced the lamp from its proper place, instead of on the other peak beside a small Ganesha temple. In the end, the Munnani was forced to back down, although it fruitlessly reiterated its demand year after year. The Tirupparankundram agitation has never excited large numbers of Hindus, although many fewer people, fearing trouble, now attend the festival compared with the past. Nevertheless, in Tirupparankundram as in Thane, the Hindu nationalists have interfered in a popular festival to project their message that Hindus are completely different from Muslims and that Hindu "rights" over Muslim holy sites must be reclaimed.

The evidence about Ramdev Pir and the Muslim saints in Saundatti, Thane, and Tirupparankundram demonstrates that many Hindu devotees continue to worship them, whatever nationalists say. In this respect, these four are not unusual and all kinds of popular religious beliefs and practices that combine Hindu and non-Hindu elements still flourish throughout India. Nevertheless, the evidence also shows a clear trend toward increasing Hinduization and the separation of mixed religious elements. Among more and more people, even if they continue in old ways, the nationalists' assertion that Hinduism is radically distinct from Islam (and Christianity) and Hindus are radically different from non-Hindus is making real headway.

CONCLUSION

The Hindu nationalist movement's primary objective is to unite all Hindus into a single "community" that can be the foundation of a strong, Hindu Indian nation. Disunity among Hindus, especially caste divisions, must therefore be overcome and marginal groups must be integrated into the body of Hindu society; at one and the same time, the distinction between Hindus and non-Hindus, particularly Muslims, has to be reinforced. Polytheism and hierarchical differentiation within Hinduism are plainly problematic for the nationalists. Multiple gods and goddesses, popular with different sets of people in different parts of the country, do not easily translate into symbols of unity, and the problem is exacerbated by the existence of diverse beliefs and practices, evaluated as superior or inferior, which define and constitute hierarchical relationships among Hindus belonging to different social categories and groups.

Hindu nationalist intellectuals, leaders, and activists are conscious of these difficulties and have sought to overcome them. Gods and goddesses who are revered by large numbers of people and whose characteristics best lend themselves to nationalist ideology have become the movement's chosen deities. Ganesha, Rama, the "epic" Krishna, Durga, and some other goddesses—these deities in particular have been transformed into "celestial nationalists" who can be inspirational, unifying symbols of Hindutva in major regions of India. Rama, the perfect Hindu king, is preeminent among them, but his potency as a nationalist symbol is restricted by his relative lack of popularity outside Hindi-speaking north India. Some great deities—notably Shiva the ascetic renouncer—have attributes that make them less suitable for nationalist purposes; the little deities whose tutelary functions are almost always confined to local social units cannot symbolize pan-Hindu unity at all. Partly for that reason, worshipers of little deities—especially low-caste and tribal people—are often encouraged to become devotees of the great deities of an ideally pan-Indian Hinduism.

In promoting Hindu unity, public rituals, festivals, and processions play a key role, because they encourage people to join together in collective worship and they also manifest Hindu strength and ubiquity through physical control over the streets and other public arenas. In developing a more politicized, public form of religious expression, Hinduism—as Daniel Gold (1991) observes—had to become more "organized" under Sangh Parivar leadership than pluralistic "traditional" religion ever was. Converting private devotion into demonstrative public worship has been a consistent strategy of the Hindu nationalists, whose broader aim is to transform the polity and civil society, and the public sphere as a whole, so that they become infused with Hindu religious signs and symbols. In fact, no solid "wall" between religion and the state was ever built in independent India, but since the mid-1980s the divide between them has been very visibly crumbling. And, as Thomas Blom Hansen rightly insists, the "saffron wave" of Hindu nationalism "has emerged and taken shape neither in the political system as such nor in the religious field," but in the broader "public space in which a society and its constituent individuals and communities imagine, represent, and recognize themselves" in various discursive and institutional ways (1999: 4).

Although the public space or sphere has become increasingly Hinduized, it should be noted that politicized religion is not the sole cause, for other significant religious developments are under way. In many regions of India, there is evidence of a broader wave of Hindu revivalism and in Tamilnadu, for example, as I discuss elsewhere (Fuller 2003: chap. 5), this revivalism has been particularly visible in Brahmanical temple Hinduism since the early 1990s, most spectacularly and expensively in the temple renovation rituals that have become increasingly frequent. Another important development all over India is the exponential growth in the number and popularity of modern gurus, especially among the educated, affluent middle class, as well as the overseas "Non-Resident Indian" population. Among these gurus, who abound in "contemporary India's dense religious supermarket with its global networks and transnational connections" (Warrier 2003: 248), is Mata Amritanandamayi of Kerala, whose popularity—together with the wealth and endeavor of her ashram—has expanded spectacularly since the 1980s. Partly on the basis of evidence about another guru popular with leading businessmen in Chennai (Fuller and Harriss n.d.; Harriss 2003), I concur with Maya Warrier's conclusion (2003: 247–49) that the Mata's appeal nowadays has less to do with middle-class devotees' sense of anomic rootlessness (as argued above, pp. 179–81) than with the freedom of choice she offers them as individuals. Flourishing gurus, like some other latter-day changes, owe at least as much to economic liberalization as they do to politics and religious nationalism, but in

this chapter, limitations of space and available ethnography have prevented a fuller discussion.

Taken as a whole, the evidence presented in this Afterword suggests
that the religion increasingly filling the public sphere has been modified
by politics in two partly opposed directions, for the impact of Hindu
nationalism on popular religion is both less and more than it might at first
appear. Less, because the Sangh Parivar cannot determine what all Hindus do and Hindutva ideology is not hegemonic; in particular, people's
understandings and actions are always intimately connected to their own
local position and interests, which may be opposed to those of Hindu
nationalists, so that Hindutva ideology is changed into an array of diverse
and contested meanings. More, because religious beliefs and practices
have often been affected, to a greater or lesser extent, by nationalist discourse and agitation, even for people who certainly do not support the
nationalist movement; examples include the "non-political" participants
in Ganesha's festival in Maharashtra and Tamilnadu, the protagonists in
Kota's Ram Lila who pursued their own political aims apart from the
BJP's, the Yadavs in Mathura whose Krishna defends their caste interests
against the BJP, or the ordinary Hindu women who see their own public
acts of worship as signs of faith, not politics. Hindu nationalism is not an
all-powerful force transforming all popular religion into its own image,
so that people still "imagine, represent, and recognize themselves" very
variably, but its impact is considerable even in domains of belief and
practice that appear untouched by or resistant to it.

Peter Gottschalk investigated "multiple identities" among Hindus and
Muslims in a Bihar village and concluded that many villagers "recognize
a definite increase in communal polarization, especially . . . as demonstrated in religious performance," so that they see rituals as "more of an
expression of religious identity *alone* and less of local affiliation *among
others*" (2000: 33). More generally, the villagers, like many other Indians, "increasingly see one another as singular in identity, particularly religious identity," although, conversely, Hindus and Muslims do still interact and are "sharing identities beyond their religious ones" (ibid.: 34).
My own observations and those reported to me by others suggest that
Gottschalk's Bihari villagers are typical of very many Indians today.

In the final analysis, therefore, probably the most significant single
change since 1992 in particular is that for more and more people in contemporary India—Hindu or non-Hindu—"Hindu" has become a more
singular, marked identity than it was, and this applies irrespective of anyone's stance toward religious nationalism. Practicing Hinduism, especially worship of a deity who has become a nationalist symbol, has
therefore become a more marked activity as well, more constitutive of a

distinctive religious affiliation and identity than it used to be. Rama can still dwell in people's hearts, as the Hindu quoted on p. 261 said he should, and he can still be worshiped with devotion, but the act of worshiping him, especially if done in public, has unavoidably become a more pronounced expression of fixed religious identity than it ever was before the campaign to "liberate" his birthplace gathered pace.

APPENDIX

THE HINDU CALENDAR

In modern India, for secular purposes, the western Gregorian calendar or the reformed Indian National Calendar, which is exactly aligned with the former, is generally used. But for religious purposes, Hindus use various traditional calendrical systems, which I outline in this appendix.

All Hindu calendrical systems are based on a geocentric universe in which the earth is orbited by the "nine planets" (*navagraha*): the sun (Surya), the moon (Chandra), Mars (Mangala), Mercury (Budha), Jupiter (Brihaspati), Venus (Shukra), Saturn (Shani), and two mythical planets, Rahu and Ketu. There are seven weekdays named after the first seven planets (Sunday to Saturday); each day starts at sunrise, rather than midnight.

In most of India and in Nepal, a lunar calendar is used. The year is divided into synodical lunar months, ending on full-moon or new-moon day, and each month is divided into thirty lunar days (*tithi*). The mean length of a lunar day is slightly less than twenty-four hours. The period of fifteen lunar days ending on full-moon (*purnima*), while the moon waxes, is known as the "bright fortnight" (*shuklapaksha*), and that ending on new-moon (*amavasya*), while the moon wanes, is the "dark fortnight" (*krishnapaksha*). Except for *purnima* and *amavasya*, the names of the lunar days are forms of the Sanskrit words for "first," "second," and so on, up to "fourteenth." In most of India, lunar months end on full-moon day (*purnimanta* system), but in much of the west and south, as well as Nepal, they end on new-moon day (*amanta* system). The bright fortnights of each month always coincide, but the dark fortnights do not, because the dark fortnight of a month precedes the bright one in the *purnimanta* system and follows it in the *amanta* system. Because a year of twelve lunar months falls short of a solar year by around ten days, an intercalary month, which "repeats" a month, is normally inserted into the lunar year every three years to realign it regularly with the solar year. As a result, Hindu lunar months more or less coincide with the same solar months every year.

Table 4 lists the lunar months, with their approximate western equivalents. In the table, Sanskrit names are given; these are slightly modified in standard Hindi and more so in other vernacular languages. Where a lunar calendar is used, New Year usually begins on the first day of *chaitra* bright fortnight, but there are some regional variations.

Apart from a few events observed on particular weekdays within lunar months, almost all important pan-Indian festivals occur on particular

TABLE 4
Lunar Months

---

chaitra (March–April)
vaishakha (April–May)
jyaishtha (May–June)
ashadha (June–July)
shravana (July–August)
bhadrapada (August–September)
ashwina (September–October)
karttika (October–November)
margashirsha (November–December)
pausha (December–January)
magha (January–February)
phalguna (February–March)

---

lunar days within particular lunar months; except in the far south, this is also true of the majority of regional festivals. Because lunar days vary in length, one lunar day can be current on two consecutive weekdays, or two lunar days can be current during one weekday. Hence a festival lasting a specified number of lunar days can continue for more or fewer weekdays. For example, Navaratri, which is held on the first nine lunar days of *ashwina* bright fortnight, lasted for eight weekdays in 1987 (24 September–1 October), nine in 1988 (11–19 September), and ten in 1989 (30 September–9 October). Unlike a festival occurring in a bright fortnight, one celebrated during a dark fortnight—although held on the same day everywhere—is dated by different months in the two systems of reckoning. Throughout this book, the date of any festival falling in a dark fortnight is given according to the *purnimanta* system. Thus, for example, I say (in chap. 6) that Holi falls on the first day of the dark fortnight of *chaitra*, but in the *amanta* system it falls on the same lunar day of *phalguna*.

Although lunar calendars generally prevail, solar calendars are traditionally used as well in eastern India (West Bengal, Orissa, and Assam) and most systematically in the far south (Tamilnadu and Kerala). Indeed, in Tamilnadu and Kerala, although pan-Indian festivals are fixed as elsewhere by the lunar calendar, a large proportion of regional and temple festival dates are determined by the solar calendar. The year is divided into twelve solar months, each normally lasting thirty or thirty-one days. As in western astronomy, the ecliptical zone—the heavenly belt through which the sun apparently orbits the earth—is divided into twelve equal segments. These are the zodiacal houses (*rashi*), which are identified by the same set of constellations recognized in the west. Table 5 lists the Sanskrit names of the zodiacal houses and their equivalent solar months,

TABLE 5
Zodiacal Houses and Solar Months

House	Month
mesha (Aries)	*chittirai* (April–May)
vrishabha (Taurus)	*vaigasi* (May–June)
mithuna (Gemini)	*ani* (June–July)
karka (Cancer)	*adi* (July–August)
simha (Leo)	*avani* (August–September)
kanya (Virgo)	*purattasi* (September–October)
tula (Libra)	*aippasi* (October–November)
vrishchika (Scorpio)	*karttigai* (November–December)
dhanus (Sagittarius)	*margali* (December–January)
makara (Capricorn)	*tai* (January–February)
kumbha (Aquarius)	*masi* (February–March)
mina (Pisces)	*panguni* (March–April)

whose Tamil names are supplied because they are repeatedly referred to in chapter 8.

A Hindu solar month is defined as the period during which the sun remains in a particular zodiacal house. (The sun moves into a house in the Hindu system approximately three weeks after it moves into the equivalent house in the western astronomical system.) The Hindu solstices and equinoxes coincide with the sun's transition from the preceding houses into *karka* (summer), *makara* (winter), *mesha* (spring), and *tula* (autumn). The six months between the winter and summer solstices, when the sun appears to move north, are the *uttarayana* ("northern path"), and the other six months, when the sun appears to move south, are the *dakshinayana* ("southern path"). In Tamilnadu, New Year begins on 1st *chittirai* and in Kerala on 1st *chinnam* (= *avani*).

Typically, a festival's date by south Indian solar reckoning is given by a particular *nakshatra* within a particular solar month. The path of the moon's orbit around the earth (one sidereal lunar month) is divided into twenty-seven equal segments, identified by constellations, whose names are given to the *nakshatra*s, a term variously translated as "star," "lunar asterism," or "lunar house." As a unit of time, a *nakshatra* is the period (lasting approximately twenty-four hours) during which the moon remains in one segment. Thus, for example, the Tiruvadirai festival (see chap. 8) falls on *ardra nakshatra* in *margali*.

To ascertain the dates of festivals, the overwhelming majority of ordinary Hindus rely on calendars and almanacs, or on the advice of astrologers or other literate people able to read them. Modern calendars always supply dates according to both Indian and western systems, so that it is never difficult to determine the correct date for a festival.

Traditionally, numerous eras were and are used to record the year in different regions of India and Nepal. One of them, the Shaka era (beginning A.D. 78), is the basis of the Indian National Calendar, although the Christian era is more widely used for secular purposes. As mentioned several times in this book, we are also now living in the degenerate era known as the *kaliyuga*. There are four *yugas*—*satya*, *treta*, *dwapara*, and *kali*—and the *kaliyuga*, the shortest, lasts 432,000 years; in modern India, it is conventionally said to have begun on 18 February 3102 B.C. (Kane 1968–77, 3:869), so that things will continue to worsen for a long time before cosmic dissolution occurs.

For Hindus—as chapters 5, 6, 8, and 10 in particular have shown—the calendrical system does not merely define a set of technical divisions of duration, because time and its units are themselves ritually significant. Thus, for example, auspiciousness and inauspiciousness are partly determined temporally, so that "light" periods are generally auspicious and "dark" periods inauspicious. Moreover, all units of time can be treated as divine and worshiped, and many are linked with specific deities as well. For example, in most of India Monday and Friday are regarded as days sacred to Shiva and the goddess respectively; Saturday is always inauspicious, because it is governed by malevolent Shani (Saturn). Similarly, the eleventh lunar day (*ekadashi*) is universally recognized as sacred to Vishnu, whereas the eighth (*ashtami*) and, in dark fortnights, the fourteenth (*chaturdashi*) are respectively days for the goddess and Shiva. Numerous other links between deities and units of time, of greater or lesser importance in different regions of India, could also be listed, and classical astronomical texts provide elaborate, although divergent, explanations for these links, and hence for the whole annual cycle. In some places, such as the discussion in chapter 5 of the timing of Navaratri, I have indirectly drawn on analyses derived from either classical or popular ideas about the ritual significance of time, but nowhere have I attempted to deal with the latter topic in depth.

The literature on Hindu calendrical systems and the ritualization of time is uneven in quality, and some sources are technically inaccurate, interpretatively unconvincing, or both. The classical systems are accurately described by Basham (1971: 494–97) very briefly, by Renou and Filliozat (1953: 720–38) in more detail, and by Kane (1968–77, 5:chaps. 14–19) at great length. On the contemporary Tamil religious calendar (with brief comparative remarks), see Fuller (1980b); for a specific illustration from north India, see Freed and Freed (1964a). Merrey (1982) is excellent on the calendar and the symbolism of time, which Pugh (1983b) and Wadley (1983) also discuss; Brown (1970: chap. 3) explores the significance of eras and cycles of time. Madan (1987a: chap. 2) examines time and auspiciousness.

GLOSSARY

All names and terms are transliterated from Sanskrit, Hindi (H), or Tamil (T).

abhisheka — bathing ritual performed during *puja*; anointment

acharya — guru; spiritual leader of devotionalist order

Agama — text (or collection of texts) expounding Shaiva doctrine and governing worship of Shiva; sometimes also refers to equivalent texts for Vishnu (Samhita) and the Goddess (Tantra)

Aiyanar (T) — village god in Tamilnadu, commonly paired with and superior to Karuppan

Aiyappan (T) — son of Shiva and Vishnu (Mohini); popular god in Tamilnadu and Kerala with major pilgrimage temple at Sabarimalai

alankara — decoration ritual performed during *puja*

amman (T) — goddess, particularly village or clan goddess, in south India

arati — display of camphor flame (or lamps) before deity's image; by extension, *puja*

asura — demon

avatara — "avatar"; incarnation of Vishnu

bali — sacrifice, especially animal sacrifice

Bhagavad Gita — "Song of the Lord"; celebrated section of *Mahabharata*, Book 6

bhagavan — god, lord; common honorific term of address for god or guru

Bhairava — fierce form of Shiva and often prominent village or clan god

bhajana — devotionalist hymn; collective singing of hymns

bhakti — devotion; attitude of loving devotion to deity; refers to stream of Hinduism emphasizing such devotion

bhu — earth, soil (personified by Bhudevi and Bhumiya)

Bhudevi — goddess of earth, soil; Vishnu's second wife

Bhumiya — god of earth, soil; tutelary village god in north India

bhuta-preta — spirit-ghost; collective term for malevolent spirits and ghosts of the dead

brahm (H) — malevolent ghost of dead Brahman

Brahma — one of the three great gods, but less important in popular Hinduism than Vishnu or Shiva

Chandi — form of Durga or Kali

Chellattamman (T) — village goddess in Tamilnadu, usually guarding north of settlement

churail (H) — malevolent ghost of childless woman

darbar (H) — court assembly of king; anglicized as "durbar"

darshana — sight, vision of deity or image

deva — god; generally refers to Vishnu, Shiva, or other great gods

devata — god or deity; generally refers to village, clan, or other little deities

devi — goddess; refers to all goddesses or specifically to the Great Goddess (Mahadevi)

dharma — religious duty, law, and custom, classically set out in *dharmashastra* texts; by extension, sociocosmic moral order in its entirety

diparadhana — display of lamps, lamp service during *puja*

dishti (T) — evil eye

dosha — taint, fault, defect; malevolent force emanating from and causing such defects

Draupadi — heroine of *Mahabharata* and popular village goddess in parts of south India

Durga — fierce goddess and slayer of Mahishasura

gaddi (H) — seat or throne of king

Ganesha — elephant-headed god, Shiva's first son and god of beginnings and obstacles; especially popular in Maharashtra

Ganga — river Ganges; the Ganges (and all rivers) personified as a goddess

gopi — cowherdess and lover of Krishna

goswami — devotee of Krishna; spiritual leader of Krishnaite devotionalist order

grahadosha — "fault of planets"; inauspicious force exerted by planets and defect in human beings produced by it

gramadevata — village deity

Hanuman — "monkey-god," Rama's faithful servant and god of immense strength

homa — act of making oblations into sacrificial fire

Indra — king of the gods

ishtadeva(ta) — favorite deity "chosen" by individual worshiper

Jagannatha — form of Krishna in his famous temple in Puri

jnana — "knowing"; contemplative religious knowledge

jutha (H) — left-over food polluted by saliva and touch of eater

Kali — fierce goddess especially revered in Tantrism

kaliyuga — fourth and last degenerate era in which we now live

karma — action and its meritorious or unmeritorious consequence in the future, either in this or subsequent lives

Karuppan (T) — important village god in Tamilnadu; commonly a subordinate "guardian deity"

Kherapati (H) — tutelary village god in north India

Krishna — incarnation of Vishnu; one of the most popular gods in Hinduism, especially in devotionalist religion *kuladeva(ta)* — clan or family deity

kunkuma — red powder emblematic of goddesses

Lakshmi — goddess of good fortune; Vishnu's principal wife

lila — divine "play"

linga — aniconic phallic emblem of Shiva, normally resting on base representing *yoni*, female sexual organ

Mahabharata — longer of the two great Hindu epics

Mahishasura — buffalo-demon slain by Durga

mangala — "auspicious" (cf. *sumangali*)

mantra — sacred formula or chant; magical spell

mantravadin — magician, especially one relying on *mantra*s

Manusmriti — "The Laws of Manu," the most famous *dharmashastra* text

Mariyamman (T) — tutelary village goddess and goddess of smallpox in south India

mata (H) — goddess, particularly village or clan goddess, in north India

Minakshi — form of goddess in her temple in Madurai and wife of Sundareshwara

moksha — liberation or salvation from cycle of rebirth

murti — image of deity; form of deity (especially Shiva)

naivedya — food offering made during *puja*

najar (H) — evil eye

namaskara — gesture to greet and show respect to deities or other people

Narasimha — "man-lion" incarnation of Vishnu; fierce form of Vishnu and prominent village god in parts of India

Nataraja — form of Shiva as "Lord of the dance"

ojha (H) — exorcist

Parvati — Shiva's principal wife

pativrata — faithful wife devoted to her husband

pey (T) — anonymous malevolent spirit and ghost of the dead in Tamilnadu

pradakshina — auspicious, clockwise circumambulation

prasada — "grace"; sanctified food or other substances distributed to worshipers at end of *puja*

puja — worship, normally comprising series of offerings and services (*upachara*)

Purana — myth (or collection of myths) about deities

purusha — "male"; the primeval Man sacrificed to create the world

Radha — Krishna's principal lover among the *gopi*s

raja — king (*maharaja*, great king)

Rama — incarnation of Vishnu; model king and husband, and one of the most popular gods in Hinduism, especially in devotionalist religion

Ramayana — shorter of the two great Hindu epics, which recounts story of Rama

Ravana — demon king of Lanka, vanquished by Rama

sampradaya — "tradition"; by extension, religious order (or sect) following its own tradition

samsara — ceaseless cycle of rebirth and redeath

sanatana dharma — "eternal religion"; Hinduism in the language of modern reformism

sannyasin — ascetic renouncer

Saraswati — goddess of learning; Brahma's wife

sati — faithful wife who burns herself on husband's funeral pyre; anglicized as "suttee" to refer to ritual of wife's immolation

seva — "service"; especially devotee's selfless service to deity

Shaiva — of or pertaining to Shiva; worshiper of Shiva

shakti — divine power, personified as feminine; also refers to the Goddess as personification of power, especially as Shiva's consort

Shankaracharya — spiritual successor to the great philosopher Shankara and ascetic head of a monastery founded by him

shishya — disciple or pupil of guru

Shitala (H) — tutelary village goddess and goddess of smallpox in north India

Shiva — alongside Vishnu, one of the two most important great gods of Hinduism

shubha — "good," "auspicious" (opposite is *ashubha*)

sindura — vermilion streak of red lead worn in parting of hair by married women

Sita — Rama's wife

Skanda — Shiva's second son; especially popular in Tamilnadu as Murugan

sumangali — auspicious woman, who is married to living husband

Sundareshwara — form of Shiva in his wife Minakshi's temple in Madurai

swami — god, lord; common honorific term of address for god or guru

tapas — power, heat of asceticism

tejas — power, splendor, glory, energy of deities

tilaka — forehead mark; red roundel worn by married women, or "sect-mark" worn by worshipers of particular deity

tirtha — "ford, crossing-place"; pilgrimage center

upachara — offering or service that is constituent element of *puja*

utsava — festival

vaikuntha — heaven of Vishnu

Vaishnava — of or pertaining to Vishnu; worshiper of Vishnu

varna — one of four social "classes" (Brahmans, Kshatriyas, Vaishyas, and Shudras); opposite is *avarna*, referring to fifth "class" of Harijans outside *varna* hierarchy

Veda — "knowledge"; revealed, authoritative sacred knowledge or the four texts containing it: Rig, Yajur, Sama, and Atharva Vedas

Venkateshwara — form of Vishnu in his famous temple in Tirupati

vibhuti — white ash smeared on Shiva's body and used in his worship

vira — deified hero

Virabhadra — angry, fierce form of Shiva

Vishnu — alongside Shiva, one of the two most important great gods of Hinduism

Vishwanatha — "Lord of all"; form of Shiva in his principal temple in Benares

Vithoba — form of Vishnu in his major pilgrimage temple in Pandharpur

yajamana — royal or lordly patron of Vedic sacrifice

yajna — Vedic sacrifice

yatra — journey, pilgrimage

BIBLIOGRAPHICAL GUIDE

A principal purpose of this bibliographical guide, which is arranged thematically, is to list relevant sources that have not been specifically cited in the text. The guide does not pretend to be comprehensive, and most works listed will be familiar to specialists. But for nonspecialists and students, I hope that the first and fuller part will be a useful source of further anthropological readings on popular Hinduism and that the second part will signal some of the mainly textual scholarship that is important for anthropologists. When an article has been reproduced in a later book, I normally cite only the latter, and although much valuable material exists in unpublished theses, only those that I have actually used are cited. Dates of first publication, when relevant, are given in square brackets.

ANTHROPOLOGICAL STUDIES

1. Monographs on Popular Hinduism

Srinivas's monograph on the Coorgs (1965 [1952]) is the pioneering modern study. Dumont's on the Pramalai Kallar (1986 [1957]: pt. 3) contains a long section on religion. Several ethnographies contain valuable material on popular Hinduism, but the principal ones devoted to the subject are Babb (1975) on Chhattisgarh in Madhya Pradesh, Babb (1987) on modern movements in Delhi, Gold (1988a) on a Rajasthan village, Hanchett (1988) on family festivals in two Karnataka villages, Herrenschmidt (1989) on an Andhra Pradesh village, Morinis (1984) on pilgrimage temples in West Bengal, Östör (1980) on a West Bengal town, Pocock (1973) on central Gujarat, Reiniche (1979) on a Tamilnadu village, Tapper (1987) on an Andhra Pradesh village, Tarabout (1986) on festivals in Kerala, van der Veer (1988) on the pilgrimage town of Ayodhya in Uttar Pradesh, and Wadley (1975) on an Uttar Pradesh village. One-line reviews are invidious, but Gold's monograph is specially recommended for its excellent ethnography, sensitive interpretation, and clarity of expression.

2. The Deities of Popular Hinduism

In addition to Mayer (1960) and Reiniche (1979), sources for the principal ethnographic illustrations in chapter 2, all the monographs listed in section 1 contain much information on popular Hindu deities and their rituals. Other ethnographic monographs containing useful data include

Beck (1972: 110–21, 140–45; Tamilnadu), Berreman (1963: chap. 3 and app. 1 [2d ed., 1972, omits appendixes]; Himalayan Uttar Pradesh), Chauhan (1967: chap. 6; Rajasthan), Dube (1955: chap. 4; Andhra Pradesh), Hiebert (1971: chap. 7; Andhra Pradesh), Lewis (1958: chap. 6; Uttar Pradesh), Majumdar (1958: chap. 10; Uttar Pradesh), Moffatt (1979: chap. 6; Tamilnadu), Planalp (1956: chaps. 2 and 8; Uttar Pradesh), Srinivas (1976: chap. 10; Karnataka), and Dirks (1987: chap. 9; an ethnohistory of a Tamil kingdom). Articles that look at the deities and their rituals include Babb (1970), Biardeau (1989c), Blackburn (1985), Bradford (1983), Burkhart (1987), Carstairs (1961), Coccari (1989), Delfendahl (1971), Dumont (1970b: chap. 2), Dumont and Pocock (1959: 40–74), Fuller (1988a), Galey (1986), Harper (1959; 1964), Kolenda (1982), Lapoint (1978), Marriott (1969), Nicholas (1982), Reiniche (1975; 1988), Sharma (1970), and Stanley (1989). Early works that modern anthropologists find useful include O'Malley (1935), still the only general book on popular Hinduism, and Crooke (1926), Elmore (1925), Enthoven (1924), and Whitehead (1921); more recent (although theoretically outdated) is Diehl (1956). Quite different, but worthy of mention, is Hardiman (1987) on a transformed village goddess's cult in Gujarat in the 1920s.

3. Village Festivals

In addition to Srinivas (1965), the analysis of festivals in chapter 6 (cf. chap. 4) is mainly based on Beck (1981), Biardeau (1989b: pt. 2), Brubaker (1979), Dirks (1987: chaps. 9 and 12), Dumont (1986: pt. 3A), Good (1985), Gough (1970), Hanchett (1982), Herrenschmidt (1989: chaps. 4–5), Hiltebeitel (1985), Moffatt (1979: chap. 6), Nishimura (1987: chaps. 2–3), Reiniche (1979: chaps. 3–6), and Tapper (1987: chaps. 5–7) for south India; Dube (1955: chap. 4), Ghurye (1960: chap. 3), Hiebert (1971: 150–55), and Orenstein (1965: 199–204) for central India; Chauhan (1967: chap. 6), Lewis (1958: chap. 6), Majumdar (1958: chap. 10), Marriott (1968a; 1969), Mayer (1960: 99–111), D. B. Miller (1973), Planalp (1956: chap. 3), and Wadley (1975: chap. 8) for north India. Other interesting studies of festivals or related topics include Beals (1964), Berreman (1963: chap. 4 and app. 2), Freed and Freed (1962), Good (1983), Hanchett (1988), Hiltebeitel (1982), McGilvray (1983), Reiniche (1987), and Toffin (1981; 1982).

The long debate about the nature of the Indian village forms part of the background to chapter 6; see in particular Dumont (1970a: chaps. 7–8; 1970b: chap. 6) and Srinivas (1987, especially "The Indian Village: Myth and Reality" [1975]).

4. Temples, Deities, and Rituals

Anthropological research on temples is reviewed by Fuller (1988c) and Galey, introducing an edited collection (1985–86) of articles by anthropologists and textual scholars. Monographs about major urban temples, concentrating on different themes, include Appadurai (1981a) on the Partasarati temple in Madras, Fuller (1984) on the Minakshi temple in Madurai, Marglin (1985) on the Jagannatha temple in Puri, Morinis (1984) on three West Bengal temples, and Reiniche (1989) on the Shiva temple in Tiruvannamalai, Tamilnadu. Eschmann et al. (1978), also about the Jagannatha temple, is a multidisciplinary collection, as is Stein (1978) on south Indian temples.

The material on the Minakshi temple in chapters 3, 4, and 8 comes mainly from my own fieldwork. In chapter 3 in particular, I have modified some of my earlier arguments in Fuller (1979; 1984: chap. 1); parts of chapter 4 are revised versions of Fuller (1988a; 1991: 554). Other studies of other south Indian temples also relevant to chapters 3 and 4 are Appadurai (1981a: chaps. 1–2; 1981b), Appadurai and Breckenridge (1976), Burgess (1883), Fuller (1987), Good (1987a), Pillay (1953), Reiniche (1979: chap. 3), and van den Hoek (1979). Chapter 8 builds on other work about ritual in the Minakshi temple, especially Fuller (1980a; 1985a), Fuller and Logan (1985), Harman (1989), and Hudson (1978; 1982). Logan (1980), as well as work by two Tamil scholars, Shulman (1980) and Yocum (1982; 1986), are also drawn on.

Other useful studies include Béteille (1965b), Fuller (1985b), Good (1989a), Pocock (1981), Shankari (1984), and van der Veer (1988: chap. 4) on temple organization and officiants, and Good (1987b; 1989b), Martin (1982), Moreno (1985), Moreno and Marriott (1989), Nicholas (1981), Östör (1980), Preston (1980), and Stanley (1977) on temple rituals and festivals.

For the history of the Babri Masjid-Ramjanmabhumi dispute in Ayodhya (see chap. 11), I have mainly relied on van der Veer (1987b) and, for events in 1989–91, on reports in the news magazine *India Today* and the British newspaper, the *Guardian*.

5. Worship and Sacrifice

Ethnographic descriptions of worship (*puja*) and sacrifice (*bali*) are contained in many studies listed in sections 1–4. Several anthropologists have written specifically about the analysis of worship. Babb (1983b; 1987: chap. 3) and Logan (1980: chap. 2) emphasize identity between deity and worshiper. In the work relating to "worship and social hierarchy" discussed in chapter 3, Babb (1975: chap. 2) and Harper (1964) focus on exchange between deity and worshiper; so do Appadurai and Brecken-ridge (1976) and Appadurai (1981a: chap. 1; 1981b)—although they refer to "a process of redistribution"—and Dirks (1987: 38–39, 99–103, 130–35, 285–97 and *passim*), who develops their model. Marriott (1976) has been one particularly important influence on the latter authors. Against American "transactionalism," French "structuralism" approaches the analysis of worship from a completely different direction— although neither school pays much serious attention to the other. Coupled with Dumont's theory of caste, Biardeau's analysis of Hindu sacrifice (1976) (see chap. 4) is most fully developed ethnographically in relation to both worship and sacrifice by Reiniche (1979: 299–38 and *passim*), but it has also strongly influenced other French anthropologists, such as Galey (1986), Herrenschmidt (1989), Tarabout (1986), and Toffin (1981; 1982).

Important as background to anthropological analysis of worship and sacrifice is work on purity and pollution, and on food exchange; from a vast literature, most of it part of the wider literature on caste, Dumont (1970a: chap. 2), Harper (1964), Herrenschmidt (1989: chap. 6), Madan (1987a: chap. 2), Marriott (1968b; 1976), and Srinivas (1965: chap. 4) may be cited. Also important is the work on purity and auspiciousness in Carman and Marglin (1985), as well as recent studies of Hindu gift exchange and food symbolism, especially Parry (1982; 1985b; 1986; 1989) and Raheja (1988a).

6. *Kingship and Royal Rituals*

So important is kingship to the temple, worship, and sacrifice that many references in sections 4 and 5 are also relevant, especially for royal ritual. On royal Navaratri and *shami*-tree worship, see Biardeau (1989b: 299–317, 328–30); on the Benares Ram Lila, Schechner (1985: chap. 4) is supplemented by Hess (1983), Kapur (1985), Lutgendorf (1989), and (from the nineteenth century) Prinsep (1834). Detailed anthropological studies of Hindu kingship itself are sparse. Dumont (1970b: chap. 4) has been influential but much criticized; valuable ethnography and analysis are in Burghart (1978a; 1983a; 1987), Galey (1984; 1989), Gold (1989), Mayer (1981a; 1985), and Raheja (1988b); ethnohistorical work includes Breckenridge (1978), Cohn (1983), Dirks (1987), and Rudner (1987). Allen and Dwivedi (1984), a glossy product for the nostalgia market, contains some illuminating testimony from former kings and courtiers. My description of Navaratri in Mewar and Dasara in Mysore has benefited from information collected by Adrian Mayer and kindly supplied to me.

7. Goddesses and Women

Anthropological material on Hindu goddesses is contained in many studies already listed. Collections edited by Biardeau (1981) and Hawley and Wulff (1982) contain some anthropological, as well as textual, articles. Hanchett (1988: chap. 5 and *passim*) is an interesting study of women's festivals in rural Karnataka; L. Bennett (1983), on Nepali high-caste Hindus, is a detailed ethnographic analysis of the relationship between goddesses and women; see also Marglin (1985) on the Jagannatha temple dancers, and Wadley (1975) on female rituals in an Uttar Pradesh village. Other relevant sources include Allen (1976), Babb (1987: chap. 6), Bouillier (1982), Egnor (1980), Fruzzetti (1982), Harper (1969), Hershman (1977), Jacobson (1978), Kolenda (1984), Ojha (1981), Reynolds (1980), Robinson (1985), Tapper (1979), Wadley (1980), and Wulff (1985).

8. Devotionalism and the Guru

On devotionalism, most of the main anthropological sources are cited in chapter 7. Dumont (1970b: chap. 3) has been influential and also much criticized. For the Radha-Krishna associations in Madras, consult Singer (1968; 1972: chap. 6); for the Ramanandi order, Burghart (1978b; 1983a; 1983b) and van der Veer (1987a; 1988: chap. 3; 1989); for the Pushti Marga, P. J. Bennett (1983; 1990), Lynch (1988), and Pocock (1973: chap. 5); for the Swaminarayan order, Pocock (1973: chap. 6) and Williams (1984). Babb (1987) covers three modern movements, the Radhasoamis, Brahma Kumaris, and followers of the "god-man" Sathya Sai Baba, for which see also Swallow (1982). Kakar (1983) contains valuable insights into modern movements and related topics. Other useful sources include Babb (1972) on the Satnamis, Bradford (1985) and Vail (1985) on the Lingayats, Cantlie (1985) on Assamese Vaishnavism, Deleury (1960) and Engblom (1987) on the Varkaris, Holmström (1971) on modern devotionalism in Bangalore, Lorenzen (1987) on the Kabir Panth, Morinis (1984: chap. 5) on Bengali Vaishnavism, Parry (1982) on Aghori ascetic gurus in Benares, and Toomey (1990) on Krishnaite devotionalism in Braj. Also interesting is the address by a Marathi guru in Dandekar (1988), and information on the Kanchipuram Shankaracharya in Mines and Gourishankar (1990).

9. Pilgrimage

On pilgrimage, many of the main anthropological sources are cited in chapter 9: Deleury (1960), Engblom (1987), Karve (1988 [1951]), and

Mokashi (1987 [1964]) on the Pandharpur pilgrimage, Daniel (1984: 245–87) and Kjaerholm (1986) on Aiyappan's pilgrimage, Gold (1988a) on pilgrimage from a Rajasthani village, and Morinis (1984) on West Bengali temple pilgrimage. See also Binford (1976) on a pilgrimage to a Rajasthani center and Guilmoto et al. (1990: chap. 2) on pilgrimage to Tiruvannamalai. On particular pilgrimage centers, many studies on temples listed in section 4 are relevant, but see also Eck (1983) and Parry (1981) on Benares, Hawley (1981) on Brindavan, van der Veer (1988) on Ayodhya, and Vidyarthi (1961) on Gaya.

10. Misfortune

Most ethnographic works listed in sections 1 and 2 contain data on mystical causes and explanations of misfortune in popular Hinduism. Those cited in chapter 10 include Babb (1975), Gold (1988a), Planalp (1956), Pocock (1973), and Srinivas (1976). Other cited sources include Carstairs (1983), Gough (1976), Kakar (1983), Knipe (1989), Moffatt (1979: chap. 6), Parry (1980), Raheja (1988a), and, specifically on *karma*, Babb (1983a), Pugh (1983a), Sharma (1973), and Wadley and Derr (1989). I have also benefited from unpublished work by Parry (n.d.) and other data kindly supplied by him. Further relevant literature includes Caplan (1987: chaps. 7–8), Dumont (1986: pt. 3B), Dumont and Pocock (1959: 55–74), Egnor (1984), Freed and Freed (1964b), Gold (1988b), Harper (1969), Prakash (1986), Stanley (1988), Wadley (1976), and for more on *karma*, articles in Keyes and Daniel (1983).

TEXTUAL STUDIES

11. General Works on Hinduism

Hiltebeitel (1987) and Weightman (1985) are recommended as short introductions by two textual scholars knowledgeable about popular Hinduism. Biardeau (1981; English translation 1989a) presents a powerful, structuralist synthesis—based on texts but informed by a knowledge of popular Hinduism—which has influenced my approach in this book; see Fuller (1991) and Hiltebeitel (1983) for reviews of Biardeau's work. Many modern books survey Hinduism through its texts, mainly from a historical perspective and without much attention to popular religion; four useful works are Basham (1971: chap. 7), Brockington (1981), Renou (1953), and Sen (1961), but numerous others could be listed. Kinsley (1982) pays more attention than most to ritual; Brown (1970) is illuminating, but does not pretend to be comprehensive. Renou and Filliozat's encyclopedic manual (1947; 1953) remains invaluable. Of the many older books, Monier-Williams (1974 [1883]) may be the best and most useful today. Sourcebooks of readings from Hindu texts are numerous, but anthropologists may be more interested in compilations of mythology, such as Dimmitt and van Buitenen (1978) and O'Flaherty (1975).

Radhakrishnan's influential writings (1941; 1971 [1927]; 1975 [1937, with postscript by Basham]) are the quintessence of modern, reformist, intellectualist Hinduism, whose development is covered by most general works. For a brief account of reformism, see Jordens (1975b). Srinivas (1966) discusses the sociological significance of reformism in several places. Derrett (1968) shows that the impact of reformist legal definitions of Hinduism transcends the confines of the law itself; see also Fuller (1988b) and Galanter (1971). Frykenberg (1989) contends that all modern definitions of "Hinduism" are misleadingly dangerous; Madan (1987b; cf. 1987a: epilogue) is skeptical about secularism's future in India; Thapar (1989) discusses modern religious change in long-term historical perspective. The views of the last three scholars (and others) have been significantly influenced by the rise of Hindu fundamentalism.

12. Gods and Goddesses

Most general works on Hinduism provide similar information about Vishnu, Shiva, the goddess, and other deities, but they are often discussed fragmentarily, partly owing to the historical perspective of most textual authors. Biardeau (1981: 77–171; cf. 1976; 1989b) is important for the discussion of Vishnu, Shiva, and the goddess in chapter 2, and so too are O'Flaherty (1973) and Shulman (1980), innovative and influential analyses of the mythology of Shiva (and the goddess). These three scholars, despite differing methodologies, all present their work in a way that connects with the anthropology of popular Hinduism, and they have been particularly influential in closing the gap between anthropological and Indological scholarship in recent years. Hiltebeitel (1988) on the goddess Draupadi is a major work in the same vein; see also Meyer (1986) on the goddess Angalamman.

Other important monographs on the great gods, although less accessible to anthropologists, include Gonda (1970) on Vishnu and Shiva, Hiltebeitel (1976) on Krishna, and Kramrisch (1981b) on Shiva. On Ganesha in Maharashtra, see Courtright (1985), and on Murugan in Tamilnadu, see Clothey (1978). Archer (1957) evokes Krishna the lover, Kinsley (1975; 1987) explores Krishna and Kali and the many forms of the goddess, and Hawley and Wulff (1982) is a collection on Radha and other goddesses. O'Flaherty (1976; 1980a) investigates the deities' relationships with each other and humanity in mythology.

13. Temples, Images, Worship, and Festivals

The standard textual work on the Hindu temple is Kramrisch's vast study (1976 [1946]); Michell (1977) is shorter and more accessible. Aspects of the symbolism of the temple are discussed by Beck (1976), Inden (1985a), and Reiniche (1985). A short, practical introduction to iconography is Mitchell (1982); for Shiva's iconography, see Kramrisch (1981a), which is also an illuminating introduction to the god.

On the meaning of images and their role in ritual (see chap. 3), Eck (1981a) is excellent. The textual model of worship (*puja*) is outlined by Gonda (1970: 75–86 and chap. 4 *passim*), citing a host of sources; Kane (1968–77, 2: chap. 19) covers much the same material. Scholarly work on ritual texts (Agamas, Samhitas, and Tantras) is highly specialized, but their significance is explained by Brunner (1975–76); see also Filliozat (1983). Many descriptions of worship are idealized, because they partly or wholly reproduce textual models; an example is Stevenson's description of temple worship (1920: chaps. 14–15), but her book is still recommended for its valuable material on Gujarati Brahman ritualism. Studies on particular temples that variously combine textual, historical, and some ethnographic material include Eschmann et al. (1978) on the Jagannatha temple, Pillay (1953) on Suchindram temple, and Raman (1975) on a Kanchipuram temple.

Studies of particular festivals combining textual and observational data include Clothey (1969), Hein (1972; 1976), Hiltebeitel (1982; 1988), Long (1982), and Younger (1982a; 1982b); for annual festival cycles, Eck (1983: chap. 6) on Benares and Stevenson (1920: chaps. 10–13) on Kathiawar (Gujarat) are recommended. Classical data on the major festivals are in Kane (1968–77, 5: chaps. 4–13), chapter 13 being a 200-page annotated list.

The most celebrated recension of the Navaratri myth of Durga and Mahishasura is the *Devimahatmya* (from the *Markandeya Purana*), translated by Coburn (1991); for translated extracts, see Dimmitt and van Buitenen (1978: 232–40) and (partly from the *Skanda Purana*) O'Flaherty (1975: 238–49).

14. Sacrifice and Gifts; Brahmans, Renouncers, and Kings

For students of contemporary popular Hinduism, technical exegeses of Vedic sacrifice are largely irrelevant. Far more important is research on sacrificial texts and other material, especially mythology, which examines the relationship between Vedic sacrifice and popular Hindu ritual, the connection among sacrifice, worship, and gift giving, the significance of sacrifice for concepts of the Brahman, ascetic renouncer, and king, and so on. This body of scholarship is germane to much of this book, especially chapters 4, 5, and 6.

Biardeau (1976; 1989b) insists on the centrality of sacrifice and the continuity that persists despite its transformations. This argument reappears in her discussion of the ideal Brahman (1981: 23–76 and *passim*); Malamoud (1976) analyzes *dakshina*, the priest's gift or payment, and Malamoud (1975) is also relevant. Heesterman (1959; 1971; 1985: chaps. 1–7 and *passim*) emphasizes, against Biardeau, a radical disjunctive transformation of the archaic Vedic sacrifice, and he interprets *dakshina* differently from Malamoud, but much in Heesterman's discussion of the Brahman, renouncer, and king complements the French authors'. On those three key figures, see also Burghart (1978a; 1983a; 1990) and Das (1977: chap. 2); on *dakshina* and gifts, see also Shulman (1985b) and Trautmann (1981: 277–93). Throughout this literature, Dumont's theory of caste is directly or indirectly criticized. In mythological analysis, sacrifice is also a central theme, notably in Shulman (1980), but also in the work of Biardeau, Hiltebeitel, O'Flaherty, and others.

The writings of Biardeau, Burghart, Das, and Heesterman (1985: chaps. 8–10 and *passim*; 1986) are also important for the analysis of kingship, and Dumont is again a focus for much critical discussion. Other valuable studies are Derrett (1959; 1975; 1976), Gonda (1969), Inden (1981), Reiniche (1989: chap. 6), articles in Richards (1978), and Shulman (1985a) analyzing south Indian mythology. Relevant historical work on Indian kingship that focuses on the king's ritual role, especially in relation to temples, includes Kulke's chapters in Eschmann et al. (1978) for eastern India, and Appadurai (1981a: chap. 2 and *passim*), Dirks (1987), articles in Stein (1978), and Stein (1980: chaps. 7, 8, and *passim*) for south India.

For many writers listed above, classical religious law—the *dharmashastra*—is inevitably a central concern. The monumental, standard work on the *dharmashastra* is Kane's five volumes (1968–77 [1930–62]); volumes 2 and 3 contain most of the material relevant to the topics of this section. Derrett (1968) and Lingat (1973), both important books, make the *dharmashastra* accessible.

15. Devotionalism, Pilgrimage, and Karma

Most general works on Hinduism cover the theology, scripture, and history of devotionalism more or less thoroughly; see Jordens (1975a) for a brief account. The large literature on particular devotionalist orders and bodies of scripture is mainly relevant to anthropologists specializing in the field. Textual studies that evince any interest in anthropological approaches to devotionalism are not numerous; they include Biardeau

(1981: 98–133, 161–71), Dimock (1989), which is also the best work on Tantrism, Hawley (1981) on Krishna's dramas in Brindavan, which is also relevant to pilgrimage, Ramanujan's introduction to his translation of Lingayat hymns (1973), and articles in Singer (1968). Other works focusing specifically on pilgrimage include Bharati (1963), Bhardwaj (1973), and Eck (1981b); Kane (1968–77, 4: chaps. 11–16) contains classical material on pilgrimage centers, chap. 16 being a 100-page annotated ' list of them.

Every general work on Hinduism discusses *karma* in relation to *dharma*, *samsara*, and *moksha*, although often only the "orthodox," Brahmanical version of the theory is examined. This bias is corrected by O'Flaherty's edited collection (1980). O'Flaherty (1976) explores the concept of evil in mythology and Inden (1985b) considers it in Vaishnava thought. There is also material in Hiltebeitel's edited volume (1989) and Shulman (1985a) that is relevant to popular notions, but to date relatively few textual scholars discussing misfortune escape from the Indologists' preoccupation with *karma*.

ANTHROPOLOGICAL AND TEXTUAL STUDIES PUBLISHED SINCE 1991

16. Popular Hinduism

Anthropological monographs on popular Hinduism include Assayag (1992) on the goddess Yellamma's cult in Karnataka, Berti (2001) on possession rituals in Himachal Pradesh, Caldwell (1999) on the goddess Bhadrakali's cult in Kerala, Nabokov (2000) on ritual and possession in Tamilnadu, and Sax's two monographs on the goddess Nandadevi and pilgrimage in Uttaranchal (formerly Himalayan Uttar Pradesh) (1991), and on the performance of the *Mahabharata* in the same region (2002). Khan (1997a; 1997b) explores the cult of Ramdev Pir in Rajasthan ethnographically and historically. Gellner (1992) and Laidlaw (1995), monographs about Tantric Buddhism in Nepal and Jainism in Jaipur respectively, both examine in detail Hinduism's relationship with two cognate religions.

Nicholas (2003) brings together earlier articles on Bengali Hinduism. Two edited collections on Hindu deities and rituals are Assayag and Tarabout (1999) and Bouillier and Toffin (1993). Ethnographies containing significant material on popular Hinduism include Kapadia (1995: chaps. 4, 6; Tamilnadu village), Osella and Osella (2000: chap. 5; Izhavas in Kerala), Pache Huber (2002: chaps. 3, 5; Maheshwaris in Jaipur), and Wadley (1994, *passim*; Uttar Pradesh village), as well as Charsley and

Karanth (1998: chap. 6 and *passim*; Dalits in Karnataka). Some interesting articles are De Neve (2000), D. P. Mines (2002), and Mosse (1994), as well as Vidal (1998) on Ganesha's milk-drinking "miracle" in 1995.

Two monographs about temple ritual are Claveyrolas (2003) on the Sankat Mochan (Hanuman) temple in Benares, and L'Hernault and Reiniche (1999) on the Shiva temple in Tiruvannamalai, Tamilnadu. Articles on temple rituals include Fuller (1993; 1995; 2004), Good (2000), and Tarabout (1997). Fuller (2003) is about the changing position of the Minakshi temple priests in Madurai. Two studies of Tamil temples that are mainly historical and textual are Ghose (1996) on Tiruvarur and Younger (1995) on Chidambaram. Two ethnohistorical monographs about kings, temples, and other Hindu institutions are Clémentin-Ojha (1999) and Toffin (1993). On Dasara and royal rituals in "tribal" kingdoms, see Schnepel (1995; 2002), as well as Gell (1997) and Sundar (2001).

Hawley and Wulff (1996; a revision of the 1982 edition) includes some new anthropological and textual studies about the goddess. Harlan (1992) is about Rajasthani Rajput women's religion, including *sati*, on which there is interesting controversy in Hawley (1994); see also Hardgrove (1999) on the Marwaris. Harlan (2003) explores "heroes" in Rajasthani religion, especially in relation to gender. Hancock (1999) includes ethnography on women's religion in Chennai.

Monographs on devotionalist and ascetic orders include P. J. Bennett (1993) on the Pushti Marga, Bouillier (1997) on Kanphata Yogis in Nepal, and Juergensmeyer (1991) on the Radhasoamis. On modern gurus, see Fuller and Harriss (n.d.), Harriss (2003), and Warrier (2003). Two interesting and very different edited volumes are Babb and Wadley (1995) on modern media and religion, and Sax (1995) on divine "play" (*lila*). Misfortune is discussed in Parry (1994: chap. 7 and *passim*), which focuses on death in Benares but examines many other features of Hinduism as well. Knipe (1995) discusses inauspicious Saturn.

General works on Hinduism continue to be published; noteworthy are Michaels (1998 [English translation, 2004]), which takes an unusually comprehensive view, and Smith (2003), which concentrates on Hinduism's relationship with modernity. Huyler (1999) is a personal account illustrated by superb photographs. Important books on Hindu deities and ritual, mostly based on textual scholarship, include Davis (1991) on Shaiva ritual, Erndl (1993) on the goddess in northwestern India, Hiltebeitel's further explorations of Draupadi and the *Mahabharata* (1991; 1999; 2001), and McDermott (2001) on the goddess in Bengal. Lutgendorf (1994; 1997; 2002) writes about Hanuman. Vaudeville (1996) collects her essays on Krishna and north Indian devotionalism. Richman

(1991; 2001) has edited two important books about the *Ramayana*; Lutgendorf (1991) explores the *Ramcharitmanas* as performed in north India. Two disparate volumes containing some valuable articles are Dalmia and von Stietencron (1995) and Dalmia, Malinar, and Christof (2001).

17. Hindu Nationalism

The literature on Hindu nationalism, which is now extensive, has expanded rapidly (and sometimes repetitiously) since the early 1990s. Two earlier contributions by anthropologists that still deserve attention are Madan (1997) and van der Veer (1994). Jaffrelot (1996) is the standard political history; D. Gold (1991) is probably the clearest short religious history. Assayag (2001), Corbridge and Harriss (2000), Deshpande (2003), and Khilnani (1997) place contemporary Hindu nationalism in its wider context from different perspectives; Rajagopal (2001), which contains the best concise discussion of the rise of modern Hindu nationalism, is about much more than "politics after television."

T. Basu et al. (1995) is still one of the best studies of the Hindu nationalist movement, mainly in north India. Other studies from north India that contain valuable ethnographic or firsthand reportage include Brass (1997, esp. chap. 7), Froerer (2002), Jaffrelot (2002), McKean (1996a), Michelutti (2002), Nandy et al. (1995), Peabody (1997), and Rajagopal (2001). On the Shiv Sena in Mumbai and western India, see especially the insightful books by Hansen (1999; 2001), as well as Eckert (2003), Heuzé (1995), and Kaur (2003). On the south, the material is thinner: see Assayag (1993; 1995 [English translation, 2004]) on Hindu-Muslim relations in Karnataka, as well as Kakar (1995) on violence; see also Fuller (2001). On the VHP processions, see Assayag (1998) and Davis (1996). Jeffery and Basu (1998) and Sarkar and Butalia (1995) both contain chapters about women and Hindu nationalism; Hansen and Jaffrelot (1998) covers regional variations in the nationalist movement. Gottschalk (2000) on Hindu and Muslim identities in a Bihar village contains much relevant data and analysis.

BIBLIOGRAPHY

Allen, Charles, and Sharada Dwivedi. 1984. *Lives of the Indian Princes*. London: Century.

Allen, M. R. 1976. "Kumari or 'Virgin' Worship in Kathmandu Valley." *Contributions to Indian Sociology*, n.s. 10: 293–316.

Anandhi, S. 1995. *Contending Identities: Dalits and Secular Politics in Madras Slums*. New Delhi: Indian Social Institute.

Appadurai, Arjun. 1981a. *Worship and Conflict under Colonial Rule: A South Indian Case*. Cambridge: Cambridge University Press.

———. 1981b. "The Past as a Scarce Resource." *Man*, n.s. 16: 201–19.

Appadurai, Arjun, and Carol A. Breckenridge. 1976. "The South Indian Temple: Authority, Honour and Redistribution." *Contributions to Indian Sociology*, n.s. 10: 187–211.

Archer, W. G. 1957. *The Loves of Krishna in Indian Painting and Poetry*. London: Allen and Unwin.

Assayag, Jackie. 1992. *La Colère de la Déesse Décapitée: Traditions, Cultes et Pouvoir dans le Sud de l'Inde*. Paris: CNRS Éditions.

———. 1993. "The Goddess and the Saint: Acculturation and Hindu-Muslim Communalism in a Place of Worship in South India (Karnataka)." *Studies in History* 9: 219–45.

———. 1994. "Homo Hierarchicus, Homo Symbolicus: Approche Structurale ou Hérmeneutique en Anthropologie Sociale (de l'Inde) (Note Critique)." *Annales HSS* 49, 1: 133–49.

———. 1995. *Au Confluent de Deux Rivières: Musulmans et Hindous dans le Sud de l'Inde*. Paris: École Française d'Extrême Orient.

———. 1998. "Ritual Action or Political Reaction? The Invention of Hindu Nationalist Processions in India during the 1980s." *South Asia Research* 18: 125–48.

———. 2001. *L'Inde: Désir de Nation*. Paris: Odile Jacob.

———. 2004. *At the Confluence of Two Rivers: Muslims and Hindus in South India*. New Delhi: Manohar.

Assayag, Jackie, and Gilles Tarabout, eds. 1999. *La Possession en Asie du Sud: Parole, Corps, Territoire. Puruṣārtha* 21.

Babb, Lawrence A. 1970. "Marriage and Malevolence: The Uses of Sexual Opposition in a Hindu Pantheon." *Ethnology* 9: 137–48.

———. 1972. "The Satnamis: Political Involvement of a Religious Movement." In J. Michael Mahar, ed., *The Untouchables in Contemporary India*. Tucson: University of Arizona Press.

———. 1975. *The Divine Hierarchy: Popular Hinduism in Central India*. New York: Columbia University Press.

———. 1983a. "Destiny and Responsibility: Karma in Popular Hinduism." In Charles F. Keyes and E. Valentine Daniel, eds., *Karma: An Anthropological Inquiry*. Berkeley: University of California Press.

———. 1983b. "The Physiology of Redemption." *History of Religions* 22: 293–312.

Babb, Lawrence A. 1987. *Redemptive Encounters: Three Modern Styles in the Hindu Tradition*. Delhi: Oxford University Press.

Babb, Lawrence A., and Susan S. Wadley, eds. 1995. *Media and the Transformation of Religion in South Asia*. Philadelphia: University of Pennsylvania Press.

Basham, A. L. 1971 [1954]. *The Wonder that Was India*. London: Fontana.

Basu, Amrita. 1998. "Hindu Women's Activism in India and the Questions It Raises." In Patricia Jeffery and Amrita Basu, eds., *Appropriating Gender: Women's Activism and Politicized Religion in South Asia*. New York: Routledge.

Basu, Tapan, Pradip Datta, Sumit Sarkar, Tanika Sarkar, and Sambuddha Sen. 1993. *Khaki Shorts and Saffron Flags: A Critique of the Hindu Right*. New Delhi: Orient Longman.

Bayly, Susan. 1989. *Saints, Goddesses and Kings: Muslims and Christians in South Indian Society, 1700–1900*. Cambridge: Cambridge University Press.

Beals, Alan R. 1964. "Conflict and Interlocal Festivals in a South Indian Region." *Journal of Asian Studies* 23 (special issue): 95–113.

Beck, Brenda E. F. 1969. "Colour and Heat in South Indian Ritual." *Man*, n.s. 4: 553–72.

———. 1972. *Peasant Society in Konku: A Study of Right and Left Subcastes in South India*. Vancouver: University of British Columbia Press.

———. 1976. "The Symbolic Merger of Body, Space and Cosmos in Hindu Tamil Nadu." *Contributions to Indian Sociology*, n.s. 10: 213–43.

———. 1981. "The Goddess and the Demon: A Local South Indian Festival and Its Wider Context." *Puruṣārtha* 5: 83–136.

Bennett, Lynn. 1983. *Dangerous Wives and Sacred Sisters: Social and Symbolic Roles of High-caste Women in Nepal*. New York: Columbia University Press.

Bennett, Peter J. 1983. "Temple Organisation and Worship among the Puṣṭimārgīya-Vaiṣṇavas of Ujjain." Ph.D. thesis, University of London.

———. 1990. "In Nanda Baba's House: The Devotional Experience in Pushti Marg Temples." In Owen M. Lynch, ed., *Divine Passions: The Social Construction of Emotion in India*. Berkeley: University of California Press.

———. 1993. *The Path of Grace: Social Organisation and Temple Worship in a Vaishnava Sect*. Delhi: Hindustan.

Berreman, Gerald D. 1963. *Hindus of the Himalayas*. Berkeley: University of California Press.

———. 1972. *Hindus of the Himalayas: Ethnography and Change* (revised edition). Berkeley: University of California Press.

Berti, Daniela. 2001. *La Parole des Dieux: Rituels de Possession en Himayala*. Paris: CNRS Éditions.

Béteille, André. 1965a. *Caste, Class, and Power: Changing Patterns of Social Stratification in a Tanjore Village*. Berkeley: University of California Press.

———. 1965b. "Social Organization of Temples in a Tanjore Village." *History of Religions* 5: 74–92.

Bharati, Agehananda. 1963. "Pilgrimage in the Indian Tradition." *History of Religions* 3: 135–67.

Bhardwaj, Surinder M. 1973. *Hindu Places of Pilgrimage in India: A Study in Cultural Geography*. Berkeley: University of California Press.

Biardeau, Madeleine. 1976. "Le Sacrifice dans l'Hindouisme." In Madeleine Biardeau and Charles Malamoud, *Le Sacrifice dans l'Inde Ancienne*. Paris: Presses Universitaires de France.

———. 1981. *L'Hindouisme: Anthropologie d'une Civilisation*. Paris: Flammarion.

———. 1984. "The Śamī Tree and the Sacrificial Buffalo." *Contributions to Indian Sociology*, n.s. 18: 1–23.

———. 1989a. *Hinduism: The Anthropology of a Civilization*. Delhi: Oxford University Press.

———. 1989b. *Histoires de Poteaux: Variations Védiques autour de la Déesse Hindoue*. Paris: École Française d'Extrême Orient.

———. 1989c. "Brahmans and Meat-eating Gods." In Alf Hiltebeitel, ed., *Criminal Gods and Demon Devotees: Essays on the Guardians of Popular Hinduism*. Albany: State University of New York Press.

———, ed. 1981. *Autour de la Déesse Hindoue*. Puruṣārtha 5.

Binford, Mira R. 1976. "Mixing in the Color of Rām of Rānuja." In Bardwell L. Smith, ed., *Hinduism: New Essays in the History of Religions*. Leiden: Brill.

Blackburn, Stuart H. 1985. "Death and Deification: Folk Cults in Hinduism." *History of Religions* 24: 255–74.

Bouillier, Véronique. 1982. "Si les Femmes Faisaient la Fête: À Propos des Fêtes Féminines dans les Hautes Castes Indo-népalaises." *L'Homme* 22 (3): 91–118.

———. 1997. *Ascètes et Rois: Un Monastère de Kanphata Yogis au Népal*. Paris: CNRS Éditions.

Bouillier, Véronique, and Gérard Toffin, eds. 1993. *Classer les Dieux? Des Panthéons en Asie du Sud*. Puruṣārtha 15.

Bradford, Nicholas J. 1983. "Transgenderism and the Cult of Yellamma: Heat, Sex, and Sickness in South Indian Ritual." *Journal of Anthropological Research* 39: 307–22.

———. 1985. "The Indian Renouncer: Structure and Transformation in a Lingayat Community." In Richard Burghart and Audrey Cantlie, eds., *Indian Religion*. London: Curzon.

Brass, Paul R. 1997. *Theft of an Idol: Text and Context in the Representation of Collective Violence*. Princeton: Princeton University Press.

Breckenridge, Carol A. 1978. "From Protector to Litigant: Changing Relations between Hindu Temples and the Raja of Ramnad." In Burton Stein, ed., *South Indian Temples: An Analytical Reconsideration*. Delhi: Vikas.

Brockington, J. L. 1981. *The Sacred Thread: Hinduism in its Continuity and Diversity*. Edinburgh: Edinburgh University Press.

Brown, W. Norman. 1970. *Man in the Universe: Some Continuities in Indian Thought*. Berkeley: University of California Press.

Brubaker, Richard L. 1979. "Barbers, Washermen, and Other Priests: Servants of the South Indian Village and Its Goddess." *History of Religions* 19: 128–52.

Brunner, Helene. 1975–76. "Importance de la Littérature Āgamique pour l'Étude des Religions Vivantes de l'Inde." *Indologica Taurinensia* 3–4: 107–24.

Burgess, James. 1883. "The Ritual of Rāmēśvaram." *Indian Antiquary* 12: 315–26.

Burghart, Richard. 1978a. "Hierarchical Models of the Hindu Social System." *Man*, n.s. 13: 519–26.

―――. 1978b. "The Founding of the Ramanandi Sect." *Ethnohistory* 25: 121–39.

―――. 1978c. "The Disappearance and Reappearance of Janakpur." *Kailash* 6: 257–84.

―――. 1983a. "Renunciation in the Religious Traditions of South Asia." *Man*, n.s. 18: 635–53.

―――. 1983b. "Wandering Ascetics of the Rāmānandī Sect." *History of Religions* 22: 361–80.

―――. 1987. "Gifts to the Gods: Power, Property and Ceremonial in Nepal." In David Cannadine and Simon Price, eds., *Rituals of Royalty: Power and Ceremonial in Traditional Societies*. Cambridge: Cambridge University Press.

―――. 1990. "Ethnographers and Their Local Counterparts in India." In Richard Fardon, ed., *Localizing Strategies: Regional Traditions of Ethnographic Writing*. Edinburgh: Scottish Academic Press.

Burkhart, Geoffrey. 1987. "Family Deity Temples and Spatial Variance among Udayars of Northern Tamil Nadu." In V. Sudarsen, G. Prakash Reddy, and M. Suryanarayana, eds., *Religion and Society in South India*. Delhi: B. R. Publishing.

Caldwell, Sarah. 1999. *Oh Terrifying Mother: Sexuality, Violence and Worship of the Goddess Kali*. Delhi: Oxford University Press.

Cantlie, Audrey. 1985. "Vaishnava Reform Sects in Assam." In Richard Burghart and Audrey Cantlie, eds., *Indian Religion*. London: Curzon.

Caplan, Lionel. 1987. *Class and Culture in Urban India: Fundamentalism in a Christian Community*. Oxford: Clarendon.

Carman, John B., and Frédérique A. Marglin, eds. 1985. *Purity and Auspiciousness in Indian Society*. Leiden: Brill.

Carstairs, G. Morris. 1957. *The Twice-born: A Study of a Community of High-caste Hindus*. London: Hogarth.

―――. 1961. "Patterns of Religious Observance in Three Villages of Rajasthan." In L. P. Vidyarthi, ed., *Aspects of Religion in Indian Society*. Meerut: Kedar Nath Ram Nath.

―――. 1983. *Death of a Witch: A Village in North India 1950–1981*. London: Hutchinson.

Cashman, Richard I. 1975. *The Myth of the* Lokamanya: *Tilak and Mass Politics in Maharashtra*. Berkeley: University of California Press.

Census of India 1981, Series-1 India, Paper-4 of 1984. New Delhi: Government of India.

Charsley, Simon R., and G. K. Karanth, eds. 1998. *Challenging Untouchability: Dalit Initiative and Experience from Karnataka*. New Delhi: Sage.

Chauhan, Brij Raj. 1967. *A Rajasthan Village*. New Delhi: Associated Publishing House.

Claveyrolas, Mathieu. 2003. *Quand le Temple Prend Vie: Atmosphère et Dévotion à Bénarès*. Paris: CNRS Éditions.

Clémentin-Ojha, Catherine. 1999. *Le Trident sur le Palais: Une Cabale Anti-*

Vishnouite dans un Royaume Hindou à l'Époque Coloniale. Paris: École Française d'Extrême Orient.

Clothey, Fred W. 1969. "Skanda-ṣaṣṭi: A Festival in Tamil India." *History of Religions* 8: 236–59.

———. 1978. *The Many Faces of Murukaṉ: The History and Meaning of a South Indian God.* The Hague: Mouton.

Coburn, Thomas B. 1991. *Encountering the Goddess: A Translation of the* Devī-Māhātmya *and a Study of Its Interpretation.* Albany: State University of New York Press.

Coccari, Diane M. 1989. "Protection and Identity: Banaras's Bīr Babas as Neighbourhood Guardian Deities." In Sandria B. Freitag, ed., *Culture and Power in Banaras: Community, Performance, and Environment, 1800–1980.* Berkeley: University of California Press.

Cohn, Bernard S. 1983. "Representing Authority in Victorian India." In Eric Hobsbawm and Terence Ranger, eds., *The Invention of Tradition.* Cambridge: Cambridge University Press.

Corbridge, Stuart, and John Harriss. 2000. *Reinventing India: Liberalization, Hindu Nationalism and Popular Democracy.* Cambridge: Polity.

Courtright, Paul B. 1985. *Gaṇeśa: Lord of Obstacles, Lord of Beginnings.* New York: Oxford University Press.

Crooke, William. 1926. *Religion and Folklore of Northern India.* London: Oxford University Press.

Dalmia, Vasudha, Angelika Malinar, and Martin Christof, eds. 2001. *Charisma and Canon: Essays on the Religious History of the Indian Subcontinent.* Delhi: Oxford University Press.

Dalmia, Vasudha, and Heinrich von Stietencron, eds. 1995. *Representing Hinduism: The Construction of Religious Traditions and National Identity.* New Delhi: Sage.

Dandekar, G. N. 1988. "The Last Kīrtan of Gadge Baba." In Eleanor Zelliott and Maxine Berntsen, eds., *The Experience of Hinduism: Essays on Religion in Maharashtra.* Albany: State University of New York Press.

Daniel, E. Valentine. 1984. *Fluid Signs: Being a Person the Tamil Way.* Berkeley: University of California Press.

Das, Veena. 1977. *Structure and Cognition: Aspects of Hindu Caste and Ritual.* Delhi: Oxford University Press.

Davis, Richard H. 1991. *Ritual in an Oscillating Universe: Worshiping Śiva in Medieval India.* Princeton: Princeton University Press.

———. 1996. "The Iconography of Rama's Chariot." In David Ludden, ed., *Contesting the Nation: Religion, Community, and the Politics of Democracy in India.* Philadelphia: University of Pennsylvania Press.

De Neve, Geert. 2000. "Patronage and 'Community': The Role of a Tamil 'Village' Festival in the Integration of a Town." *Journal of the Royal Anthropological Institute,* n.s. 6: 501–19.

Deleury, G. A. 1960. *The Cult of Vithoba.* Poona: Deccan College.

Delfendahl, Bernard. 1971. "Parenté, Fonction et Territoire dans les Cultes Champêtres d'un Village de l'Inde." *L'Homme* 11 (1): 52–67.

Deliège, Robert. 1988. *Les Paraiyars du Tamil Nadu.* Nettetal: Steyler.

Derrett, J. Duncan M. 1959. "Bhū-bharaṇa, Bhū-pālana, Bhū-bhojana: An Indian Conundrum." *Bulletin of the School of Oriental and African Studies* 22: 108–23.

———. 1968. *Religion, Law and the State in India.* London: Faber.

———. 1975. "Social and Political Thought and Institutions." In A. L. Basham, ed., *A Cultural History of India.* Oxford: Clarendon.

———. 1976. "Rājadharma." *Journal of Asian Studies* 35: 597–609.

Deshpande, Satish. 2003. *Contemporary India: A Sociological View.* New Delhi: Viking.

Diehl, Carl G. 1956. *Instrument and Purpose: Studies on Rites and Rituals in South India.* Lund: Gleerup.

Dimmitt, Cornelia, and J. A. B. van Buitenen. 1978. *Classical Hindu Mythology: A Reader in the Sanskrit Purāṇas.* Philadelphia: Temple University Press.

Dimock, Edward C. 1989 [1966]. *The Place of the Hidden Moon: Erotic Mysticism in the Vaiṣṇava-sahajiyā Cult of Bengal.* Chicago: University of Chicago Press.

Dirks, Nicholas B. 1987. *The Hollow Crown: Ethnohistory of an Indian Kingdom.* Cambridge: Cambridge University Press.

Dube, Ishita Banerjee. 2001. *Divine Affairs: Religion, Pilgrimage, and the State in Colonial and Postcolonial India.* Shimla: Indian Institute of Advanced Study.

Dube, S. C. 1955. *Indian Village.* London: Routledge and Kegan Paul.

Dumont, Louis. 1970a [1966]. *Homo Hierarchicus: The Caste System and its Implications.* London: Weidenfeld and Nicolson.

———. 1970b. *Religion, Politics and History in India.* Paris: Mouton.

———. 1986 [1957]. *A South Indian Subcaste: Social Organization and Religion of the Pramalai Kallar.* Delhi: Oxford University Press.

Dumont, Louis, and David F. Pocock. 1959. "Pure and Impure; On the Different Aspects or Levels in Hinduism; Possession and Priesthood." *Contributions to Indian Sociology* 3: 9–74.

Eck, Diana L. 1981a. *Darśan: Seeing the Divine Image in India.* Chambersburg: Anima.

———. 1981b. "India's Tīrthas: 'Crossings' in Sacred Geography." *History of Religions* 20: 323–44.

———. 1983. *Banaras: City of Light.* London: Routledge and Kegan Paul.

Eckert, Julia M. 2003. *The Charisma of Direct Action: Power, Politics, and the Shiv Sena.* Delhi: Oxford University Press.

Egnor, Margaret. 1980. "On the Meaning of Śakti to Women in Tamil Nadu." In Susan S. Wadley, ed., *The Powers of Tamil Women.* Syracuse: Maxwell School of Citizenship and Public Affairs, Syracuse University.

———. 1984. "The Changed Mother or What the Smallpox Goddess Did When There Was No More Smallpox." *Contributions to Asian Studies* 18: 24–45.

Elmore, Wilber T. 1925 [1915]. *Dravidian Gods in Modern Hinduism: A Study of the Local and Village Deities of Southern India.* Madras: Christian Literature Society.

Engblom, Philip C. 1987. Introduction. In D. B. Mokashi, *Palkhi: An Indian Pilgrimage.* Albany: State University of New York Press.

Enthoven, R. E. 1924. *The Folklore of Bombay*. Oxford: Clarendon.

Erndl, Kathleen M. 1993. *Victory to the Mother: The Hindu Goddess of Northwest India in Myth, Ritual, and Symbol*. New York: Oxford University Press.

Eschmann, Anncharlott, Hermann Kulke, and Gaya Charan Tripathi, eds. 1978. *The Cult of Jagannath and the Regional Tradition of Orissa*. New Delhi: Manohar.

Filliozat, Jean. 1983. "The Role of the Śaivāgamas in the Śaiva Ritual System." In Fred W. Clothey and J. Bruce Long, eds., *Experiencing Śiva: Encounters with a Hindu Deity*. New Delhi: Manohar.

Forster, E. M. 1983 [1953]. *The Hill of Devi*. Harmondsworth: Penguin.

Freed, Ruth S., and Stanley A. Freed. 1962. "Two Mother Goddess Ceremonies of Delhi State in the Great and Little Traditions." *Southwestern Journal of Anthropology* 18: 246–77.

———. 1964a. "Calendars, Ceremonies, and Festivals in a North Indian Village: Necessary Calendric Information for Fieldwork." *Southwestern Journal of Anthropology* 20: 67–90.

———. 1964b. "Spirit Possession as Illness in a North Indian Village." *Ethnology* 3: 152–71.

Froerer, Peggy. 2002. "From Local Tensions to Ethnic Conflict: The Emergence of Hindu Nationalism in a Christian/Hindu 'Tribal' Community in Chhattisgarh, Central India." Ph.D. thesis, University of London.

Fruzzetti, Lina. 1982. *The Gift of a Virgin: Women, Marriage, and Ritual in Bengal*. New Brunswick: Rutgers University Press.

Frykenberg, Robert E. 1989. "The Emergence of Modern 'Hinduism' as a Concept and as an Institution: A Reappraisal with Special Reference to South India." In Gunther D. Sontheimer and Hermann Kulke, eds., *Hinduism Reconsidered*. New Delhi: Manohar.

Fuller, C. J. 1979. "Gods, Priests and Purity: On the Relation between Hinduism and the Caste System." *Man*, n.s. 14: 459–76.

———. 1980a. "The Divine Couple's Relationship in a South Indian Temple: Mīnākṣī and Sundareśvara at Madurai." *History of Religions* 19: 321–48.

———. 1980b. "The Calendrical System in Tamilnadu (South India)." *Journal of the Royal Asiatic Society* (1980): 52–63.

———. 1984. *Servants of the Goddess: The Priests of a South Indian Temple*. Cambridge: Cambridge University Press.

———. 1985a. "Royal Divinity and Human Kingship in the Festivals of a South Indian Temple." *South Asian Social Scientist* 1: 3–43.

———. 1985b. "Initiation and Consecration: Priestly Rituals in a South Indian Temple." In Richard Burghart and Audrey Cantlie, eds., *Indian Religion*. London: Curzon.

———. 1987. "Sacrifice (*Bali*) in the South Indian Temple." In V. Sudarsen, G. Prakash Reddy, and M. Suryanarayana, eds., *Religion and Society in South India*. Delhi: B. R. Publishing.

———. 1988a. "The Hindu Pantheon and the Legitimation of Hierarchy." *Man*, n.s. 23: 19–39.

———. 1988b. "Hinduism and Scriptural Authority in Modern Indian Law." *Comparative Studies in Society and History* 30: 225–48.

Fuller, C. J. 1988c. "The Hindu Temple and Indian Society." In Michael V. Fox, ed., *Temple in Society*. Winona Lake: Eisenbrauns.

———. 1991. "Hinduism and Hierarchy (Review Article)." *Man*, n.s. 26: 549–55.

———. 1993. " 'Only Śiva Can Worship Śiva': Ritual Mistakes and their Correction in a South Indian Temple." *Contributions to Indian Sociology*, n.s. 27: 169–89.

———. 1994. "La 'Cohérence' à la Lumière de l'Hindouisme Populaire (Réponse à J. Assayag)." *Annales HSS* 49, 1: 151–57.

———. 1995. "The 'Holy Family' of Shiva in a South Indian Temple." *Social Anthropology* 3: 205–17.

———. 2001. "The 'Vinayaka Chaturthi' Festival and Hindutva in Tamil Nadu." *Economic and Political Weekly* 34 (12 May): 1607–16.

———. 2003. *The Renewal of the Priesthood: Modernity and Traditionalism in a South Indian Temple*. Princeton: Princeton University Press.

———. 2004. "The Renovation Ritual in a South Indian Temple: The 1995 Kumbhābhiṣeka in the Mīnākṣī Temple, Madurai." *Bulletin of the School of Oriental and African Studies* 67: 40–63.

Fuller, C. J., and John Harriss. n.d. "Globalising Hinduism: The 'Traditional' Teaching of Swami Dayananda Saraswati and Modern Businessmen in Chennai." In Jackie Assayag and C. J. Fuller, eds., *The Anthropology of Globalisation in India*. London: Anthem.

Fuller, C. J., and Penny Logan. 1985. "The Navarātri Festival in Madurai." *Bulletin of the School of Oriental and African Studies* 48: 79–105.

Galanter, Marc. 1971. "Hinduism, Secularism and the Indian Judiciary." *Philosophy East and West* 21: 467–87.

Galey, Jean-Claude. 1984. "Souveraineté et Justice dans le Haut-Gange: La Fonction Royale au-delà des Écoles Juridiques et du Droit Coutumier." In Jean-Claude Galey, ed., *Différences, Valeurs, Hiérarchie: Textes Offerts à Louis Dumont*. Paris: École des Hautes Études en Sciences Sociales.

———. 1986. "Totalité et Hiérarchie dans les Sanctuaires Royaux du Tehri-Garhwal (Himalaya Indien)." *Puruṣārtha* 10: 55–95.

———. 1989. "Reconsidering Kingship in India: An Ethnological Perspective." *History and Anthropology* 4: 123–87.

———, ed. 1985–86. *L'Espace du Temple* 1: *Espaces, Itinéraires, Médiations*; *L'Espace du Temple* 2: *Les Sanctuaires dans le Royaume*. *Puruṣārtha* 8, 10.

Geetha, V., and T. Y. Jayanthi. 1995. "Women, Hindutva and the Politics of Caste in Tamil Nadu." In Tanika Sarkar and Urvashi Butalia, eds., *Women and Right-wing Movements: Indian Experiences*. London: Zed.

Gell, Alfred. 1997. "Exalting the King and Obstructing the State: A Political Interpretation of Royal Ritual in Bastar District, Central India." *Journal of the Royal Anthropological Institute*, n.s. 3: 433–50.

Gellner, David N. 1992. *Monk, Householder, and Tantric Priest: Newar Buddhism and its Hierarchy of Ritual*. Cambridge: Cambridge University Press.

Ghose, Rajeshwari. 1996. *The Lord of Ārūr, the Tyāgarāja Cult in Tamilnāḍu: A Study in Conflict and Accommodation*. Delhi: Motilal Banarsidass.

Ghurye, G. S. 1960. *After a Century and a Quarter: Lonikand Then and Now.* Bombay: Popular Book Depot.

Gilsenan, Michael. 1982. *Recognizing Islam: An Anthropologist's Introduction.* London: Croom Helm.

Gold, Ann G. 1988a. *Fruitful Journeys: The Ways of Rajasthani Pilgrims.* Berkeley: University of California Press.

———. 1988b. "Spirit Possession Perceived and Performed in Rural Rajasthan." *Contributions to Indian Sociology*, n.s. 22: 35–63.

———. 1989. "The Once and Future Yogi: Sentiments and Signs in the Tale of a Renouncer-king." *Journal of Asian Studies* 48: 770–86.

Gold, Daniel. 1991. "Organized Hinduisms: From Vedic Truth to Hindu Nation." In Martin E. Marty and R. Scott Appleby, eds., *Fundamentalisms Observed.* Chicago: University of Chicago Press.

Gombrich, Richard, and Gananath Obeyesekere. 1988. *Buddhism Transformed: Religious Change in Sri Lanka.* Princeton: Princeton University Press.

Gonda, Jan. 1969. *Ancient Indian Kingship from the Religious Point of View.* Leiden: Brill.

———. 1970. *Viṣṇuism and Śivaism: A Comparison.* London: Athlone.

Good, Anthony. 1983. "A Symbolic Type and Its Transformations: The Case of South Indian Poṅkal." *Contributions to Indian Sociology*, n.s. 17: 223–44.

———. 1985. "The Annual Goddess Festival in a South Indian Village." *South Asian Social Scientist* 1: 119–67.

———. 1987a. "Divine Coronation in a South Indian Temple." In V. Sudarsen, G. Prakash Reddy, and M. Suryanarayana, eds., *Religion and Society in South India.* Delhi: B. R. Publishing.

———. 1987b. "The Religious, Economic and Social Organization of a South Indian Temple." *Quarterly Journal of Social Affairs* 3: 1–25.

———. 1989a. "Law, Legitimacy, and the Hereditary Rights of Tamil Temple Priests." *Modern Asian Studies* 23: 233–57.

———. 1989b. "Divine Marriage in a South Indian Temple." *Mankind* 19: 181–97.

———. 2000. "Congealing Divinity: Time, Worship and Kinship in South Indian Hinduism." *Journal of the Royal Anthropological Institute*, n.s. 6: 273–92.

Goswami, B. B., and S. G. Morab. 1975. *Chamundesvari Temple in Mysore.* Calcutta: Anthropological Survey of India (Memoir no. 35).

Gottschalk, Peter. 2000. *Beyond Hindu and Muslim: Multiple Identity in Narratives from Village India.* New York: Oxford University Press.

Gough, E. Kathleen. 1960. "Caste in a Tanjore Village." In E. R. Leach, ed., *Aspects of Caste in South India, Ceylon and North-west Pakistan.* Cambridge: Cambridge University Press.

———. 1970. "Palakkara: Social and Religious Change in Central Kerala." In K. Ishwaran, ed., *Change and Continuity in India's Villages.* New York: Columbia University Press.

———. 1976 [1959]. "Cults of the Dead among the Nāyars." In Milton Singer, ed., *Traditional India: Structure and Change.* Austin: University of Texas Press.

Gough, E. Kathleen. 1989. *Rural Change in Southeast India: 1950s to 1980s.* Delhi: Oxford University Press.

Guilmoto, Christophe, Marie-Louise Reiniche, and Pierre Pichard. 1990. *Tiruvannamalai: Un Lieu Saint Śivaïte du Sud de l'Inde 5: La Ville.* Paris: École Française d'Extrême Orient.

Hanchett, Suzanne. 1982. "The Festival Interlude: Some Anthropological Observations." In Guy R. Welbon and Glenn E. Yocum, eds., *Religious Festivals in South India and Sri Lanka.* New Delhi: Manohar.

———. 1988. *Coloured Rice: Symbolic Structure in Hindu Family Festivals.* Delhi: Hindustan.

Hancock, Mary. 1999. *Womanhood in the Making: Domestic Ritual and Public Culture in Urban South India.* Boulder: Westview.

Hansen, Thomas Blom. 1999. *The Saffron Wave: Democracy and Hindu Nationalism in Modern India.* Princeton: Princeton University Press.

———. 2001. *Wages of Violence: Naming and Identity in Postcolonial Bombay.* Princeton: Princeton University Press.

Hansen, Thomas Blom, and Christophe Jaffrelot, eds. 1998. *The BJP and the Compulsions of Politics in India.* Delhi: Oxford University Press.

Hardgrove, Anne. 1999. "*Sati* Worship and Marwari Public Identity in India." *Journal of Asian Studies* 58: 723–52.

Hardiman, David. 1987. *The Coming of the Devi: Adivasi Assertion in Western India.* Delhi: Oxford University Press.

Harlan, Lindsey. 1992. *Religion and Rajput Women: The Ethic of Protection in Contemporary Narratives.* Berkeley: University of California Press.

———. 2003. *The Goddesses' Henchmen: Gender in Indian Hero Worship.* New York: Oxford University Press.

Harman, William P. 1989. *The Sacred Marriage of a Hindu Goddess.* Bloomington: Indiana University Press.

Harper, Edward B. 1959. "A Hindu Village Pantheon." *Southwestern Journal of Anthropology* 15: 227–34.

———. 1964. "Ritual Pollution as an Integrator of Caste and Religion." *Journal of Asian Studies* 23 (special issue): 151–97.

———. 1969. "Fear and the Status of Women." *Southwestern Journal of Anthropology* 25: 81–95.

Harriss, John. 2003. "The Great Tradition Globalizes: Reflections on Two Studies of 'The Industrial Leaders' of Madras." *Modern Asian Studies* 37: 327–62.

Hawley, John S. 1981. *At Play with Krishna: Pilgrimage Dramas from Brindavan.* Princeton: Princeton University Press.

———, ed. 1994. *Sati, the Blessing and the Curse: The Burning of Wives in India.* New York: Oxford University Press.

Hawley, John S., and Donna M. Wulff, eds. 1982. *The Divine Consort: Rādhā and the Goddesses of India.* Berkeley: Berkeley Religious Studies Series.

———, eds. 1996. *Devī: Goddesses of India.* Berkeley: University of California Press.

Heesterman, J. C. 1959. "Reflections on the Significance of the *Dakṣiṇā.*" *Indo-Iranian Journal* 3: 241–58.

————. 1971. "Priesthood and the Brahmin." *Contributions to Indian Sociology*, n.s. 5: 43–47.

————. 1985. *The Inner Conflict of Tradition: Essays in Indian Ritual, Kingship, and Society*. Chicago: University of Chicago Press.

————. 1986. "The King's Order." *Contributions to Indian Sociology*, n.s. 20: 1–13.

Hein, Norvin. 1972. *The Miracle Plays of Mathura*. New Haven: Yale University Press.

————. 1976 [1959]. "The Rām Līlā." In Milton Singer, ed., *Traditional India: Structure and Change*. Austin: University of Texas Press.

Herrenschmidt, Olivier. 1989. *Les Meilleurs Dieux sont Hindous*. Lausanne: L'Âge d'Homme.

————. 2002. "Pêcheurs en Mer de l'Andhra Pradesh, de 1960 à Nos Jours: Réflexion sur l'Ethnologie et les Problèmes de Développement." *Puruṣārtha* 23: 85–110.

Hershman, Paul. 1977. "Virgin and Mother." In Ioan Lewis, ed., *Symbols and Sentiments: Cross-cultural Studies in Symbolism*. London: Academic.

Hess, Linda. 1983. "Ram Lila: The Audience Experience." In Monika Thiel-Horstmann, ed., *Bhakti in Current Research, 1979–1982*. Berlin: Dietrich Reimer.

Heuzé, Gérard. 1995. "Cultural Populism: The Appeal of the Shiv Sena." In Sujata Patel and Alice Thorner, eds., *Bombay: Metaphor for Modern India*. Bombay: Oxford University Press.

Hiebert, Paul G. 1971. *Konduru: Structure and Integration in a South Indian Village*. Minneapolis: University of Minnesota Press.

Hiltebeitel, Alf. 1976. *The Ritual of Battle: Krishna in the Mahābhārata*. Ithaca: Cornell University Press.

————. 1981. "Draupadī's Hair." *Puruṣārtha* 5: 179–214.

————. 1982. "Sexuality and Sacrifice: Convergent Subcurrents in the Firewalking Cult of Draupadī." In Fred W. Clothey, ed., *Images of Man: Religion and Historical Process in South Asia*. Madras: New Era.

————. 1983. "Toward a Coherent Study of Hinduism." *Religious Studies Review* 9: 206–12.

————. 1985. "On the Handling of the Meat, and Related Matters, in Two South Indian Buffalo Sacrifices." *L'Uomo* 9: 171–99.

————. 1987. "Hinduism." In Mircea Eliade, ed., *The Encyclopedia of Religion* 6: 336–60. New York: Macmillan.

————. 1988. *The Cult of Draupadī*, 1: *Mythologies: from Gingee to Kurukṣetra*. Chicago: University of Chicago Press.

————. 1989. "Draupadī's Two Guardians: The Buffalo King and the Muslim Devotee." In Alf Hiltebeitel, ed., *Criminal Gods and Demon Devotees: Essays on the Guardians of Popular Hinduism*. Albany: State University of New York Press.

————. 1991. *The Cult of Draupadī*, 2: *On Hindu Ritual and the Goddess*. Chicago: University of Chicago Press.

————. 1995. "Draupadī Cult Līlās." In William S. Sax, ed., *The Gods at Play: Līlā in South Asia*. New York: Oxford University Press.

Hiltbeitel, Alf. 1999. *Rethinking India's Oral and Classical Epics: Draupadī among Rajputs, Muslims, and Dalits.* Chicago: University of Chicago Press.

———. 2001. *Rethinking the Mahābhārata: A Reader's Guide to the Education of the Dharma King.* Chicago: University of Chicago Press.

———, ed. 1989. *Criminal Gods and Demon Devotees: Essays on the Guardians of Popular Hinduism.* Albany: State University of New York Press.

Holmström, M. 1971. "Religious Change in an Industrial City in South India." *Journal of the Royal Asiatic Society* (1971): 28–40.

Hubert, Henri, and Marcel Mauss. 1964 [1898]. *Sacrifice: Its Nature and Function.* London: Cohen and West.

Hudson, Dennis. 1978. "Śiva, Mīnākṣī, Viṣṇu—Reflections on a Popular Myth in Madurai." In Burton Stein, ed., *South Indian Temples: An Analytical Reconsideration.* Delhi: Vikas.

———. 1982. "Two Citrā Festivals in Madurai." In Guy R. Welbon and Glenn E. Yocum, eds., *Religious Festivals in South India and Sri Lanka.* New Delhi: Manohar.

Huyler, Stephen P. 1999. *Meeting God: Elements of Hindu Devotion.* New Haven: Yale University Press.

Inden, Ronald. 1981. "Hierarchies of Kings in Medieval India." *Contributions to Indian Sociology,* n.s. 15: 99–125.

———. 1985a. "The Temple and the Hindu Chain of Being (Kashmir)." *Puruṣārtha* 8: 53–73.

———. 1985b. "Hindu Evil as Unconquered Lower Self." In David Parkin, ed., *The Anthropology of Evil.* Oxford: Blackwell.

———. 1986. "Orientalist Constructions of India." *Modern Asian Studies* 20: 401–46.

Jacobson, Doranne. 1978. "The Chaste Wife: Cultural Norm and Individual Experience." In Sylvia Vatuk, ed., *American Studies in the Anthropology of India.* New Delhi: Manohar.

Jaffrelot, Christophe. 1994. "Processions Hindoues, Stratégies Politiques et Émeutes entre Hindous et Musulmans." *Puruṣārtha* 16: 261–87.

———. 1996. *The Hindu Nationalist Movement and Indian Politics, 1925 to the 1990s.* London: Hurst.

———. 2002. "Les Nationalistes Hindous Face à la Mobilisation des Basses Castes." *Puruṣārtha* 23: 328–63.

Jeffery, Patricia, and Amrita Basu, eds. 1998. *Appropriating Gender: Women's Activism and Politicized Religion in South Asia.* New York: Routledge.

Jenkins, Rob. 1998. "Rajput Hindutva, Caste Politics, Regional Identity and Hindu Nationalism in Contemporary Rajasthan." In Thomas Blom Hansen and Christophe Jaffrelot, eds., *The BJP and the Compulsions of Politics in India.* Delhi: Oxford University Press.

Jordens, J. T. F. 1975a. "Hindu Religious and Social Reform." In A. L. Basham, ed., *A Cultural History of India.* Oxford: Clarendon.

———. 1975b. "Hindu Religious and Social Reform in British India." In A. L. Basham, ed., *A Cultural History of India.* Oxford: Clarendon.

Juergensmeyer, Mark. 1991. *Radhasoami Reality: The Logic of a Modern Faith.* Princeton: Princeton University Press.

Kakar, Sudhir. 1983. *Shamans, Mystics and Doctors: A Psychological Inquiry into India and its Healing Traditions*. Boston: Beacon.

———. 1995. *The Colours of Violence*. New Delhi: Viking.

Kalra, Mandira. n.d. "Banjaras and the RSS." Unpublished manuscript, London School of Economics.

Kane, P. V. 1968–77 [1930–62]. *History of Dharmaśāstra*. 5 vols. Poona: Bhandarkar Oriental Research Institute.

Kapadia, Karin. 1995. *Siva and Her Sisters: Gender, Caste, and Class in Rural South India*. Boulder: Westview.

Kapur, Anuradha. 1985. "Actors, Pilgrims, Kings and Gods: The Ramlila at Ramnagar." *Contributions to Indian Sociology*, n.s. 19: 57–74.

———. 1993. "Deity to Crusader: The Changing Iconography of Ram." In Gyanendra Pandey, ed., *Hindus and Others: The Question of Identity in India Today*. New Delhi: Viking.

Karve, Irawati. 1988 [1951]. "On the Road: A Maharashtrian Pilgrimage." In Eleanor Zelliott and Maxine Berntsen, eds., *The Experience of Hinduism: Essays on Religion in Maharashtra*. Albany: State University of New York Press.

Kaur, Raminder. 2002. "Martial Imagery in Western India: The Changing Face of Ganapati since the 1890s." *South Asia* 25: 69–96.

———. 2003. *Performative Politics and the Cultures of Hinduism: Public Uses of Religion in Western India*. Delhi: Permanent Black.

Keyes, Charles F., and E. Valentine Daniel, eds. 1983. *Karma: An Anthropological Inquiry*. Berkeley: University of California Press.

Khan, Dominique-Sila. 1997a. *Conversions and Shifting Identities: Ramdev Pir and the Ismailis in Rajasthan*. New Delhi: Manohar.

———. 1997b. "La Tradition de Rāmdev Pīr au Rajasthan: Acculturation et Syncrétisme." *Puruṣārtha* 19: 121–40.

Khilnani, Sunil. 1997. *The Idea of India*. London: Penguin.

Kinsley, David R. 1975. *The Sword and the Flute: Kālī and Kṛṣṇa, Dark Visions of the Terrible and the Sublime in Hindu Mythology*. Berkeley: University of California Press.

———. 1982. *Hinduism: A Cultural Perspective*. Englewood Cliffs: Prentice-Hall.

———. 1987. *Hindu Goddesses: Visions of the Divine Feminine in the Hindu Religious Tradition*. Delhi: Motilal Banarsidass.

Kjaerholm, Lars. 1986. "Myth, Pilgrimage and Fascination in the Aiyappa Cult: A View from Fieldwork in Tamilnadu." In Asko Parpola and Bent Smidt Hansen, eds., *South Asian Religion and Society*. London: Curzon.

Knipe, David M. 1989. "Night of the Growing Dead: A Cult of Vīrabhadra in Coastal Andhra." In Alf Hiltebeitel, ed., *Criminal Gods and Demon Devotees: Essays on the Guardians of Popular Hinduism*. Albany: State University of New York Press.

———. 1995. "Softening the Cruelty of God: Folklore, Ritual and the Planet Śani (Saturn) in Southeast India." In David Shulman, ed., *Syllables of Sky: Studies in South Indian Civilization in Honour of Velcheru Narayana Rao*. Delhi: Oxford University Press.

Kolenda, Pauline. 1982. "Pox and the Terror of Childlessness: Images and Ideas of the Smallpox Goddess in a North Indian Village." In James J. Preston, ed., *Mother Worship: Theme and Variations*. Chapel Hill: University of North Carolina Press.

———. 1984. "Woman as Tribute, Woman as Flower: Images of 'Woman' in North and South India." *American Ethnologist* 11: 98–117.

Kramrisch, Stella. 1976 [1946]. *The Hindu Temple*. 2 vols. Delhi: Motilal Banarsidass.

———. 1981a. *Manifestations of Shiva*. Philadelphia: Philadelphia Museum of Art.

———. 1981b. *The Presence of Śiva*. Princeton: Princeton University Press.

Laidlaw, James. 1995. *Riches and Renunciation: Religion, Economy, and Society among the Jains*. Oxford: Clarendon.

Lapoint, Elwyn C. 1978. "The Epic of Guga: A North Indian Oral Tradition." In Sylvia Vatuk, ed., *American Studies in the Anthropology of India*. New Delhi: Manohar.

Lewis, Oscar. 1958. *Village Life in Northern India: Studies in a Delhi Village*. Urbana: University of Illinois Press.

L'Hernault, Françoise, and Marie-Louise Reiniche. 1999. *Tiruvannamalai: Un Lieu Saint Śivaïte du Sud de l'Inde, 3, Rites et Fêtes*. Paris: École Française d'Extrême Orient.

Lingat, Robert. 1973 [1967]. *The Classical Law of India*. Berkeley: University of California Press.

Logan, Penelope. 1980. "Domestic Worship and the Festival Cycle in the South Indian City of Madurai." Ph.D. thesis, University of Manchester.

Long, J. Bruce. 1980. "The Concepts of Human Action and Rebirth in the *Mahābhārata*." In Wendy D. O'Flaherty, ed., *Karma and Rebirth in Classical Indian Traditions*. Berkeley: University of California Press.

———. 1982. "Mahāśivarātri: The Śaiva Festival of Repentance." In Guy R. Welbon and Glenn E. Yocum, eds., *Religious Festivals in South India and Sri Lanka*. New Delhi: Manohar.

Lorenzen, David N. 1987. "Traditions of Non-caste Hinduism: The Kabir Panth." *Contributions to Indian Sociology*, n.s. 21: 263–83.

Ludden, David, ed. 1996. *Contesting the Nation: Religion, Community, and the Politics of Democracy in India*. Philadelphia: University of Pennsylvania Press.

Lutgendorf, Philip. 1989. "Rām's Story in Shiva's City: Public Arenas and Private Patronage." In Sandria B. Freitag, ed., *Culture and Power in Banaras: Community, Performance, and Environment, 1800–1980*. Berkeley: University of California Press.

———. 1991. *The Life of a Text: Performing the* Rāmcaritmānas *of Tulsidas*. Berkeley: University of California Press.

———. 1994. "My Hanuman is Bigger than Yours." *History of Religions* 33: 211–45.

———. 1997. "Monkey in the Middle: The Status of Hanuman in Popular Hinduism." *Religion* 27: 311–32.

———. 2002. "Evolving a Monkey: Hanuman, Poster Art and Postcolonial Anxiety." *Contributions to Indian Sociology*, n.s. 36: 71–112.

Lynch, Owen M. 1988. "Pilgrimage with Krishna, Sovereign of the Emotions." *Contributions to Indian Sociology*, n.s. 22: 171–94.

McDermott, Rachel F. 2001. *Mother of my Heart, Daughter of my Dreams: Kālī and Umā in the Devotional Poetry of Bengal.* New York: Oxford University Press.

McGilvray, Dennis B. 1983. "Paraiyar Drummers of Sri Lanka: Consensus and Constraint in an Untouchable Caste." *American Ethnologist* 10: 97–115.

McKean, Lise. 1996a. *Divine Enterprise: Gurus and the Hindu Nationalist Movement.* Chicago: University of Chicago Press.

———. 1996b. "Bhārat Mātā." In John S. Hawley and Donna M. Wulff, eds., *Devī: Goddesses of India.* Berkeley: University of California Press.

Madan, T. N. 1987a. *Non-renunciation: Themes and Interpretations of Hindu Culture.* Delhi: Oxford University Press.

———. 1987b. "Secularism in its Place." *Journal of Asian Studies* 46: 747–59.

———. 1997. *Modern Myths, Locked Minds: Secularism and Fundamentalism in India.* Delhi: Oxford University Press.

Majumdar, D. N. 1958. *Caste and Communication in an Indian Village.* London: Asia.

Malamoud, Charles. 1975. "Cuire le Monde." *Puruṣārtha* 1: 91–135.

———. 1976. "Terminer le Sacrifice." In Madeleine Biardeau and Charles Malamoud, *Le Sacrifice dans l'Inde Ancienne.* Paris: Presses Universitaires de France.

Mandelbaum, David G. 1970. *Society in India.* Berkeley: University of California Press.

Mankekar, Purnima. 1999. *Screening Culture, Viewing Politics: An Ethnography of Television, Womanhood, and Nation in Postcolonial India.* Durham: Duke University Press.

Marglin, Frédérique A. 1985. *Wives of the God-king: The Rituals of the Devadasis of Puri.* Delhi: Oxford University Press.

Marriott, McKim. 1968a. "The Feast of Love." In Milton Singer, ed., *Krishna: Myths, Rites, and Attitudes.* Chicago: University of Chicago Press.

———. 1968b. "Caste Ranking and Food Transactions: A Matrix Analysis." In Milton Singer and Bernard S. Cohn, eds., *Structure and Change in Indian Society.* Chicago: Aldine.

———. 1969 [1955]. "Little Communities in an Indigenous Civilization." In McKim Marriott, ed., *Village India: Studies in the Little Community.* Chicago: University of Chicago Press.

———. 1976. "Hindu Transactions: Diversity without Dualism." In Bruce Kapferer, ed., *Transaction and Meaning.* Philadelphia: Institute for the Study of Human Issues.

———. 1989. "Constructing an Indian Ethnosociology." *Contributions to Indian Sociology*, n.s. 23: 1–39.

Martin, James L. 1982. "The Cycle of Festivals at Pārthasārathī Temple." In Guy R. Welbon and Glenn E. Yocum, eds., *Religious Festivals in South India and Sri Lanka.* New Delhi: Manohar.

Mayer, Adrian C. 1960. *Caste and Kinship in Central India: A Village and Its Region.* London: Routledge and Kegan Paul.

Mayer, Adrian C. 1981a. "Perceptions of Princely Rule: Perspectives from a Biography." *Contributions to Indian Sociology*, n.s. 15: 127–54.

———. 1981b. "Public Service and Individual Merit in a Town of Central India." In Adrian C. Mayer, ed., *Culture and Morality: Essays in Honour of Christoph von Fürer-Haimendorf*. Delhi: Oxford University Press.

———. 1985. "The King's Two Thrones." *Man*, n.s. 20: 205–21.

Mehta, Gita. 1981. *Karma Cola*. London: Fontana.

Merrey, Karen L. 1982. "The Hindu Festival Calendar." In Guy R. Welbon and Glenn E. Yocum, eds., *Religious Festivals in South India and Sri Lanka*. New Delhi: Manohar.

Meyer, Eveline. 1986. *Aṅkāḷaparamēcuvari: A Goddess of Tamilnadu, Her Myths and Cult*. Stuttgart: Steiner.

Michaels, Axel. 2004 [1998]. *Hinduism: Past and Present*. Princeton: Princeton University Press.

Michell, George. 1977. *The Hindu Temple: An Introduction to its Meaning*. London: Paul Elek.

Michelutti, Lucia. 2002. "Sons of Krishna: The Politics of Yadav Community Formation in a North Indian Town." Ph.D. thesis, University of London.

Miller, Barbara S. 1977. *Love Song of the Dark Lord: Jayadeva's Gītagovinda*. New York: Columbia University Press.

Miller, D. B. 1973. "Holi-Dulhendi: Licensed Rebellion in a North Indian Village." *South Asia* 3: 15–22.

———. 1975. *From Hierarchy to Stratification: Changing Patterns of Social Inequality in a North Indian Village*. Delhi: Oxford University Press.

Mines, Diane P. 2002. "Hindu Nationalism, Untouchable Reform, and the Ritual Production of a South Indian Village." *American Ethnologist* 29: 58–85.

Mines, Mattison, and Vijayalakshmi Gourishankar. 1990. "Leadership and Individuality in South Asia: The Case of the South Indian Big-man." *Journal of Asian Studies* 49: 761–86.

Mitchell, A. G. 1982. *Hindu Gods and Goddesses*. London: Victoria and Albert Museum/Her Majesty's Stationery Office.

Moffatt, Michael. 1979. *An Untouchable Community in South India: Structure and Consensus*. Princeton: Princeton University Press.

Mokashi, D. B. 1987 [1964]. *Palkhi: An Indian Pilgrimage*. Albany: State University of New York Press.

Monier-Williams, M. 1974 [1883]. *Religious Thought and Life in India: Vedism, Brahmanism and Hinduism*. New Delhi: Oriental Books.

Moreno, Manuel. 1985. "God's Forceful Call: Possession as a Divine Strategy." In Joanne P. Waghorne and Norman Cutler, eds., *Gods of Flesh, Gods of Stone: The Embodiment of Divinity in India*. Chambersburg: Anima.

Moreno, Manuel, and McKim Marriott. 1989. "Humoral Transactions in Two Tamil Cults: Murukan and Mariyamman." *Contributions to Indian Sociology*, n.s. 23: 149–67.

Morinis, E. Alan. 1984. *Pilgrimage in the Hindu Tradition: A Case Study of West Bengal*. Delhi: Oxford University Press.

Mosse, David. 1994. "Catholic Saints and the Hindu Village Pantheon in Rural Tamil Nadu, India." *Man*, n.s. 29: 301–32.

Nabokov, Isabelle. 2000. *Religion Against the Self: An Ethnography of Tamil Rituals*. New York: Oxford University Press.

Nandy, Ashis, Shikha Trivedy, Shail Mayaram, and Achyut Yagnik. 1995. *Creating a Nationality: The Ramjanmabhumi Movement and Fear of the Self*. Delhi: Oxford University Press.

Nicholas, Ralph W. 1981. "Understanding a Hindu Temple in Bengal." In Adrian C. Mayer, ed., *Culture and Morality: Essays in Honour of Christoph von Fürer-Haimendorf*. Delhi: Oxford University Press.

———. 1982. "The Village Mother in Bengal." In James J. Preston, ed., *Mother Worship: Theme and Variations*. Chapel Hill: University of North Carolina Press.

———. 2003. *Fruits of Worship: Practical Religion in Bengal*. New Delhi: Chronicle Books.

Nishimura, Yuko. 1987. *A Study on Māriyammaṉ Worship in South India: A Preliminary Study on Modern South Indian Village Hinduism*. Tokyo: Institute for the Study of Languages and Cultures of Asia and Africa.

Obeyesekere, Gananath. 1968. "Theodicy, Sin and Salvation in a Sociology of Buddhism." In E. R. Leach, ed., *Dialectic in Practical Religion*. Cambridge: Cambridge University Press.

———. 1984. *The Cult of the Goddess Pattini*. Chicago: University of Chicago Press.

O'Flaherty, Wendy Doniger. 1973. *Asceticism and Eroticism in the Mythology of Śiva*. London: Oxford University Press.

———. 1975. *Hindu Myths*. Harmondsworth: Penguin.

———. 1976. *The Origins of Evil in Hindu Mythology*. Berkeley: University of California Press.

———. 1980a. *Women, Androgynes, and Other Mythical Beasts*. Chicago: University of Chicago Press.

———. 1980b. "Karma and Rebirth in the Vedas and Purāṇas." In Wendy D. O'Flaherty, ed., *Karma and Rebirth in Classical Indian Traditions*. Berkeley: University of California Press.

———. 1981. *The Rig Veda: An Anthology*. Harmondsworth: Penguin.

———, ed. 1980. *Karma and Rebirth in Classical Indian Traditions*. Berkeley: University of California Press.

Ojha, Catherine. 1981. "Feminine Asceticism in Hinduism: Its Tradition and Present Condition." *Man in India* 61: 254–85.

O'Malley, L. S. S. 1935. *Popular Hinduism: The Religion of the Masses*. Cambridge: Cambridge University Press.

———. 1941. "Mechanism and Transport." In L. S. S. O'Malley, ed., *Modern India and the West: A Study of the Interaction of Their Civilizations*. London: Oxford University Press.

Orenstein, Henry. 1965. *Gaon: Conflict and Cohesion in an Indian Village*. Princeton: Princeton University Press.

Osella, Filippo, and Caroline Osella. 2000. *Social Mobility in Kerala: Modernity and Identity in Conflict*. London: Pluto.

Östör, Ákos. 1980. *The Play of the Gods: Locality, Ideology, Structure, and Time in the Festivals of a Bengali Town*. Chicago: University of Chicago Press.

Pache Huber, Véronique. 2002. *Noces et Négoces: Dynamiques Associatives d'une Caste de Commerçants Hindous*. Neuchâtel: Éditions de l'Institut d'Ethnologie; Paris: Éditions de la Maison des Sciences de l'Homme.

Pandey, Gyanendra. 1995. "The Appeal of Hindu History." In Vasudha Dalmia and Heinrich von Stietencron, eds., *Representing Hinduism: The Construction of Religious Traditions and National Identity*. New Delhi: Sage.

Parry, Jonathan. 1980. "Ghosts, Greed and Sin: The Occupational Identity of the Benares Funeral Priests." *Man*, n.s. 15: 88–111.

———. 1981. "Death and Cosmogony in Kashi." *Contributions to Indian Sociology*, n.s. 15: 337–65.

———. 1982. "Sacrificial Death and the Necrophagous Ascetic." In Maurice Bloch and Jonathan Parry, eds., *Death and the Regeneration of Life*. Cambridge: Cambridge University Press.

———. 1985a. "The Brahmanical Tradition and the Technology of the Intellect." In Joanna Overing, ed., *Reason and Morality*. London: Tavistock.

———. 1985b. "Death and Digestion: The Symbolism of Food and Eating in North Indian Mortuary Rites." *Man*, n.s. 20: 612–30.

———. 1986. "The Gift, the Indian Gift and the 'Indian Gift.'" *Man*, n.s. 21: 453–73.

———. 1989. "On the Moral Perils of Exchange." In Jonathan Parry and Maurice Bloch, eds., *Money and the Morality of Exchange*. Cambridge: Cambridge University Press.

———. 1994. *Death in Banaras*. Cambridge: Cambridge University Press.

———. n.d. Spirit Possession as "Superstition" [now published as Parry 1994: ch. 7].

Peabody, Norbert. 1997. "Inchoate in Kota? Contesting Authority through a North Indian Pageant-play." *American Ethnologist* 24: 559–84.

Pillai, T. K. Velu. 1940. *The Travancore State Manual*. Vol. 4. Trivandrum: Government of Travancore.

Pillay, K. K. 1953. *The Śucīndram Temple*. Madras: Kalakshetra.

Planalp, Jack M. 1956. "Religious Life and Values in a North Indian Village." Ph.D. thesis, Cornell University.

Pocock, David F. 1973. *Mind, Body and Wealth: A Study of Belief and Practice in an Indian Village*. Oxford: Blackwell.

———. 1981. "The Vocation and the Avocations of the Guggali Brahmans of Dvaraka." *Contributions to Indian Sociology*, n.s. 15: 321–36.

Prakash, Gyan. 1986. "Reproducing Inequality: Spirit Cults and Labor Relations in Colonial Eastern India." *Modern Asian Studies* 20: 209–30.

Preston, James J. 1980. *Cult of the Goddess: Social and Religious Change in a Hindu Temple*. New Delhi: Vikas.

Prinsep, James. 1834. *Benares Illustrated in a Series of Drawings*. 3rd ser. London: Smith, Elder.

Pugh, Judy F. 1983a. "Astrology and Fate: The Hindu and Muslim Experiences." In Charles F. Keyes and E. Valentine Daniel, eds., *Karma: An Anthropological Inquiry*. Berkeley: University of California Press.

———. 1983b. "Into the Almanac: Time, Meaning and Action in North Indian Society." *Contributions to Indian Sociology*, n.s. 17: 27–49.

Radhakrishnan, S. 1941. "Hinduism and the West." In L. S. S. O'Malley, ed., *Modern India and the West: A Study of the Interaction of Their Civilizations*. London: Oxford University Press.

———. 1971 [1927]. *The Hindu View of Life*. London: Unwin.

———. 1975 [1937]. "Hinduism." In A. L. Basham, ed., *A Cultural History of India*. Oxford: Clarendon.

Raheja, Gloria G. 1988a. *The Poison in the Gift: Ritual, Prestation, and the Dominant Caste in a North Indian Village*. Chicago: University of Chicago Press.

———. 1988b. "India: Caste, Kingship, and Dominance Reconsidered." *Annual Review of Anthropology* 17: 497–522.

Rajagopal, Arvind. 2001. *Politics After Television: Religious Nationalism and the Reshaping of the Indian Public*. Cambridge: Cambridge University Press.

Raman, K. V. 1975. *Srī Varadarājaswāmi Temple—Kāñchi: A Study of Its History, Art and Architecture*. New Delhi: Abhinav.

Ramanujan, A. K. 1973. *Speaking of Śiva*. Harmondsworth: Penguin.

Rao, C. Hayavadana. 1936. *The Dasara in Mysore: Its Origin and Significance*. Bangalore: Bangalore Printing and Publishing.

Redfield, Robert, and Milton B. Singer. 1954. "The Cultural Role of Cities." *Economic Development and Cultural Change* 3: 53–73.

Reiniche, Marie-Louise. 1975. "Les 'Démons' et leur Culte dans la Structure du Panthéon d'un Village du Tirunelveli." *Puruṣārtha* 2: 173–203.

———. 1979. *Les Dieux et les Hommes: Étude des Cultes d'un Village du Tirunelveli, Inde du Sud*. Paris: Mouton.

———. 1985. "Le Temple dans la Localité: Quatre Exemples au Tamilnad." *Puruṣārtha* 8: 75–119.

———. 1987. "Worship of Kāḷiyamman in Some Tamil Villages: The Sacrifice of the Warrior-weavers." In V. Sudarsen, G. Prakash Reddy, and M. Suryanarayana, eds., *Religion and Society in South India*. Delhi: B. R. Publishing.

———. 1988. "Un Nom, une Forme, un Lieu: L'Invention Hindoue de l'Autre et du Même." *Revue de l'Histoire des Religions* 205: 367–84.

———. 1989. *Tiruvannamalai: Un Lieu Saint Śivaïte du Sud de l'Inde 4: La Configuration Sociologique du Temple Hindou*. Paris: École Française d'Extrême Orient.

Renou, Louis. 1953. *Religions of Ancient India*. London: Athlone.

Renou, Louis, and Jean Filliozat, eds. 1947. *L'Inde Classique: Manuel des Études Indiennes*, 1. Paris: Payot.

———. 1953. *L'Inde Classique: Manuel des Études Indiennes*, 2. Hanoi: École Française d'Extrême Orient.

Reynolds, Holly B. 1980. "The Auspicious Married Woman." In Susan S. Wadley, ed., *The Powers of Tamil Women*. Syracuse: Maxwell School of Citizenship and Public Affairs, Syracuse University.

Richards, John F., ed. 1978. *Kingship and Authority in South Asia*. Madison: University of Wisconsin.

Richman, Paula, ed. 1991. *Many Rāmāyaṇas: The Diversity of a Narrative Tradition in South Asia*. Berkeley: University of California Press.

Richman, Paula, ed. 2001. *Questioning Ramayanas: A South Asian Tradition*. Berkeley: University of California Press.

Robinson, Sandra P. 1985. "Hindu Paradigms of Women: Images and Values." In Yvonne Y. Haddad and Ellison B. Findly, eds., *Women, Religion, and Social Change*. Albany: State University of New York Press.

Rocher, Ludo. 1980. "Karma and Rebirth in the Dharmaśāstras." In Wendy D. O'Flaherty, ed., *Karma and Rebirth in Classical Indian Traditions*. Berkeley: University of California Press.

Rudner, David W. 1987. "Religious Gifting and Inland Commerce in Seventeenth-Century South India." *Journal of Asian Studies* 46: 361–79.

Sangren, P. Steven. 1987. *History and Magical Power in a Chinese Community*. Stanford: Stanford University Press.

Sarkar, Tanika. 2001. "Aspects of Contemporary Hindutva Theology: The Voice of Sadhvi Rithambhara." In Vasudha Dalmia, Angelika Malinar, and Martin Christof, eds., *Charisma and Canon: Essays on the Religious History of the Indian Subcontinent*. Delhi: Oxford University Press.

Sarkar, Tanika, and Urvashi Butalia, eds. 1995. *Women and Right-wing Movements: Indian Experiences*. London: Zed.

Sax, William S. 1991. *Mountain Goddess: Gender and Politics in a Himayalan Pilgrimage*. New York: Oxford University Press.

———. 2002. *Dancing the Self: Personhood and Performance in the Pāṇḍav Līlā of Garhwal*. New York: Oxford University Press.

———, ed. 1995. *The Gods at Play: Līlā in South Asia*. New York: Oxford University Press.

Schechner, Richard. 1985. *Between Theater and Anthropology*. Philadelphia: University of Pennsylvania Press.

Schnepel, Burkhard. 1995. "Durga and the King: Ethnohistorical Aspects of Politico-Ritual Life in a South Orissan Jungle Kingdom." *Journal of the Royal Anthropological Institute*, n.s. 1: 145–66.

———. 2002. *The Jungle King: Ethnohistorical Aspects of Politics and Ritual in Orissa*. New Delhi: Manohar.

Sen, K. M. 1961. *Hinduism*. Harmondsworth: Penguin.

Shankari, Uma. 1984. "Brahmin, King and Bhakta in a Temple in Tamil Nadu." *Contributions to Indian Sociology*, n.s. 18: 169–87.

Sharma, Kalpana. 1995. "Chronicle of a Riot Foretold." In Sujata Patel and Alice Thorner, eds., *Bombay: Metaphor for Modern India*. Bombay: Oxford University Press.

Sharma, Ursula M. 1970. "The Problem of Village Hinduism: 'Fragmentation' and Integration." *Contributions to Indian Sociology*, n.s. 4: 1–21.

———. 1973. "Theodicy and the Doctrine of Karma." *Man*, n.s. 8: 347–64.

Shulman, David D. 1980. *Tamil Temple Myths: Sacrifice and Divine Marriage in the South Indian Śaiva Tradition*. Princeton: Princeton University Press.

———. 1985a. *The King and the Clown in South Indian Myth and Poetry*. Princeton: Princeton University Press.

———. 1985b. "Kingship and Prestation in South Indian Myth and Epic." *Asian and African Studies* 19: 93–117.

Singer, Milton. 1968. "The Rādhā-Krishna *Bhajanas* of Madras City." In Milton Singer, ed., *Krishna: Myths, Rites, and Attitudes*. Chicago: University of Chicago Press.

———. 1972. *When a Great Tradition Modernizes*. London: Pall Mall.

———, ed. 1968. *Krishna: Myths, Rites, and Attitudes*. Chicago: University of Chicago Press.

Singh, Andrea M. 1976. *Neighbourhood and Social Networks in Urban India*. Delhi: Marwah.

Slocum, Carolyn. 1988. "Shakti: Women's Inner Strength." In Eleanor Zelliott and Maxine Berntsen, eds., *The Experience of Hinduism: Essays on Religion in Maharashtra*. Albany: State University of New York Press.

Smith, David. 2003. *Hinduism and Modernity*. Oxford: Blackwell.

Srinivas, M. N. 1965 [1952]. *Religion and Society among the Coorgs of South India*. Bombay: Asia.

———. 1966. *Social Change in Modern India*. Berkeley: University of California Press.

———. 1969 [1955]. "The Social System of a Mysore Village." In McKim Marriott, ed., *Village India*. Chicago: University of Chicago Press.

———. 1976. *The Remembered Village*. Delhi: Oxford University Press.

———. 1987. *The Dominant Caste and Other Essays*. Delhi: Oxford University Press.

Staal, J. F. 1963. "Sanskrit and Sanskritization." *Journal of Asian Studies* 23: 261–75.

Stanley, John M. 1977. "Special Time, Special Power: The Fluidity of Power in a Popular Hindu Festival." *Journal of Asian Studies* 37: 27–43.

———. 1988. "Gods, Ghosts, and Possession." In Eleanor Zelliott and Maxine Berntsen, eds., *The Experience of Hinduism: Essays on Religion in Maharashtra*. Albany: State University of New York Press.

———. 1989. "The Capitulation of Maṇi: A Conversion Myth in the Cult of Khandoba." In Alf Hiltebeitel, ed., *Criminal Gods and Demon Devotees: Essays on the Guardians of Popular Hinduism*. Albany: State University of New York Press.

Stein, Burton. 1980. *Peasant State and Society in Medieval South India*. Delhi: Oxford University Press.

———, ed. 1978. *South Indian Temples: An Analytical Reconsideration*. Delhi: Vikas.

Stevenson, Margaret (Mrs. Sinclair). 1920. *The Rites of the Twice-born*. London: Oxford University Press.

Stewart, Tony K., and Edward C. Dimock. 2001. "Kṛttibāsa's Apophatic Critique of Rāma's Kingship." In Paula Richman, ed., *Questioning Ramayanas: A South Asian Tradition*. Berkeley: University of California Press.

Sundar, Nandini. 2001. "Debating Dussehra and Reinterpreting Rebellion in Bastar District, Central India." *Journal of the Royal Anthropological Institute*, n.s. 7: 19–35.

Swallow, Deborah A. 1982. "Ashes and Powers: Myth, Rite and Miracle in an Indian God-man's Cult." *Modern Asian Studies* 16: 123–58.

Tapper, Bruce E. 1979. "Widows and Goddesses: Female Roles in Deity Symbolism in a South Indian Village." *Contributions to Indian Sociology*, n.s. 13: 1–31.

———. 1987. *Rivalry and Tribute: Society and Ritual in a Telugu Village in South India*. Delhi: Hindustan.

Tarabout, Gilles. 1986. *Sacrifier et Donner à Voir en Pays Malabar: Les Fêtes de Temple au Kerala (Inde du sud): Étude Anthropologique*. Paris: École Française d'Extrême Orient.

———. 1997. "L'Évolution des Cultes dans les Temples Hindous: L'Exemple du Kerala (Inde du Sud)." In Catherine Clémentin-Ojha, ed., *Renouveaux Religieux en Asie*. Paris: École Française d'Extrême Orient.

Thapar, Romila. 1989. "Imagined Religious Communities? Ancient History and the Modern Search for a Hindu Identity." *Modern Asian Studies* 23: 209–31.

Tod, James. 1914 [1829]. *Annals and Antiquities of Rajast'han*. Vol. 1. London: Routledge.

Toffin, Gerard. 1981. "Culte des Déesses et Fête du Dasai chez les Néwar (Népal)." *Puruṣārtha* 5: 55–81.

———. 1982. "Analyse Structurale d'une Fête Communale Néwar: le *Deś Jātrā* de Panauti." *L'Homme* 22 (3): 57–89.

———. 1993. *Le Palais et le Temple: La Fonction Royale dans la Vallée du Népal*. Paris: CNRS Éditions.

Toomey, Paul M. 1990. "Krishna's Consuming Passions: Food as Metaphor and Metonym for Emotion at Mount Govardhan." In Owen M. Lynch, ed., *Divine Passions: The Social Construction of Emotion in India*. Berkeley: University of California Press.

Trautmann, Thomas R. 1981. *Dravidian Kinship*. Cambridge: Cambridge University Press.

Turner, Victor. 1974. "Pilgrimages as Social Processes." In Victor Turner, *Dramas, Fields, and Metaphors*. Ithaca: Cornell University Press.

Vail, Lise F. 1985. "Founders, Swamis, and Devotees: Becoming Divine in North Karnataka." In Joanne P. Waghorne and Norman Cutler, eds., *Gods of Flesh, Gods of Stone: The Embodiment of Divinity in India*. Chambersburg: Anima.

van Buitenen, J. A. B. 1968. "On the Archaism of the *Bhāgavata Purāṇa*." In Milton Singer, ed., *Krishna: Myths, Rites, and Attitudes*. Chicago: University of Chicago Press.

van den Hoek, A. W. 1979. "The Goddess of the Northern Gate: Cellattamman as the 'Divine Warrior' of Madurai." In Marc Gaborieau and Alice Thorner, eds., *Asie du Sud: Traditions et Changements*. Paris: Éditions du Centre National de la Recherche Scientifique.

van der Veer, Peter. 1984. "Structure and Anti-structure in Hindu Pilgrimage to Ayodhya." In Kenneth Ballhatchet and David Taylor, eds., *Changing South Asia: Religion and Society*. Hong Kong: Asian Research Service/School of Oriental and African Studies.

———. 1987a. "Taming the Ascetic: Devotionalism in a Hindu Monastic Order." *Man*, n.s. 22: 680–95.

———. 1987b. "'God Must be Liberated!' A Hindu Liberation Movement in Ayodhya." *Modern Asian Studies* 21: 283–301.

———. 1988. *Gods on Earth: The Management of Religious Experience and Identity in a North Indian Pilgrimage Centre*. London: Athlone.

———. 1989. "The Power of Detachment: Disciplines of Body and Mind in the Ramanandi Order." *American Ethnologist* 16: 458–70.

———. 1994. *Religious Nationalism: Hindus and Muslims in India*. Berkeley: University of California Press.

Vaudeville, Charlotte. 1996. *Myths, Saints and Legends in Medieval India*. Delhi: Oxford University Press.

Vidal, Denis. 1998. "When the Gods Drink Milk! Empiricism and Belief in Contemporary Hinduism." *South Asia Research* 18: 149–71.

Vidyarthi, L. P. 1961. *The Sacred Complex in Hindu Gaya*. Bombay: Asia.

Wadley, Susan S. 1975. *Shakti: Power in the Conceptual Structure of Karimpur Religion*. Chicago: University of Chicago, Department of Anthropology.

———. 1976. "The Spirit 'Rides' or the Spirit 'Comes': Possession in a North Indian Village." In A. Bharati, ed., *The Realm of the Extra-human: Agents and Audiences*. The Hague: Mouton.

———. 1980. "The Paradoxical Powers of Tamil Women." In Susan S. Wadley, ed., *The Powers of Tamil Women*. Syracuse: Maxwell School of Citizenship and Public Affairs, Syracuse University.

———. 1983. "The Rains of Estrangement: Understanding the Hindu Yearly Cycle." *Contributions to Indian Sociology*, n.s. 17: 51–85.

———. 1994. *Struggling with Destiny in Karimpur, 1925–1984*. Berkeley: University of California Press.

———. 2000. "The Village in 1998." In William H. Wiser, Charlotte V. Wiser, and Susan S. Wadley, *Behind Mud Walls: Seventy-five Years in a North Indian Village*. Berkeley: University of California Press.

Wadley, Susan S., and Bruce W. Derr. 1989. "Eating Sins in Karimpur." *Contributions to Indian Sociology*, n.s. 23: 131–48.

Warrier, Maya. 2003. "Processes of Secularization in Contemporary India: Guru Faith in the Mata Amritanandamayi Mission." *Modern Asian Studies* 37: 213–53.

Weber, Max. 1967 [1917]. *The Religion of India: The Sociology of Hinduism and Buddhism*. New York: Free Press.

———. 1978 [1920]. *Economy and Society*. Berkeley: University of California Press.

Weightman, Simon. 1985. "Hinduism." In John R. Hinnells, ed., *A Handbook of Living Religions*. Harmondsworth: Penguin.

Whitehead, Henry. 1921. *The Village Gods of South India*. London: Oxford University Press.

Wilks, Mark. 1869 [1810–17]. *Historical Sketches of the South of India*. Vol. 1. Madras: Higginbotham.

Williams, Raymond B. 1984. *A New Face of Hinduism: The Swaminarayan Religion*. Cambridge: Cambridge University Press.

Wiser, William H. 1969 [1936]. *The Hindu Jajmani System*. Lucknow: Lucknow Publishing House.

Wiser, William H., and Charlotte V. Wiser. 1971 [1963]. *Behind Mud Walls, 1930–1960*. Berkeley: University of California Press.

Wulff, Donna M. 1985. "Images and Roles of Women in Bengali Vaiṣṇava *Paḍāvalī Kīrtan.*" In Yvonne Y. Haddad and Ellison B. Findly, eds., *Women, Religion, and Social Change.* Albany: State University of New York Press.

Yocum, Glenn E. 1982. *Hymns to the Dancing Śiva: A Study of Maṇik-kavācakar's* Tiruvācakam. Columbia: South Asia Books.

————. 1986. "Brahmin, King, Sannyāsi, and the Goddess in a Cage: Reflections on the 'Conceptual Order of Hinduism' at a Tamil Śaiva Temple." *Contributions to Indian Sociology,* n.s. 20: 15–39.

Younger, Paul. 1982a. "Ten Days of Wandering and Romance with Lord Raṅkanātaṉ : The Paṅkuṉi Festival in Śrīraṅkam Temple, South India." *Modern Asian Studies* 16: 623–56.

————. 1982b. "Singing the Tamil Hymnbook in the Tradition of Rāmānuja: The Adyayanōtsava Festival in Śrīraṅkam." *History of Religions* 21: 272–93.

————. 1995. *The Home of Dancing Śivaṉ: The Traditions of the Hindu Temple in Citamparam.* New York: Oxford University Press.

INDEX